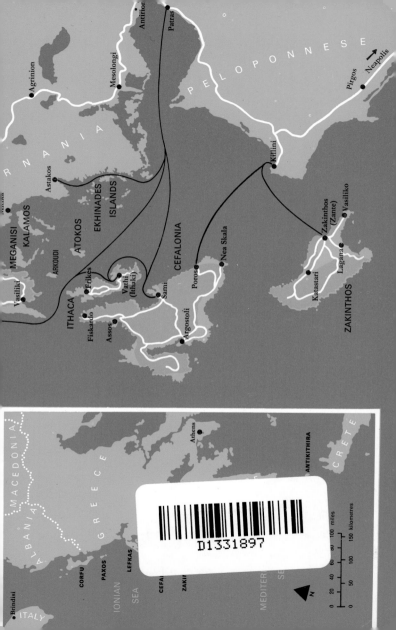

Corfu
and the other
Ionian Islands

Travellers' Guide

Corfu and the other Ionian Islands

by Martin Young

Jonathan Cape London

To My Mother

First published 1971
Reprinted 1973
Second edition 1977
Third edition 1981
Text and maps © Copyright Helga Greene 1971, 1977, 1981
Maps drawn by Janet Landau
General Editors: Judith Greene and June Gordon-Walker

Jonathan Cape Ltd
30 Bedford Square, London WC1

British Library Cataloguing in Publication Data

Young, Martin
    Corfu and the other Ionian islands. — 3rd ed. — (Travellers'
    guide).
    1. Ionian Islands — Description and travel — Guide-books
    I. Title   II. Series
    914.95'50476   DF901.16

ISBN 0-224-01952-X

Typeset by Computape (Pickering) Ltd
and printed in Great Britain by Thomson Litho Ltd, East Kilbride

CONTENTS

MAPS AND CHARTS

Acknowledgments

The help and advice of many friends in the Ionian Islands and elsewhere improved this book; the kindness and hospitality of many others added to the pleasure of writing it. In particular, my warm thanks go to Mr John Damaskinos, Mr George Dondas, Mr Peter Kalligas, Mr and Mrs John Kollas, Mrs Andrée Kavadias and Mr John Tranakas on Corfu; to Mr Panos Rondoyannis and Mr Epaminondas Vayenas on Lefkas; to Mrs Helen Kosmetatos and Mr and Mrs Alex Reid on Cefalonia; to Mr John Komouto and Mr Dionysios Romas on Zakinthos; to Mr Nicholas Coldstream, Mr Byron Dapontes and Professor George Huxley on Kithira; to Miss Sylvia Benton, Mr and Mrs Leo Kollas, Professor A. W. Lawrence, Mr Peter Megaw, Mrs Jane Rabnett and Mrs Rosemary Bultzo in Athens; and to Mrs Helga Greene, Mr Roger Lubbock and Dr Theodore Stephanides in London. I am also grateful to June and Robin Gordon-Walker for some useful additions to the 1977 edition.

The author and publishers gratefully acknowledge permission to quote passages from *The Latins in the Levant* by W. Miller (John Murray, London, 1908), *A Handbook for Travellers in Greece* by John Murray (John Murray, London, 1840), *Byzantine Civilization* by Steven Runciman (Edward Arnold, London, 1933), *Memoirs of Hadrian* by Marguerite Yourcenar (Secker and Warburg, London, 1955; Farrar, Straus and Giroux Inc., New York) and *The Letters of Private Wheeler* ed. by B. H. Liddell Hart (Michael Joseph, London, 1962; copyright-holder Mrs F. E. Ellis).

Thanks are also due to the Loeb Classical Library (William Heinemann, London; Harvard University Press, Cambridge, Massachusetts) for permission to use extracts from the Loeb editions of Plutarch, Strabo, Livy and Pausanias, and to Penguin Books Ltd, London, for permission to use extracts from E. V. Rieu's translation of Homer's *Odyssey* (© E. V. Rieu 1946) and Aubrey de Selincourt's translation of Herodotus' *The Histories* (© The Estate of Aubrey de Selincourt 1954).

Chart of Excursions

Island	Town sights *Major*	*Secondary*
CORFU	*Corfu Town* Esplanade Archaeological Museum Palace of St Michael and St George Platitera Convent *Environs* Church of SS Jason and Sosipater Analipsis Kanoni (for Mouse Island and Vlakherena Convent)	*Corfu Town* Citadel New Fort Town Hall Church of St Spiridon Kambielo Quarter Church of the Panayia Kremasti Pandokrator Church Orthodox Cathedral Tomb of Menekrates British Cemetery *Environs* Paleopolis Church
PAXOS	*Gaio* Gaio as a whole	*Gaio* Former British Residency Castle
LEFKAS	*Lefkas Town* Museum and Public Library *Environs* Castle of Ayia Mavra	*Lefkas Town* Church of Isodia tis Theotokou
ITHACA	*Vathi* Archaeological Museum	*Environs* Arethusa's Fountain

Out of town

Major	*Secondary*

Route 1
Church of the Panḍokrator at
  Ayos Markos (17 km.)
Mt Panḍokrator (35·5 km.)
Kassiopi (37 km.)
 	
Route 3
Paleokastritsa (25 km.)
 	
Route 5a
Fortress of Gardiki (25 km.)
 	
Route 5b
Akhillion (9 km.)
	Route 1
	Venetian Arsenal at Gouvia (8 km.)
	Chapel of Ayos Merkourios
	  (18·5 km.)
	
	Route 2
	Canal d'Amour (36 km.)
	
	Route 4
	Kaiser's Throne (13 km.)
	Mirtiotissa (16 km.)
	
	Route 5c
	Benitses (10·5 km.)
	
	Route 6
	Arkoudillas Monastery (30·5 km.)

Paxos as a whole	*Route 2* Church of Ipapanḍi (5 km.) *Route 3* Sea-caves on west coast

Route 1
Ancient Lefkas (2·5 km.)
Nidri (17·5 km.)
 	
Route 2
Monastery of the Panayia Odiyitria
  (3 km.)
Livadi sump (13 km.)
Mt Meganoros (22 km.)
 	
Route 3
Sappho's Leap (55 km.)
	Route 1
	Poros (28·5 km.)
	Monastery of Ayos Ioannis sto
	  Rodaki (34 km.)

Route 1 Mt Aetos (5 km.) Stavros Museum (18 km.)	*Route 1* Cave of the Nymphs (4 km.) Homer's School (20 km.)

Chart of Excursions

Island	Town sights Major	Secondary
CEFALONIA	*Argostoli* Koryalenios Museum	*Argostoli* Archaeological Museum *Environs* Sea Mill St Theodore's Lighthouse Ancient Krani
ZAKINTHOS	*Zakinthos Town* Zakinthos Museum Church of Our Lady of the Angels Church of the Faneromeni *Environs* Castle Hill	*Zakinthos Town* Church of St Nicholas-on-the-Mole Church of Ayos Dionisios Solomos Museum British Cemetery *Environs* Akrotiri
KITHIRA	*Khora* Kastro	*Khora* Museum Stavromenos Church

Out of town

Major	Secondary
Route 1 Castle of Ayos Yeorgos (9 km.)	*Route 1* Tombs of Mazarakata (9 km.)
Route 4 Mt Enos (23 km. + 1 hour)	*Route 2* Nea Skala mosaics (40 km.)
Route 5 Fortress of Assos (41 km.) Fiskardo (53 km.)	*Route 3* Cave of Drongarati (21·5 km.) Ancient Sami (24 km. + 50 minutes)
	Route 5 Chapel of the Panayia Kouyanna (49 km.)
	Link Route B Pot-Hole of Melissani (3 km.)
Route 2 Pitch Springs (17 km.) Keri Church (21 km.)	*Route 3* Ipapanḍi Church (11 km.)
Route 3 Makherado Church (11 km.) Anafonitria Monastery (38·5 km.)	*Route 4* Church of Ayia Paraskevi, Volimes (34 km.)
Route 4 Monastery of St John the Baptist (19·5 km.) Monastery of Ayos Yeorgos Kremna (33·5 km. + ¾ hour)	*Route 5* Kalipado Church (8 km.)
Route 1 Church of Ayos Dimitrios (7 km.)	*Route 1* Monastery of Ayia Elesa (8 km.) Katouni Bridge (2·5 km.) Mirtidia Monastery (13 km.)
Route 2 Church of Ayos Petros (12·5 km.) Kato Khora (12·5 km.) Milopotamo Cave (13 km. + ½ hour)	*Route 2* Panayia Orfani Monastery (17 km.)
Route 3 Church of Ayos Theodoros (15·5 km.)	*Route 4* Chapel of Ayos Yeorgos (28 km. + ½ hour)
Route 5 Ancient Kithira (Paleopolis) and the Church of Ayos Kozmas (15 km. + 20 minutes)	*Route 5* Kastri (20·5 km.)

INTRODUCTION

At about the time of the Fourth Crusade (A.D. 1204) the Ionian Islands were seized by Frankish adventurers and, with the exception of Lefkas, were not later snapped up by the Ottoman Turks like similar foreign settlements elsewhere (Rhodes of the Knights in 1522, Genoese Chios in 1566 and Venetian Crete in 1669, to mention only a few), but were early on acquired by Venice and remained within 'the safeguard of the West' until the long life of the Serene Republic was finally snuffed out by Napoleon in 1789. Thereafter they came under French, Russian and British protection for another seventy-five years.

By 1864, when the islands were united with Greece, these six hundred years of Western domination had produced a distinct Ionian society with its own artists, architects and poets, landed gentry and peasantry, polite manners and administrative experience, prosperous olive groves and well-tended countryside. Today, the Anglo-Venetian relics of this society — churches, castles, country-houses, music, costume and cuisine — are still visible on all the Ionian Islands (though more so on some than others) and give them a peculiar and attractive 'Ionian stamp' which distinguishes them from the rest of Greece.

Each island, of course, also possesses a character of its own which has nothing to do with this 'Ionian stamp' but is made up of its own myths and mountains, people and landscape, ancient monuments and modern development. 'Comparisons are odorous', perhaps, but a guide-book on seven different islands cannot do without them. In the first half of this book I have therefore compared the islands of Corfu, Paxos, Lefkas, Ithaca, Cefalonia, Zakinthos and Kithira under such headings as accommodation, climate, architecture, bathing, accessibility and so on; the table of contents contains a full list of these headings and is therefore a sort of subject index. From the excursion table on pages 14–17 it is possible to make comparative judgments concerning the various islands since they show the number of outstanding sights on each.

The second half of the book contains separate descriptions of the islands. Each island chapter is preceded by a few pages of practical information and an introduction. If I have succeeded in writing something true about each island in these introductions, they and the introductions to the seven capitals which follow them will provide a quick way of deciding which is most likely to appeal to you. As for the changes that have taken place since this book was first published ten years ago, they have become a matter of history and are dealt with, sadly, under that heading.

GETTING TO THE IONIAN ISLANDS

Details of all methods of approach to each island are given at the beginning of the island chapters, and the end-paper maps illustrate the different types of connection. (See also Travel between the Ionian Islands.)

AIR

Corfu is the only one of the seven islands with an international airport; in summer Olympic Airways operate weekly flights from London, and there are also many charter flights from England. From Athens there are daily flights to Corfu, Cefalonia, Aktion (for Lefkas, 16 km. away) and Kithira, and five flights a week to Zakinthos.

SEA

All of the large international car ferries which ply between Brindisi or Bari and Patras or Igoumenitsa stop at Corfu (see p. 105 for details). Between April and September there is a ferry every day. From late March to mid-October car ferries of the Linée Canguro also sail four times a week from Ancona to Igoumenitsa and Patras.

For travellers approaching Corfu from mainland Greece there are frequent daily car ferries from Igoumenitsa. Cefalonia and Ithaca are served by fast daily car ferries from Patras, and Zakinthos by frequent car ferries from Killini, an hour's drive south of Patras. A new car ferry service from Killini to Poros on Cefalonia was due to start late in 1980. Lefkas is in practice a peninsula, closer by road to Igoumenitsa than to Patras. Kithira is reached by a ship and a car ferry sailing from Piraeus, and a small car ferry from Neapolis.

BUS

Daily Pullman coaches belonging to the island bus co-operatives (K.T.E.L.) link Athens with the capitals of Corfu, Cefalonia, Lefkas and Zakinthos, taking the ferries in their stride. Ithaca shares a bus with Cefalonia; for Paxos one can take a bus to Parga, and for Kithira one to Neapolis.

RAIL

The railway from Athens to Killini via Patras can also be used by travellers catching the ferries to Corfu, Cefalonia, Ithaca, and Zakinthos.

Athens Ticket Offices of the S.E.K. (Hellenic Rail): 1 Karolou Street (tel. 5222491) and 6 Sina Street (tel. 3624402/6).

CAR DOCUMENTS

To take a British-registered car into Greece for up to four months you need your car's log-book to get it through customs. Alternatively you can obtain a 'Carnet de Passages en Douanes' or 'triptyque' from your own British automobile club in advance; this is valid for one year from the date of issue. Though insurance is not compulsory, to drive in Greece without adequate *third party* coverage is madness. To get to Greece by road you will need an International Green Card in any case. You will only need your national driving licence.

PASSPORT AND CUSTOMS

Holders of valid British passports of *most* descriptions, or of valid British Visitors' passports, can visit Greece for up to three months without a visa; but holders of passports of some British dependent territories do not benefit from this concession. (British Visitors' passports are not valid for travel through Yugoslavia.)

Customs concessions cover up to two hundred cigarettes (or fifty cigars, or the equivalent in tobacco); a *portable* radio, record-player and typewriter; a camera and movie-camera, and one litre of spirits, one of wine and 90 c.c. of perfume. If any of your equipment looks unusually expensive it may be registered in your passport as a guarantee that you take it with you when you leave.

TRAVEL BETWEEN THE IONIAN ISLANDS

A Greek car ferry sailing weekly between Brindisi and Patras calls at Corfu, Paxos, Ithaca and Cefalonia en route; two or three of these islands are therefore easy to fit into one holiday. In addition, Cefalonia and Ithaca are linked by a daily car ferry, and there are also daily services between Corfu and Paxos. Though Zakinthos has no direct sea links with its close neighbour Cefalonia, a new car ferry service from Poros on Cefalonia to mainland Killini means that a journey between the two islands can now be made entirely by sea, even though by a roundabout route. No ferry calls at Lefkas; but it is only 122 km. by a fast road from Igoumenitsa, so can be visited by car from Corfu without any difficulty. And the new car ferry service from Neapolis (400 km. from Killini by a spectacular drive over the Taygetos mountains) means that Kithira too can be visited by anyone hiring a car in one of the other islands, providing of course that the terms of rental allow you to take the car off the island where it was originally hired.

TRANSPORT ON THE ISLANDS

LOCAL BUSES

In the last ten years comfortable new Pullman buses have replaced old village rattletraps; full of hens, baskets, sacks of vegetables, priests and mustachioed peasants, they are a slow but entertaining means of travel. They are also cheap: about two drachmas a mile. But they are often crowded and it is best to book a seat at the bus station the day before you go.

Though the island bus services are designed to meet the needs of villagers going into town, to market or to work and not those of tourists going out of town to lunch, bathe or sightsee, it is possible to get out to most places and back in a day, though often for much longer or shorter than one needs. In Lefkas there is a convenient round-the-island service. In Zakinthos and Cefalonia there are frequent summer services to and from the best beaches near the capital and in Corfu the bus schedules often take account of tourist traffic. Where a day-return service existed along an island route in 1980 it is mentioned after the route instructions for each island. But schedules are constantly being improved. Travellers intending to use buses regularly should collect a printed timetable and itinerary (*dromolóyo*) from the office of the island bus co-operative — the K.T.E.L. — and ask their hotel or a Greek-speaking friend to help them work out the possibilities. In Corfu the National Tourist Office produces an island bus timetable in English.

GUIDED TOURS

In Corfu and Cefalonia, travel agencies run three or four pleasant coach or caique excursions. The grander out-of-town hotels also have their own minibus services and though these are used mainly for commuting between the hotel and the town, excursions are also arranged. Compared with K.T.E.L. prices, these excursions are, of course, extremely expensive.

TAXIS

In 1980 the official rate for taxis throughout the islands was Drs 20 a kilometre one way or Drs 12 a kilometre return, with a charge of Drs 150 an hour for waiting. There is a minimum charge of Drs 40. In some of the islands rather more expensive 'hire' cars (labelled *Agoraion*) ply side by side with taxis; they have no meters and their rates are given on fare charts.

CAR, SCOOTER AND BICYCLE HIRE

In 1980 cars could be hired in Corfu, Lefkas, Cefalonia, and Zakinthos. The large mainland firms (Avis Rent-a-Car, Hellas Cars, and Hertz) and the smaller Corfu, Zakinthos and Argostoli enterprises have a number of different renting schemes (hourly with unlimited mileage, daily with a fixed mileage allowance, weekly and so on). The relative advantages of each firm for each traveller obviously cannot be worked out in this book and the following Hertz rates for the 1980 high season in Corfu are quoted simply to give an idea of car-hire prices as a whole: the basic rate for a Fiat 127 was Drs 570 daily (100 km. minimum), Drs 3,570 weekly (700 km. minimum), plus Drs 7·60 a kilometre; or Drs 10,700 a week with unlimited mileage.

In 1980 scooters could be hired in all the islands except Kithira and Cefalonia, and bicycles everywhere but Kithira; scooters cost Drs 250 a day and bicycles Drs 100.

In Corfu and Zakinthos bicycling is a surprisingly easy and pleasant way of getting about, since the roads near the capitals are tarred and fairly level; but in Lefkas and Cefalonia a bicycle is worth having only for the immediate environs.

CARRIAGES

In 1980 the official rate for the horse-drawn victorias of Corfu was Drs 500 an hour.

MOTORING

Chiefly as a result of British industry in the nineteenth century (see p. 68), the motorist will find on the Ionian Islands a road network denser than in any other part of Greece outside Attica; in some places — the central part of Corfu and the plain of Zakinthos — the lanes are as haphazard as Gogol's Russian roads, wandering off in all directions 'like crayfish spilt out of a sack'. In the last ten years so many of these village roads have been tarred that unsurfaced ones are now the exception. But the tarred lanes are often steep, narrow and serpentine, and the huge Pullman buses which completely fill them and novices on motor-scooters are constant hazards, especially since half of everyone's attention is on avoiding potholes. Jaywalking too is as much an Ionian custom as it was in Viscount Kirkwall's day. 'In Cefalonia, where the carriages are very few indeed, the people habitually walk in the middle of the streets and roads. This is generally the case even in Corfu where vehicles and equestrians are, comparatively speaking, plentiful.'

Animals add to the risk and excitement of island driving: frenzied dogs will leap suddenly from a ditch and pursue your car, snapping and snarling at your wheels in a most unnerving way; car-shy mules will show you the whites of their eyes and threatening hindquarters, or stampede with the cursing old crones who ride them; and often not even the shrillest of whistles from the goat-herd, or a shower of stones, will drive a herd of goats out of the way on to the hillside before you are among them.

Members of the A.A. and the R.A.C. can call on the Automobile and Touring Club of Greece (E.L.P.A.) for help.

Athens office: Athens Tower, 2 Mesongeion Street. Tel. 7791-615

Corfu office: 120 Kapodistriou Street. Tel. 29528

Patras office: Othonos and Amalias Street. Tel. 76920

PETROL

Apart from Corfu, petrol stations are scarce outside the island capitals, and it is always wise to start a long excursion with a full tank. In 1980 'Super', with an octane rating of ninety-six, cost Drs 33·70 a litre and 'Regular', with an octane rating of eighty-four, Drs 29·60.

MAPS AND SIGNPOSTS

The tourist maps on sale in the islands vary in accuracy. In 1980 the only map on sale on Zakinthos was very impressionistic and contained several bad mistakes; and some of those on sale on Corfu were not much better. But both Corfu and Paxos are well covered by the Road-Touristic Map published by the Automobile and Touring Club of Greece. There are two maps of Cefalonia and Ithaca, an old one good on contours and a new one (published by Kalligas Wines) up to date on roads. The only map of Lefkas is attractive and nearly up to date; and that of Kithira (by E. Sophios) is a proper survey map, though lettered only in Greek.

Apart from maps the motorist can now count on an excellent signposting system using large blue-painted metal sign-boards written in both Greek and Roman alphabets.

CAIQUES

In Corfu caiques run daily up the east coast to Kassiopi, in Lefkas daily down the east coast to Nidri, in Ithaca daily from Vathi to Kioni, and in Paxos daily from Gaio to Lakka. They are a pleasant and inexpensive way of travelling.

ACCOMMODATION AND RESTAURANTS

Just over a hundred years ago the Earl of Carlisle pronounced that 'anyone who wishes to condense the attractions of southern scenery, and see it all in the utmost comfort and luxury, need only come to Corfu'. Corfu is still way ahead of the other islands in comfort and luxury, as the table below shows; but the pressure of tourists there is much greater — some 500,000 visitors a year compared with 200,000 to Zakinthos, the only island which begins to compete as a tourist resort. In the summer months many hotels are almost entirely given over to group tours, and bookings for July and August should be made well ahead.

Number of Ionian Island Hotels in 1980

	LUXURY	A	B	C	D	E
Corfu	8	19	16	50	21	9
Zakinthos	0	0	6	29	15	6
Cefalonia	0	2	3	10	7	3
Leffkas	0	0	2	2	1	2
Ithaca	0	0	2	0	0	0
Paxos	0	0	1	0	0	1
Kithira	0	0	0	1	0	0

A list of hotels on each island is given in the information sections of the island chapters. They are listed alphabetically within their categories, from L (luxury) to E class. The comments are designed to give a quick idea of the size, position and type of each hotel but do not touch on their merits.

CATEGORIES AND PRICES

Hotels in Greece are divided into six categories: Luxury, A, B, C (Γ), D (Δ) and E. At present, the controlled price brackets of the first four are as follows (there is no controlled ceiling price for rooms in Luxury class hotels):

Daily hotel bed and breakfast prices in 1980

TYPE OF ROOM	LUXURY	A	B	C	D
Single room					
Without bath	—	388–585	334–451	278–379	247–310
With bath	From 845*	613–946	451–730	337–524	310–376
Double room					
Without bath	—	675–1043	531–770	410–592	397–448
With bath	From 1180*	928–1371	611–1068	519–700	448–578

*With air conditioning and without breakfast

For a stay of only one or two days the price may be increased by 10 per cent. An extra bed costs 20 per cent extra. From July 1st to September 15th a 20 per cent high season surcharge may be added. In L, A, B and C class hotels obligatory demi-pension prices may be charged. A single person pays 80 per cent of the price for a double room. Air conditioning costs Drs 64 a day extra for a single room, Drs 96 for a double.

Hoteliers are allowed to *reduce* prices by any amount they wish in the off-season period. This varies from hotel to hotel, but in general reductions of between 30 per cent to 40 per cent are common from

November 1st to March 31st, with lesser reductions (approx. 10 per cent) in October and May. Special rates for groups are available on request. The foregoing price ranges *include* a 15 per cent service charge and a 6 per cent government (VAT) tax. The inclusive price, and how it is made up, is displayed on a card inside each hotel room. This card will also note the price of optional extras such as a hot or cold shower or bath in a public bathroom.

In Greece an old hotel is seldom promptly downgraded if it fails to keep up with the current standards of comfort. Over the years official criteria have also been somewhat elastic. The result is that you do not always know exactly what to expect from a hotel in any given category. For example, you may find a private shower or bath with every room, central heating and a restaurant in one C class hotel and none of these things in another. In general, the Luxury class hotels fully deserve their rating; in all A, almost all B and many C class hotels most rooms have private showers or baths; and it is only in D and E class hotels that you run a considerable risk of finding curiously sway-backed beds, hard mattresses, a long delay while the water for your public shower (or much more rarely bath) is heated, and inefficient and disagreeable lavatories.*

The majority of C, D and E class hotels in the islands do not have restaurants, and many do not even provide breakfast. Quite a number of them are in fact no more than lodging-houses; they are called hotels because the tax law classifies as a hotel any building which contains more than six rooms for rent (when these are registered by a single owner). Except for their higher prices rooms in such hotels are often indistinguishable from those described in the next paragraph.

ROOMS IN PRIVATE HOUSES

There are a large number of rooms to be hired in all the islands. Details of their number and whereabouts are given in the island chapters. In the towns rooms to rent are often in private houses. Here the decor may include an oleograph of troikas and wolves, of an Alpine lake or of nymphs bathing, a relief model of a warship and a large photograph of a mustachioed grandfather. In the

---

* On the question of lavatories generally, the best plan if caught short in a town is to aim for the nearest expensive hotel, and in a village to make rapidly for the countryside. The W.C. is called *to apokhoritírio, i toualéta*, or, more colloquially, *to méros*.

country they are more often in small blocks built specially for tourists. In either case they come in three categories whose prices are correlated with hotel-room rates as follows:

A class private room = C class hotel room
B class private room = D class hotel room
C class private room = E class hotel room

When the room has been officially licensed there will be a price-card on the door. But there are many unofficial rooms which offer identical facilities at the same price or cheaper. Rooms are not always advertised. If you like the look of some seaside place, tell the café or restaurant proprietor that you want a *domátio* and he will ask one or two householders to show you what is available. In the villages of the interior, tourists are not expected and the accommodation is seldom attractive. In particular, the village doss-house called a *pandokhíon* should be avoided except in an emergency.

HOLIDAY CAMPS

The *Club Méditerranée*, well known all over the Mediterranean, has three properties on Corfu and an undeveloped site on Zakinthos. In an exceptionally beautiful site at Dassia on Corfu (p. 150), there is a 'summer village' of the original romantic type with Tahitian straw huts under the trees. At Nisaki (p. 151) and Ayos Ioannis Peristeron (p. 167) large and luxurious hotel complexes have been acquired to accommodate the older and richer type of member.

You can join the club in London (40–41 Conduit Street, W1; tel. 01-499 1965) or through its Athens branch office (Hotel Minoa, 12 Karolou Street. Tel. 539-868).

The *Barracuda Club* is the name of a small German holiday association which has taken over a hotel with fifteen double rooms at Paleokastritsa on Corfu. Inquiries about membership should be made to 2110 Buchholz b, Hamburg.

The Lassi Holiday Centre (tel. Argostoli 0671-28054) on Cefalonia has accommodation in eight-bedded bungalows and is for under-twenty-fives only.

YOUTH HOSTELS

There are youth hostels in the villages of Ayos Yannis (p. 160) and Kondokali on Corfu (p. 147). In 1980 a bed cost Drs 107 a night.

CAMPING

There are nine camping sites on Corfu, two on Lefkas, and two in Kithira, all with electricity, water and W.C.s. Their daily charges in 1980 were as follows: caravan Drs 60–105; car and tent, Drs 50–95; motor-bicycle, Drs 30–40; and a charge of Drs 60–70 per person per day with Drs 10–30 for electricity. In the islands without camping sites few land-owners will show anything but curiosity and kindness if you camp on an uncultivated piece of their land; and if you keep away from main roads, public beaches and houses the police will have no objection. In the dry summer months, though, they may be anxious about fires.

VILLAS

In Corfu and Paxos there is an organized market for summer 'villas', which range from accommodation in converted village cottages to custom-built holiday homes grouped in olives groves close to the sea. Prices for these, as well as for the few genuine villas (in other words private houses in their own grounds let for a few months by their generally British owners) vary enormously. In 1980 a very simple and unfavourably sited 'villa' containing two double bedrooms, sitting-room, kitchen, bathroom and terrace cost Drs 900 a day in the Low Season, Drs 1200 in the High, and Drs 1500 during July, August and September. The agencies listed on p. 104 will send details to England. A few houses can also be found in the other islands, especially on Zakinthos and Cefalonia, but are difficult to hire by post.

FURNISHED FLATS

Half way between villas and rooms in private houses (where one can often use the kitchen) are furnished flats. There are several blocks of these on the east coast of Corfu (details from the N.T.O.) and one at Argasi in Zakinthos. In 1980 rates for a double bedroom flat varied between Drs 800 a day in Argasi and Drs 2,300 a day in Benitses.

RESTAURANTS

There are five categories of restaurants — Luxury to D. It is the size, comfort and amenities of a restaurant and not its cuisine which determine its category. In a Luxury class restaurant you will find a bar, linen table-cloths and napkins, comfortable chairs, a place to wash and a plethora of waiters. In a D class restaurant the forks will bend double if you lean on them, the table will be covered with a sheet of paper, there may be no wash-basin and the owner may be both cook and waiter. Prices are uncontrolled in Luxury class restaurants, controlled in all the others. Whether or not the menus have two columns of prices (the second showing the total when service and taxes are added), the final bill always includes both these extras.

There are different types as well as different categories of restaurant — the *tavérna*, the grilled-meat place, the *estiatórion* and the *kéndro*. These, and the sort of food you will find in them, are described in the section on food and drink.

PRACTICAL INFORMATION

TOURIST INFORMATION

The National Tourist Organization has a large and exceptionally efficient office in Corfu, and a small one in Argostoli. Its London office is at 195 Regent Street, W1R 8DL, and its head office at 4 Stadiou Street, Athens. On Corfu and Zakinthos the Tourist Police are helpful and generally speak at least one foreign language. Other policemen, though notably polite, seldom speak English. Since they are not allowed to serve in the district they come from they can in any case often help you less than a local hotelier, shop-keeper or knowledgeable resident. In the capitals of Ithaca and Kithira the Town Halls are the best sources of information. If you need help in a remote village, ask for the *próedros* (the president of the local community) or the *kinotikó grafío* (the rural district office).

CLIMATE AND CLOTHES

Though the Ionian Islands have a much higher winter rainfall than most of Greece, the summer is as fine as it is in the Aegean. Temperature and rainfall in each of the six northern islands will not differ greatly from the following averages based on readings over thirty years in Corfu, Argostoli and Zakinthos:

Month	Jan	Feb	Mar	Apr	May	June	July	Aug	Sept	Oct	Nov	Dec
Mean maximum temperature (C)	14	15	17	19	24	28	31	31	28	23	19	16
Mean minimum temperature (C)	6	7	9	11	15	18	21	19	16	16	12	9
Average number of rainy days	13	12	10	8	5	4	1	1	4	11	13	16

As these means suggest, the temperature can soar in July and August, and fall below freezing point in January and February. May and the first half of June, or September and the first half of October, are the best times for any holiday which is not going to be devoted entirely to bathing. In a dry year, April and the second half of October are exhilarating times, the first for its outburst of wild flowers, the second for cool sunny days and skies washed clean by September's sudden Wagnerian thunderstorms.

The Ionian Sea is spared the tyranny of the Aegean's fierce northerly, the *meltémi*. The prevailing wind in the summer is the *máestros*, a fresh north-westerly breeze. The moister southerly, the *óstria*, is also common. In some years the *sirókos*, a hot, sticky south-easterly, blows for days at a time in July and August, leaving everyone fretful and exhausted.

In Kithira, cooled by a prevailing westerly, the mean maximum temperatures are always a degree or two lower than in the other islands, though the mean minima from April to November are as high as in Zakinthos, the warmest of the northern six. Total rainfall is much lower, and you would be unlucky in Kithira to have more than five or six rainy days between the beginning of April and the end of September.

Rainfall Table

	ZAKINTHOS	CORFU	CEFALONIA	KITHIRA	ATHENS
Average annual rainfall (cm.)	115	114	89	66	40
Average number of rainy days a year	105	101	90	44	102

In May and October a light topcoat is often welcome in the evenings, and you will need a jacket or a jersey for cool nights and breezy days even in midsummer. An umbrella is well worth taking for spring showers and autumn rainstorms.

HEALTH AND DRINKING WATER

All the islands are healthy places — the Ithacans are famed for their longevity — and the only trouble you are likely to suffer from is an upset stomach. This can of course be caused by one unlucky mouthful of stale food; but it is much more often produced by too sudden an indulgence in hot sun and cold sea-water on top of food which, though perfectly clean, is rich and strange. It is wise to wash fruit and vegetables bought for picnics, since their skins may retain traces of toxic sprays as well as dust.

The Greeks are great connoisseurs of water and you will never be *offered* drinking water which is unsafe. In the towns the mains are pure; and if your hotelier is surprised to find you drinking out of the tap, this will be only because you have not asked for a carafe of the tap-water which he keeps iced in his refrigerator. In the villages the water in the taps or in the painted tin reservoir over the washstand may not be drinking water.

A glance at the population figures of the capitals will suggest what medical facilities you are likely to find on each island: almost everything on Corfu, a lot on Cefalonia, Zakinthos and Lefkas, and very little on Ithaca, Kithira and Paxos. In the first three islands, the tourist offices or police will help you find a doctor or dentist who speaks English.

MONEY AND BANKS

There are banks or banking agencies in all the island capitals, in Lixouri and Sami on Cefalonia, and in Potamos on Kithira. They are open from 08.00–14.00 and are shut on Saturdays and Sundays. Most hotels and some shops and restaurants are authorized to change money at the official rate. In practice you may get *fractionally* less at such places than at the banks since they tend to cover themselves against the daily fluctuations in the rate of exchange.

SHOPPING AND SOUVENIRS

In the summer months shops are open from about 08.00–13.00 and 17.00–20.00. Early closing day varies from island to island and according to the type of shop: hairdressers, butchers, grocers, etc. close on different afternoons. Most picnic ingredients can be bought at a grocer's (*pandopolíon*), though for butter (*voútiro*) you may have to go to a dairy (*galaktopolíon*), for bread (*psomí*) to a baker's (*foúrnos*) and for *draught* wine (*krassí khíma*) to a wineshop (*inopolíon*).

In 1980 Greek filter cigarettes cost between Drs 17 and 32 for twenty; in the towns they are sold chiefly at the ubiquitous newspaper-kiosks (*períptero*), where you can also buy sweets, razor-blades, toothpaste, etc., and sometimes make a telephone call. English, French and American cigarettes can be found in one or two souvenir shops and in the more expensive hotels, but English pipe tobacco is hard to get and extremely expensive. In the villages you will find local cigarettes in a café. In the town of Corfu two or three newsagents stock English, French and American books, magazines and newspapers (the last arrive the same day), but in the other islands English reading matter is limited to two small English-language Athens newspapers and a handful of paperbacks.

There are few genuine peasant handicrafts, but some quite ordinary utilitarian objects like brooms and earthenware casseroles make good presents, though these are not always made locally. There is a flourishing souvenir industry in Corfu, and among the bags, scarves, hats, clothes and carved olive wood it is possible to find attractive things, some brought from other parts of Greece, some produced locally for the tourist trade. Corfu also has several antique shops; but travellers from countries rich in nineteenth-century bric-à-brac will not often be tempted by their contents or their prices.

TIPPING

Except in one or two special cases, tipping is governed by the same uncertain conventions as everywhere else. In general, 10–15 per cent of an amount charged is a satisfactory tip, whether you are in a café or at a hairdresser's. Service is included in hotel bills, and the amount of additional largesse you distribute at the end of your stay is best treated by acting as you would at home. In most restaurants there are two people to tip, the waiter who takes your order and brings your food, and the boy who looks after your bread, water and wine. (You address the second as *mikré* — 'small one' — even if he is older and larger than you.) The waiter need not be, and in a modest place often is not tipped, since he gets a cut of the service charge which is included in the bill; but you should leave a coin for the *mikrós*, who will otherwise get nothing. If you give the waiter the extra 5 per cent which he will hope for in a prosperous place, leave his tip on the plate and the boy's on the table. No tip is necessary in small cafés and restaurants where the owner serves you himself. Taxi-drivers and cabbies do not expect tips.

Most tourists will be faced with the problem of how to show gratitude for unexpected acts of helpfulness or hospitality: the fisherman who gives you a lift in his boat, the priest who walks a mile to open a church for you, the villagers who pull your car out of a ditch or the cottager who offers you a bunch of grapes or a glass of ouzo. In ninety-nine cases out of a hundred an offer of money will be received with astonishment if not indignation, and the best thing is to travel with a bag of sweets for children and packets of English cigarettes for men. A photograph will give tremendous pleasure — but only if you remember to send it!

CINEMAS AND NIGHT-LIFE

Except for one new air-conditioned cinema in Corfu, cinemas in all the island capitals are out of doors in the summer. (You can therefore smoke, which you are not allowed to do at indoor cinemas.) The girl who looks as if she were there to show you to your seat expects a drachma, whether she does so or not. Foreign films are subtitled in Greek rather than dubbed, but the sound-track is often turned down rather too low. In many villages weekly cinema shows are provided by a touring van. On Corfu you can dance to an orchestra at one or two of the grander hotels and restaurants, and on all the islands there are (unfortunately) disco-theques wherever any considerable number of tourists stays; but they are obliged to close at 2 a.m. The casino in the *Akhillion* in Corfu (p. 164) provides roulette, baccarat, *chemin de fer* and fruit-machines.

HOLIDAYS AND FEAST-DAYS

PUBLIC HOLIDAYS

January 1st
January 6th (Epiphany).
March 25th (Independence Day).
Clean Monday (first day of Orthodox Lent).
Orthodox Good Friday.
April 21st (1967 Revolution).
May 21st (SS Constantine and Helen's Day. Anniversary of the union of the Ionic Islands with Greece).
August 15th (Assumption of the Virgin)
September 14th (Holy Cross Day).
October 28th (*Ókhi* Day — Greece said 'No' to the Italian ultimatum in 1940).
Christmas Day.

FEAST-DAYS

Palm Sunday	St Spiridon saves **Corfu** from the plague. Procession at 11.00.
Good Friday	*Epitáfios* processions in the afternoon and evening on all the islands.
Easter Even	03.00 **Zakinthos** procession. 09.00 Procession in **Corfu**. St Spiridon saves the island from famine. 11.00 Smashing of crockery on **Corfu**. 23.30–24.00 Services and processions on all the islands. Midnight announcement that Christ is risen.
Friday in Easter week	*Panayíri* at **Paleokastritsa** on Corfu.
Sunday after Easter	Procession in honour of St Yerasimos in the **Omala** on Cefalonia.
Whit Monday	Lefkas' chief *panayíri* at **Faneromeni Monastery**.
May 3rd	St Mavra's Day. *Panayíri* at **Makherado** in Zakinthos.
August 6th	Transfiguration. *Panayíria* at **Kassiopi** and on **Mt Pandokrator** on Corfu.
August 11th	St Spiridon saves **Corfu** from siege in 1716. Procession. Festival of St Spiridon in **Karia**, Lefkas, lasts two days, with traditional costumes and customs.
August 15th	*Panayíria* at **Markopoulo**, Cefalonia, **Kathara Convent**, Ithaca, **Mirtiotissa**, Kithira and many other churches dedicated to the Virgin Mary.
August 10th–20th (approx.)	Music and folk-dancing festival on **Lefkas**.
August 16th	Death of St Yerasimos. Procession in the **Omala**, Cefalonia.
August 24th	Return of St Dionisios' remains from the Strofades Islands. Procession in **Zakinthos**.
October 20th	Beatification of St Yerasimos. Procession in the **Omala**, Cefalonia.
First Sunday in November	St Spiridon saves Corfu from plague (1673). Procession.

| December 12th | Death of St Spiridon. Service in his church in **Corfu**. |
| December 17th | Death of St Dionisios. Procession in **Zakinthos**. |

SPORTS

BATHING
'Let's have a swim. I detest antiquarian twaddle,' Byron exclaimed during his visit to Ithaca in 1823.

Bathing almost everywhere in the Ionian Islands is from sand, shingle or pebble beaches, rather than rocks. Corfu has the widest choice, though its best sand beaches are on the west coast some way from the town. Lefkas and Cefalonia have superb bathing within a few minutes of their capitals; and shallow water at most of the beaches in Zakinthos makes them particularly suitable for children. The beaches in Kithira and Ithaca are not so good, so numerous or so easy to get to as in the other five islands. The best places to bathe are listed at the beginning of each island chapter. If you bathe from rocks, beware of sea-urchins. Sharks are very rare, but the myth that they are small and harmless dies tragically every year with one or two unfortunate bathers somewhere in the Mediterranean. It is foolish to swim far out to sea, or to bathe where very deep water comes right up to the shore, as it does for instance on the west coast of Paxos. Most of the more expensive seaside hotels and, of course, the holiday clubs provide water ski-ing for their residents, and several have wind-surfers and sailing dinghies too. Tourists staying elsewhere can queue for a turn at any touristic beach.

TENNIS
There is a tennis club in Corfu (p. 117). Many Corfu hotels and a few on Cefalonia and Zakinthos have their own tennis courts.

CRICKET
Cricket, planted by the British in the gravel of the Esplanade and kept alive after 1864 by annual visits of the Mediterranean Fleet, has taken firm root in Corfu, and on Saturday (and sometimes Wednesday) afternoons you can watch nineteenth-century under-arm bowling and listen to passionate appeals in Greek. The tourist office will help to make arrangements for anyone who would like to play.

SHOOTING

The Ionian Islanders are keen hunters and in the spring on Zakinthos almost every tree on the Keri and Vasiliko promontories hides a patient sportsman waiting for the exhausted doves to land 'on their passage from Barbary to Bessarabia' (Murray, 1900). In Kithira in the autumn you will see the islanders out to intercept the migrating quail which, in the nineteenth century, they were adept in catching 'on the wing in a sort of landing net' (Murray, 1872). There is rough shooting on all the islands for hare and partridge. There are also woodcock on Zakinthos and Corfu, and a few duck and snipe in the Corfiot marshes and lagoons. But only Greeks and resident foreigners are allowed shooting licences.

YACHTING

The Ionian Sea is an admirable cruising-ground for yachts and the Yacht Cruising Association (Old Stone House, Judges Terrace, Ship Street, East Grinstead, Sussex RH19 1AQ, tel. (0342) 311366-8) organizes fortnightly cruising holidays there. The yachtsman's *vade mecum* in these waters is *The Ionian Islands to Rhodes; a Sea Guide* by H. M. Denham (John Murray, 1978).

POSTAL AND TELEPHONE INFORMATION

In the island capitals post offices are open from 07.30–19.30 on weekdays and are shut on Sundays. In the larger villages their weekday hours are 08.00–14.30. In the towns stamps are also sold at one or two souvenir shops and kiosks.

Postal rates in Greece, as everywhere in the world, increase so often that it would be misleading to give specific figures. But it should be kept in mind that there is a basic fee for air mail letters (the first 20 grammes for Europe, including the United Kingdom; the first 10 grammes for the U.S.A. and Canada); then a fee for the next weight (20–50 grammes for Europe; 10–20 grammes for the U.S.A. and Canada); and then extra fees for successive increments.

In the capitals of Corfu, Lefkas, Cefalonia and Zakinthos telegraph offices (known as *Oté* from the initials of their name in Greek) are separate from post offices and are open day and night. Opening times in the capitals of the other three islands vary slightly but are approximately 08.00–12.00 and 16.00–20.00 on weekdays and 09.00–12.00 and 17.00–19.00 on Sundays.

Telecommunications are very good in Greece and there are

automatic telephone links with Britain, Europe and the U.S.A. (The U.K. Code is 0044.) Direct dialling rates are quite reasonable.

WEIGHTS AND MEASURES

The metric system is used in Greece. Liquids are not bought by the litre but by the kilogram; when ordering draught wine in a shop or restaurant you would thus ask for 'a half-kilo of wine' (*misó kiló krassí*). Land is measured in *strémata*, each stréma containing 1,000 square metres (i.e., about a quarter of an acre). Temperature is measured on the Centigrade scale. To convert Centigrade to Fahrenheit, multiply by 9/5 and add 32; to convert Fahrenheit to Centigrade, subtract 32 and multiply by 5/9.

ELECTRICITY

In the last few years electricity has spread everywhere in the islands. Current is 220-volt AC. Plugs and bulb sockets vary in shape, size and type and it is safest to buy any plugs you may need when you arrive.

TIME

Time in Greece is one hour ahead of British Summer Time (i.e., two hours ahead of Greenwich Mean Time).

GEOGRAPHY

The Ionian Islands take their name from the sea which lies between the sole of Italy and the west coast of Greece. Known as the Ionian Gulf or Sea since at least the sixth century B.C., it confusingly suggests Ionia on the Turkish coast or at any rate the Ionians of Attica. But whereas Ionia and the Ionians take their name from their founder hero Ion, the Sea (according to Aeschylus) is called after the nymph or goddess Io. (In Greek the two names are spelled with a different 'o'.) The title 'Ionian Islands' was coined in 1800 when Admiral Uschakow used it in a proclamation to the inhabitants of what the Venetians had known as the 'Isole di Levante'. Geographically speaking, Kithira is not an Ionian island at all and is included in this book because it was administered as one of the group between 1718 and 1864 and shares much of their earlier history. The Ionian Islands are also known as the *Eptánisos*, from

the 'seven islands' which formed the constituent units of a Septinsular Republic set up in 1800. Apart from the main seven there are
seventeen other inhabited islets in the group (see the end-paper
maps); Meganisi is nearly as large and populous as Paxos, the
smallest of the seven.

Visitors to more than one island may notice that each has its own
typical village-name. On Corfu many village-names end in '-ades'
or '-ada', on Lefkas and Cefalonia in '-ata', on Paxos in '-atika' and
on Kithira in '-adika' or '-anika'. The prettiest name in the Seven
Islands is 'Kalisperianika' on Kithira (i.e., 'Good-evening-ham').

GEOLOGY

Geologically speaking, the Ionian Islands are the offshore peaks of
ranges belonging to the intensely deformed belt of mountains which
runs down through Yugoslavia and western Greece and on under
the sea to Crete. On Kithira the central nucleus of these mountains
is visible in an area of crystalline schist which is probably
Palaeozoic; but in the other islands the oldest rocks of the highlands
are the Mesozoic limestones which lie over the central core and
were crushed against it when the ranges were thrown up in the
Tertiary period. Folded in with the limestones are a great variety of
later Tertiary formations — marls, siltstones, sandstones, clays,
shales and conglomerates — and the coastal plains and valley bottoms are covered by even more recent Quaternary deposits. These
different geological groundnotes account for a surprising number of
modulations in the landscape.

As always in limestone areas the softer deposits have been
gnawed out by the sea or leached away by the rain to form caves and
grottoes. The finest sea-caves are on the west coast of Paxos; the
best land-caves are at Milopotamo on Kithira and Drongarati on
Cefalonia. Other features of the islands are curious sump-like
valleys and corries which have no outlet to the sea but are drained
by *katavóthres* or swallow-pits. The most spectacular of these sumps
is the Livadi valley on Lefkas. As Davy has remarked, 'there is
much that is mysterious in the physical history of these islands,
especially in connection with the distribution of water'. On
Cefalonia an underground water-gallery runs beneath the
mountains from one sea to another; fresh water springs up in the

middle of the sea in several places; Paxos has sulphuretted springs; and on Zakinthos there are the famous pitch springs described by Herodotus.

Corfu, Paxos and Kithira are more or less immune to earthquakes, as their surviving old buildings show. But the other four islands have a long history of seismic shocks due to two separate faults, one running south from the mainland mountains to peter out south of Lefkas, the other running west from the Gulf of Corinth to an epicentre between Cefalonia and Zakinthos. The second is the more damaging, for Zante and Argostoli are exposed to its slightest shudder and the repercussions of a severe earthquake reach as far as Ithaca and the south of Lefkas. The last bad earthquake on Lefkas was in 1948 and on the other three islands in 1953. The latter was appallingly catastrophic, destroying or damaging beyond all hope of repair something like 70 per cent of all the buildings on Zakinthos, Cefalonia and Ithaca. In spite of generous help from many foreign countries and the determined efforts of the local inhabitants, the islands still bear innumerable scars of the cataclysm. Prospective visitors can be comforted by four considerations: first, the last earthquake of comparative severity before 1953 was in 1514; second, in spite of earthquakes, Zante survived as a virtually complete seventeenth- and eighteenth-century town until 1953; third, even the 1953 earthquake did not seriously damage the few modern buildings which existed at that date; and fourth, since 1953 all buildings have been constructed to withstand a shock as bad as the one of that year.

POPULATION

Corfu and Lefkas are the two most densely populated rural areas in Greece. Zakinthos and Paxos take fourth and sixth place; and the southern half of Cefalonia is high up on the national list. These dense populations were built up during the centuries before 1864 when the islands were more secure and prosperous than the rest of the country. But on the more rugged islands of Kithira and Ithaca and on northern Cefalonia the population has been halved in the last sixty years by emigration to Australia, the United States, southern Africa and, more recently, Germany. Even the more fertile islands have lost population since 1945, and only on Corfu has the tourist boom begun to halt the flow. The population figures given in each island chapter are based on the 1971 census and may now be as much as 10 per cent too high.

ECONOMY

Though tourism is a major source of revenue on Corfu and Zakinthos and is becoming increasingly important to the other islands, their economy remains essentially agricultural. Olive-oil, wine and currants are the main cash crops. Olives now cover over half the cultivated area of Corfu (which has more than 2,700,000 trees) and 90 per cent of that of Paxos. On Lefkas (750,000 trees) and Zakinthos (850,000 trees) olives share the farmed land more equitably with vines and cereals; and though there are densely planted areas on Cefalonia, Ithaca and Kithira, on these three islands it is the mountainsides of evergreen scrub and the terraces of fresh young wheat or golden stubble which dominate the landscape.

The main vine islands are Corfu, Cefalonia, Zakinthos and Lefkas, the first three exporting a little white table-wine (see p. 101), the last sending the bulk of its coarse red production to western Europe where it is used for blending or as the base for fortified aperitifs. Currants, though still an important crop on Zakinthos and the Lixouri peninsula of Cefalonia, are no longer the source of extraordinary wealth they were in the seventeenth and early nineteenth centuries (see p. 58).

Corfu has a few valuable acres under tobacco, and its flat pasturelands feed enough cows to support a dairy industry which exports butter all over Greece. Sheep and goats are numerous on all the islands, and their milk is made into a variety of cheeses (see p. 100).

Apart from a little light industry and one or two other minor cash crops — salt and fish from Lefkas and Corfu, and magnesite from Mount Skopos on Zakinthos — the only other notable source of wealth is seafaring. On Cefalonia and Ithaca something like half the adult population have worked at one time or another with lines owned by Cefalonian ship-owners, or under foreign flags, and on Ithaca the proper ambition for every small boy is to be a 'sea-captain'. This marine tradition, as old as Homer, goes back in modern times to the eighteenth century when Cefalonian barks deserted the Venetian for the Russian flag, and sailed to the Black Sea to trade.

FAUNA

BIRDS

The islands provide a wide variety of habitat for birds, and bird-watchers will be glad of their binoculars and a good bird book. While bigger birds like golden orioles, blackbirds and hoopoes are fair game for a peasant *stifádo*, you will never see, as D. H. Lawrence saw in the Italian markets, 'whole yard-lengths of robins, like coral and onyx necklaces . . . offered along with strings of sausages'; and apart from caged linnets and finches to charm you or set you in a rage, the Ionian Islanders leave songbirds alone, half a dozen names and the generic name *pouláki* ('little bird') summing up their interest in the winged kingdom.

Waders and herons are restricted to one or two salt-pans, swamps and lagoons (Keri on Zakinthos and Korissia and Andinioti on Corfu, where you can see Black-winged stilts), and the Sea Lake of Lefkas, where pelicans and cormorants are common. In the late summer kingfishers preside over seaside coves: they are enchanting bathing companions. Kestrels and buzzards are the commonest birds of prey, but Golden and other eagles are not rare, especially on Cefalonia, whose western cliffs the osprey haunts in winter, and above whose mountains you can often see the huge Griffon vulture sailing. Ravens can be seen in large numbers on Mt Enos, and please half, at any rate, of the Homeric scholars by still frequenting what they believe to be the 'Raven's Crag' above Arethusa's Fountain on Ithaca (*Odyssey* Book 13). Hoopoes are common on all the islands, but are particularly numerous on Corfu and Zakinthos. Jays on the other hand, outside the pinewoods of Zakinthos, the stands of cypress on the Fiskardo peninsula of Cefalonia and the forest on Mt Enos, are rare enough to seem exotic; and one does not see golden orioles as frequently as one would like. The variation in the bird population of each island is considerable and cannot always be easily explained. Magpies, which are two a penny along the west coast of the Peloponnese, seem not to like sea journeys; and while you will find plenty of them on Corfu and Lefkas, near the mainland, you may not see one on the other islands. More mysteriously, blackbirds whistle all over Cefalonia, but don't seem to care for Zakinthos or Corfu. A lot of garden birds common in western Europe are migrants and put in a very short appearance on these islands; all the tits except the Coal tit are uncommon, and wrens, robins and thrushes are seldom seen; their place as a background to the bird population is taken by three of the four wheatears, red-starts, whinchats and stonechats, and a large variety of warblers. Blackcaps, whitethroats, the Sardinian, Cetti's, Rüppell's and the Grasshopper warbler are easy to recognize; but there are many others to be identified by anyone with enough skill and patience. Other birds which are common are goldfinches and greenfinches, Pied and Collared flycatchers — always fluttering among the olive groves — and Woodchat shrikes, which like to use cypresses and telephone wires as vantage points to survey the countryside. The most beautiful and exciting of all the birds found on the Seven Islands is undoubtedly the Blue Rock thrush. It is not particularly rare and you may well see one as close to civilization as the far scarps of the castle hill on Zakinthos.

BEASTS

The wolves which were driven out of the Akarnanian hills by the fighting in the 1820s and took refuge in Lefkas have long since disappeared; but Corfu is still the most westerly place in Europe where jackals are common. The only other wild mammals which you are now likely to see are foxes, hares, bats, seals and small rodents of various sorts. The villagers of Agalas used to lower themselves perilously down the western cliffs of Zakinthos on ropes in order to get at the seals in the caves below; according to Grasset their fat gave a brighter light than olive-oil but had an unbearable smell.

In spring you will come across tortoises scrambling around in the aromatic undergrowth, and there are frogs and terrapins in most perennial pools. There are *basso profondo* frogs, alto frogs, piping pale-green tree-frogs and frogs that sing as shrilly as parakeets. Lizards of various sorts — the handsomest are large green ones — are responsible for most of the sinister rustles in the under-growth; but there is also an entertaining variety of snakes — except on Paxos, where St Paul is said to have performed the same apo-tropaic function as St Patrick in Ireland. It is always difficult to separate fact from fiction where snakes are concerned. There seem to be two varieties of viper, called *okhiá* and *saprokhiá*, the first like an English adder, the second more brightly coloured. There is a long thin snake called *saítas* (arrow) which if disturbed in the breeding season will launch itself at you. Though not poisonous, it is the only snake in the world known to have teeth on both its upper and lower jaws, and can thus cling on to you disconcertingly. Then there is a large, polished, brown snake (or possibly a scincoid lizard) called *tiflitás* or 'blind one'; though harmless, it can give you a tremendous start as it lashes around in a fury of alarm when it belatedly hears your footsteps near it in the grass. The peasants on Corfu say that the *tiflitás* is the dragon St George killed, and that it regains its sight on April 23rd; but even this presents St George in a new and rather unsporting light. Another snake with legendary attributions is a white snake with a black cross on its head which is said to appear only at the village of Markopoulo on Cefalonia (see p. 244).

'Scorpions and centepees' infested the barracks in Private Wheeler's time. Though they can easily be located if you are a knowledgeable scorpion addict like the young Gerald Durrell, they are seldom seen otherwise; but campers should keep their eyes open. Among the insects, cicadas, fireflies and, more literally, mosquitoes are the most striking. In the late summer the frenzied stridency of the cicadas is so unrelenting that, like some kinds of pain, one ceases to be consciously aware of it. Fireflies, at their densest in May, fill the parklands of Corfu with a swirl of embers. They have a special passion for the ditch of the Citadel, and it is an extraordinary sight to look down from the Esplanade on their turmoil of aerial traffic, navigation lights greenly winking.

FLORA

With their high rainfall (see p. 31), the northern six Ionian Islands are extraordinarily rich in wild flowers. As you approach Zakinthos by ferry in the spring you will be assailed by a scent as sweet and strong as ever Conrad met as he lay off eastern shores. Other parts of Greece can boast of their riots of colour; only on Corfu and Zakinthos are there whole island uprisings. It is impossible here to mention more than some of the more striking effects: the pools of pale-blue *Anemone blanda* in the moss under the firs on Mt Enos; the clusters of *Orchis provincialis*, *quadripunctata* and *purpurea* among the hummocks of yellow spurge on Mt Enos and Mt Pandokrator; the sheets of gold produced by the various brooms along the foothills of Zakinthos; the almonds and the Judas trees in flower high on the west coast of Lefkas; the magenta stipples of *Gladiolus segetum* or *communis* in the young corn; or the untilled fields covered with blue thistles and white asphodel. Fortunately the amateur botanist now has an excellent guide which will enable him to identify most of the more attractive plants: *Flowers of Greece and the Aegean* by Anthony Huxley and William Taylor (Chatto and Windus, 1977).

Though the summer visitor will miss many of the most interesting flowers, he will still find the islands green. Unlike the burned hillsides of the Cyclades, sparsely covered by *garigue*, the uncultivated slopes are almost everywhere densely thicketed with evergreen *maquis* in which the lentisk, arbutus and the holly-leaved kermes oak are the dominant species. In one or two places this scrub has grown up into proper woods: above Perakhori and on Aetos on Ithaca, and in the valley leading up to the pass of Agrapidies behind Sami on Cefalonia. Apart from the primeval forest of silver firs on the ridge and slopes of Mt Enos — the most exciting botanical experience in the Seven Islands — pines are common only on Zakinthos, where there are woods of Aleppo pine above the cliffs in the hilly region to the north-west, and clumps and groves of handsome stone-pine on the Vasiliko peninsula. Cypresses — particularly buxom and Italianate on Corfu — everywhere flatter the landscape with their black spires. In places they are either indigenous or have acclimatized themselves: in the north of the Fiskardo peninsula they grow as impenetrably as bristles in a hair-brush. Though plane trees grow beside the streams of the Milopotamo valley on Kithira and in the Vale of Arakli on Cefalonia, they are not as common as one would expect on such well-watered islands. Perhaps the custom of planting them by fountains is really more Turkish than Greek, for only on Lefkas does nearly every village have one or two round its well or spring. The park-like character of much of Corfu and the plain of Zante is given by clumps of magnificent deciduous oak, *ostrya* (hop hornbeam), silver poplar and eucalyptus trees. The *Robinia* from North America is an import which has become acclimatized, and the dusty island roads are often lined by this false acacia with its white early-summer flowers and finely fringed leaves.

And, of course, there are the olives — more than five million of them in the Seven Islands. It is no exaggeration to say that on Paxos and parts of Zakinthos, Lefkas and Corfu they look like natural woods, for the contours of the foothills break up all but a soothing hint of order in their arrangement. As often as not — through idleness or difficulty of terrain — the ground beneath the trees is left uncultivated, and the lawns of grass, first starred with daisies and camomile, then knee-high in wild flowers, and last mown or cropped by tethered sheep, stay green until late into the summer. Each island has its own indigenous form of olive as well as a heavy-fruiting variety imported from around Koroni in the Peloponnese. On Corfu the olives are enormous, their huge corded trunks riddled with eyes; unmanageable and uneconomical, they are as beautiful as forest trees. Where they have been belatedly pruned they are unsightly and absurd, with thin new arms sticking out of the tops of their decapitated trunks like sticks out of an umbrella-stand. On Paxos the olives are not 'massy and dark like those of Corfu, but straggling and long-armed' (Lear, *Views*); and on Kithira they are small and shrubby, pruned to grow into flat-topped treelets.

HISTORY

PREHISTORY (c. 70,000 B.C. to 850 B.C.)

The earliest inhabitants of the Ionian Islands were Middle and Upper Palaeolithic peoples (*c.* 70,000 B.C.–*c.* 40,000 B.C.). Their tools have been discovered at various seaside sites on Corfu and in a cave shelter near Gardiki (p. 162). Flint factories on the beaches of Cefalonia and Zakinthos suggest that the central islands were first settled during the Mesolithic period (*c.* 10,000 B.C.–*c.* 6000 B.C.).

The Neolithic period in Greece is marked by the rather sudden arrival and subsequent slow dispersal over the whole Aegean area of a new people whose pottery owes its inspiration to prototypes in Asia Minor. To judge from the stray sherds which have been found, this widespread culture quite early on reached all the Ionian Islands except Corfu and Paxos, whose Neolithic contacts seem to have been more with south Italy than mainland Greece: pottery dated to the very beginning of the period from Sidari on the north coast of Corfu, and to the very end from Afionas on the west, shows affinities with wares found in Apulia.

In about 3000 B.C. another influx of people from Asia Minor brought new metal-working techniques to the east and south-east coasts of Greece, and their culture soon spread to the Ionian Islands. Pre-Greek names ending in '-nthos' and '-ssos' such as 'Zakinthos', 'Assos' and 'Erissos' on Cefalonia — go back to these Early Bronze Age people. Traces of them have been found in all the islands but Corfu, which continued to evolve an isolated sub-Neolithic culture of its own until well on into the Bronze Age, as a site at Ermones shows. Those who settled at Nidri on Lefkas seem to have been of slightly different stock from the rest, for they cremated their dead before burying them, a practice unknown elsewhere in Early Bronze Age Greece.

In about 2000 B.C. another new racial element appeared on the mainland — the first Greek-speaking peoples. Their wheel-made 'Minyan' pottery has been found on Lefkas, Ithaca and Cefalonia, and on Lefkas their circular grave-plots recall the Grave Circles at Mycenae. But it took nearly five hundred years of dull pupation in a stream of Cretan influences before this Middle Bronze Age civilization on the mainland was ready to shed its dowdy chrysalis and emerge as the glittering and rapacious Mycenaean dragonfly of the Late Bronze Age (c. 1500–1150 B.C.). With the earlier flowering of Minoan civilization this book is not concerned, except to note that Kithira was colonized from Crete in about 1900 B.C. and peacefully abandoned in about 1450 B.C. — the date at which Mycenae assumed the hegemony of the Aegean world. There is no evidence of Minoan settlement beyond Cape Maleas and up into the Ionian Sea, and even the later spread of Mycenaean influence along the Gulf of Corinth in this direction was slow. Mycenaean pottery first appears in the central Ionian Islands in the fourteenth century B.C., and most of the rock-cut chamber tombs of Cefalonia (see p. 240) are a century or more later. But Mycenaean settlement during this late period is all that is needed to square with the Homeric account of an island confederation of sea-raiders whose ruler fought at the siege of Troy (c. 1200 B.C.). The excavations made at Polis and Pelikata (see pp. 220–21) by no means prove that a historical character called Odysseus lived on the island now called Ithaca — perhaps only a Linear B tablet could do that — but they do show that the island was inhabited by Mycenaeans at the right time and provide evidence that his name was associated with the island from a very early age. On Corfu on the other hand there is no evidence in the twelfth or thirteenth century of any such people as Homer makes the Phaeacians out to be. The voyage of the Argonauts may well be a poetic record of a Late Bronze Age expedition in search of the overland amber route to the Baltic, but if on their way home Jason and Medea called at Corfu when it was known as Drepane they left no more Mycenaean pottery in King Alkinous's realm than Odysseus did when it was known as Scheria.

As the Dorian invaders pushed down in successive waves into central Greece and the Peloponnese in the twelfth century, Mycenaean ruling families and their followers moved out of their path and took refuge in as yet unconquered corners of the mainland, in the neighbouring islands and overseas. If Strabo's story that Saguntum was colonized from Zakinthos is ever borne out by excavation at Murviedro in Spain, it will probably turn out to have taken place at this time. Some refugees certainly went to Cefalonia, for there is evidence there of a sub-Mycenaean influence between 1150 and 1050 B.C. Pausanias has a curious story about the return of the descendants of Cephalus to Attica from this island 'after ten generations', and it is tempting to think that this may be a garbled version of a further exodus to Athens in the eleventh century as the Dorians invaded Cefalonia in its turn. Cefalonian participation in the great migration to colonize Ionia in the eleventh century would not only account for the ancient but mysterious tradition that Sami on Cefalonia was the founder of Samos in the Dodecanese, but also explain the survival on the neighbouring island of Chios of a topographically detailed Cefalonian epic for Homer to incorporate in the *Odyssey* three hundred years later.

The centuries following the Dorian invasions are the great age of Phoenician maritime activity. Herodotus says that it was Phoenicians from Syria who founded the temple to Aphrodite on Kithira, and they may have had a station on the island to collect the murex shells of the Laconian coast for their purple dye. The story that Aeneas built another temple to Aphrodite on Lefkas suggests Phoenician influence farther north. Hyrie — another name for Zakinthos — and Scheria are both Semitic names, and Bérard ingeniously derives the name of Kerkira from the Semitic word which Herodotus uses for a fast Phoenician boat — *kerkoúros*. But if the easiest explanation of the seafaring Phaeacians and their magic ships is that they were in fact Phoenicians, no sign of their trading-post on Corfu has yet been found.

ARCHAIC, CLASSICAL AND HELLENISTIC TIMES (850 B.C. to 229 B.C.)

The Ionian Islands emerge from the Dark Ages with the first Greek exploratory voyages to the west in the ninth century B.C. Pottery found at Aetos on Ithaca shows that the Corinthians were using the island as a regular staging-post to south Italy by 850. In 733 they ejected a few earlier Euboean colonists and the indigenous Liburnians from Corfu and founded the colony of Corcyra at the landward end of the Paleopolis peninsula. Corcyra grew rich and proud and won her freedom from Corinth in the first recorded sea-battle of Greek history (*c*. 664 B.C.). Cypselus, tyrant of Corinth from *c.* 657 to 627 B.C., founded Lefkas (*c.* 625 B.C.) and other colonies to hem the rebellious island in, but it was not finally brought to heel until the reign of his son Periander (*c.* 625–586 B.C.). Herodotus tells how Periander sent off three hundred Corfiot youths to Lydia to be castrated, as a savage reprisal for the assassination of his son Lycophron, and how they escaped in Samos (Book 3). With the downfall of the tyranny in Corinth in 582 B.C. Corcyra became independent again, and the remains of her monuments in the Corfu Archaeological Museum testify to her wealth and culture at the time.

We know almost nothing of the history of the other islands before the sixth century B.C. Kithira belonged to the kings of Argos until their defeat by Sparta in 546 B.C., after which it was administered by a special Spartan commissioner called the Kithiroides. Zakinthos seems to have been a dependency of the Achaeans in 708 B.C.: it is associated with the colony of Kroton in the Gulf of Taranto which they founded at that date. The stages by which Cefalonia grew into a confederation of four small city states are obscure. There is no record of colonization, and the towns of Krani, Sami, Pali and Proni are probably indigenous growths of the sixth century B.C. But a shrine near the summit of Mt Enos must be much older, since it is mentioned by Hesiod (eighth-century?).

The Ionian Islands were too remote from the central stage of Athens in the fifth century B.C. to play any important role in that golden age of politics, art and war. The Lefkadians sent three ships to Salamis in 480 B.C. and fought side by side with a small contingent from Pali on Cefalonia at the battle of Plataea in the following year. Corcyra promised to provide sixty ships to fight against the Persians, but ignobly hedged her bet on an Athenian victory and made sure that they did not arrive in time. During the long struggle for ascendancy between Athens and Sparta in the fifth and fourth centuries B.C. the islands had strategic importance as naval bases from which the Athenians could harry the Peloponnese, and we hear of them from time to time as they are raided or won over: in 456 B.C. when Tolmides sacked Kithira and persuaded Zakinthos and Cefalonia to join the Athenian side; in 431 B.C. when an Athenian fleet made sure of the friendship of Cefalonia and Zakinthos at the outset of the Peloponnesian War; in 424 B.C. when Nicias captured Kithira from the Spartans; in 375 B.C. when Corcyra and Cefalonia were pressured into joining the Second Athenian Alliance; and so on. Corcyra, of course, has a greater claim to fame: it was her dispute with Corinth over their joint colony of Epidamnus and Athenian intervention to prevent her defeat in the sea-battle of Sybota in 433 B.C. which provided the main *casus belli* of the Peloponnesian War. And the bloody revolution which broke out on the island in 427 B.C. started a chain reaction in the Hellenic world which continues to this day. In the whole literature of antiquity there is nothing more contemporary in feeling than Thucydides' account — in Book 3 of his *Peloponnesian War* — of the pattern of ideological conflict which was first formulated on the pleasant island of Corfu.

The rise of Macedon in the fourth century B.C. had little impact in the west, and there is nothing of interest to note in the Ionian Islands during the confused century which followed the break-up of Alexander's Empire.

ROMAN PERIOD (229 B.C. to A.D. 330)

In 229 B.C. Queen Teuta of the Illyrians captured Corfu and provoked Rome to send over a fleet to free the island and suppress Illyrian piracy. Though allowed to govern herself, Corcyra was in effect a Roman protectorate from this time on. Strabo writes of this period that the island was 'proverbially derided as a joke because it was humbled by its many wars . . . And later on, although it was set free by the Romans, it got no commendation, but instead as an object of reproach, got a proverb: "Corcyra is free, dung where thou wilt".' (Book 7). The other islands came into Roman hands as a result of the ambition of Philip V of Macedon, whose impudent alliance with Hannibal in 215 B.C. brought a Roman fleet to the Ionian Sea in 212 B.C. and a formal declaration of war in 200 B.C. Lefkas — the capital of Philip's staunchest allies, the Acarnanians — was taken by siege in 197 B.C., Zakinthos in 191 B.C. and Cefalonia — after a heroic defence by Sami — in 188 B.C. Though the islands were attached to the new Roman province of Macedonia after 148 B.C., they seem to have been administered rather loosely. Strabo tells us that when Gaius Antonius went into fifteen years' exile in Cefalonia in 59 B.C. 'he held the whole island in subjection as though it were his private estate.' Gaius had been Cicero's friend and fellow-consul and his sojourn in the Ionian Islands may have something to do with a curious memorial to Cicero which was found in Zakinthos in A.D. 1547. John Locke saw it in 1553 and writes that 'under the same stone was found a glasse somewhat proportioned like an urinall . . . wherein were the ashes of the head and right arme of Mar. T. Cicero, for . . . his wife having got his head and right arme

. . . went from Rome, and came to Zante, and there buried his head and arme, and wrote upon his tombe this style M. T. Cicero. Have. Then followeth in other letters, Et tu Terentia Antonia . . .'

During the Roman civil wars of the first century B.C. the islands were forced willy-nilly to take one side or the other: in 48 B.C. Corfu helped in the Dyrrhachium campaign which ended in Caesar's defeat of Pompey at Pharsalus, and all the islands suffered as a result of having served as fleet stations for Antony and Cleopatra during the winter before Actium. Lefkas was stormed by Agrippa before the battle in 31 B.C. and Corfu's monuments razed after it as a punishment for aiding and abetting the enemy. A few years later Augustus gave Kithira to Julius Eurycles, tyrant of Sparta, as a reward for his part in the campaign, and Strabo tells us that he thereafter regarded the island 'as his private property'. With Augustus's accession in 27 B.C. the other Ionian Islands were attached to the new Roman province of Achaia. Lefkas seems to have been a port of entry at this time and was linked to the mainland by a stone causeway and bridge (see p. 193).

A strange story Plutarch tells about Paxos in the time of Tiberius (42 B.C.–A.D. 37) may describe the first tidings of Christianity in the islands.

Epitherses . . . said that once upon a time in making a voyage to Italy he embarked on a ship carrying freight and many passengers. It was already evening when near the Echinades Islands, the wind dropped, and the ship drifted near Paxi. Almost everybody was awake, and a good many had not finished their after-dinner wine. Suddenly from the island of Paxi was heard the voice of someone loudly calling Thamus, so that all were amazed. Thamus was an Egyptian pilot, not known by name even to many on board. Twice he was called and made no reply, but the third time he answered; and the caller, raising his voice, said, 'When you come opposite to Palodes (Butrinto) announce that Great Pan is dead.'

So, when he came opposite Palodes, and there was neither wind nor wave, Thamus from the stern, looking towards the land, said the words as he had heard them, 'Great Pan is dead.' Even before he had finished there was a great cry of lamentation not of one person, but of many, mingled with exclamations of amazement. As many persons were on the vessel the story was soon spread abroad in Rome, and Thamus was sent for by Tiberius Caesar.

There are local traditions that St Paul visited Lefkas and Paxos, but neither these nor the Kithiran belief that St John wrote parts of his *Revelation* in a hermitage above Kapsali Bay can be reconciled with what is known of the movements of these early Church Fathers.

Of the Ionian Islands during the first three centuries A.D. we know very little. Suetonius recounts that Nero gave a song recital at Kassiopi on Corfu on his way to Greece in A.D. 66. In the second century the islands were attached to the new province of Epirus, and Cefalonia was wealthy enough for Hadrian to earmark its taxes to pay for his public works in Athens. Most of the Roman villas which have been discovered on Corfu and Cefalonia date from these centuries, which seem to have been prosperous and peaceful.

BYZANTINE PERIOD (A.D. 330 to 1204)

For nearly nine hundred years after the dedication of Constantine's new capital on the Bosphorus, the Ionian Islands remained part of what has come to be known as the Byzantine Empire. For most of this period barely a chronicle, hardly a building, survives. On the far fringe of the prefecture of Illyria, the islands were exposed to the raids of barbarian tribes such as the Vandals, who invaded the moribund carcass of the old Roman world and in about 466 pillaged the northern islands. To judge by the scale of the sixth-century basilica of Paeleopolis and frequent mentions of Corfiot participation in Byzantine sea-battles, Corfu at least seems to have remained powerful and prosperous until about 562, when the old town was devastated by Totila the Ostrogoth in a savage reprisal for Belisarius's campaigns in Italy. At the end of the sixth century the Slavs who in Justinian's day had plundered the Balkan provinces only to withdraw behind the Danube with their loot, began to settle in Greece. According to the *Chronicle of Monemvasia* almost the whole of the Peloponnese was under Slav control from 587–805 and the fate of the Ionian Islands during these two hundred years is particularly obscure. Since the Slavs were competent sailors — they reached Crete in 623 — all the islands must have been raided and some may have been settled. There are no remains of churches of this period in any of the islands but many Slavic place names. 'Cerigo', the medieval Italian name for Kithira, is almost certainly a corruption of the Slavic name 'Tsirigo'.

When the Slavs were being brought under control at the end of the eighth century a system of administrative districts called 'themes' (after the regiments— *thémata* — stationed in the Anatolian provinces) was introduced into Greece, and by 809 the northern six islands had been formed into a new maritime theme of Cefalonia under a *stratigós* or military governor. The fact that his capital was on Cefalonia suggests that St George's castle but not the Citadel of Corfu existed by this date. Later in the ninth century the new theme was given a naval establishment to protect it from the raids of the Arabs based on Crete and Sicily. In 961 Crete was retaken and Kithira was brought under control and repopulated.

By the tenth century Constantinople had begun to treat the former Byzantine province of Venice as an independent ally, and in the eleventh century brought her on to the Ionian scene by a call for help against the Norman, Robert Guiscard. By 1071 the Normans had taken the last Byzantine possession in the south of Italy and in 1081 they launched an attack on the Empire, capturing Corfu. Venice's services in driving the Norman army out of Dyrrhachium on the Albanian coast in 1083 and defeating the Norman fleet off Corfu in 1084 were paid for (in advance) by a chrysobull granting her unrestricted trade throughout the Empire, free of customs dues. Once having locked her teeth into the life-giving jugular of the Oriental markets, Venice was reluctant to let go, and when her trading privileges were reduced in 1122 in favour of her Pisan rivals, the Doge himself led the fleet down for a belligerent demonstration in front of Corfu. When Guiscard's nephew Roger II of Sicily took Corfu again in 1147 the Venetians once more came to the help of the Greeks and in 1149, after a long siege, helped the Emperor Manuel Comnenus to drive the Normans out of the Citadel. Relations between the two allies were so bad that at one point in the siege the Venetians seized an imperial vessel, hung it with gold and purple brocades and enthroning a Negro in it went through a mocking pantomine of Byzantine court ceremonial in front of the dark-skinned Emperor. In 1182 when William II of Sicily launched the third Norman attack against the Empire the Venetians refused to help, and William's piratical admiral Margaritone took Corfu, Cefalonia and Zakinthos without any difficulty before sailing on into the Aegean. When peace was made in 1187 neither side was in a position to make terms and though Corfu was evacuated and handed back, Cefalonia, Zakinthos and Ithaca were kept as spoils of war by Margaritone.

Of the Norman years we know only that the islanders did not have to pay the heavy Byzantine hearth tax: 'Nicetas Acominatus, punning about the tax, says that at the end of the twelfth century the

Corfiotes preferred the fire of foreign slavery (to the Normans) to the smoke of the tax' (Runciman).

Venice's bitterness and greed were largely responsible for the downfall of the Byzantine Empire in 1204. In 1199 plans were afoot in Europe for a new Crusade against Islam. The land route to the Holy Land had been cut by Turks and Bulgars, and for the sum of 85,000 silver marks and half the crusaders' territorial conquests Venice agreed to transport the army and its train by sea to Egypt, the weak point of the Saracen Empire. But unknown to most of the crusaders a deal was brewing behind their backs: Doge Dandolo, Alexius the son of a deposed Byzantine Emperor and several leading crusaders were all more interested in aiming at Constantinople than at Alexandria. Nudged by these schemers' experienced hands, events fell into a sequence which favoured their plans, and in 1203, while the crusading armada lay at anchor off Corfu, Alexius signed a treaty in which he undertook to foot the outstanding Venetian bill if the fleet would call first at Constantinople and put him on the Imperial throne. Thus on the eve of Pentecost the fleet set sail from Corfu on what was to become the sack of the greatest city in the world. The weather was typical of Corfu in May and the Provençal chronicler records: 'Et li jorz fu bels et clers, et li venz dolz et soes; et il laissent aler les voiles al vent.'

MIDDLE AGES (A.D. 1204 to 1502)

After the fall of Constantinople the Byzantine world was divided up on paper between Venice, the crusaders and the Latin Emperor. Venice's share included the western part of Greece and all the Ionian Islands as well as the Morea (as the Latins called the Peloponnese) and various possessions in the Aegean. It was a greedy helping which the Republic had no real appetite for and was quite incapable of digesting. A mercantile city-state, she had neither the population nor the motive for mainland conquest. All she needed was a string of defensible ports along her trade route to the Levant. Though Corfu at first sight seemed an obvious candidate, and was settled for a few years in 1207, the twin ports of Modon and Koroni in the Morea turned out to be better staging points. They were also insulated against Greek attacks by the powerful Principality of the Morea which the Provençal crusader Geoffrey de Villehardouin had set up in the hinterland. For the time being Venice could therefore afford to leave the Ionian Islands to the Greek and Italian adventurers who occupied them. How they came variously under the despots of Epirus, the Sicilian House of Hohenstaufen, the Angevins and their Italian vassals the Orsini and Tocco families, the Venetian family of Venier, the Monemvasiote family of Daimoyannes, and finally under the direct rule of the Republic is described in the Historical Chart of Island Suzerains on pages 66–7. Many of the changes in ownership came about peacefully as the result of dynastic marriages or feudal transfers of sovereignty. But if, until the last quarter of the fifteenth century, the islands were embroiled in no major wars, they were often savagely raided by their European rulers' enemies: by the Aragonese in 1292 and the Catalan Company in 1303 when they were under the Angevins, by the Genoese in 1403 and 1432 and the Turks in 1431 when they were under the Venetians.

Under all their medieval rulers alike life followed the feudal tenor of the age. Salt, wine and oil were the rulers' chief sources of revenue, to which it was no breach of contemporary etiquette to add the fruits of a little steady piracy. Land was divided between the ruler's domain, church estates and feudal fiefs. Under the Angevins Corfu had twenty-four baronies, Zakinthos twelve and Cefalonia five. On Corfu at the end of the fourteenth century there was a special fief for the gypsies who were probably encouraged to settle on the island because of their skill at horse-breeding. Ithaca (which was also known in the Middle Ages as 'Val di Compare') was one barony and Paxos another. Kithira, like gold, was divided into twenty-four *carati*, all owned in 1204 by the Venier family, who — claiming descent from Venus — regarded her birthplace as their rightful if rather belated inheritance. The Salic law did not apply in the Latin Empire of Romania to which the Ionian Islands theoretically belonged, and in course of time and intermarriage most of the baronies came to be held by families which though Italian in name were Greek in faith and speech. On Corfu the barons formed a General Assembly even before the Venetian take-over in 1386, and by 1440 a smaller Council existed whose members filled various administrative and judicial posts. As serfs the common people had no rights at all.

With the arrival of the Angevins and their Catholic vassals, the Orthodox Church — which on Corfu had flourished under the despots of Epirus — went into a sharp decline. Orthodox bishops were deprived of their sees and cathedrals, and the Minorites seized most of the Greek monastic lands. Their new monasteries on Corfu, Zakinthos and Cefalonia attracted many Frankish pilgrims on their way to the east. Corfu exerted a horrid fascination because of the tradition that Judas Iscariot (i.e., 'the Skheriot') had come from the island when it bore the name of 'Skheria'. Though the Venetians were less bigoted than the Angevins and treated the Orthodox dignitaries with respect, they did not alter the status quo which they inherited, and it was not until the Russians landed in 1798 that the Greek Church recovered its rightful status.

The barons did service for their liege lords in innumerable campaigns on the mainland, or commuted it for money, jousted and tilted at the ring (a sport still practised on Corfu at carnival-time in the nineteenth century) and exploited their estates either directly or through tyrannical bailies.

The last great Frankish medieval rulers in the Ionian Islands — and indeed in the whole of Greece — were the Tocco family, whose four islands of Cefalonia, Zakinthos, Ithaca and Lefkas had formed a Palatine County of the Principality of Achaia ever since their predecessors, the Orsini, had chosen Geoffrey de Villehardouin as their liege lord in about 1218. In 1404 this feudal tie with the Peloponnese — now largely retaken by the Greeks — was abolished, and by 1418 Carlo Tocco II had added Epirus, Akarnania and Aetolia to his domains. When Cyriac of Ancona visited him in Ioannina he styled himself 'King of the Epirotes'. But the days of the Franks in Greece — and of the Greeks themselves — were now numbered. Under Murad II and Muhammad II the Ottoman Turks resumed the inexorable advance that had been checked for a few years in 1402 by Timur and his Mongols. Ioannina was taken from Carlo Tocco in 1430, and in 1449 his son Leonardo III was driven back into his islands. Constantinople fell to Muhammad II in 1453, Athens in 1456, and by 1460 the whole of the Morea had been overrun. In 1463 war was declared on Venice, and Venetian subjects swelled the stream of refugees who sought asylum in Zakinthos and Lefkas. Now at last Venice found the time ripe to claim 'her' islands, and when Leonardo stubbornly refused to hand them over to the Republic, left him out of the peace treaty she signed with the Turks in 1479. The result was their immediate sack by an Ottoman fleet. Zante was burned to the ground and thousands of Cefalonian peasants were 'carried off to Constantinople where the Sultan separated husbands from wives and mated both sexes to Ethiopians to produce a race of grey slaves' (Miller). In 1481 Leonardo's brother recaptured Cefalonia and Zakinthos with the help of a Catalan squadron but was dislodged from Zakinthos in the following year by a Venetian squadron from Modon. In 1483 his Cefalonian garrison murdered him and handed over the island to the Republic. Zakinthos was retained on payment of an annual tribute of 500 ducats to the Porte, but the Sultan insisted on the return of Cefalonia in 1485. During the war of 1499–1503 it was retaken by the Venetians with the help of Gonzalo de Cordoba, the greatest admiral of the day, and Lefkas was also captured in 1502. But while Cefalonia thereafter remained Venetian, Lefkas had to be handed back before the Turks would agree to make peace.

VENETIAN COLONIES (A.D. 1502 to 1797)

Between 1463 and 1718 seven wars with the Ottoman Empire slowly drained Venice of her wealth and energy, until in 1797 nothing was left of her greatness but an absurd charade. The background and chronology of these wars, and the fortunes of the Ionian Islands during them, is given in the table of Venice's wars with the Turks on p. 59. Apart from the sieges of Corfu in 1537 and 1716, the Seven Islands were never the main target of an Ottoman attack, but they were raided and savagely pillaged from time to time. Lefkas (which the Venetians called Santa Maura) changed hands five times, and in the eighteenth century Kithira (Cerigo) was lost to the Turks for four years. But in general the islands gained rather than suffered from Venice's long struggle to keep her trade with the Porte — to feed from the hand whose sublimest pleasure it was from time to time to smite her Christian cheek. With each new setback — in Euboea, Crete and the Morea — new nobles, merchants, artists, soldiers and craftsmen (both Greek and Venetian) fell back on the islands which the Republic was to hold on to till the end — at first because they were useful naval bases, arsenals and trading stations, later because they provided her with salt, oil and currants for her own consumption, and finally because they were an important source of customs revenue when British, French and Dutch vessels captured the Mediterranean carrying trade.

At the end of the fifteenth century, however, Venice was still one of the Great Powers of Europe. Every year six great trading fleets set off to collect wine, currants, sugar, linen, spices, precious stones, muslins, dyes and gold from the ports of the eastern Mediterranean. The bustle of military and administrative activity which followed the wars of 1463–79 and 1499–1503 invigorated the economies of the Ionian Islands. Modon and Koroni, lost to the Ottomans in 1499, had been for Venice 'the receptacle and special nest of all our galleys, ships and vessels on their way to the Levant' (Miller); now

Zante (as the Venetians called Zakinthos) took their place, its population and that of Cefalonia swollen by settlers from the lost settlements in the Morea. Another consequence of the loss of the Koroni olive groves, Venice's chief source of oil, was the introduction of a state subsidy of twelve gold pieces for every hundred olive trees planted in the Ionian Islands. Ithaca, deserted since its devastation by a Turkish fleet in 1479, was resettled from Cefalonia in 1503. The fortifications of the islands were speedily put into better shape. The old castle of St George on Cefalonia was virtually rebuilt from its foundations by engineers sent out from Venice, and on Kithira (which had gained new importance since the loss of the Morean fortresses and now came to be known as 'an eye of Crete') new landward ramparts were added to the medieval castle above Kapsali.

Corfu, where a colonial superstructure had been gradually added to the feudal foundations of governments inherited by Venice in 1386, provided a ready-made model for the administration of the new colonies, and on Cefalonia, Zakinthos and Kithira a *Provveditore* was now appointed by the Venetian Senate to carry out the duties of civil and military governor for a term of two years. Posts of particular importance under him, such as the chief of police and the salt commissioner, were reserved for patrician civil servants sent out from Venice, but other administrative offices were shared in rotation by the members of a council elected from the ranks of each island's nobility, who were registered in a Golden Book. During the war of 1499–1503 a new post of *Provveditore Generale del Levante* was established. This important official, a sort of Governor-General who resided in Corfu, was appointed for a term of three years and descended on each of the northern islands in turn to inspect its administration, economy and defences and to listen to any complaints of abuses. In the sixteenth century these were corrected immediately, for the odious but efficient Venetian system of state inquisitors, secret police and official boxes for denunciatory letters made it impossible for any Venetian offical to lapse with impunity from the high standards of integrity still demanded by the Senate.

In the sixteenth century, and even more in the seventeenth, Zakinthos and Cefalonia became enormously wealthy from the currant trade. The currant vine seems to have been introduced into these islands by refugees from the Peloponnese in the early sixteenth century. By the middle of the century the first consignment of currants had arrived in England; in 1586 a traveller men-

Table of Venice's wars with the Turks

1463–79	Venice lost Euboea and all her possesions in the Peloponnese except Modon, Koroni and Monemvasia.
1499–1503	Venice lost Modon and Koroni (1499), but captured *Cefalonia* (Christmas Eve 1500) and *Lefkas* (August 1502). *Lefkas* had to be handed back in 1503. Ithaca, abandoned by the Turks, was resettled in the same year.
1537–40	In Spring 1537 a huge Ottoman fleet passed *Corfu* amid mutual salutes and courtesies on its way to attack the Kingdom of Naples. Turkish transports tangled accidentally with Venetian galleys as they ferried troops across to south Italy from Albania, Suleiman II took affront, and 5,000 men and 30 cannon were landed to besiege the *Citadel of Corfu*. It was a half-hearted siege which was raised without a major assault, though the Turks sailed off with 15,000 slaves. On its way back to Turkey the fleet stopped at *Kithira* to sack the capital of Ayos Dimitrios and carry off another 7,000 slaves. Venice made peace in 1540, losing Monemvasia and various Aegean islands.
1570–73	Venice lost Cyprus to Selim II. Evacuated villages on *Kithira, Zakinthos, Cefalonia* and *Corfu* were sacked by the Turkish fleet which was later annihilated at the Battle of Lepanto by an allied fleet under Don John of Austria (October 7th, 1571). Many of the Venetian galleys were manned or captained by Corfiots, Cefalonians and Zantiots. The Republic sued for an independent peace in 1573 and had to increase her tribute for *Zakinthos* to 1,500 ducats a year.
1645–69	Venice lost Crete.
1684–99	The Venetians under Francesco Morosini captured *Lefkas* (August 6th, 1684) — the opening blow of a campaign which recovered the whole of the Peloponnese and Athens (1688). Under the Treaty of Carlowitz (1699) Venice kept *Lefkas*, the whole of the Peloponnese and Aegina and stopped paying tribute for *Zakinthos*.
1713–18	The Turks retook the Peloponnese in 1713. *Kithira* and *Lefkas* were abandoned without a struggle in 1714 as the Venetians fell back on *Corfu*, which a Saxon soldier of fortune — Count John Matthias von der Schulenburg — and some foreign regiments had been hired to defend. In 1716 the Turks disembarked 30,000 men for a siege which was to last forty-two days. On August 17th and 18th a Turkish general assault forced the defenders back to the Esplanade, but Schulenburg at the head of 800 men drove them out of the town again. On the night of the 18th one of Corfu's stupendous thunderstorms demoralized the Turkish camp and on the following night the whole force sailed secretly away, leaving their guns and baggage-train behind. Later in the autumn Schulenburg retook *Lefkas* but Prince Eugen's capture of Belgrade led to Venice's allies making peace just as a promising campaign had started in Epirus; so under the Treaty of Passarowitz (July 1718) Venice got *Kithira* back as a sop, but retained none of her mainland conquests.

tions the English house in Zante; and in 1592, when the Turkey and Venice Companies were merged in the new Levant Company, currants were the staple of the English trade. By 1609 Lithgo could write of Zakinthos that 'this little Ile maketh yearely onely of Currants 160,000 Chickins . . . every Chickin of Gold being nine shillings English . . . A rent or summe of mony which these silly Ilanders could never affoord (they being not above 60 yeares agoe, but a base beggarly people, and an obscure place) if it were not here in England of late for some Liquorous lips, who forsooth can hardly digest Bread, Pasties, Broth . . . without these currants.' For many years this English craze for currants was a mystery to the Ionian islanders. 'The Zantiots have not long known what we doe with them; but have been perswaded that we use them only to Dye Cloth with; and are yet strangers to the luxury of Christmas Pies, Plum-potage, Cake and Puddings, etc.,' commented Wheler in 1675. At that date the English 'had a little factory' in Zante 'consisting of a Consul, and five or six Merchants' who supervised the loading of the currants from 'Warehouses they call Seraglios; into which they are powred through a hole above, until the room be filled up to the top. By their own weight they cake so together, that they are forced to dig them out with piked Irons' (Wheler).

The sudden great wealth of the islands had social and artistic consequences. A new class of prosperous burghers sprang up between the nobility and the peasantry. On Zakinthos artisans and tradesmen formed themselves into guilds of ropemakers, butchers, hairdressers and so on, which vied with each other and the nobles in commissioning handsome baroque churches to replace the modest Byzantine buildings of the sixteenth century. The decoration of these churches and of the nobles' new *palazzi* stimulated an influx of refugee artists from Crete, where the Ottomans had embarked on a twenty-five year struggle to take the island in 1645 (see Church art, p. 91). Other refugees brought with them the rhythms of the Cretan folk epics and a tradition of demotic Greek which Ionian poets were to develop and use in the nineteenth century.

The new middle classes bitterly resented the feudal privileges of the nobility, who were still the only members of Ionian society to have a say in the administration of the islands. In 1628 the Zantiot guilds challenged their authority in the first of a series of bloody uprisings. Venice could not afford to suppress them, for on their wealth and social ambition she now increasingly relied to finance her wars, and in 1647 — two years after the Turkish attack on Crete — a law was published in the Ionian Islands which allowed the bourgeoisie to buy the rights and titles of nobility. By this time lethargy and corruption had begun to infect the Venetian civil service and the islanders were left to resolve their social tensions in their own way. The blood-feud had earlier on been introduced by refugees from the Mani, and the picture of assassination and extortion by hired ruffians or *bravi* throughout the seventeenth century is as relentless and horrifying as that described by Manzoni in *I Promessi Sposi*. ' . . . they make more conscience to break a Fast, than to commit a Murther', wrote George Sandys of the Zantiots in 1610, and in 1675 Wheler noted, 'The inhabitants of Corfu are of a very revengeful nature, never forgetting any injury done them; which is often the ruin of whole families . . . They themselves confess and relate most barbarous adventures . . .'

In the eighteenth century 'Bribery, and every mode of illegal practice, were carried on openly; toleration for a crime might easily be purchased, and the laws, in many respects imperfect themselves, were rendered wholly null by the corruption of the judges' (Holland). Justice could be bought for a trifling sum: 'I would shoot you had I thirty piastres to pay for your skin', was a comment overheard by Sibthorp during his stay in Zakinthos. The residence of the *Provveditore Generale del Levant*— once a proud patrician — was now furnished by a Jewish rental firm on Corfu who provided even the cutlery and linen for his table and the livery for his servants. At the *repas d'étiquette* which Grasset tells us that this official gave five times a year, each guest slid a voucher for a certain amount of oil (or its equivalent in cash) under his plate, and the Governor-General's politeness as he said good night was gauged to a nicety by the amount written on it, discreetly whispered to him by an aide-de-camp. In the opera-houses of Corfu, Zante and Cefalonia the audience turned their backs on the *opéra bouffes* and ballets to watch the goings-on in the *Provveditore*'s box, or ate and played at cards. The petty regulations which governed protocol and dress in Venice were scrupulously applied: while the *Protópapas*— the chief dignitary of the Orthodox Church in each island— was entitled to a ducal mantle and an immense peruke, the painter Nicholas Koutouzis was considered lacking in the proper punctilio when he insisted on wearing red silk stockings with gold garters, trimming his beard and keeping his hat off to show the elegant parting in his hair while only abbot of St Nicholas-on-the-Mole in Zante. On Zakinthos the women wore black velvet masks in the street, and on Cefalonia they stuck their feet through special little traps in their doors so that their legs should not be seen when they were measured for their shoes. There was no public education during the whole period of Venetian rule and though such scholarly priests as Vikentios Damodos (1679–1759) on Cefalonia, and Evyenios Voulgaris (1716–1806) and Nikiforos Theotokis (1736–1805) on Corfu taught privately and were the first to write in demotic Greek, the only evidence of the experimental and scientific temper of the age was the attempt of Count Kharvouris to introduce cotton and indigo on to Cefalonia. He was murdered by the peasants for his pains.

In the last quarter of the eighteenth century Russian expansion into the Mediterranean brought a breath of political and economic fresh air into the stale atmosphere of frivolity and corruption. Since the outbreak of her war with Turkey in 1768 Russia had tried to stir up discontent on the Greek mainland, and by 1774 was the self-appointed champion of its fellow-Orthodox population. A few years later a sort of diplomatic and military guerrilla centre was set up for Greeks in St Petersburg and several of the Zantiots, Corfiots and Cefalonians who were enrolled by the Russian consuls at this time were to return and play a part in the political life of the islands after 1800. Many island ship-owners also took advantage of a Russo-Turkish commercial treaty of 1783 to sail to Constantinople and the Black Sea under the Russian flag and thus escape from restrictions which channelled Ionian trade exclusively through Venice.

It is easy to paint too lurid a picture of the Ionian Islands in the period of Venice's decline. That their lot was even then fortunate compared with the mainland can be judged by the impression which Zante made on Richard Chandler as he returned from a tour of Turkish-occupied Greece just twenty years before the fall of the Republic: 'A capacious harbour filled, besides other vessels, with large ships and glittering galleys, a flourishing city with steeples and noble edifices, the sound of bells, the dress and manners of Italy, were all articles to which we had been long disused. The transition from misery and desolation was as striking as it had been sudden.' On many of the islands earthquakes have destroyed all testimony to the Republic's long presence except castles and olive groves. On Corfu, however, the legacy is more generous. 'It is to Venice that Corfu, almost more than any other place in Greece, owes its present appearance. The streets, the fortifications, the houses are all Venetian rather than Greek . . . The whole fabric of modern Corfiote society, the conditions of land tenure, and the habits of the people are still largely based upon the Venetian polity' (Miller).

NAPOLEONIC WARS (A.D. 1797 to 1815)

One of the first decisions taken by General Bonaparte after he had occupied Venice in the spring of 1797, at the end of his brilliant diversionary attack on Austria, was to dispatch two thousand men to take the Ionian Islands, which he regarded as bases essential to the success of an Eastern policy in general and of his Egyptian campaign in particular. 'Les îles de Corfu, Zante et Céphalonie sont plus intéressantes pour nous que toute l'Italie ensemble,' he wrote to the Directory (Matton). By August all the islands had been occupied and in October the Treaty of Campo Formio retrospectively legalized the position. The social and political reforms which the French introduced were at first greeted with enthusiasm by all but the former ruling class. The islands were grouped into three *départements*, each to be represented in Paris by an elected deputy; the feudal regime was abolished and the Golden Books of the nobility symbolically burned; the winged lions of St Mark were chipped off the stone tablets on many castle walls, and trees of liberty were planted in village squares. But the popularity won by such measures was rapidly offset by French anti-clericism and mockery of religion, by a decision to grant the much-hated Jews a civic status equal to the Orthodox Christians, and by a suspect alliance with the islanders' nearest Turkish enemy, Aly Pasha of Ioannina. So when Russia and Turkey joined the Second Coalition against France and — profiting from the French defeat at the battle of the Nile in August 1798 — dispatched a joint fleet under Admiral Uschakow to retake the islands, the Orthodox Russian — if not the Turkish — landing-parties were greeted as liberators. Only on Corfu did the French have a big enough garrison to put up a fight; but after several months of siege hunger forced them to surrender the town and citadel in February 1799.

Under the terms of a Russo-Turkish convention of May 1800 the Seven Islands now became an independent federal republic under the protection of the Tsar and paying tribute to the Porte. The new regime was thoroughly reactionary and aristocratic and even before the last Russian and Turkish troops had left in 1801 there was a democratic uprising in Zakinthos. In 1802 the Septinsular Republic had to call on two British frigates to deal with an insurrection on Corfu, and it was not till the return of a strong Russian force at the end of the year that order was restored on the islands. Its commander, Count Mocenigo, a Venetian born in Zante and trained at St Petersburg, remained in the islands as Russian plenipotentiary until

1807. Meanwhile the secretary to the Septinsular Government, the Corfiot Count John Kapodistrias, introduced one new constitution after another in an attempt to satisfy factions as adamantly opposed to each other as they had been at the time of the Peloponnesian War.

When war broke out again between Britain and France in 1803 it seemed at first as if the Great Powers would respect the islands' independence. But Napoleon still had the old bee in his bonnet about Corfu, and a fortnight after his Austrian and Prussian campaigns had brought Tsar Alexander to a floating conference-table in the middle of the River Niemen he had dispatched a letter to Italy ordering General Berthier to sail for the islands and strongly garrison Corfu — 'la clef de l'Adriatique' (Matton). Their formal transfer from Russian to French protection was subsequently arranged in an annexe to the Treaty of Tilsit in 1807.

This setback to British *amour propre* in the Mediterranean was followed by the ignominious loss of Capri to the French in 1808, and the commander-in-chief, Collingwood, decided to retrieve the position by retaking as many as possible of the Ionian Islands. He had learned from a deputation of Cefalonian and Zantiot merchants that they were eager to regain their independence. The strong force which sailed under sealed orders from Sicily in 1809 had no difficulty in capturing Zakinthos, Cefalonia, Ithaca and Kithira by October; but Corfu — now stocked with sufficient equipment for an army of forty to fifty thousand men (according to Napoleon's later recollection) and fortified by five hundred new pieces of artillery — was much too well defended to make an assault anything but foolhardy. It was therefore neutralized by blockade, and for the next six years a curious position persisted in which the military representatives of two Powers engaged in bitter fighting in Europe each peacefully pursued similar policies in islands almost within sight of each other. It could be argued that the agricultural, social and cultural reforms of the new French commander on Corfu, General Donzelot, were virtues of necessity forced on him by his blockaded position. But the blockade was something of a farce. 'All agree in thinking it the most imperfect act of hostility ever enforced,' wrote William Turner in 1813. 'Telegraphs are established all along the coasts of the island, and as soon as these report the two frigates, the only force we have on the station, to be out of sight, boats immediately run over to the coast of Albania and bring back plentiful supplies of corn and cattle.' Donzelot was in fact a man of exceptional charm and ability — 'the most popular ruler who ever landed in the Seven Islands' (Kirkwall). During his six-year term an Ionian Academy was set up to encourage the arts and sciences, and several periodicals were published in French and Italian on presses imported from France, providing an intellectual stimulus unknown during the days of Venetian censorship.

Of the regime in the 'British' islands with its H.Q. in Zante, William Turner was able to report that 'Every mode of conciliation is adopted, and the national and religious prejudices of the islanders are as much consulted as is consistent with good government.' But since murder was still 'an organized system' and 'the most revolting and unnatural crimes' were common, good government involved a sterner administration of justice than had been known for several hundred years, and it was rare that the public gibbets were un-occupied. A certain amount of persuasion was also necessary to persuade the islanders to accept the impartial but unpopular *corvée* system of building new roads. On Cefalonia William Turner was 'shocked' to see two soldiers of the Corsican Rangers supervising work 'by no means idle, with whips in their hands'. Ignorance and superstition had also to be overcome. When the military governor of Cefalonia, Major de Bosset, 'wished to introduce the culture of the potato some of the priests laboured to convince the peasants, that this was the very apple with which the serpent seduced Adam and Eve in Paradise' (Holland). The islanders were partly won over to accept the strange British passion for justice and social order by the success and prestige of the new regiments which Major Richard Church was raising on Zakinthos from among local volunteers and Greeks from Epirus and the Peloponnese. By March 1811 the 1st Regiment, Duke of York's Greek Light Infantry was ready to acquit itself pluckily at the capture of Santa Maura from the French, and in November of that year Church wrote to his mother, 'I have now, thank God, divested those men of prejudices rooted by ages, and converted them from the most lawless of mankind, not only into good soldiers, but also into praiseworthy members of civilized society. These men, who once knew no law but their sword, are now the admiration of the inhabitants for their correct, quiet, and obedient conduct . . . ' (Lane-Poole). A second regiment, raised on Cefalonia and officered almost entirely by Greeks, took part in the capture of Paxos in February 1814. Though both regiments were disbanded at the end of the Napoleonic Wars, many of their Greek officers and men were later to turn their experience of modern discipline and tactics to good use as leaders in the Greek War of Independence, notably Theodore Kolokotronis, whose portraits

Historical Chart: Suzerains of

	CORFU AND PAXOS	LEFKAS
Sicily	1185–7a	
Greek Emperor	1187–c. 1200c	1185–c. 1204
Venice (1st period)	1207–c. 1214c	
Despots of Epirus	c. 1214–57e	c. 1204–c. 1295f
Latin Emperor		
Manfred of Sicily	1257–66e	
Angevins	1267–1368g	c. 1295–1404g
Tocco family		1404–79h
Venice (2nd period) (See table on p. 59)	1386–1797i	1502–3 1684–1714 1716–97
Ottoman Turks (See table on p. 59)		1479–1502h 1503–1684 1714–16
French Republic	1797–9	1797–8
Russian Protection	1799–1807	1798–1807
French Empire	1807–14	1807–11
British Protection	1814–64	1811–64

a Held by the Normans during William II's campaign against the Greek Emperor.

b Under the Sicilian admiral Margaritone until 1194 when they passed to his son-in-law Matthew Orsini, an adventurer from Apulia. The Orsini were vassals of the Sicilian House of Hohenstaufen until 1209, of Venice until c. 1218 and then of the de Villehardouins, princes of Achaia, whose suzerain was the Latin Emperor in Constantinople.

c Seized from the Greek Emperor in about 1200 by the Genoese pirate Vetrano and held by him until 1207 when he was caught and hanged by the Venetians.

d Captured from the Venetian Venier family in c. 1270 by a Vicenzan ally of the Greek Emperor, who gave the island to the Daimoyannes family of Monemvasia.

e After the fall of Constantinople a local official in Epirus, Michael Ducas, set himself up as an independent ruler and in c. 1214 treacherously seized Corfu from its early Venetian settlers. His son, Michael Ducas II, despot of Epirus, gave the island to King Manfred of Sicily. Manfred had been campaigning as a free-lance in Epirus and was bribed into an alliance by the hand of the despot's daughter and her island dowry.

f Probably under the despots of Epirus from the date of the fall of Constantinople until c. 1295 when it was given as a dowry to John Orsini. Thereafter it became a duchy of the Palatine County of Cefalonia.

g In 1266 Charles of Anjou, papal candidate for the crown of Sicily, defeated and killed King Manfred of Sicily at the battle of Benevento. Charles had the grand ambition of re-taking Constantinople, from which the Latin Emperor, Baldwin II, had recently been ejected by the Greeks. Like Napoleon five centuries later and

the Ionian Islands from 1185 to 1864

ITHACA	CEFALONIA	ZAKINTHOS	KITHIRA
1185–1209b	1185–1209b	1185–1209b	
			1185–1204 c. 1270–1309d
1209–c. 1218b	1209–c. 1218b	1209–c. 1218b	1204–c. 1270d
c. 1218–67b	c. 1218–67b	c. 1218–67b	
1267–1404g	1267–1404g	1267–1404g	
1404–79h	1404–79h 1481–3h	1404–79h 1481–2h	
1503–1797	1483–5h 1500–1797	1482–1797h	1309–1714j 1716–97
1479–1503h	1479–81h 1485–1500	1479–81h	1714–18
1797–8	1797–8	1797–8	1797–8
798–1807	1798–1807	1798–1807	1798–1807
1807–9	1807–9	1807–9	1807–9
1809–64	1809–64	1809–64	1809–64

the Normans before him, he regarded Corfu as an essential springboard for his eastern adventure and made a point of getting his rights to Corfu accepted in the Treaty of Viterbo of 1267. William de Villehardouin, prince of Achaia, was present at Viterbo and placed his kingdom under Charles's suzerainty. In accordance with the feudal custom of the age, suzerainty over the Palatine County of Cefalonia passed at the same time. Though the Sicilian Vespers of 1282 put an end to Charles's plans of conquest and lost him Sicily, his successors as kings of Naples retained their suzerainty over Corfu and the Palatine County while bestowing the enjoyment of the islands on the princes of Taranto. In 1324 Robert of Taranto deposed the Orsini for refusing fealty and in 1357 he gave the Palatine County to William Tocco of Benevento, a court favourite whose father had once governed Corfu.

h In 1404 the feudal tie which bound the Tocco family to the Angevins was abolished, and they became independent rulers until thrown out of their islands, first by the Turks in 1479 and then by the Venetians in 1482 and 1483.

i Charles III of Durazzo seized the crown of Naples and by 1382 had taken possession of Corfu. When he died a year or two later leaving an infant son, a Venetian squadron persuaded the Corfiots that Venice was the only state willing and able to protect the island. So in 1386 a delegation of Corfiots left for Venice to negotiate the terms of their voluntary sentence as a Venetian colony. It was to last just over four hundred years.

j The Venieri regained ownership by intermarrying with the Daimoyannes, but had the island taken out of their control by the Republic in 1363 as punishment for their part in a rebellion in Crete.

and statues all show him still sentimentally attached to his British helmet. And it was because of Church's success with these regiments in the Ionian Islands that a Greek national assembly elected him commander-in-chief of all their land forces in 1827.

BRITISH PROTECTORATE (A.D. 1815 to 1864)

In November 1815 the plenipotentiaries of Great Britain, Prussia, Austria and Russia — the last represented by Count John Kapodistrias — agreed at the reconvened Congress of Vienna that the Ionian Islands should henceforth be an independent state under the protection of Great Britain, and should be governed in accordance with a constitution to be promulgated by a Lord High Commissioner. The first 'Lord High', Sir Thomas Maitland, was also governor of Malta. (For Napier's comments on his personal habits see p. 127.) He had no doubts about the kind of rule the islanders needed. Before he even arrived in 1816 he wrote:

> Least of all can I think for a moment with temper of anything like a representative government. We tried that experiment in Siciliy, and the result was what one naturally would have expected where the whole community was divided into two classes, viz. tyrants and slaves. Neither the one nor the other are fitted to enjoy the blessings of a free government. We may hereafter prepare them for it. In the meantime, all we can do is to correct the abuses that may exist, to rule them with moderation, and turn their thoughts gradually to improvements that may be made as they advance in their ideas, and in their knowledge of true and sound policies.

While the constitituion which he devised in 1817 provided a flattering appearance of parliamentary government it kept all the executive power firmly in his hands. 'His Highness' the President of the Ionian Senate and the 'most illustrious' Senators, though elected, were his creatures by right of veto, and the 'most noble' members of the Legislative Assembly were therefore unable to force through any measure with which he disagreed. In the last resort he could always dissolve the parliament altogether. Maitland's constitution was not substantially altered until 1849, with the result that he and his successors were able to introduce the economic, social and judicial reforms they wanted, and carry out the public works which took their fancy — roads, schools, bridges, prisons, palaces and lunatic asylums. There is no disputing the level of prosperity and security which their measures achieved over the years. 'Here what roads! what joyous hamlets! . . . What security! what inviolable respect for property, both from those governing and those governed,' wrote a Greek visitor to Zakinthos in 1851 (Jervis). 'Here you can proceed, loaded with gold from one end of the islands to the other without the least fear. At home, we cannot without the greatest danger go even from Athens to Kifissia . . .'

But the price of efficient administration was foreign rule, and after Greece had achieved her independence in 1828 such rule became increasingly irksome to a population which, in spite of six hundred years of Italian domination, had never ceased to feel Greek. During the War of Independence itself, the official neutrality of the Ionian state had placed the islanders in an impossible position. Every patriotic instinct urged them to send help to the mainland or to take savage revenge on any Turk unlucky enough to fall into their hands, and the punishment exacted for such natural acts of belligerence or barbarity seemed all the more incomprehensible when people such as Guilford (see p. 127) and Byron (see p. 240) — 'the semi-delirious lords', as De Quincey called them — were preaching or waiting to practise philhellenism on Corfu and Cefalonia.

For several reasons the movement for union with Greece was slow to gather momentum among the islanders. In the first place, until the grant of a constitution in 1844, the regime of King Otho and his Bavarian advisers on the independent mainland at times seemed almost as foreign and authoritarian as their own. In the second place, as the years went by various sections of Ionian society acquired a vested interest in becoming 'Protectionists' rather than 'Unionists'. Many of the Ionian gentry were tempted by the status of senator or island regent or the reward of a K.C.M.G. (see p. 128) to throw in their lot with the British Establishment as their predecessors had with the Venetian. Some land-owners and merchants, especially on Cefalonia and Zakinthos, were 'glued to the English market' in currants (Napier), which had suddenly boomed as result of Ibrahim Pasha's devastation of the vineyards of the Peloponnese. But the chief reason was undoubtedly a Government control of the press so complete that the Unionists were unable to propagate their ideas.

By the mid 'forties, however, sympathy for the movement was widespread, and when early in 1848 Lord Seaton, the sixth 'Lord High', underwent a strange liberal conversion and announced a revised constitution and freedom of the press, the immediate results were a formal demand for Union in the Legislative Assembly and the publication of two outspokenly Unionist newspapers on Cefalonia, always the most disputatious and hot-headed of the islands. This was not at all what Lord Seaton had foreseen. 'He did not perceive that the great mass of Ionians cared little for reform, and desired only Union' (Kirkwall). An armed insurrection broke out on Cefalonia and was put down only after a year of martial law and the execution of twenty-one ringleaders.

It took fifteen more years to persuade successive 'Lords High' and the British Government that Union was the wish of the majority of the Ionian Islanders and not just the ambition of 'demagogues or . . . traffickers in place', as Mr Gladstone bitterly concluded. In 1858 he had been appointed Lord High Commissioner Extraordinary to look into the islands' troubles; but the only result of his patient inquiry and recommendations was a stubborn petition for Union to the Queen. This was promptly turned down and the politician, 'who had come out such a warm Philhellene, departed thoroughly disgusted with the Greeks in general, and with the Ionians in particular' (Kirkwall).

By 1859 there seemed to be no way out of the impasse into which Ionian obstinacy had driven the British Government. But in 1862 the unexpected dethronement of King Otho of Greece provided Lord Palmerston with the opportunity for a face-saving retreat. He made it known to the Greek National Assembly that the cession of the Ionian Islands would follow the election of a suitable new King of the Hellenes. In Queen Victoria's opinion Palmerston's attempt to disguise a bow to the inevitable as a disinterested gesture was 'grievously messed and bungled' (Prevelakis). But the man in the street knew nothing of the tortuous *quid pro quos* of diplomacy, and when, on May 21st, 1864, a year after the satisfactory choice of Prince William of Denmark, the Ionian Islands were reunited to Greece, he was stirred by this manifestation of British selflessness and hailed the transfer as 'one of the most extraordinary events of the day' (Kirkwall).

FROM A.D. 1864 TO THE PRESENT DAY

After 1864 the Ionian Islands became separate provinces of Greece (see p. 75). The Ionian Academy (p. 127) was merged with the National University of Athens and the Ionian Church (see p. 72) with the Church of Greece. Another local institution — the Ionian titled gentry — was also fated to lose its privileged position. A few families put their experience to good use on the less sheltered stage of national politics, but the majority retired to their estates with memories of senatorial posts and the gold and enamel links of their Orders.

With its palaces still used in the summer by Greek kings, Corfu never quite lost the aura of a capital city. The visits of Elizabeth of Austria and, later, the German Kaiser to the Akhillion evoked memories of old pomp and circumstance, and the annual visits of the Mediterranean fleet and sportsmen bent on wild-fowling in Albania provided nostalgic glimpses of familiar British whiskers. Some of the other islands also attracted a little attention. To Lefkas, Ithaca and Cefalonia as well as to Corfu scholars, topographers and archaeologists, including Heinrich Schliemann, were lured by the siren voices of Homeric geography (see p. 81). Paxos and Zakinthos claimed the attention of the encyclopedic Archduke Ludwig Salvator of Austria, who, in the last quarter of the nineteenth century, cruised round the Ionian Sea on his steam-yacht *Nixe*, compiling valuable but exhausting works on these two islands. Zakinthos too was the home of five British families who stayed on to look after the dwindling currant trade, and this nucleus attracted a small stream of visiting friends and relations bringing with them Scottish nannies and novelties from Europe. Not only the currant trade but the whole agricultural economy of the islands suffered when the protective British cloche was removed, and between 1880 and 1940 emigration drastically thinned the populations of Kithira, Ithaca and northern Cefalonia (see p. 40).

During the First World War Greece's ally Serbia was invaded from Bulgaria, and Corfu became the refuge of the evacuated Serbian army: the cemetery on Vidos island suggests the scale and misery of the operation. In 1923 Corfu's peace was again shattered by an Italian bombardment which Mussolini senselessly ordered in reprisal for the assassination of the Italian delegate on the Albanian boundary commission, and a little later its prosperity as the chief doorway from Europe into Greece was undermined by the completion of the new rail link between Belgrade and Athens.

After the German invasion of Greece in 1941 the Ionian Islands were transferred to nominal Italian control like most of the mainland, and it is clear from the special currency printed for them and the renaming of streets and squares that they would have been formally annexed to Italy after the war. During the war the towns of Corfu and Zakinthos both suffered from Axis and Allied bombing.

By about 1958, after a long and difficult post-war period, Greece had recovered enough political and economic stability to begin to invest in tourism. Owing partly to her pre-eminence as a resort island and partly to the earthquake which shattered Zakinthos, Cefalonia and Ithaca in 1953 (see pp. 40 and 265), Corfu was at first the only island to benefit. But by 1968 (when the first edition of this book was being finished) all the islands except Kithira had modest modern hotels, and in Corfu there were two or three new ones which seemed rather too large for the scale of the island's scenery. Unfortunately, during the regime of the Colonels, controls on the size, number and siting of new hotels were relaxed as part of a deliberate policy of mortgaging Greece's landscape, monuments and traditional way of life to the tourist industry. And once under way almost nothing can stop the momentum of mass tourism; for it draws into its wake innumerable beneficiaries (including the writers of guidebooks such as this one); and these become unwitting accomplices in the crimes it commits: noise, overcrowding, ugliness and pollution. In the summer months all these are now manifest in Corfu, plain to see in Zakinthos, and coming into sight in Lefkas.

RELIGION

In the seventeenth century Wheler found the Ionian Church 'much Latinized in doctrine'. He may have been misled by the Italianate appearance of Ionian church art (see p. 91). Today, at any rate, there is no doctrinal difference between the Ionian sees and the rest of the Church of Greece with which, after more than a thousand years of direct dependence on the Oecumenical Patriarch in Constantinople, they were united in 1866. In their veneration of their patron saints and in their Easter processions, the Ionian Islands do however show certain religious peculiarities. The veneration of relics is of course as much a practice of the Orthodox Church as it is of the Roman Catholic. But in Greece most of the important relics were grabbed by the Franks after the Fourth Crusade; and the Turks naturally discouraged any elaborate Christian celebration of those that remained. So only round the mummified remains of St Spiridon (p. 135) on Corfu could a processional ceremonial evolve — or, perhaps, continue on early Byzantine lines. To the cynical, the rivalry between the three main islands will be the obvious reason why the figures of St Yerasimos (p. 246) and St Dionisios (p. 268) appeared on Cefalonia and Zakinthos so soon after Corfu's acquisition of St Spiridon; and even to the uncynical, emulation will explain why their remains are mummified, housed and carried in procession in exactly the same way. As for Easter processions, though these take place all over the Orthodox world, a combination of Italianate art, Venetian civic pomp and military bands makes them particularly spectacular (p. 79) in the Ionian Islands.

ORTHODOX

The Ionian Islanders are as devout as all Greeks from rural areas. A farmer lunching in a Corfu restaurant will 'make his Cross' before he starts to eat; and there will be a flutter of pious fingers each time the women in a bus catch sight of a distant chapel. Such simple people will think it slightly unnatural if, when you visit their village church, you do not spend a drachma or two on a candle, light it and put it in front of one of the icons. Politeness and religious conviction apart, this is often the only way in which you can indirectly pay for the coffee or the ouzo which the priest or the monk will generally offer you. In an Orthodox church women need not cover their heads or their bare arms but should, of course, be modestly dressed. Women should never go behind the screen, and men should ask permission before doing so.

ROMAN CATHOLIC

Though the great majority of the islanders are Orthodox there are Roman Catholic minorities in Corfu and Argostoli. For reasons which stem from her rivalry with the Papacy as a temporal power in Italy, Venice did not allow all the consequences of Catholicism to fall on the Ionian Islands, any more than she did on her mainland territories. The Inquisition was never introduced; and, more important for the future, mixed marriages were allowed. The consequence, in a predominantly Orthodox society, was that younger sons and all the daughters of such marriages became Orthodox, and most Roman Catholics are not, as one might expect, descendants of early Venetian families but of Maltese farmers brought over during the British Protectorate (p. 244) and Italian artisans who found work on Corfu at the end of the nineteenth century. A Roman Catholic archbishop — one of only three in Greece — still resides in

Corfu, and Catholic churches are open there (p. 137) and in Argostoli (p. 231).

JEWISH

Since the establishment of the state of Israel the once numerous Jewish population has disappeared from all the Ionian Islands except Corfu, where a community of about a hundred and fifty Jews have a synagogue. The Jews were encouraged to settle on Corfu by the Angevins. By 1386 they had become such an important element in the community that the six-man delegation which set out for Venice to negotiate the charter of the island with its new rulers contained two of them. Their numbers increased after the expulsion from Spain and Portugal, and again after 1572 when the Republic exempted the Jews of the Ionian Islands from expulsion from Venetian territory. In 1889 one in every nine townsmen of Corfu was a Jew. Though prosperous and tolerated by the authorities, until the nineteenth century their treatment was as unenviable as elsewhere. The gates of the ghettos (which survived until British times) were locked each night, and they were obliged to wear a distinguishing yellow patch on their breast: '. . . a Venetian ordinance naively remarks that this was "a substitute for the custom of stoning which does so much injury to the houses"' (Miller). There is an interesting old Jewish cemetery on the way up the castle hill on Zakinthos (p. 272).

PROTESTANT

During the British Protectorate the drums and fifes of the garrison church-parades used to gladden the heart of patriotic and worthy Britons. 'Their mustering and marching off afterwards with their full band under the high rock of the citadel is very picturesque,' wrote the Earl of Carlisle on a visit to Corfu in 1854. An Orthodox church was usually borrowed by the authorities and assigned to Anglican services, and the Doric church inside the Citadel of Corfu (p. 134) is the only surviving church specifically built for a garrison; it is now Orthodox. Since the destruction of the Anglican Church of the Holy Trinity in the last war, a room in the middle of the unused Ionian Parliament building (p. 128) has been open on Sundays for private worship from 10.30 to 12.00. But the localities most evocative of Protestantism are now the cemeteries on Corfu (p. 139), Zakinthos (p. 271) and near Argostoli (p. 251).

GOVERNMENT AND ADMINISTRATION

Greece is divided into districts called nomes administered by a prefect called a *nomárkhis*. Some nomes are divided into sub-districts called eparchies. Lefkas and Zakinthos are nomes without eparchies, the two smallest in Greece. Paxos and Antipaxos together form an eparchy of the nome of Kerkira (Corfu). The nome of Kefallinia (Cefalonia) is divided into four eparchies: the three sub-districts of the island of Cefalonia itself — Pali, Sami and Krani — and Ithaca and the Ekhinades Islands. Kithira and Anti-kithira now form an eparchy of the nome of Attica. The commercial, administrative and cultural ties which linked the islands under Venetian, French and British rule have withered away. They have no place in the highly centralized Hellenic Republic where each nome competes with its neighbour for the attention of the authorities in Athens. Few Lefkadians have visited Corfu and even fewer Zantiots have been to Cefalonia only eight miles away.

LANGUAGE

The differences in accent, vocabulary and idiom between country people in various parts of Greece are about the same as they are in Great Britain. The most striking characteristic which an Athenian will notice in the Ionian Islands is the chanting lilt of the voices which on Zakinthos amounts almost to a sing-song. The long Venetian domination accounts for rather more Italian loan-words than usual, but many of the Italianate words you will hear, especially seafaring terms, are part of demotic Greek everywhere. The modification of the Greek genitive plural in '*ón*' into an Italianate '*óne*' is a musical local peculiarity, and on Kithira you will often hear a soft Cretan 'ch' in place of the usual hard 'k'.

On Corfu and Lefkas, with their rural economies, the illiteracy rate is quite a lot higher than the 1972 national average of 12 per cent; on Ithaca and Cefalonia, renowned for their appetite for learning, it is considerably lower. But if you should show your map to an elderly peasant on any of the islands he may tell you with engaging simplicity that he is 'not so good at his letters'.

In Corfu English is spoken in many shops and restaurants, and in the outlying villages of Cefalonia, Kithira, Ithaca and Zakinthos you will almost always find at least one returned emigrant to help you, sometimes in accents straight out of Faulkner or Tennessee Williams. Many of the older inhabitants of all the islands also speak a bit of Italian. The educated Corfiot, Zantiot or Cefalonian speaks English or French or Italian as a matter of course, often all three of them.

Note on transliteration. In the transliteration used in this book for Ionian Island place-names, every letter has its usual English value except those below, which should be pronounced as shown:

a   as in c*u*t
e   as in b*e*t
i   as in *ee*l
o   as in *o*ught
ou   as in r*oo*t
d   as in *th*em
ḍ   as in *d*og
g   as in the Spanish fue*g*o (i.e. softer than in English)
kh   as in lo*ch* (but not rasped)
ng   as in a*ng*er (not as in si*ng*ing)
th   as in *th*in
s   as in *s*ibilant
y   as in *y*es

Except for the dipthong 'ou' every vowel should be given its own value; 'u' on its own appears only in the name Corfu; and 'c' rather than 'k' has been retained only in 'Corfu' and 'Cefalonia'. The spelling of place-names in passages quoted from other authors has been left unchanged, and most proper names are transliterated in the usual English way, i.e. 'Odysseus' rather than 'Odisséfs', 'Aphrodite' rather than 'Afrodíti'.

In Greek the stressed syllable of a word sometimes, and its case ending nearly always, changes in the genitive case, i.e. 'Kérkira' becomes 'Kerkíras'. In this book place-names are usually given in the nominative case; but whatever the case they appear in, the syllable to stress is shown by an acute accent — in the index and on the black-and-white island maps, but not in the text.

CUSTOMS

On Corfu and Lefkas the peasant women still wear their traditional costume. On Lefkas this consists of a black or russet-brown woollen dress with a deeply cut bodice and long tight sleeves. An overskirt is always girded up and fastened behind the waist, and a satin neckerchief is so arranged that two stiff points conceal the *décolletage*. 'Sunday best' is of the same eighteenth-century Venetian cut, but is made of blue, green or brown satin. The costume is worn by the majority of village women at all times and adds greatly to the character of the island.

On Corfu the everyday costume is more sombre and medieval-looking. Worn only by the older women of the villages of the interior, it consists of a black skirt and overskirt, a loose white cotton blouse with drawstring neck and very full sleeves, a black bodice like a vestigial waistcoat, and a white headkerchief carelessly arranged in any number of graceful ways. Feast-day dresses are of shot silks with embroidered muslin aprons, magnificent short velvet jackets in the Epirot style encrusted with gold embroidery, and frothy head-dresses of lace, ribbons and flowers. These enchanting costumes are now fancy dress, and the only time you are likely to see them is at exhibitions of Corfiot folk-dancing. In the summer these are held once or twice a week at the Akhillion (p. 164).

On the other five islands the traditional dresses have quite disappeared. According to Lear (*Views*), that of Kithira was 'among the most picturesque of any in the islands'. The women carried 'peculiar long sacks made of gorgeous-coloured carpets, slung from the shoulders . . . and . . . universally used as cradles during their outdoor labour . . .'

Corfu, Cefalonia, Zakinthos and Lefkas are all renowned for their bands, which often play in the central squares on summer evenings as well as at Easter and on other festive occasions. Dressed in colourful uniforms and wearing neat kepis or plumed shakos, the bandsmen are of all ages from twelve to seventy. The oldest band — the Corfu Philharmonic — was founded in 1840 when the authorities decided that St Spiridon no longer rated an accompaniment of British regimental music on his processions. It still wears the blue and crimson colours of the Ionian state.

There are several intriguing Easter customs. At exactly eleven o'clock on the morning of Easter Saturday all the old pottery crocks and jugs are thrown from the top storeys of Corfu town houses to smash on the pavements below. Most likely this is a stylized version of the gauntlet any Jew had to run in the Middle Ages if he were rash enough to venture into the streets in Holy Week. The best place from which to watch this satisfying spectacle is the middle or south end of the Liston. In Zakinthos the young men go secretly round the town on Easter Saturday night turning the shop-signs upside down or stacking them outside the museum. This may be a vestige of horse-play and rivalry among the youths of the seventeenth-century guilds or the relic of a spring Saturnalia — in Grasset's day several pagan fertility rites survived as Easter customs on Corfu. On Easter Saturday too the pretty white lambs which for a week or two have been led around by children on red silk ribbons are slaughtered for the Easter feast, and in the suburbs of Corfu many doorways are signed with three bloody crosses — a curious Christian adaptation of the Jewish Passover custom. Though the lamb itself is generally eaten at midday on Easter Sunday, after the ceremonies at midnight on Saturday everyone goes home for a substantial meal which includes either *avgolémono* (a broth bound with egg and lemon) or a special Easter soup of chopped lamb's inwards called *mayirítsa*. On the table will be a basket of Easter eggs, 'the shels of them collared lyke a damaske Rose' (as Thomas Dallam noted on a visit to Zakinthos in 1599), and everyone tries his fortune by testing the strength of his egg against his neighbours'.

A custom which is not peculair to the Ionian Islands (or indeed to Greece) is the evening stroll or *vólta*. In summer the social life of the islands unfolds after dark, gratefully, like some night-scented flower. These are the hours of respite, almost of truce, and the central *platía* fills up with relaxed and leisurely people. Mothers sit gossiping over ices as their children scramble round tables, fly into tantrums, are soothed by doting fathers. Youths with combed and glistening hair and sharp polished shoes go by in self-conscious groups; old men in yellowing linen suits lift their grey Homburg hats to faded old ladies; girls pass by in fresh and pretty dresses, apparently engrossed in chat, apparently absorbed in thought, apparently quite unaware of hungry and admiring eyes. Whether you sit under the arches of the Liston, in the main square of Argostoli or on the quaysides of Vathi or Gaio, or more energetically stroll up and down Zante's Platia Rouga or Lefkas' wooden-galleried main street, the whole gamut of each town's residents, as well as all its bizarre tourist migrants, will be paraded in front of you. It is a very beguiling ritual.

On the Ionian Islands as in the rest of Greece the feast-day of the saint to whom a church is dedicated is celebrated by a special service and a feast called a *panayíri*. When a saint is particularly revered, a monastery richly endowed, or an icon believed to have miraculous powers, the *panayíri* will draw people from all over the island and the occasion becomes something like a Bank Holiday race-meeting, with sweating traffic-police, food-stalls, ice-cream tricycles and so on. The most attractive *panayíria* are small pastoral affairs where, after the service, sheep are roasted over charcoal pits and the villagers picnic under the olive trees, drinking a great deal of wine and dancing. In a village, chairs and tables will fill the *platía* or water-front and a juke-box will often provide the music rather than a clarinet and fiddle.

Three of the islands have patron saints whose mummified remains are carried in procession in ornate glass-fronted sedan chairs several times a year — St Spiridon (p. 135) and St Dionisios (p. 268) through the streets of Corfu and Zante respectively, St Yerasimos (p. 246) up and down the avenue leading to his church in the Omala of Cefalonia.

Easter, the main feast of the Orthodox Church, is celebrated with particular splendour in the towns of Zakinthos and Corfu. In Zakinthos the whole town and all its thousands of visitors participate in three processions designed to underline the religious significance of the Easter sequence of events. At about three o'clock on Good Friday afternoon a long procession leaves the church of St Nicholas-on-the-Mole in time to the noble Easter Hymn of the Zantiot Paul Karrer (1829–96). Behind the slowly pacing scouts, guides and school-children comes an icon of the Virgin carried under a black canopy by four sailors, and then the Cross with a life-size painted effigy of Christ upon it. Apart from the solemn tubas of the bands there is no sound but the doleful scrape of feet along the Platia Rouga. The blue and white flags hang at half-mast and are twined with ribbons of black crêpe. This funeral procession takes an hour to return to Solomos Square, where the Bishop takes the Cross and dips it in blessing to the crowd.

At three o'clock on Saturday morning a similar procession forms up. Now the dark streets are lit by long eighteenth-century lanthorns carried on poles and the fluttering of a thousand candles. A red quarter-moon is reflected in the still waters of the harbour and the night air is heavy with incense and the scent of bees-wax. This time the Cross is bare and the painted effigy of the dead Christ lies in a gilded bier — the *Epitáfios*. There are many exclamations of pity as it passes.

At half-past-eleven the following night a smaller procession walks swiftly from the Orthodox cathedral to St Mark's Square. Now there is neither Cross nor *Epitáfios*, and as the Bishop in his glittering mitre mounts a bay-decked dais to lead a final litany all eyes are on the clock-tower. The tension is enormous. Then the first stroke of midnight chimes and there is complete pandemonium. Rockets whizz up, squibs explode, plates are smashed, the band strikes up, and church bells swing madly from every surviving bell-tower. *'Khristós anésti'* ('Christ is risen') goes round the greeting; *'Alithós anésti'* ('He is risen indeed') comes the reply.

In the other island capitals each church has its own *Epitáfios* and the squares are criss-crossed by competing processions. Between six and eleven o'clock on Good Friday evening the narrow streets of Corfu are full of bands playing the Dead March from *Saul*, strings of schoolgirls carrying baskets of flowers, and detachments of the armed forces slow-marching with arms reversed. The spectacle is colourful, but too confused and spun out to focus the whole town's emotion like Zante's artistically stage-managed performance. But midnight on Saturday in Corfu is a magical occasion. As the clock strikes in the Citadel, flame runs swiftly along every balcony over-looking the Esplanade until each tall house is dressed overall in candle-light, the pale green underleaves of the Judas and horse-chestnut trees gleam eerily in the glow of thousands of tapers, the band bursts into an Easter hymn, cannons roar, bells peal and fireworks burst in a tumult of noise and golden spangles.

ARCHAEOLOGY

THE 'ITHACA QUESTION' AND ARCHAEOLOGICAL EXCAVATION

It is hardly an exaggeration to say that until the Second World War the 'onlie begetter' of excavation in the Ionian Islands was Homer, and that the avowed or unavowed object of archaeologists was the solution of some aspect of what has come to be known as the 'Ithaca Question'.

The Ithaca Question arises from the difficulty of reconciling Homer's account of Ithaca's position with the geographical situation of the island now called by that name. Remembering that Lefkas lies to its north and Cefalonia to its west, it is difficult to see how the present high and narrow island can be said to lie 'low in the sea' or 'farthest out to sea', 'farthest up towards the north' or 'slanting to the west', the likely alternative meanings of Homer's obscure and archaic Greek. Another difficulty is that if Cefalonia is the Homeric island of *Same* (a town called Sami survives there), then the only candidate for the island of Asteris — from whose 'windy heights' the suitors kept watch for the returning Telemachus — is the flat islet of Daskalio.

To Sir William Gell and Colonel Leake, the first geographers since Strabo to identify the present island with the Homeric Ithaca, these geographical discrepancies did not seem so inexplicable or striking as the fact that its topography tallied so well with the demands of the action of the *Odyssey*; on their separate visits in 1806 they were even able to discover various bays, springs and grottoes whose relative positions were right for the Bay of Phorcys, Arethusa's Fountain and the Cave of the Nymphs. Their conclusions (published respectively in 1807 and 1835) were convincing enough to tempt Heinrich Schliemann to inaugurate his astonishing archaelogical career. On his first visit to Greece in 1867 he dug in the north-east corner of the acropolis of Aetos on Ithaca (p. 218), where 'according to his calculations' the olive tree which Odysseus used as his bedpost must have grown. When he hit bedrock only sixty-six centimetres below the surface he consoled himself with the observation that 'there were cracks in this rock into which the roots of the olive tree could have penetrated'. Of a large Greek 'D' cut into a rock he remarked reverently that Odysseus himself might have cut it.

Wilhelm Dörpfeld, a German archaeologist who had dug with Schliemann after 1882, was not satisfied by the identification of Aetos with Odysseus's stronghold. After excavating perfunctorily in North Ithaca in search of an alternative site, he became convinced that the only consistent way of explaining both Homer's geography and his topography was to assume that Lefkas was the original Ithaca, and that the present Ithaca's name had been carried to the next island down the line during migrations at the time of the Dorian invasions. His theory is more convincingly argued (in *Alt-Ithaka*) than many of his critics give him credit for, but unfortunately very few of the interesting finds he made during many seasons of excavation in Lefkas tally chronologically with the fact that the Homeric Odysseus should be a late-Mycenaean ruler.

Dörpfeld's claims provoked Lord Rennell of Rodd into trying to vindicate the traditional Ithaca's good name, and under his patronage the British School of Archaeology at Athens spent several seasons between 1930 and 1935 excavating various sites in the island. Though these excavations provided only rather frail evidence of a late-Mycenaean palace in North Ithaca, they showed that the name of Odysseus had been associated with the island as early as Hellenistic times and that there were contacts between Ithaca and Ionia (Homer's supposed birthplace) in the seventh century B.C. More surprisingly, they provided solid bronze evidence for Homer's story of the thirteen tripod-cauldrons given to Odysseus by the Phaeacians (see p. 220). Aetos was eliminated as a Mycenaean site but produced a rich store of later pottery.

Twenty years previously a rich Dutch Homeric enthusiast, A. E. H. Goekoop, had been inspired by Dörpfeld's radical new approach to the Ithaca Question and some surprising Mycenaean finds made at Mazarakata in 1909 (p. 240) to advance the ingenious theory that Ithaca, Dulichium and Same (three of the four islands mentioned by Homer) were really different parts of the one large island of Cefalonia: effectively cut off from each other by Cefalonia's mountainous terrain, they were island peoples rather than 'peopled islands' who habitually communicated with each other only by sea (a state of affairs which persisted on Cefalonia until roads were built in the early nineteenth century). In defence of this theory (which aroused little scholarly interest) and in the face of Lord Rennell's mounting Ithacan campaign, Goekoop's widow sponsored a series of excavations under the direction of a Cefalonian archaeologist, S. Marinatos. Though Professor Marinatos (later head of the Greek Archaeological Service and well known for his Thera excavations) did not locate the site of any town or palace, the various tombs he excavated revealed that Cefalonia had undoubtedly been the site of a flourishing late- or sub-Mycenaean community.

Meanwhile various attempts had been made to prove that Corfu was the land of Scheria from which, in less than twenty-four hours, Odysseus was at last to reach his home. It was about the right distance away from the central group of islands and Thucydides had recorded that its inhabitants accounted for their naval skill by the fact 'that those famous sailors the Phaeacians had inhabited Corfu before them'. In 1867 Schliemann had 'easily' identified the site of the Phaeacian capital on the Paleopolis peninsula (p. 140) and, stripped to his shirt, waded out to sea off the mouth of the River Potami (p. 169) to inspect two large stones on which Nausicaa had done her washing. But in 1901 the French scholar V. Bérard decided on topographical rather than archaeological grounds that

Paleokastritsa (p. 159) was a likelier site, and following this lead various archaeologists, Dörpfeld included, explored other promising places on the north-west coast, such as Afionas (p. 155) though without discovering any evidence of the right Mycenaean date.

By the outbreak of the Second World War most archaeologists had been forced by the inconclusive or negative evidence of all these Homeric excavations to conclude that the Ithaca Question was a horse which — if not quite dead — was no longer worth flogging, and since the war the only two major archaeological campaigns in the islands have been directed to other subjects. Since 1954 the Greek Archaeological Service has been gradually clarifying the topography and architectural history of the Corinthian town of Kerkira on the Paleopolis peninsula, and in 1963 and 1965 the British School at Athens undertook the exploration of a Minoan site at Kastri in Kithira (p. 308).

ANCIENT MONUMENTS

'Fools looking for old stones' (in Sir Thomas Maitland's phrase) will not find a rich hunting-ground in the Ionian Islands. Apart from Corfu in her ex-colonial days none of the islands was powerful or wealthy, and what buildings they did put up have been shaken down by earthquakes, sacked by barbarians or robbed by medieval builders. So even where sites have been excavated there is astonishingly little visible evidence of antiquity. To the Minoan trading station at Kastri on Kithira (p. 308) and the late-Mycenaean settlement on Cefalonia (p. 240) only a few impressive rock-cut tombs bear witness. At Nerikos on Lefkas (p. 193), Aetos on Ithaca (p. 218), Krani, Proni and Sami on Cefalonia (pp. 234, 245 and 248) and Paleopolis on Kithira, town walls survive whose huge irregular polygonal boulders — wonderfully hewn and fitted — have an air of mythical age, perhaps because this type of masonry comes to an evolutionary dead-end and forms no part of western Europe's architectural inheritance. But in Greece it continued to be used for defensive walls and revetments long after coursed masonry had become common and on stylistic grounds alone these walls can therefore be only vaguely dated to somewhere between the seventh and fourth centuries B.C. Little else survives of this period. A few small columns of the visually unexciting sixth-century Doric temple of Kardaki (p. 144) are visible over the wall of the royal park on Corfu, and the 'altar' of the great temple of Artemis (p. 141) is still *in situ*. The only complete monument is the seventh- or sixth-century tomb of Menekrates (p. 139). More evocative than this squat but important little rotunda are the Doric capitals — like flattened querns — the blocks of fine-grained stone, the smooth or fluted marble columns and the lion-head waterspouts ensconced in the churches of Ayos Kozmas on Kithira (p. 307), Ayos Ioannis sto Rodaki on Lefkas (p. 198), Ayos Dimitrios on Zakinthos (p. 283) and Paleopolis and SS Jason and Sosipater (p. 141) on Corfu; for from these clues one can build in one's imagination the temples to Aphrodite, Hera or Demeter which once stood close by. The Hellenistic and Roman periods are even more meagerly represented: there is a substantial ruined Hellenistic tower at Poros on Lefkas (p. 197) and attractive Roman mosaics at Nea Skala on Cefalonia (p. 243), but nothing else worth a detour.

ARCHAEOLOGICAL MUSEUMS

The archaeological museums would reflect the history of the islands better if so many objects had not been carried off in the days of the British and Venetians. In the early days of the British Protectorate tomb-robbing was a favourite occupation of the visiting antiquary. John Lee, F.R.S., for instance, records that in 1812, 'we engaged some labourers with spades and pickaxes; and, being shown where Major de Bosset and other travellers had been successful, we were delayed only by the rain.' Not for long; in no time he had scooped the contents out of more than a dozen graves of an ancient Ithacan cemetery. Major de Bosset, the Resident on Cefalonia, was an indefatigable collector, and his discoveries and purchases now form the De Bosset Collection in Neuchâtel. Another fine collection, chiefly of coins (not all found on the Ionian Islands), was bequeathed to the British Museum in 1866 by James Woodhouse, a former treasurer-general of the Ionian Islands.

The Venetians, though less systematic, did not hesitate to carry off anything which they thought would embellish their watery *palazzi*. Nicolas de Nicolai records a *provveditore*'s decapitation of 'une statue de femme vêtue à la grecque, de grandeur démesurée', which still lay on the site of ancient Kithira when he passed by in 1551. Grasset mentions the disappearance from Zakinthos of Cicero's 'tombstone' (p. 50): 'peut-être existe-t-il encore dans quelque musée d'Italie,' he adds musingly. And Jacob Spon (Wheler's more learned French travelling companion) tells us that the statue which the Corfiots put up to Germanicus in about A.D. 12 was 'emportée à Venise par le Provéditeur Vallier'.

The contents of the various museums, therefore, consist largely of finds made during the last fifty years during the archaeological excavations described in the previous section: at Corfu (p. 130), of the Archaic, Classical and Hellenistic temple decorations (including the famous Gorgon pediment) and burial goods discovered at Paleopolis chiefly by members of the Greek Archaeological Service, as well as miscellaneous earlier finds from other scattered sites; at Argostoli (p. 233), of the sub-Mycenaean pottery and jewellery found by Professor Marinatos; at Stavros (p. 220) and Vathi (p. 212) of the Archaic bronzes and pottery dug up by the British School at Athens; at Lefkas (p. 188) of the Neolithic and Early and Middle Bronze Age finds made by Dörpfeld, and some Hellenistic terracottas; and on Kithira (p. 293) of a few pieces of the Minoan pottery found by the British School at Kastri.

No large-scale excavation has ever been undertaken on Zakinthos, and the chance finds which had accumulated were destroyed in the 1953 earthquake. Paxos has no museum. Opening hours and admission prices are given in the island chapters. Museums are closed on public holidays.

ART AND ARCHITECTURE

MILITARY ARCHITECTURE

The most imposing architectural remains in the Ionian Islands are Byzantine, medieval and Venetian fortresses. Corfu has five: the two Byzantine fortresses of Gardiki (p. 162) and Angelokastro (p. 157), the Angevin fortress of Kassiopi (p. 152), the Citadel (p. 133) and the New Fort (p. 134). Though the visible defences of the Citadel are Venetian work of the sixteenth and seventeenth centuries, it was first fortified in Byzantine times and much extended under the Angevins. The late-sixteenth-century New Fort is military architecture at its most professional, a huge and complex lump of masonry more impressive than attractive. The castle of Ayia Mavra on Lefkas (p. 189) is unusual both because it lies like a stranded hulk in the middle of the sea, and because the architectural styles of three successive owners — Angevin, Turkish and Venetian — can be discerned in its towers and bastions. On Cefalonia the castle of St George (p. 237), built from scratch on a Byzantine site in the first years of the sixteenth century, is arguably the most elegant in the whole of Greece; and though the fortress of Assos

(p. 252), built a century later, cannot compete with it architecturally, its site is even more remarkable. Zakinthos' one castle, on a hill behind the capital, has an elaborately ornamented seventeenth-century Venetian side entrance and impressive main defences of the same date to the north-west. On Kithira the Kastro (p. 292) is almost as dramatically perched on a great acropolis of rock as Lindos on Rhodes, but its fourteenth- and sixteenth-century walls are not themselves very interesting. Kato Khora (p. 299) is a Kithiran fortified village with a sixteenth-century grand entrance on an agreeable rustic scale.

DOMESTIC ARCHITECTURE

There is a certain amount of attractive domestic building on Lefkas, Kithira and Paxos and a lot on Corfu; on the other three islands only a few cottages or houses of any architectural distinction survived the earthquake of 1953.

The curious half-timbered town and country houses of Lefkas are described on pp. 184 and 201. In the capital of Kithira and one or two of its villages — e.g., Milopotamo (p. 298) and Kato Khora (p. 299) — old houses with flat roofs in the Cycladic style are almost as common as nineteenth-century ones with pitched roofs of tile. Where these flat roofs have not been concreted over in recent years, they are made of a thick layer of special earth which is added to from time to time and recompacted with a roller often made of a length of an old column. The façades are extremely plain and the only clues by which one can allot them to the sixteenth, seventeenth and eighteenth centuries are odds and ends of agreeable stone decoration — corbels, lintels, balusters and carved scutcheons, tall, round or octagonal chimneys, and the moulding of an occasional doorway. The only striking nineteenth-century constructions on the island are two neo-Gothic Lancastrian schools (pp. 298 and 299) and two great bridges (pp. 296 and 297) built by a British Resident in the 1820s.

If most of Corfu's domestic architecture is the result of the building boom which accompanied the island's chief period of prosperity and thus belongs to the first half of the nineteenth century, its style often appears earlier. This is because the walled town of Corfu grew chiefly upwards, and owners who added new storeys to the low but solid buildings which characterized the city in the days of Grasset and Bellaire were obliged to continue in the original style. Both in Corfu town and in Gaio a tiled string-course frequently marks the level of earlier eaves; but this is not always the case: there is nothing but Cartwright's drawing of 1821 to show that the Liston (p. 126) was originally only three storeys high. The style that persisted is a handsome one even if not very exciting: stone architraves flush with the mortar stucco, painted jalousies, and tiled drip-courses jutting out like eyebrows over the windows are the only features of otherwise undecorated façades. Stone string-courses and moulded lintels to the doors and windows are uncommon, for unlike Zakinthos, Corfu had neither great wealth to spend on richly ornamented town houses in the seventeenth and eighteenth centuries, nor an easy freestone to work with. The Town Hall (p. 125), the Grimani barracks (p. 127), the former Law Courts and half a dozen colonnaded or porticoed houses are the only surviving early buildings with architectural pretensions.

Outside the walled town, in the suburbs and villages, the nineteenth-century style is more neo-classical. But in the Ionian Islands the early neo-classical is marked not so much by the sudden introduction of niches, fluted pilasters and terracotta capitals as it is in Othonian Greece, as by an increased use of the simple decorative elements already present in the façades of the 'Ionian Baroque' churches and grander eighteenth-century houses. It thus represents a Palladian rather than a Greek revival; the Renaissance arcade of the Liston and not the austere Doric colonnades of the Palace of St Michael and St George (p. 128) or Napier's vanished market building in Lixouri remained the conservative ideal in nineteenth-century Corfu.

The material in which the decoration is carried out depends on the resources of each island. On Ithaca and Cefalonia the raised quoins, cornices, architraves and string-courses are made of finely dressed limestone. A few houses on the east side of Vathi Bay (p. 212) and in Fiskardo (p. 254) are almost the only undamaged specimens of this very handsome nineteenth-century architecture, though many Cefalonian villages contain ruined examples. On Corfu, for lack of freestone, the decorative elements in the design are carried out in raised bands of stucco, painted white to contrast with the ochre, mulberry, lemon or chartreuse ground of the façade; the arches of the nineteenth-century arcades — whether in the suburbs or villages — are outlined in the same way. The elegance with which this simple technique endows a small tiled box is quite remarkable, and Corfu, happily, is full of this delightful poor man's Palladian. In the country houses of the Corfiot gentry the use of stone embellishments adds to the sophistication. Unfortunately most of these houses are hidden away behind the olives and cypresses of their private estates, but the Youth Hostel in Ayos Yannis (p. 160), the former British Residency on Paxos (p. 174) and the Valaorites home on Lefkas are good examples which can be seen by everybody.

Other attractive features of nineteenth-century Corfiot architecture are the tiled lean-to loggias which provide the villager with an outdoor terrace shielded from sun and rain. Running out sometimes to square whitewashed piers, sometimes to plastered columns, and occasionally to an arcade on an upper storey, their long sway-backed slopes of weathered tiles lend grace and interest to even the plainest cottage.

CHURCH ARCHITECTURE

The surviving churches of architectural interest on the Ionian Islands belong to two main periods and styles — the Byzantine 'cross-in-square' church of the twelfth and thirteenth centuries, and the 'Ionian Baroque' church of the seventeenth and eighteenth.

Though the 'cross-in-square' (or 'inscribed-cross') church was a type common in the Byzantine world from the tenth to the fifteenth centuries, earthquakes on the central islands and the Catholic domination of Corfu from the beginning of the thirteenth century prevented its survival on any island except Kithira, which the bigoted Angevins never possessed (p. 55). Outside Kithira only one 'cross-in-square' church survives, that of SS Jason and Sosipater on Corfu (p. 141). On Kithira the best examples are the churches of Ayos Theodoros (p. 302), Ayos Petros (p. 300) and Ayia Varvara (p. 302). Apart from some fine antique marble columns inside and some mock Cufic tile decoration outside SS Jason and Sosipater, all these churches are very plain. They are also comparatively small. It is therefore easy to pass them by without carrying away any more striking impression than that made by the pleasant texture and colour of their whitewashed or masonry walls and their roofs of weathered pink tiles or (often on Kithira) stone. They are, however, all examples of a masterly if repetitive design.

The tall shape and centralized plan of the 'cross-in-square' church goes back to the martyrs' tomb shrines of the fourth to sixth centuries. (The little chapel of Our Lady on Kithira (p. 306) may be a martyrium of this sort.) Inside the rectangular floor-plan the shape of the Cross is not firmly suggested by a solid line of walls as it is by the walls of the nave, choir and transepts in most Western churches, but only by a dotted line of piers and columns. At floor level the church thus appears to have a squarish open plan made up of various compartments all opening into each other through arches. But look up and you will see the shape of the Cross firmly outlined in mid air by two high intersecting barrel-vaults; and where they intersect your eye will rise to a yet higher central space formed by an octagonal drum and the smooth hemisphere of a dome. The square plan, the Cross and the dome together constitute a deliberate act of architectural symbolism: from the confused and much divided ground level of the human world you look up to see the unifying symbol of Christianity and, beyond this intermediary level and at the summit of aspiration, the dome of heaven. Though the remarkable harmony and proportions of these churches can best be seen in their vaulted interiors, the grouping and shape of their superimposed tiers of symbolic spaces can be recognized more easily from outside.

At first sight, the shape of the 'Ionian Baroque' church — a tall 'shoe-box' lit by segmental side-windows and covered with a pitched roof of tiles ending in triangular gables — seems a sudden innovation. But though this shape came into full fashion again only in the seventeenth century, its Ionian history is as old as the sixth-century church of Paleopolis on Corfu (p. 142), as the surviving central aisle of this once five-aisled basilica shows. Under Western influence it began to be reintroduced into the islands in the fifteenth century as a rival to the barrel-vaulted churches and chapels of Angevin and early Venetian times. The chapel of the Odiyitria (p. 200) on Lefkas, built in 1450, has a typical 'Ionian Baroque' shape, though it is constructed in a Byzantine style of masonry; and the surviving fifteenth-century churches of Anafonitria (p. 282) and Maries on Zakinthos (though these have side-aisles) suggest that the basilica plan was more popular in the fifteenth century than appears now after so much seventeenth-century rebuilding. At any rate, the churches of St Nicholas-on-the-Mole (p. 267) on Zakinthos (built in 1560), St Spiridon (p. 135) on Corfu (built in 1596), and Evangelistria on Cefalonia, of about the same date (p. 239), show that the flat-ceilinged single-aisled basilica had become the fashionable model by the end of the sixteenth century. In the seventeenth century the external decoration was added which gives this plain shape its baroque appearance. For 'Ionian Baroque' consists, with only one or two exceptions (e.g., the church of the Faneromeni (p. 268) on Zakinthos) more of enrichment to doors and windows than of any deliberate rhythmical design of the whole elevation. Pillared and pilastered doors and windows with Tuscan or Corinthian capitals, rusticated or fluted quoins, broken and swan-necked pediments, shells, lozenges and garlands are 'stuck on' to almost identical stone or plastered façades. The result is always pleasing, but should perhaps be termed baroque decor rather than baroque architecture. The most richly furbished seventeeth- and early-eighteenth-century façades — all on Zakinthos — are to be seen in the churches of the Faneromeni (p. 268), Our Lady of the Angels (p. 267), Our Lady of Keri (p. 279), Ipapandi (p. 281) and Ayia Paraskevi (p. 284). The best nineteenth-century façade belongs to the church at Kaligata on Cefalonia (p. 241) where the applied decoration is nearly rococo.

Inside, the sumptuousness of some of these 'Ionian Baroque' churches is astonishing. Though the screen (see below) across the east end, the women's gallery projecting from the west end, and lines of high-backed 'standing' pews along the north and south walls are the only features which give structural interest to the empty rectangle of space, the profusion of carved and gilded wood, painted ceilings, silver, bronze or carved wood candelabra and crystal chandeliers provide the interiors with a richness reminiscent of Thornhill or Wren. The most completely decorated interiors are those of the Platitera Convent (p. 137) and St Spiridon (p. 135) on Corfu and of the church in Makherado (p. 280) on Zakinthos. The best time to see Greek churches is in the week after Easter. Then all the silver glistens and the smooth marble floors, still strewn with sprigs of lentisc and myrtle, look like embroidered silk counter-panes.

The 'Ionian Baroque' church is distinguished by one other feature, its belfry. The belfry of a Byzantine church generally consists of a more or less ornamented wall which is pierced with arches for the bells to hang in and stands up above the façade of the church or over its courtyard gate. This type persists to the present day; but near many 'Ionian Baroque' churches the bells are hung in an immensely tall free-standing campanile topped by a painted cement dome or a pyramidal tiled roof. On Zakinthos and Cefalonia many of these Italianate campaniles were destroyed in the 1953 earthquake, but they are still common landmarks on Corfu. Two bells only, tuned a semitone apart, are used in a peal. This is apt to sound dismal or, when the bells are cracked — as they often are by earthquakes — positively discordant to a Western ear; but some of the bells themsleves, cast in Venice in the seventeeth century, have a lovely tone. Cefalonia was once famous for its ringing, and the campanile of the church in Makherado still sends out silvery notes across the plain of Zante.

CHURCH ART

SCREENS

With their tall campaniles and their baroque exteriors many Ionian churches look more Roman than Greek. But the liturgical differ- ence between the two churches is always clearly stated in an Orthodox church by the screen with triple doors which separates the sanctuary and altar from the rest of the building. This screen — or *témplo*, as it is generally called in the Ionian Islands — is the main monument of Ionian church art. For its deco- ration local craftsmen in the second half of the seventeenth century evolved a fusion of styles and techniques, where Byzantine motifs were carried out in the newly fashionable Venetian material of carved and gilded wood and subordinated to an overall Renais- sance or baroque design. In spite of the fire which destroyed the screens of so many of the Zakinthos town churches in 1953, the finest examples are still to be found on that island, in the museum or re-erected in the restored or rebuilt churches of Our Lady of the Angels (p. 267) and Ayia Ekaterini (p. 274) in the town and envi- rons, and in the country churches of Keri (p. 279), Meso Volimes (p. 284) and Exokhora (p. 282). There are also handsome screens on Kithira and Cefalonia, but most of them are more simply carved and later than those of Zakinthos and have often been cheaply regilded. On Lefkas, a poor island and only retaken from the Turks in 1684, the screens are often painted white and mostly belong to the eighteenth century. Corfu and Paxos have little or no pine-wood and their early screens are generally made of stone or marble. There are finely carved examples in the city churches of Pan- dokrator (p. 136) and the Panayi Kremasti (p. 136) and a very grand one, imitating the façade of a church, in the church of St Spiridon (p. 135).

As its technical name — *ikonostásis* (icon-stand) — implies, the screen provides a framework into which holy pictures are set in a determined order. It adds greatly to the interest of a church, and to the identification of the icons, to know what this order is. The bottom tier usually contains four principal icons: that on the far left is of the saint to whom the church is dedicated; those to the left and right of the central door are of the Virgin Mary and of Christ as High Priest; and the icon on the far right is of St John the Baptist.

When, as is often the case, a church is dedicated to the Virgin or St John, there will generally be two icons of each, in the two appropriate places. The right- and left-hand screen doors depict angels or hierarchs, and the central door, Christ in majesty. The twelve icons in the second tier generally depict the Apostles or the principal feasts of the Church; and the higher tiers often portray Church Fathers or Old Testament prophets. In addition to these icons and others round the walls of the church, there is generally one particularly venerated icon on the wall to the right of the screen, or on an individual stand in the body of the church. (On Cefalonia many screens hold five or six rather than four principal icons.)

ICONS

At the end of the eighteenth century Grasset dismissed the icons of the Ionian Islands as worthless because 'on n'y reconnaissoit pas même l'ombre de principes de dessin, et le coloris étoit, dans tous, le même.' At one's first encounter with Byzantine painting it is easy to have Grasset's reaction. The difficulty of distinguishing between sixteenth- and seventeenth-, eighteenth- and even nineteenth-century icons is increased by their dirty and damaged state, and by the gloom of the churches. But in recent years many of the more important icons have been cleaned by restorers from the Byzantine Museum in Athens and this programme continues.

The icons reflect the geographical position of the Ionian Islands halfway between two sources of artistic inspiration — Crete and Italy. In the icons of the fourteenth to sixteenth centuries the Italo-Byzantine style — deriving through Italian painting from Ravenna and centred, after its foundation by a Zantiot in 1539, on the Orthodox church of St George in Venice — can sometimes be fairly easily distinguished by its simplicity from the more mannered Byzantine style which evolved on Crete after the fall of Constantinople. After the lovely 'Entry into Jerusalem' in the Lefkas museum (p. 186), the icon of Ayia Mavra in the church of Makherado on Zakinthos (p. 280) is probably the finest example of this Italianate style; it has something of the noble severity of Mantegna. Like all the other surviving works of this type it can be attributed to no known painter. Many of the icons of the late-sixteenth- and seventeenth-century Cretan school, on the other hand, are known to be by such masters as Michael Damaskinos, George Klondzas, Emmanuel Lombardos the Corfiot, Emmanuel Tzanfournari and Dimitrios and George Moskhos. There are numerous examples in the island churches and museums.

As the seventeenth century progressed, the painters of the Cretan school adopted two divergent styles. With pictures whose subjects had never formed part of the Byzantine canon of religious illustration they felt free to experiment with western ideas of form, colour and composition: their painting became more realistic in its treatment of nature and the human body, and laws of perspective began to govern their architecture. With pictures illustrating traditional subjects, or the other hand, their treatment remained rigorously conventional. The result (to the inexperienced eye) is pictures apparently by quite different hands. Many of these painters visited or settled in the Ionian Islands and there is a larger collection of their works in Ionian churches and museums than anywhere in Greece outside Athens. The most famous are Emmanuel Tzanes, Viktoros of Crete, Stephen Tzangarola (a Venetian naturalized on Crete), Theodore Poulakis and John Moskhos.

With the fall of Crete to the Turks in 1669, the last stronghold of the Byzantine artistic conscience vanished and the Ionian painters of the eighteenth and nineteenth centuries were obliged to turn for inspiration to the West. Though their works are rightly studied by Greek art historians and celebrated on Zakinthos, their appeal to a western European visitor is likely to be more academic than aesthetic; for while it is certainly surprising that seven small islands should have produced so many competent painters, nothing their artists did has not been done better elsewhere. The founder of the school, Panayotis Doxaras (1662–1729), studied in Rome and Venice and filled his notebook with precepts to be learned from the paintings of Poussin, Claude and Lebrun as well as of the Italian masters. His only major work — the ceiling of the church of St Spiridon on Corfu — was unfortunately painted over in 1850. The major work of his son Nicholas Doxaras (c. 1710–75), who studied for eighteen years in Venice as a protégé of Marshal Schulenburg, was equally ill-fated; for his nine years' work on the church of the Faneromeni on Zakinthos was almost all lost in the fire which followed the earthquake of 1953. The bright colours and vigorous drawing of a few surviving panels in the museum are reminiscent of G. B. Piazzetta and suggest that he had a lively talent. His main followers, the two eccentric priests Nicholas Koutouzis (1741–1813) and Nicholas Kandounis (1767–1834), are extremely eclectic painters. Many of the paintings by which they are represented in the Zakinthos museum are sticky, brown, emotional studies in the manner of Annabile Caracci or Lucca Giordano. Both appear to much greater advantage in the Platitera Convent on

Corfu, where Koutouzis in particular reveals a palette of clear Venetian colours and a spontaneous touch.

Many of the icons in Ionian churches are partially covered by repoussé silver-work, a method of enrichment that goes back to Paleologue times. When tinny crowns and silver mittens are nailed to a fine icon with tacks, or a sheet of uninspired metal turns the icon into a silver bagatelle board, with angels' and cherubs' faces peering out of little breathing holes, this enrichment is either irritating or absurd. But George Diamandis Baffas (c. 1775–1854), an Epirot silversmith who worked mostly on Zakinthos, raised this pious but misguided habit to an art and produced icon-casings which are masterpieces of movement and design as well as of technical skill. He also make fine Bible-covers and alms-dishes; and the splendid coffer of St Dionisios is by his hand.

WALL-PAINTINGS

On the central five islands few early churches have survived constant tremors or the spate of rebuilding in the sixteenth and seventeenth centuries, and the remaining wall-paintings mostly date from the seventeenth and eighteenth centuries. There are, however, two or three very beautiful eleventh-century fragments left on Corfu, from the church of St Nicholas (to be seen in the Palace of St Michael and St George) and in the church of Ayos Merkourios (p. 150). On Kithira several churches still contain two or three layers of superimposed frescoes painted between the twelfth and fifteenth centuries: Ayos Dimitrios (p. 296), Ayos Petros (p. 300), Ayia Sofia in the Milopotamo cave (p. 300) and Ayos Antonios (p. 302). In Ayos Antonios, as in the chapel of the Odiyitria on Lefkas (p. 200), the fifteenth-century wall-paintings are in a distinctly Italianate style. The church of Ayos Markos on Corfu (p. 150) contains the most complete set of sixteenth-century painting in the islands, and the work of the seventeenth century can best be judged in the chapels of Kato Khora (p. 300) on Kithira, the church of Anoyi (p. 223) on Ithaca and the Zakinthos Museum, to which the wall-paintings from a complete church in Volimes have been transferred.

OTHER MUSEUMS

Apart from the archaeological museums mentioned on p. 84, there are a few museums concerned with the art and history of the islands in medieval and modern times: the Palace of St Michael and

St George on Corfu (p. 128), the Zakinthos Museum (p. 269) and the Solomos Museum on that island (p. 269), the Lefkas Museum (p. 186) and the Koryalenios Museum on Cefalonia (p. 231). In particular all but the third have extremely interesting collections of icons.

FOOD AND DRINK

Apart from one or two recipes and local specialities (see p. 99), food in the Ionian Islands is much the same as in the rest of Greece. Cooking is one of the very few activities at which the Greeks seem never to have excelled. Simple and appealing as far as it goes, their cuisine is limited, repetitive and very conservative in its ideas and techniques, more of a peasant handicraft than an art. In the course of a short holiday its limitations are not likely to worry you, even if you regard eating as a purely gastronomic exercise; for there are enough new succulent tastes and smells to last you a few weeks at any rate. And if, like the Greeks, because of a tradition of frugality, you regard eating out more as an occasion round which to build a sense of shared well-being, then the simplicity of a Greek meal will offer you a new and happy type of experience. As Marguerite Yourcenar makes the Emperor Hadrian say, 'In the merest hole of a place in Aegina or Phaleron I have tasted food so fresh that it remained divinely clean despite the dirty fingers of the tavern waiter; its quantity, though modest, was nevertheless so satisfying that it seemed to contain in the most reduced form possible some essence of immortality.'

Hotel meals are apt to be of an interdenominational but faintly Western European type. Though the menu will probably include one or two of the 'safer' and better-known Greek dishes, it will too often tail off into stewed fruit or *crème caramel* (the last generally delicious). On Corfu several hotels have their own restaurants; but on the other islands you will find it hard to avoid both the hazards and delights of genuine Greek restaurant cooking. On Ithaca, Kithira and Lefkas the former outnumber the latter.

In Greece, if you want the whole standard European sequence of a meal — preceded by an aperitif, ending with something sweet and followed by coffee — you may have to move two or three times unless you are eating at a hotel. You will start in a café with a drink. If you order the national aperitif, *oúzo* (a colourless grape-spirit flavoured with fennel, coriander and anise, which clouds if you add water), a *mezés* will be included in the price. In the Ionian Islands the choice of *mezédes* is not very large — and the two or three titbits brought to you on a saucer will not include anything more exotic than an olive, a potato chip, a quarter of tomato, a slice of cucumber, a little square of bread supporting a morsel of cheese, anchovy, salami or a dab of *taramosaláta*— a purée of pink salted cod's roe pounded and beaten up with oil and mashed potato. If you drink anything other than ouzo, you will have to order a plate of *mezédes* specially and pay extra for them.

If you are on one of the islands where the wine is good you can more adventurously take your aperitif in a *tavérna*. Strictly speaking, a *tavérna* is a pub, characterized by a row of wine-barrels along one side of the room. In certain parts of Greece, particularly Athens, *tavérnes* have developed into restaurants and the term is now inaccurately but conveniently used for any simple eating-place. In the Ionian Islands *tavérnes* are drinking-places and are common only in the town of Zante — rustic and bucolic haunts where you can order a measure of wine and a simple *mezés*. But in the side-streets of most of the towns there are indeterminate little places — part wine-shop, part *ouzería*, part café — to whose door-ways you may be drawn by the scent of various foods being prepared on charcoal grills: spicy little sausages (*loukánika*), or *kokorétsi*— yard-long sausages of coarsely chopped inwards and herbs wound in a sheep's gut and looking like the knotted elastic of a huge toy aeroplane. After Easter a whole sheep, or on Lefkas in the autumn a whole pig, may be turning on a spit and you can order 'a little bit' (*'éna komatákî'*) to try, or a helping of half a kilo. It will be brought to you on a sheet of grease-proof paper, sprinkled with salt, together with a lump of bread; accompanied by a salad nothing could make a better main course for a meal. Sometimes such places develop into proper restaurants specializing in grilled meats; and in the last ten years grilled chicken restaurants have become a useful standby in most of the island capitals.

The ordinary restaurant (*estiatórion*), unlike the grilled-meat place, is somewhere you can count on finding at least one or two and, in the towns, sometimes a large selection of ready-cooked foods, either baked or stewed gently over the fire: mutton, beef (euphemistically called veal) or chicken *kokkinistó*— that is, simmered in oil and water (sometimes wine) flavoured with herbs, garlic and tomato paste until nothing remains but a piece of very tender meat surrounded by an unctuous and aromatic orange gravy (the characteristic Greek stewing technique); fish baked with potatoes and tomatoes (*psári foúrno*) — generally grey mullet (*kéfalos*), sea-bream (*fangrí*) or gurnet (*sinagrída*); green peppers (*piperiés*), aubergines (*meletsánes*), tomatoes (*tomátes*) or courgettes (*kolokouthákia*) stuffed with rice or a savoury mince; *mousakás* — a dish of aubergines, potatoes and minced meat capped with a cheesy sauce; meat-balls of various sorts, both stewed (*youvarelákia* and *tsoutsoukákia*) and grilled or fried (*keftédes*); and a variety of pulses cooked in rich pottages, especially in the colder months: lentils (*fakés*), chick-peas (*revíthia*) and haricot beans, the huge ones known as 'giants' (*yígandes*). Macaroni (*makarónia*), the poor man's filler-up and nothing like so good in Greece as it is in Italy, is never accompanied by an interesting sauce, but a sort of pie of macaroni and minced meat called *pastítso* can be quite good. Rice, though plain, is known as *piláfi*; with yoghourt (*yaoúrti*) it is the safest dish for an upset stomach. The commonest separate vegetables are artichokes (*anginares*) (somtimes stuffed with broad beans and flavoured with dill, but more often stewed with potatoes), green beans (*fasolákia*) stewed with oil, tomato and garlic, cauliflower (*kounoupídi*), and the wild, often rather bitter, greens called *khórta*. The last two are also eaten cold as salads. Other salads are delicious nutty white cabbage (*lákhano*) — in the early and late months of the year — and tomatoes, cucumbers (*angoúria*) and green peppers, sliced without finesse and dressed with nothing more than a thread of oil. Lettuce (*maroúli*), on the other hand, is often carefully shredded and generally served in a wet mound tasting of vinegar.

In an unpretentious restaurant all the cooked foods, in a battery of copper or aluminium pans, will be competing (often hopelessly) for a place to keep warm in the kitchen, which is generally divided from the dining area by no more than a counter; and whether or not you can read the menu it is wise — and perfectly in order — to go and inspect them before ordering. In the refrigerator or counter there will also be meat and fish to be fried (*tiganitó*) or grilled (*skáras*), though in many restaurants the grilling will be on top of the cast-iron stove rather than over charcoal. These *tis óras* ('of the hour') provisions will probably include fillet and entrecôte steaks (*bonfilé* and *brizóles*), tender little lamb chops (*paidákia*), brochettes of beef (*souvlákia*, 'little spits'), and various kinds of fish, of which the best and commonest are red mullet (*barboúnia*), sea-perch (*lithríni*) and squid (*kalamarákia*). Behind the glass front of the counter you will also be able to see a selection of fruit — oranges (*portokália*), apples (*míla*), peaches (*rodákina*), melon (*pepóni*), water-melon (*karpoúzi*) and grapes (*stafília*), according to the season — a few pots of yoghourt, one or two sorts of cheese (*tirí*), olives (*eliés*), and perhaps a dish of *taramosaláta*.

This, then, is your choice; you can see it all, smell most of it, test the temperature of some of it discreetly with the back of you hand, appraise it for freshness. Even if you speak not a word of Greek there is really no excuse for landing yourself with a plate of stale, cold, oily food. If you see nothing that appeals to you, you can try elsewhere. If you arrive hungry on a small island late in the evening and prefer not to risk the dubious remains in the bottoms of the pans, you can always order eggs (*avgá*), bread, cheese and a tomato salad. There are worse meals to be had on the Ionian Islands — but you don't have to eat them.

Another type of eating-place is the ephemeral summer restaurant called a *kéndro*. It will vary in sophistication from a thatched shelter by the seaside where you can eat in your bathing things, to a garden terrace where you can dine at white-clothed tables and dance to a juke-box. The food at a *kéndro* will be largely *tis óras*. An excellent bathing lunch which you can order everywhere is a 'country salad' (*khoriatikí saláta*) of cucumber, tomatoes, green peppers, black olives, chopped onion and *féta* — the soft white sheep or goat's cheese found all over Greece.

According to Herodotus, the Persians claimed that 'the Greeks leave the table hungry because we never have anything worth mentioning after the first course' (Book 1). And it is true that if you want an ice, a sticky cake or a *baklavás* (flaky pastry filled with nuts and dripping with honey), you will probably have to move from the restaurant table to a pastry-shop (*zakharoplastíon*) or café. Nothing about the chocolate-box decor of most pastry-shops will invite you to linger, and you may well move once more to a café pavement for your coffee. If this is to be Turkish rather than instant coffee (which you will find in most places frequented by tourists) you should say whether you want it sugarless (*skéto*), middling-sweet (*métrio*), or sweet (*glikó*). Two cafés in the islands, one in Kapodistriou Street in Corfu and one in the Platia Rouga in Zakinthos, prepare *loukoumádes* — puff-balls of deep-fried batter swimming in honey.

Apart from inspecting the food, there are one or two other things to remember about eating in a Greek restaurant. When you order *tis óras* you will be charged according to the weight of the steak or fish you choose; for everything else on the menu you will pay for a standard helping (*merída*) unless you specifically ask for 'a little' (*olígo*), when you will be given slightly more than half a helping and pay accordingly; these half-helpings are particularly useful when trying out new dishes. A table of Greeks will often order communal helpings and dab at them in a friendly free-for-all. If you are sensitive about hygiene you can modify this sensible and economical system by distributing the contents of the shared dishes, though a Greek would find this formal and unfriendly. Lunch is the main meal of the day in Greece and food is fresher, hotter and more varied then than it is in the evening. In the islands people have adapted their meal times to those of Athens: the very reasonable hours of two o'clock in the afternoon and nine o'clock in the evening.

Though food stewed in olive-oil tastes better if not served too hot (when it can easily burn one's mouth), some tepid dishes are very discouraging, particularly soup. Luckily cooks on the Ionian Islands are now more used to the whims of tourists and can sometimes be persuaded to heat things up ('*Mípos boríte na to zesténete?*, 'I wonder whether you could heat it up?'). If you are put off by the enormous puddle of oil in which your food may arrive, ask for a clean plate (*piáto*) and transfer the solid part of your helping to it. With dishes where cold oil is added after cooking (salads), or the hot oil poured on after frying (grilled fish), you can say that you want them '*skéto*' or '*khorís ládi*' ('on its own', 'without oil').

SPECIALITIES

Early travellers with justice praised the fruit and vegetables of the Ionian Islands. Wheler thought that Zante had 'the best Mellons (I dare confidently say) in the World' and found its peaches 'extraordinarily good, and big'. Grasset remarks on the vegetables of Lefkas, the oval yellow winter-melons of Cefalonia and the currant-grape of Zakinthos — 'extrèmement agréable à manger lorsqu'il n'est pas encore tout à fair mûr. Sa très grande douceur est alors corrigée par un deu d'aigrelet.' Of all the vegetables, the local tomatoes — in the markets from June till October — are the most memorable; and of the fruits, the wild strawberries cultivated on Corfu and Zakinthos between April and June. The big seedless Californian oranges now grown all over Greece and known everywhere as 'Merlins' were introduced on to Corfu by a Mr Merlin of the Ionian Bank in the late nineteenth century.

Whatever the shortcomings of the cooking on the smaller islands and in remoter villages, one can generally count on the quality of three basic materials — bread, oil and cheese. In 1824 Private Wheeler had the curiosity to peep into a baker's shop on Corfu and 'was astonished to see five straping fellows as naked as they came into the world, their nasty, greacy pelts as yellow as saffron, the sweat running down their bodies, as if they had been basted with oil or melted butter. These dirty Devils were dancing in a long kneading-trough, they held on with their hands to something over their heads while the master was scraping a jig out of a miserable old fiddle . . . It is seldom I ever put any bread in my mouth since.' Nowadays the bread baked in Corfu and the other capitals is often too hygienic and tasteless, especially that chosen by the hotels and grander restaurants; but it is always fresh and crusty. On Paxos and in the villages of the other islands you will eat rye or whole-meal bread baked in a brushwood oven. Zakinthos has two excellent cheeses, one its own slightly Parmesan-like version of *graviéra* (a Gruyère-type cheese produced all over Greece), the other a pungent white cheese called *tirí ladíou* because it is stored and matured in barrels of oil. Paxos has a hard *féta* rather like *fromage de chèvre*, and Vasiliki on Lefkas one that tastes slightly of Roquefort. Corfu has quite a number of good Italian-type cheeses. Though the oil of Paxos has the highest reputation in the islands, that of Zakinthos ('the best Oyle of the World' — Sandys) is lighter and more to the taste of foreigners.

In past centuries local recipes seem to have been more numerous than they are today. On Ithaca, for instance, Gell records 'a kind of omelet, seasoned with onions and liver, chopped into small pieces, and profusely covered with brown sugar'. And the caviar which Cefalonians brought back from the Black Sea (and which Grasset carefully describes as 'a sort of blackish paste composed of fishes eggs') is no longer a common delicacy. But at least five good island specialities survive: *bourdétto* and *soffríto* on Corfu, *sáltsa* on Zakinthos, *savóro* on Lefkas and the tongue-twisting *Kefalonitikípitta* on Cefalonia. *Bourdétto* is a fish stew strongly flavoured with paprika; *soffríto* consists of slices of veal stewed in layers with parsley, garlic and a little vinegar; *sáltsa* is made of little squares of beef stewed gently in wine, herbs and oil; *savóro* is a salad of fried fish marinated for at least a week in oil, vinegar, raisins, garlic and rosemary; and *Kefalonitikípitta* should properly be a short-crust pie filled with morsels of kid cooked with rice and flavoured with tomato paste. Another Ionian dish with a name that sounds as old as a Greek tragedy — *aristoú* — is a corruption of nineteenth-century 'Irish stew' and is further corrupted by being cooked with currants. On Corfu you will find succulent Preveza prawns (*garídes*) at a reasonable price, and on Corfu and Paxos Mediterranean lobsters or, strictly speaking, crayfish (*astakós*) at an unreasonable one; but these are not prepared in any special way.

Zakinthos produces the best nougat (*mandoláto*), Cefalonia the best pralines (*mándoles*), quince paste (*konféto*) and honey (*méli*), and Corfu the best crystallized fruit, including kumquats. All three islands distil various sweet liqueurs (*rosólio*) and Cefalonia bottles a refreshing cordial made of almonds (*ortzáta*).

WINE

Some of the draught (as opposed to the bottled) wines of the Ionian Islands are as good as any in Greece. Except on Kithira, whose wines are mediocre, they are not resinated. The white (*áspro*) wines of the hill districts of Zakinthos and Northern Ithaca are sharp, bright and dry. The *verdéa* of Zakinthos is a little sweeter, varies in colour from greenish yellow to rosy gold, and has a strong aromatic bouquet sometimes reminiscent of·sherry, sometimes of muscat grapes. Two types are bottled by Commouto, 'Mirage' and 'Verdea', the former better and lighter than the other. The splendid white *robóla* of Cefalonia is less sharp than the hill wines of the other two islands, but less idiosyncratic than *verdéa*; that bottled locally is distinctly more alcoholic than the draught variety. The robust red *robóla* produced on these three islands makes excellent winter drinking, but summer visitors will be lucky to find any left to try. Outside these three islands it is rather a matter of luck if you come on a good draught wine. Each village has its own, and they vary greatly. Thus on the west coast of Lefkas you may be offered wine far more attractive than any you will find in the capital. (The red wine bottled on Lefkas under the name 'Santa Mavra' does nothing to enhance the reputation of the island.) On the whole the red and white wines of Lefkas and Corfu are vitiated by a sweet/sour character. The Corfiots recognize this and more often drink Greek beer (which is excellent) or wines imported from other parts of Greece, frequently *retsína*, about which (according to Miller) the metropolitan of Athens remarked at the end of the twelfth century that 'it seems to be pressed from the juice of the pine rather than from that of the grape'. There are Corfiot wines bottled by Karapiperis, Lavvano, Makris and Theotoki. The last have an almost mythical reputation. Extremely expensive by Greek standards, they disappear into diplomatic and official cellars. Antipaxos produces a bottled sparkling rosé tasting of cider; well iced it is rather intriguing. And for those who care neither for beer nor wine, on Corfu it is still possible to buy ginger beer (*tsíntsin bíra*), made according to the original early-nineteenth-century recipe.

INTRODUCTION TO ISLANDS AND ROUTES

Each island chapter contains a short factual introduction, practical information about hotels, restaurants, swimming and so on, a longer introduction, an account of the capital and its principal sights, a description of any short excursions to be made from the town and a number of routes. These routes deserve a word of explanation. Even on Cefalonia — the largest of the islands — no route is so long that you cannot get out and back from the capital in a day if you ignore some or all of the optional detours. But some routes have so many of the latter that they provide material for several separate excursions. Some have places to stay at the far end, or en route; others end at a cliff or a deserted beach. Some can be linked up with neighbouring routes, in others you will have to return by the same road. The routes have been arranged and numbered as systematically as each island's topography and road network allow, but there is no recommended order in which to follow them. Each one is prefaced by a list of the chief attractions along it and you must decide for yourself whether it offers the site, beach or monument you feel in the mood for. The roads on the island maps have been marked with the appropriate route numbers, while the route numbers in brackets indicate detours. Distances are given in kilometres and are one-way. They are marked cumulatively along each route, detours being excluded.

CORFU (KERKIRA)

Though Corfu is easily the most populous of the Ionian Islands (1971 population 92,742), it is only the second largest of the group (588 square km.). It lies alongside Epirus with its north-east cape only about 3·5 km. from the Albanian coast. Its capital is also called Corfu and ranks as a city (1971 population 28,630). In Greek both city and island are known as *i Kérkira* — a feminine name.

INFORMATION FOR VISITORS

Information
For sources of tourist information in general, see p. 30.
National Tourist Organization in the building of the Administrative Authorities, a new complex situated between S. Dessila, Mantzarou and Doukissis Marias Streets. (*Map* 30). *Tourist police* (for town queries): 31 Arseniou Street (*Map* 1). For country queries: 4 Parados Yerasimou Markova (tel. 30669) (*Map* 26).
Travel Agencies
Corfu Tourist Services, 5 Arseniou Street; *Coryfo*, 76 X. Stratigou Street; *Corfu Travel*, 76 Kapodistriou Street; *Airtour Greece*, 22 Kapodistriou Street; *Adam Bogdanos*, 7 Donzelot Street; *Hermes en Gréce*, 68, I. Theotoki Street; *Tourinvest*, 11 Arseniou Street.
    Most of the foregoing selection of larger agencies arrange island excursions.
Post Office
Map 33.
Cable Office
Map 35.
Hospital
P. Konstanḍa Street (tel. 8062). On the edge of town on the Paleokastritsa route.
British Vice-Consulate
2 N. Zambeli Street (tel. 28-055).
Map 34.
Danish Vice-Consulate
37 Ay. Spiridonas Street.
Italian Vice-Consulate
10 Alexandros Avenue.
Feast-Days
Easter (see p. 79); also processions in honour of St Spiridon on Palm Sunday, Easter Even, August 11th and the first Sunday in November (see p. 135).

GETTING TO CORFU

Air

Direct daily flights from Athens all the year round and direct weekly flights from London in summer (Olympic Airways). In summer there are also many charter flights.

Athens Offices: Olympic, 6 Othonos Street, and 96 Syngrou Avenue.

London Offices: Olympic, 141 New Bond Street, W1.

Sea

International Car Ferries
From Brindisi
The *Castalia*, *Egnatia*, *Appia* and *Espresso* (Hellenic Mediterranean Lines and Adriatica Lines, Electric Railway Station Building, Piraeus, tel. 4115611). Daily from March 14th to July 31st; every other day in early March. Journey time: 8½ hours.

The *Poseidonia* (Libra Maritime, 4 Loudovikou Square, Piraeus, tels 4117864-6). Daily in summer. Journey time: 7 hours.

The *Sant Andrea* (Achaic Lines, 15–17 Khadzikyriakou Avenue, Piraeus, tels 4531844-5). Every two or three days from June 3rd to August 31st. Journey time: 9 hours.

The *Georgios* (Fragline, 5a Rethimnou Street, Athens 147, tels 8232962 and 8222162). Every two or three days from June 1st to July 30th. Journey time: 8¾ hours.

The *Ionis* (Ionian Lines Agency, 4 Marni Street, Athens, tel. 8222068). Every two or three days from June 13th to September 21st. Journey time: 8½ hours.

From Bari
The *Vergina* (Stability Maritime Inc., 271 Alkiviadou Street, Piraeus, tels 4515954 and 4132392). Every other day from May 27th to September 30th. Journey time: 7 hours.

The *Epirus* (Epirus Line, Galasy Building, 6 Skouze Street, Piraeus, tel. 4117517). Journey time: 10½ hours.

Local Car Ferries
From Igoumenitsa: In summer there are twelve services a day between 06.00 and 21.30, in winter about half this number. The ferries berth in George II Square (*Map* 3) and the journey takes 2 hours.

From Patras: The *Ionis* (see *International Car Ferries* above) every other day via Cefalonia, Ithaca and Paxos. Journey time about 12 hours.

Caiques
From Paxos: Caiques leave Gaio every morning. For details, see p. 171.

Road

From Athens: By the same route as to Lefkas (see p. 180) as far as Amfilokhia, then via Aktion, Preveza, Nikopolis and Morfi to Igoumenitsa: 476 km.

Bus

From Athens: Three buses a day along the route above. Journey time (including the Igoumenitsa–Corfu ferry) is about 10 hours. *Athens Office of the Corfu K.T.E.L.:* 100 Kifissou Avenue (tel. 5129 443).

Rail

From Athens: Seven trains (S.E.K.) a day to Patras. Journey time 4 to 5 hours. (The Corfu ferry berth in Patras is about 0·4 km. from the railway station.)

TRANSPORT ON THE ISLAND

Buses

Corfu has both a town and a country bus service. The town buses run to and fro every half hour or so from the suburb of Manḍouki (near the New Port) to the middle of the Esplanade, and from the Esplanade to Kanoni.

Country buses leave from three different terminals: buses for all villages along Routes 1 to 4 (or excursions off them) leave from New Fort Square or King George II Square next door; buses for all villages along Routes 5abc (or excursions off them) leave from Theotoki Square. For the frequency of day-return services see the Route instructions. For detailed timetables apply to the National Tourist Organization office (*Map* 30).

Taxis

There are about 200 taxis on the island. For rates see p. 23. The main city ranks are in Kapodistriou Street (tel. 9926), E. Voulgareos Street (tel. 9911), Mandzarou Street (tel. 9970), the middle of George II Square (tel. 2993) and Theotoki Square (no telephone).

Horse-drawn carriages

Victorias painted as brightly as canal barges or gypsy caravans provide an agreeable way of exploring the environs.

Their prices are controlled: in 1980, Drs 500 an hour, or Drs 700 to Kanoni and back.

Car Hire

For general information and rates, see p. 23. The main car-hire concerns are: Avis Rent-a-Car, 31 Alexandras Avenue (tel. 23820 and 28787); International Car Hire System, 76 X. Stratigou Street (tel. 29160); Hellas Cars, 18 Kapidistriou Street (tel. 23497); Hertz, 76b X. Stratigou Street (tel. 23388); Corfu, Donzelot Street (tel. 22222); Autorent, 72 X. Stratigou Street (tel. 29674).

Scooter and bicycle hire

For general information and rates, see p. 23. There are dozens of shops hiring mopeds, scooters and bicycles. In the country you will find them wherever tourist accommodation is fairly dense. In the town the three main areas are George II Square, the New Harbour (near the Ionian Hotel) and the top of Alexandras Avenue.

Maps

The safest bet among several maps on sale, some good some bad, is the one produced by the Automobile and Touring Club of Greece (E.L.P.A.) whose office is in Psikhiatrou Square close to Theotoki Square.

Guided tours by coach or boat

Daily excursions to most places of tourist interest are organized in the season by various travel agencies, e.g., Gorgon Tours, 38 Kapodistriou Street, and Corfu Travel Ltd, 18 Kapodistriou Street.

Caiques

There is a useful daily caique service to Kassiopi (p. 152) in the north which leaves every morning from the Spilia quay, calls at Nisaki (p. 151) and Kouloura (p. 152), spends the night at Kassiopi and returns early the following morning.

ACCOMMODATION AND RESTAURANTS

Hotels in Corfu Town and Environs

L Class   *Corfu Hilton*, Kanoni. Very large hotel set in wooded grounds with splendid views. Own beach, swimming pools, tennis. L class restaurants.

Corfu Palace, Vasilias Konstandinou Avenue. Large hotel in sea-front building with garden and sea-water pool in echelon of city wall. Demi-pension obligatory. Minibus to, and exchange facilities with, Miramare Beach Hotel. Dance-band. L class restaurant. Night club, tennis courts.

A Class   *Ariti*, Kanoni. Large hotel overlooking the Khalikiopoulos Lagoon. Swimming pool, L class restaurant.

Cavalieri, 4 Kapodistriou Street. Open April 1st to October 31st. Medium-sized converted nineteenth-century mansion on Esplanade. Demi-pension obligatory. Ten L class double rooms. Bathing facilities at Corfu Nautical Club. L class restaurant. Tennis courts.

Corfu Kanoni, Kanoni. Large hotel set in landscaped olive grove overlooking the Khalikiopoulos Lagoon. Swimming pool, own minibus to Mon Repos bathing lido. L class restaurant, nightclub.

B Class   *Arion*, Anemomylos. Private beach (separated from hotel by road). Mini-golf, night club, restaurant, swimming pool, water ski-ing.

Astron, 35 Donzelot Street. Medium-sized hotel overlooking Old Port. From June 1st to September 30th, demi-pension obligatory. Roof garden. Most rooms have view of sea and Mt Pandokrator. L class restaurant. Tennis courts.

King Alkinoos, 29 Panou Zafiropoulou Street. Large hotel in garden quarter. Demi-pension obligatory. Roof garden. L class restaurant.

Marina, Anemomylos. Private beach (separated from hotel by road), restaurant, swimming pool.

Olympic, 1 Megali Doukissas Marias Avenue. Medium-sized hotel in garden quarter. Demi-pension obligatory. A class restaurant. Tennis courts.

C Class *Arcadion*, 44 Kapodistriou and Widmanou Streets. Medium-sized hotel, superficially Venetianized, on Esplanade. Single rooms have double beds. A class restaurant.

Atlantis, New Port. Large, new hotel.

Bretania, 27 Ethnikou Stadiou Street. Small, close to the airport. No restaurant.

Calypso, 4 P. Vraila Armeni Street. Small hotel in old Corfu town-house style behind Garitsa Bay. Most rooms glimpse sea. No restaurant. Tennis courts.

Dalia, 7 Ethnikou Stadiou Street. Small, near the airport. No restaurant.

Helvetia (Suisse), 13 Kapodistriou Street. Medium-sized hotel in early-nineteenth-century Liston house. No lift. Most rooms overlook Esplanade. No restaurant.

Hermes, 12 G. Markora Street. Medium-sized hotel in central side street. No restaurant.

Ionion, X. Stratigou Street. Large water-front hotel, opposite Brindisi car-ferry berth in New Harbour. Half the rooms have view of sea and Mt Pandokrator. No restaurant.

Royal, Kanoni. Large hotel overlooking airfield and Pontikonisi. Swimming pool. Restaurant.

Salvos, Kanoni. Large hotel, overlooking Pontikonisi and airfield. Restaurant. Swimming pool.

Splendid, 39 E. Voulgareos Street. Small house-type hotel opposite Town Hall in narrow main thoroughfare. No restaurant.

D Class *Acropole*, Zavitsianou Street. Small hotel in late nineteenth-century six-floor block overlooking Old Port. Views of sea and Mt Pandokrator. No restaurant.

Evropi, 10 Gitsiali Street. Medium-sized hotel in side street behind New Harbour. No restaurant.

Konstandinoupolis, 11 Zavitsianou Street. Medium-sized hotel in mid-nineteenth-century block next to and with same outlook as Acropole. No restaurant.

Mitropolis, 24 Leoforos Konstantinou Street.

New York, 21 Ipapandis Street. Medium-sized pre-war hotel overlooking Old Port. Ten rooms have view of sea and Mt Pandokrator. No restaurant.

Saroko, 1 Theotoki Street. Small hotel just off Theotoki Square. No restaurant. Tennis courts.

There are also several E class hotels offering basic accommodation; inquire at the Tourist Office for details.

Country Hotels

L Class *Astir Palace*, Kommeno. *Route* **1**. Open April 1st to October 31st. Very large hotel on private headland with fine views. Air conditioning, L class restaurants, seawater swimming pool, own beach, tennis, discotheque.

Castello, Dassia. *Route* **1**. Open April 1st to October 31st. For site and description, see p. 150. Demi-pension obligatory. Minibus service. L class restaurant. Tennis courts, sea sports.

Eva Palace, Kommeno. *Route* **1**. Open April 1st to October 31st. Very large hotel on olive-wooded promontory with fine views. Air conditioning. L class restaurants. Swimming pool, tennis, water sports.

Miramare Beach, Moraitika. *Route* **5c**. Open April 1st to October 31st. Very large bungalow style hotel in flat and narrow olive grove between road and sea. Demi-pension obligatory. Own beach, obstacle golf, tennis, water skiing, car-hire, minibus service and discotheque. L class restaurant.

A Class *Agios Gordios*, Ayos Gordis. *Route* **5a**. Open April 1st to October 31st. Very large beach-side hotel under cliffs at south end of bay. L class restaurant; swimming pool, tennis, own minibus service to town.

Acrotiri, Paleokastritsa. *Route* **3**. Open April to October. Very large hotel overlooking Bay of Alipa. L class restaurant. Swimming pool, beach, water ski-ing.

Alexandros, Perama. *Route* **5c**. Large hotel in green road-side setting. L class restaurant. Swimming pool.

Chandris Dassia, Dassia. *Route* **1**. Open April 1st to October 31st. Very large hotel back from the beach. Air conditioning; L class restaurants. Swimming pool, water ski-ing.

Corcyra Beach, Gouvia. *Route* 1. Open April 1st to October 31st. Very large, partly bungalow-style. Demi-pension obligatory. Mini bus service, car-hire, sea-water swimming pool and discotheque. Private beach, tennis. A beautifully sited and landscaped setting on the Bay of Gouvia. L class restaurant.

Corfu Chandris, Dassia. *Route* 1. Open April to October 31st. Very large road-side hotel with chalets and bungalows back from the beach. Air conditioning, L class restaurants. Private beach, night club, swimming pool, water ski-ing.

Delfinia, Moraitika. *Route* 5c. Open April 1st to October 31st. Large hotel in beach-side olive grove. Minibus service, water ski-ing, caique excursions, discotheque. L class restaurant.

Elea Beach, Dassia. *Route* 1. Large beach-side hotel in olive grove. L class restaurant. Swimming pool.

Grand Hotel Glyfada Beach, Glifada beach. *Route* 4. Open April 1st to October 31st. Very large hotel under cliffs at southern end of Glyfada beach, of which it controls a private section. Night club, restaurant, swimming pool, water ski-ing.

Hermones Beach, Ermones. *Route* 4. Open April 1st to October 31st. Very large hotel on hillside above beach. L class restaurant, mini-golf, night club, swimming pool, water ski-ing, tennis. Funicular to sands.

Kerkyra Golf, Alikes. *Route* 1. Open April 1st to October 31st. Very large beach-side hotel in acres of lawn. Private beach, restaurant, night club, swimming pool, water ski-ing, tennis, riding, but no golf.

Kontokali Palace, Kondokali. *Route* 1. Open April 1st to October 31st. Very large hotel among trees with fine views. Private beach, night club, restaurant, swimming pool, water ski-ing, tennis.

Nissaki Beach, Nisaki. *Route* 1. Open April 1st to October 31st. Very large sea-side hotel on olive-planted hillside. L class restaurant, air conditioning, night club; beach, swimming pool, sailing, water ski-ing, tennis.

Regency, Tsaki (Benitses). *Route* 5c. Open April 1st to October 31st. Large roadside hotel. Air conditioning, L class restaurants, night club. Swimming pool and private beach.

Robinson Club, Dafnila. *Route* 1. Very large hotel on olive-planted hillside above the sea. Restaurants. Swimming pool, beach, tennis and facilities for many other sports and activities.

B Class   *Achilleus*, Gaenas (Benitses). *Route* 5c. Large hotel among cypresses between road and sea. L class restaurant. Private beach.

Aelos Beach, Perama. *Route* 5c. Very large hotel discreetly hidden among hillside olive groves. L class restaurant. Private beach, restaurant, mini-golf, night club, swimming pool, water ski-ing.

Akti, Perama. *Route* 5c. Open March to November. Large hotel in an olive grove between road and sea. Own small beach and jetty. Views of Pondikonisi and Kanoni. A class restaurant. Swimming pool, water ski-ing.

Ipsos Beach, Ipsos. *Route* 1. Open April to October. Medium-sized hotel on beach-side road. Private beach, restaurant, water ski-ing.

Mesongi Beach, Moraitika. *Route* 5c. Open March to November. Very large hotel in a flat seaside site surrounded by attractive gardens and lawns. Dance-band. L class restaurant. Sea-water pool, beach and water ski-ing.

Oceanis, Paleokastritsa. *Route* 3. Private beach, restaurant, swimming pool.

Paleokastritsa, Paleokastritsa. *Route* 3. Open April 1st to October 31st. Large hotel 45 metres above sea with commanding views of Paleokastritsa (1·5 km. away) and Liapades Bay. Sea-water swimming pool by hotel; discotheque and snack-bar by small private beach. L class restaurant.

Potomaki, Benitses. *Route* 5c. Open March to October. Large hotel in narrow, green, sea-front setting beyond Benitses. Sea-wall road runs between hotel and beach jetty. A class restaurant. Water ski-ing.

Roda Beach, Roda. *Route* 2. Open April to October. Very large hotel at extreme western end of vast beach. Mini-golf, night club, restaurant, swimming pools, water ski-ing, tennis.

Tourist Pavilion, Paleokastritsa. *Route* 3. Small pre-war building on the beach of the main bay. A class restaurant.

C Class   *Aegli*, Perama. *Route* **5c**. Open April 1st to October 31st. Medium-sized hotel looking down on Pondikonisi and Kanoni. Road runs between hotel and its terrace restaurant, beach and jetty. A class restaurant.

Akhilleion, Gastouri. *Route* **5b**. Small nineteenth-century two-floor block which was once the Akhillion's staff quarters (see pp. 164–5). Fine views of interior. 1·5 km. from sea. No restaurant.

Alykes Beach, Alikes-Potamou. *Route* **1**. Small hotel on waterfront road.

Aphrodite, Roda. *Route* **2**. Small beach-side block. Restaurant.

Apollon, Paleokastritsa. *Route* **3**. Small hotel on the main bay. Restaurant.

Argo, between Vrioni and Perama. *Route* **5c**. Small hotel in dullish countryside 1 km. from the sea. No restaurant.

Arillas Beach, Arillas. *Route* **2**. Small hotel back from beach. Restaurant.

Astoria, Sidari. *Route* **2**. Small beach-side hotel. Restaurant.

Benitses Inn, Benitses. *Route* **5c**.

Boukari, Boukari. *Route* **6**. Small hotel above fishing jetty and beach. Own beach taverna.

Chrysses Folies, Ayos Gordis. *Route* **5a**.

Chryssi Akti, Liapades. *Route* **3**. Small hotel in hillside olive grove above beach. Restaurant.

Dassia Beach, Dassia. *Route* **1**. Private beach, restaurant, water ski-ing.

Emerald, Pyrgi. Open April to October. *Route* **1**. Medium-sized hotel on private beach. Restaurant.

Feakion, Gouvia. *Route* **1**. Medium, mainroad-side hotel. Restaurant.

Galaxias, Gouvia. *Route* **1**. Open April to October. Medium-sized hotel on village street. Restaurant.

Gouvia, Gouvia. *Route* **1**. Small hotel on village street. Restaurant.

Ionion Sea, Ipsos. *Route* **1**.

Konstantinos, Gouvia. *Route* **1**. Small, mainroad-side hotel. Restaurant.

Margarita, Moraitika. *Route* **5c**. Medium-sized, back from beach in bare site.

Marie, Akharavi. *Route* **2**. Small hotel back from the beach. No restaurant.

Marina Beach, Arillas. *Route* **2**. Small beach-side hotel. Restaurant.

Mega, Ipsos. *Route* **1**. Open April 1st to October 31st. Medium-sized. Road runs between hotel and beach. A class restaurant.

Melissa Beach, Mesongi. *Route* **5c**. Medium-sized, back from beach in olive grove. Restaurant.

Mimosa, Sidari. *Route* **2**. Medium-sized, back from Canal d'Amour beach (see p. 156). Restaurant.

Nausika, Ayos Stefanos-Avliotes. *Route* **2**. Small beach-side hotel. Restaurant.

Oasis, Perama. *Route* **5c**. Open April to October. Small hotel in olive grove between road and sea. Own small beach and jetty. A class restaurant. Swimming pool.

Odysseus, Paleokastritsa. *Route* **3**. Medium-sized, above Alipa Bay. Restaurant.

Rossis, Mesongi. *Route* **5c**. Medium-sized beach-side hotel. Restaurant.

Roda Inn, Roda. *Route* **2**. Small water-front hotel. Restaurant.

Roulis, Mesongi. *Route* **5c**. Small, shut off from beach.

Saint Stefanos, Ayos Stefanos-Karioton. *Route* **1**. Small hotel in fishing hamlet.

Sea Bird, Moraitika. *Route* **5c**. Small, back from beach in bare site. Restaurant.

Silver Beach, Roda. *Route* **2**. Medium-sized, back from beach. Restaurant.

D Class   *Avra*, Benitses. *Route* **5c**. Small family hotel between road and sea-wall. B class restaurant.

Benitsa, Benitses. *Route* **5c**. Small hotel in village back street.

Fivos, Benitses. *Route* **5c**. Small hotel boxed in by other buildings.

Hermes, Paleokastritsa. *Route* **3**. Annexe of C class Apollon.

Iliovassilema, Paramona. *Route* **5a**. Open June to September. Small beach-side house.

International, Ayos Gordis. *Route* **5a**.

Ionia, Ayos Markos-Piryi. *Route* **1**. Small, English-run hotel on wooded hillside 1 km. from sea. Restaurant.

Kostas, Ipsos. *Route* 1. Open April to October. Medium-sized hotel. Road runs between hotel and beach. A Class restaurant.

Skheria, Dassia. Open April to October. *Route* 1. Small hotel in beach-side olive grove. Some rooms face sea. A class restaurant.

Sidari, Sidari. *Route* 2. Small beach-side hotel. Restaurant.

Three Brothers, Sidari. *Route* 2. Small beach-side hotel. Restaurant.

Villas

For general information, see p. 29. The first three tourist agencies listed under Information, Corfu Villas Ltd, 43 Cheval Place, London, SW7, Beach Villas, 8 Market Passage, Cambridge, and The Greek Islands Club, The Villa Centre, 66 High Street, Walton-on-Thames, Surrey, KT12 1BU, specialize in providing villas.

Furnished flats

For general information see p. 29. A class flats are provided by Corfu Summerflats, Benitses with 56 beds, Intermezzo Apartments, Konḍokali with 20 beds, and Theodora, Gouvia with 20 beds; B class flats by Esperides, Tsaki (Benitses) with 32 beds, and Sunrise, Ipsos with 72 beds.

Rooms in private houses

For general information see p. 27. There are more than 3,000 licensed rooms in the island. The Town and Country offices of the Tourist Police have lists of them. In the country the largest numbers are in Kassiopi, Sidari, Paleokastritsa, Pelekas and Kavos, and all along the east coast from Moraitika to Piryi.

Holiday camps

Club Méditerranée at Dassia, Nisaki and Ayos Ioannis Peristeron; *Barracuda Club* at Paleokastritsa. For membership and details of these holiday camps, see p. 28.

Youth hostels

At Konḍokali (p. 147), and at Ayos Yannis (p. 160). Breakfast and light meals available, use of kitchen. Open all year.

Camping

At Konḍokali: Kontokali Beach-International camping. Open all year (p. 147).
At Dassia: Cartol Camping. Open April 10th to October 31st (p. 147).
At Ipsos: Ideal Camping. Open April 1st to October 31st (p. 150); and Corfu Camping.
At Kommeno: Dionyssos. Open April 1st to October 31st (p. 147).
At Piryi: Paradissos. Open May 1st to October 31st (p. 150).
At Paleokastritsa: International Camping. Open May 1st to October 31st (p. 157).

Restaurants

For information on categories of restaurants and types of food, see pp. 29 and 95–9. For country restaurants see the information section at the beginning of each route. For town hotel restaurants see above. The following are the independent luxury and A class restaurants in the town of Corfu.
(L)   *Akteon*, Esplanade (on the Moat);
(A)   *Aegli*, Liston; *Khrisi*, Sevastianou Street; *Khrisomalis*, N. Theotoki Street; *Naftikon*, Spilia Gate; *Olympia Pantheon*, and *Averof* (just behind Old Port); *Rex*, Kapodistriou Street.
     The area immediately behind the old port and George II Square is well worth exploring for other small eating places.
     Specialities — *bourdétto* and *soffrito* (p. 100), lobster, Preveza prawns, crystallized fruit, kumquat liqueur, cultivated wild strawberries (*fráoules*) and Merlin oranges (p. 99).

SPORT

Bathing

Corfu Town

The Mon Repos bathing lido (small entrance fee), round the point of Garitsa Bay, has an artificial beach, a protected swimming-area, changing-rooms, a bar and a restaurant.

Country

Sand beaches at Ayos Spiridon (Route 1); Ayos Yeorgos, Sidari, Ayos Stefanos, Astrakeri and Roda (Route 2); at Glifada and Mirtiotissa (Route 4); at Ayos Gordis and Paramona (Route 5a); and at Ayos Yeorgos and Kavos (Route 6).

Shingle beaches (with a sandy bottom out to sea) at Dassia and Ipsos (Route 1); at Arillas (Route 2); at Paleokastritsa (Route 3); at Ermones (Route 4); between Benitses and Moraitika and at Mesongi (Route 5c).

Pebble beaches at Barbati and Kassiopi (Route 1).

Rock bathing at Kassiopi (Route 1).

Water sports

Most of the larger country hotels (see hotel list), provide water ski-ing for residents and their friends. Others can queue for a turn at Dassia, Benitses or Ipsos. Windsurfers for hire are becoming more common.

The National Tourist Organization can also arrange honorary membership of the *Corfu Nautical Club*, which has coxed pairs and eights, skiffs and one or two sailing dinghies.

Tennis

The *Corfu Tennis Club*, 4 Romanou Street (tel. 37021) (*Town Map* **36**) has four hard courts. 1980 court fees: Drs 100 an hour (mornings only). Many hotels also have courts for their residents.

Cricket

The local office of the National Tourist Organization (*Town Map* **30**) can generally arrange for visitors to play on the Esplanade with one of the Corfu teams. A special sporting holiday offered by *The Cricketer Taverna*, Yefira, Paleokastritsa includes a weekly cricket fixture, squash, and reduced fees at the Ropa Valley Golf Club. Inquiries to: Cricketer Taverna Holidays, Beech Hanger, Ashurst, Kent.

Golf

The 18-hole golf course (par 72, 6,800 yards) laid out in 1970 in the

Ropa Valley 10 miles from Corfu town is famous for its billiard-table greens of Penncross Bent grass; and the hundreds of trees then planted now provide an attractive setting. An automatic watering system keeps the course in condition. Visitors rates (1980): green fees, daily Drs 450; weekly Drs 2,100. Hire of clubs: half-set Drs 200, full set Drs 250 (tels, club house and manager, 0661-94220/1).

Gambling

Roulette, baccarat, chemin de fer and fruit machines at the casino in the Akhillion (for details, see p. 165).

INTRODUCTION TO CORFU

The secret of Corfu is a Proustian one: its life and landscape belong to the Time Past of Europe and release in its European visitors those intense moments of pleasure that come from recognition.

The landscape of the island as a whole has arrived by accident at that familiar ideal of wild civility which was deliberately contrived in the great parks of eighteenth-century England. Here God and the Venetian Republic have at different times and not quite equally shared the roles of Brown and Repton, the first concentrating more on contours, the second more on trees. The contours are important. Corfu is not a hogback like Ithaca or Paxos, nor one conglomerate mountain like Cefalonia, nor a plain edged with hills like Zakinthos, nor a table-land like Kithira, nor — for lack of a better description — a thumb-prodded lump of modelling clay like Lefkas, but a loosely fallen drapery held up at one point — but not too far — between the finger and thumb of Mt Pandokrator. The gently undulating folds of its interior provide the setting for the Republic's planting scheme — now perfectly matured — of huge shady woods of olive trees which clothe the hills and run down to shallow valleys filled with sunlight and the scent of mown hay. Sited on knolls and hilltops like the obligatory temples and follies of an Augustan park stand the pink and white Palladian façades of church and cottage, the crumbling stone and mortar of deserted olive-presses and decaying country mansions, all surrounded in the grand manner by stands of cypress trees. Apart from the stepped walls of the olive terraces and wayside hedges of acacia and wild pear, the countryside is almost completely unenclosed, and this adds wonderfully to the feeling that the entire island is one great estate where the fortunate visitor is free to wander as he wills. As if to emphasize this feeling, at the start of all the meandering carriage-drives around the property stands the stateliest urban home in Greece, the city of Corfu: a little down-at-heel in parts, its behind stairs a trifle insanitary and impractical as those of so many great houses are, but with any number of comfortable rooms and a delightfully elegant façade looking out over the forecourt of the Esplanade and the blue ha-ha of the sea to the distant Albanian and Epirot mountains. For unlike an English park, which copies only the green foreground of the Italian Renaissance picture of the ideal, Corfu has the mysterious blue background too; and as Edward Lear (*The Letters*) exclaimed in 1857, 'Anything like the splendour of olive-grove and orange-garden, the blue of the sky and ivory of church and chapel, the violet of mountain, rising from peacock-wing-hued sea, and tipped with lines of silver snow, can hardly be imagined.'

Life in the countryside has preserved, through an inertia bred of too kind a climate, a rustic simplicity which we have long since lost by an excess of industry but recognize from Rowlandson's late-eighteenth-century scenes. Here astute-eared ponies trip along the lanes under huge loads of brushwood for some smoky bread-oven; there girls collect water from a village tap in sweating jars; here a milch-goat with its tether wound round its middle like an abdominal truss bounds ahead of its peasant owner like a pet retriever, while she walks intently on, spinning wool; there cows and long-tailed sheep graze not in anonymous herds but in ones and twos, pegged out under the trees; and everywhere, as in Rowlandson, the best part of the day seems to be spent at dusty roadside inns where the rickety chairs are set out under the shade of a vine or a long slope of tiles or in a dark room smelling of wine and paraffin and cheese.

In the great house of the town, cricket and ginger beer, At Homes with tea and Madeira cake, newspapers under the Liston, clanging victorias and the occasional sharp smell of horse, bandstand music and evening promenades are no less evocative of Time Past, though in this case of the nineteenth rather than the eighteenth century.

An intensive watering programme between November and March brings the whole estate to a peak of broom, rose, wistaria and jasmine-scented opulence in April, May and June, just before it is thrown open for public bathing. In July and August the cicadas begin to fret, the baked countryside is full of the dusky odours of fig trees and the sands are littered with their summer flotsam of browned bodies. But until then Corfu is not too crowded. Its visitors are spread out along the coasts in hotels of every different category and size, each with its own local life — smart and touristy or simple and remote — its own beach and its own hinterland of olive trees to walk through late in the afternoon.

'Corfu ma più,' say the Corfiots of their island, and, with all this, it is easy to see why.

CORFU TOWN

Corfu is a fortunate town. It combines the picturesqueness of a medieval town and the nostalgic appearance of a Regency spa with many of the comforts of a modern resort — and all this in an incomparable setting of distant mountains and blue sea.

Architecturally Corfu is a period piece. It is the only large town in Greece whose buildings are mostly of the eighteenth and nineteenth centuries rather than the twentieth. Though it is no longer walled, and a new residential quarter has been built since Grasset's day, the overall effect of the town is much the same now as when he described it at the end of the eighteenth century as 'a mass of houses of very simple architecture squeezed in between two fortresses'. This mass of houses is intersected by a few colonnaded streets — the great feature of the town — and a maze of stepped and flagstoned lanes decked out with prettily fluttering laundry. Some of the houses are apartment or tenement blocks as many as six or seven storeys high. Built generally of plastered brick with tiled cornices to their windows and grey or green jalousies, they would be handsome buildings if their façades were repaired and more often freshened with new whitewash. But their great height and Corfu's torrential winter rains make municipal or private house-painting an expensive business and they remain dowdier than their architecture deserves. Here and there are one or two grander buildings with stone enrichments and carved gargoyle keystones. But by and large the town contains very few really distinguished monuments; even the rich insides of the churches are hidden by dull exteriors; and the appeal of Corfu lies in the fact that here, for once in Greece, is a town which has been allowed to grow continuously from its beginnings in the Middle Ages to the present day. The assaults of Turkish armies in 1537 and 1716 destroyed parts of it, air raids in the last war others; but thanks to the good sense and taste of the Corfiots the greater part survives. A few post-war buildings inside the line of ramparts — the blocks of flats housing the British Vice-Consulate

(*Map* **34**), for example — are out of character. But the old town as a whole has now been classified as an historic monument and mistakes like these will not be allowed again. Otherwise the only unsightly evidence of the island's huge tourist trade is the increasing number of cars parked on the Esplanade.

Unless one has a clear idea of the five main ways through or round the town from this centre and main open space its topography can be remarkably confusing. These five ways are therefore described in the town routes below. The principal sights are also described separately (for page numbers see the map of Corfu Town).

TOWN ROUTE 1

At the north end of the *Esplanade*, the road which leads through the arch of St George is the main traffic route to the Old Port in *George II Square*. Opposite the west front of the *Palace of St Michael and St George* (*Map* **9**), in a house approached by an outside flight of steps, the *Corfu Literary Society* and the *Rotary Club of Corfu* have their homes. Founded in 1836, the former has a library, reading-room with European newspapers and periodicals, card-room, restaurant and bar, and can extend honorary membership for fifteen days to visitors recommended by its members. Its books, furniture and portraits delightfully evoke nineteenth-century Corfu. Just beyond the club, there is a fine neo-classical building by John Khronis, Corfu's distinguished nineteenth-century architect. It stands on the site of the house where Corfu's most famous statesman, Count John Kapodistrias, was born. The *Archbishop's Palace* (*Map* **2**), on the corner of Arseniou Street, is the first of a line of handsome sea-front houses which look out across the bay. The offices of the *Tourist Police* are in No. 31 (*Map* **1**). The town's north wall originally stood well above the level of the present road, and when Edward Lear took rooms hereabouts in 1861 his address — the 'Line Wall' — preserved their recent memory. Behind these houses is the *Kambielo Quarter*, the oldest part of the town outside the Citadel; its steep lanes — some only a yard wide — flights of steps and hilltop site are reminiscent of Corfu's daughter town Corcyra Negra (now Korcula) off the Dalmatian coast. But here the picturesque has certain disadvantages: a whiff of drains from the decrepit British sewage system is likely to strike a sudden discord with the scent of jasmine and orange-blossom from a courtyard garden, and the houses are disfigured by peeling stucco and winter-stained white-

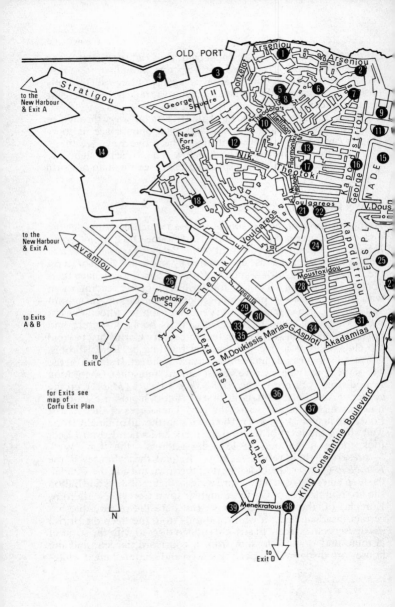

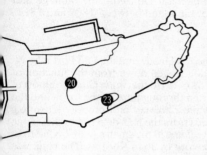

GARITSA

BAY

Corfu Town

1 Tourist Police Town Office
2 Archbishop's Palace
3 Igoumenitsa Ferry Berth
4 Paxos Caiques
5 Panayia Kremasti Church
6 Pandokrator Church
7 Corfu Literary Club & Rotary Club
8 Kokkini Well-head
9 Palace of St. Michael and St. George
  (Museum and Public Library)
10 Orthodox Cathedral
11 Adam Statue
12 St Francis R.C. Church
13 Church of St Spiridon
14 New Fort
15 Platia
16 Liston
17 Ionian Bank
18 Synagogue
19 Schulenburg Statue
20 Citadel
21 Town Hall
22 R.C. Cathedral
23 St George's Church
24 Former Law Courts
25 Spianada
26 Tourist Police Country Office
27 Maitland Rotunda
28 Former Ionian Parliament
29 Prefecture
30 National Tourist Office
31 Former Ionian Academy
32 Corfu Nautical Club
33 Post Office
34 British Vice Consulate
35 Telephone/Telegram Services (O.T.E.)
36 Corfu Tennis Club
37 Archaeological Museum
38 Douglas Obelisk
39 Tomb of Menekrates

0   100   200   300   400   500
                              metres

wash. The bombs which destroyed so many old churches in this quarter during the last war have at least opened up a few breathing-holes among the crowded tenements. The surviving *Church of the Panayia Kremasti* (*Map* 5) and *Church of the Pandokrator* (*Map* 6) are both worth a visit. The last short stretch of the seaside road is named after General Donzelot, the humane and gallant French commander of the island between 1807 and 1814.

TOWN ROUTE 2

The quickest way between the Esplanade and the Old Port is by *N. Theotoki Street*, which runs dog-legged down from the junction of the two halves of the *Liston* (*Map* 16) to the *Spilia Gate*. For most of the day it is the main pedestrian thoroughfare of the town, and the only cars allowed are the white-ribboned and proudly klaxoning taxis carrying away newly-weds from the half-dozen churches along the street. The *Ionian Bank building* in the small square on the right as you walk down is an early work by John Khronis. The bank was formed in 1839 with British capital, chiefly to provide agricultural loans at a less extortionate interest than the 25 per cent demanded by local money-lenders.

A little farther down, the main market-street cuts across N. Theotoki Street, its colourful tiers of fruit and vegetables shaded by awnings and freshened with watering-cans. Here, on the left, M. Theotoki Street takes you up to E. Voulgareos Street (Town Route 3), and on the right Filarmonikis Street leads to the Kambielo Quarter or, if you fork left down Filellinon Street, to George II Square and the Old Port. On the left of Filellinon Street there is a fine carved *stone doorway* in the same style as the screen in the church of the Panayia Kremasti. Farther down N. Theotoki Street, opposite a particularly long arcade, is the *Catholic Church of St Francis* (*Map* 12). The arcades and colonnades which run down the sides of so many of Corfu's streets are the town's main architectural feature. In the late eighteenth century the piers and arches were made of fine white Sinies limestone and had carved gargoyle key-stones. In the nineteenth century they were more often made of plastered brick like the houses above them. But whatever the quality of their construction, they are attractive both in themselves and in the constantly changing play of curving shadows they throw on to the pavements and the shop-fronts.

The town's harbour entrance at the bottom of the street was the late-sixteenth-century Spilia Gate which survives in the base of a later building. (The name 'Spilia' — 'grotto' or 'cavern' — comes from a cave halfway up to the *New Fort* (*Map* **14**).

TOWN ROUTE 3

From the south end of the Liston, *E. Voulgareos Street*, a narrow arcaded way, provides the only traffic route through the town to *Theotoki Square*. On the left is the *Town Hall* (*Map* **21**) and, in the square just behind it, the elegant Palladian front of the *Catholic Cathedral* (*Map* **22**), damaged by bombs and now restored. At the head of a flight of steps at the top of the square there is a fine restored building; originally the Residence of the Catholic Archbishop, for whom it was rebuilt in 1754, it served as the Law Courts for over a hundred years until gutted by bombs in 1943. Where E. Voulgareos Street widens into a tree-lined boulevard, and changes its name to *G. Theotoki Street*, stood the *Royal Gate*, the sixteenth-century Venetian main entrance to the walled town, pulled down early this century.

TOWN ROUTE 4

At the south end of the Esplanade, *Akadamias Street* runs west to a balustrade on top of the landward ramparts, and from here you can look down over a green and spacious residential quarter first laid out in the 1840s. *G. Aspioti Street* slants down through the ramparts into *Megali Doukissis Marias Street* to meet *Alexandras Avenue*, a fine tree-line boulevard which links Theotoki Square to Garitsa Bay (Town Route 5). The first left turn off M. Doukissis Marias Street leads, in two blocks, to the *Archaeological Museum* (*Map* **37**). In the area bounded by M. Doukissis Marias Street, S. Dessila Street and Mantzarou Street is a large new complex of buildings housing the *National Tourist Office* (*Map* **30**), the *Post Office* (*Map* **33**), and the *Telephone* and *Telegram Services* (O.T.E.).

TOWN ROUTE 5

In the 1840s the British swept away the *Venetian town wall* and *Raomonda Gate* which closed the south end of the Esplanade, and laid out the line of what is now *King Constantine Boulevard* along the Bay of Garitsa. This is the route to Kanoni (see Excursions). As you slant down from the level deck of the Esplanade you may see a coxed eight setting out from the *Corfu Nautical Club* and be reminded of the Corcyraean and Venetian galleys which patrolled these waters. On your right, the swimming pool and lawns of the *Corfu Palace Hotel* are tucked into an echelon of the fortifications; and if you turn right beyond the hotel into P. Vraila Armeni Street you will reach the new *Archaeological Museum* (*Map* 37), built chiefly to house the astonishing archaic pediment of the *Temple of Artemis*. Farther down the boulevard you will come to the *obelisk* (*Map* 38) put up to Sir Howard Douglas, Lord High Commissioner from 1835 to 1841, and can return to Theotoki Square by Alexandras Avenue. If you go up Menekratous Street, a narrow street which runs in from the obelisk and forks left, you will come to the *Tomb of Menekrates* (*Map* 39) in the grounds of a school.

ESPLANADE AND PALACE

Esplanade (Spianada and Platia)

No other town in Greece possesses an open space as historic and enchanting as Corfu's Esplanade. Here on a hot afternoon you can sit in the shade of oaks and acacias sipping ginger beer and watching cricket, or, from the gardens of an English Regency palace, look north across the sea to the mountains of Albania. Along the avenues, around the grass and gravel, bowl old victorias, their bells clanging as cheerfully as café tills. On Sundays the oldest band in Greece, the Corfu Philharmonic, from its wrought-iron bandstand, adds the strains of Sousa or Delibes to the shouts of playing children and the murmur of the throng which every day at dusk emerges from the town's close warren of streets to take the air. At Easter the balconies of the tall houses blaze with lines of candles, and amid a tumult of church bells and fireworks, strings of lights on the dark bastion of the *Venetian Citadel* announce that Christ is risen.

In the late Middle Ages the Esplanade was nothing more than a field of fire kept clear between the Citadel and the new houses springing up outside its walls; but by the time that these houses had grown into the present town and been walled in the last quarter of the sixteenth century, this open space had become what it still remains — 'the lungs of Corfu'. Under its grassy southern end (known as the *Spianada*) the Venetians excavated huge cisterns; at its northern (known as the *Platia*) a French engineer, de Lesseps, was inspired by the Rue de Rivoli to design two handsome rows of houses known as the *Liston* (*Map* 16) from the 'list' of families entitled to walk under the arcades, then as now the most social arches in Corfu. Though the southern block was started between

1807 and 1814, a well-known watercolour by Joseph Cartwright (who was paymaster-general of the forces in Corfu) shows the northern block still being built in 1821. Under the arches of the car-free Liston are Corfu's smartest and most expensive cafés, and behind them, in Kapodistriou Street, a row of tourist shops, travel agents and holiday boutiques.

Opposite the *Palace of St Michael and St George (Map 9)* the British levelled the ground for a gravel cricket-pitch and parade-ground; on Sundays 'after service the whole garrison march to the esplanade where the Major-General amuses himself two or three hours in putting them through a field day,' wrote Private Wheeler in 1823; the Major-General was the second Lord High Commissioner, Sir Frederick Adam, whose bronze *statue (Map 11)* stands on a pedestal in the pool in front of the palace. He married a Corfiot, brought water from Benitses and was 'a great favourite', according to Wheeler. But Prosalendi, Canova's Corfiot pupil, has given him a look both self-indulgent and mean. *Schulenburg's statue (Map 19)* by the bridge to the *Citadel* stands where he too may have reviewed troops he commanded in the Turkish siege of 1716; Count Schulenburg was a soldier of fortune from Saxony who made his reputation at Malplaquet and whose work *The Marshal* was a bestselling textbook on such important military matters as discipline and dress.

South of the bandstand an *Ionic rotunda* commemorates Sir Thomas Maitland, the acute little Scot who was the first Lord High Commissioner (1816–24). Napier, who served under him, says that he was 'insufferably rude and abrupt', 'particularly dirty in his person' and 'constantly drunk and surrounded by sycophants', but acknowledged that he had considerable talents (*The Life, The Colonies*). The *statue* of his most constant and brilliant critic, Count John Kapodistrias, first ruler of independent Greece, born in Corfu in 1776, stands at the south end of the Esplanade.

Near by, the shell of the fine late-seventeenth-century building on the corner, originally the *Grimani barracks*, once housed the *Ionian Academy*, founded in 1824 by that eccentric philhellene the Fifth Earl of Guilford, who had been received into the Orthodox Church in 1791 in the house a few doors away. 'Lord Guilford is here again and very pleasant,' wrote Napier in 1825. 'He goes about dressed up like Plato, with a gold band round his mad pate, and flowing drapery of a purple hue' (*The Life*). Furnished with 25,000 books from Guilford's library, the Academy became a clearing-house for the Ionian writers who were the founders of modern

Greek literary poetry.

Between the Grimani Barracks and the south end of the Liston lies a picturesque but crowded quarter, and in *Moustoxidou Street* — one of the colourful and narrow lanes which run up into it from the Esplanade — you can see a fine early-eighteenth-century portico. At the end of this lane stands the former *Ionian Parliament building*. The *British Vice-Consulate* is at the far end of N. Zambeli Street, the left turn at the end of Moustoxidou Street.

Palace of St Michael and St George
Map **9**.

It is a rather astonishing reflection on Greece's troubled history that this Regency palace is the oldest official building in the whole country to have survived in something like its original condition inside and out; and also that in Corfu the wheel of Greek architectural style should first have come full circle with an English essay in the neo-classical.

Built between 1818 and 1823 on the site of a demolished Venetian hospital, the palace had three functions: to provide a home for the Lord High Commissioner, a meeting-place for the Ionian senate, and a headquarters for the Order of St Michael and St George, instituted in 1818 by the Prince Regent to reward services in Malta and the Ionian Islands. To give the building sufficient width to fill the north end of the Esplanade, its architect, Colonel (later General Sir George) Whitmore, R.E., fronted it with a Doric colonnade and ran this out on either side to form a curving screen which he pierced with triumphal arches and terminated by balancing pavilions. The Malta sandstone that he knew and chose for its tractability has weathered to a dowdy grey on the main south façade; but one can judge the effect he aimed at from the pale gold of the sheltered western side, reminiscent of Carlton House Terrace. The central cornice above the south front contains the emblems of the Seven Islands in relief, surmounted by a Corcyraean galley. A figure of Britannia formed a focal point on the skyline of the façade but has long since been removed. Used regularly as a summer home by Greek kings between 1864 and 1913, the palace fell into disrepair during the First World War and the Republic, and was damaged by military and refugee tenants between 1940 and 1952. Now repaired, it contains a museum and the staterooms of the Order upstairs and the public library downstairs.

STATEROOMS AND MUSEUM

Open *Summer* Weekdays 09.00–15.00
Sundays 10.00–16.00
Winter Weekdays 09.00–15.30
Sundays 10.00–16.30
Closed Tuesday.
Entrance: Drs 25. Sundays free.

A visit to the museum will allow you to see some of the palace interior. This was skilfully restored to something close to its original splendour in 1954 by the Corfiot architect, Mr John Kollas, with subscriptions raised as the result of an appeal by the British ambassador in Athens, Sir Charles Peake.

The colonnaded front hall, decorated with grisailles based on Flaxman's illustrations to Homer, leads to a grand staircase. At its foot, on the left, the Senate Room contains a marble bust of George IV by Chantrey, a good bronze of Maitland by Prosalendi, and a series of stiff full-length portraits of presidents of the Ionian senate.

Upstairs, the rooms on either side of the landing have fine mahogany and palisander doors, good marble chimney-pieces, possibly by Prosalendi, and painted ceilings, one coved, the other with a saucer dome. The three staterooms of the Order, which open off the landing, are illustrated and described in detail in Sacheverell Sitwell's *Great Palaces*. The state dining-room on the right has an immense mahogany dining-table. The pediment of the *Temple of Artemis* used to be fastened incongruously over the chimney-pieces with its ends chopped off so that it would fit into the room. The central round ante-room has a blue-and-white coffer dome, its original sunburst parquet floor, and a suite of heavy Regency chairs. Behind one of the false curved walls is a little staircase leading to the musicians' gallery of the throne-room on the left. This is floridly hung with red flock wall-paper and some entertainingly bad pictures, though the copy of the Lawrence of George IV now at the Vatican is a good one. When the late King Paul used this room occasionally for official functions he sat beside, not on, the gilded throne in the style of Thomas Hope which stands on a dais at the far end of the room. Not all the Lords High Commissioner were so modest. Their aim was to impress. According to Napier (*The Colonies*), the idea of the Order was Maitland's: he saw it as a means 'to keep the inhabitants in good humour' and 'the crafty old man laughed in his sleeve when he opened, ostentatiously, the "Halls of St Michael and St George" and saw the Corfu "galaxy" glittering in all the brilliant decorations of chivalry.'

Most of the upstairs rooms are now used to house part of the fine collections of Oriental ceramics and *objets d'art* made by Grigorios Manos, a former Greek ambassador to Paris, and Hadji Vassilou. The exhibits include screens, wood carvings, silk paintings, statuary, arms, silver, ivories, jades, and ceramics from India, China, Japan, Korea, Cambodia, Thailand, and Tibet. Though quite irrelevant to the palace, and not always well labelled, they are very well worth seeing.

The two farthest rooms in the west wing contain examples of early Christian and Byzantine art: a sixth-century mosaic floor from Paleopolis Church (pp. 142–4), carved capitals and other stonework, eleventh and seventeenth-century wall paintings from the Chapel of Ayos Nikolaos, and some fine sixteenth and seventeenth-century icons (including works by Damaskinos, Tzanes and Moskhos).

PUBLIC LIBRARY
Open Weekdays *Summer* 09.00–13.30
                  Winter 10.00–14.00
Entrance: Free.

Go through St George's arch and turn right through the arch in the west wing and across the courtyard to a side-door. Apart from the usual miscellany of books, the library houses those of the islands' archives which date from 1797 to 1864. Corfu has the largest, oldest and possibly least consulted collection of archives in Greece, going back to 1396. The earlier documents are kept in the east of the palace's two pavilions or moulder in the damp of the palace cellars.

ARCHAEOLOGICAL MUSEUM
Map **37**.

Open
Summer Weekdays 09.00–15.00
          Sundays 10.00–16.00
Winter Weekdays 09.00–15.30
          Sundays 10.00–16.30
Closed Tuesdays
Entrance: Drs 25. Sundays free.

In the *dolce far niente* of a Corfu holiday it is easy to put off the serious business of a visit to the museum until the very last day or not to go at all; and this is a pity. For the museum houses one or two things which, in their way and of their period, are as impressive as anything in Greece, and deserve more than cursory inspection.

On the *landing* at the head of the stairs are several notable tomb-monuments from the Garitsa cemetery: a column surmounted by a sixth-century B.C. Doric capital with the curious decorated frill below it which is characteristic of Sicilian work of the same date; a funerary stele with a palaeographically important boustrophedon inscription of about 575 B.C.; and a fine burial pithos of the same date.

The *courtyard room* off the landing contains cases of prehistoric finds from sites at Ermones, Sidari and Roda; some fine Corinthian and Laconian pottery; a splendid bronze bowl of the sixth century B.C. from a Garitsa burial; coins; and painted terracotta antefixes and other fragments from a fifth-century B.C. Doric temple at Roda.

The *Gorgon room* next door houses a reconstruction of the whole west pediment of a *Temple of Artemis* (see p. 141) which was built in about 580 B.C. In about 520 B.C. the building's terracotta tiles, cima and antefixes were replaced by fittings in Parian marble. Examples of both types of fitting are displayed, as well as a stretch of the massive frieze with triglyphs and metopes, and a case of fragments from the vanished east pediment.

The west pediment is decorated with the most complete and monumental group of Greek archaic sculpture which has so far been found. Carved from local porous limestone, the sculptures are thought to be of Corinthian workmanship. In the middle of the pediment the colossal figure of the Gorgon kneels with her wings spread to shelter the small figures of Chrysaor and Pegasus, offspring who came to life from her dying blood. On either side of this central group lie panthers whose spots are depicted (in a metal-working technique) by concentric circles. On the right Zeus strikes down a Titan with his thunderbolt. The iconography of the balancing group on the left is disputed, some scholars maintaining that the figures represent Priam being slain on his throne in Troy, others that they depict the death of Gaia, mother of the Titans. In the left-hand angle a dead Titan lies outstretched.

Why was the Gorgon chosen as the central figure of the pediment? A Gorgon or a Gorgoneion (a roundel representing the Gorgon's head) flanked by attendant beasts seems to have been the earliest Greek device to fill up the triangle of a pediment and was a Corinthian invention. There are other early examples in Sicily. The tradition of representing heraldic beasts on either side of a central emblem goes back through Mycenaean and Minoan times to an even more ancient origin in the Middle East. The Lion Gate at Mycenae and Cretan gems, seals and pendants representing a goddess with animals on either side of her are adaptions of this theme. Did the Gorgon take the place of honour because she herself symbolized an orgiastic earth-goddess worshipped in the temple, in this case Artemis? Or, once the Perseus myth had been elaborated, was her horrifying mask or image sometimes used as a conventional warning to those bold enough to think of violating the sacred precincts of *any* temple? The pediment is now at last displayed in all its grandeur, and one can step back and view it as a whole. But the new overall effect is of little help in answering these questions, for the sculptures remain, if not completely enigmatic, at any rate ambiguous. The Gorgon who looks so terrifying from one angle appears from another to be filled with a compassionate and ecstatic glee; and the panthers who in one light look ready to spring snarling at the spectator, in another remind one of nothing so much as long-suffering and puzzled dogs tormented by their master's children.

The first part of the *Mon Repos room* (reached from the Gorgon room) contains roof fittings and other objects found during the excavation of the large temple of Kardaki (p. 144) in the grounds of Mon Repos in the 1960s. The lion, gorgon and kore antefixes from another temple (possibly a Heraion) and the painted tile ridge or cima from a smaller building in the neighbourhood all date from about 600 B.C.; with the painted clay fragments from a temple pediment they are among the finest terracottas of their sort yet found in Greece. But, even so, pride of place in this section of the room must go to part of a sculptured pediment of another Archaic temple, though this time a small one. It shows a Dionysiac supper: the bearded god and a naked youth lie at table with a wine crater to hand while a hound steps restlessly past. Its grey and silver weathering is marvellous. The fragment was discovered on the Paleopolis peninsula in 1973 and has not yet been published. The workmanship is presumably Corinthian; but something enigmatic in the composition and the features of the god and youth make one think of Etruscan parallels.

In the second part of the room the so-called limestone *Lion of Menekrates* is one of the most beautiful animal sculptures of early Greece. There is nothing in quite the same style anywhere in the world, and different experts date it to different times between

620 B.C. and 550 B.C. Nor can they agree whether or not it has in fact anything to do with the *Tomb of Menekrates* (see below), near which it was discovered in 1843. In mannered elegance the lion (or lioness) far surpasses the neo-Hittite or Assyrian models from which it must in all probability derive. The second half of the room also contains a series of terracotta votive figurines of the late sixth and early fifth centuries B.C. (those with the bow and deer depict Artemis). In the third part of the room there are some quite good second-century A.D. copies of Hellenistic marbles; and a stone-mason's lead template for shaping mouldings is interesting.

FORTS

Citadel
Map **20**.

Open 07.30 – sunset.
Entrance: Free.

Corfu traditionally takes its name from the accusative plural of the Greek for the 'peaks' of the Citadel — *korfoús*; but whether a castle already existed on the eastern peak in 968, when Bishop Liudprand of Cremona, returning from his embassy in Constantinople, first used the name in Latin and recorded that 'ad Coriphus parvenimus' (Matton), is unknown.

By 1149, however, it was certainly fortified; for in that year a Byzantine and Venetian force expelled a Norman garrison from behind walls so high that a rolling siege-tower had to be constructed, and in 1272, when Charles of Anjou took possession, the second peak had been fortified, probably by the Venetians during their brief occupation at the beginning of the century. For a couple of hundred years the town of Corfu was confined to the area now beyond the moat, though this was not dug until some years after the great siege of 1537; when John Locke visited the island in 1553 the Citadel had only just been 'trenched about with the Sea'. A few walls and semicircular bastions date from about this time, but most of them had been renewed by the nineteenth century; they seem to have had a disconcerting habit of falling down: 'a fundamentis collapsam', records one tablet of 1709 laconically. The brick and stone angled ramparts facing the Esplanade across the moat are late-seventeenth-century. Most of the Venetian buildings that clustered round the two peaks — the Cathedral, the Governor's Palace, barracks, houses and shops — were destroyed by two terrible powder-magazine explosions in 1718 and 1789; and, with the exception of the seventeenth-century vaulted *entrance-gate*, most of what remained was swept away by the British to make room for the three dull and solid *barrack-blocks* they built in the 1830s and the Doric garrison *Church of St George*, a building of the 1840s — 'the model of a heathen temple, very classical at any rate, if not exactly adapted to its present use' (Ansted). The British army was succeeded by the Greek, who used the Citadel as a recruiting centre until 1979, when it was handed over lock, stock and barrel to the Archaeological Service. Its buildings are now slowly being restored and converted to various civic purposes. Meanwhile its still military atmosphere is pleasantly offset by an old bell-tower, an ornate well and strolling peacocks, and the climb to the western peak is well worth while for the panorama of the town and island. From the summit you can see, from north to south: the island of *Vidos* (which in 1801 the French stripped of its olives, fortified, and named Île de la Paix) with *Mt Pandokrator* beyond; behind the palace, *Kambielo*, the oldest quarter of the town, on a rise, and behind that the flat top of the *New Fort*; the campanile of the *Church of St Spiridon*; a large copse of cypresses and pines marking the old *British cemetery* and the site of the demolished *Fort San Salvator*; the *Khalikiopoulos Lagoon* — the ancient Hyllaic harbour — with the *Ayi Deka range* behind; and the peninsula of *Paleopolis*, with the cupola of the former royal villa of *Mon Repos* (built for Sir Frederick Adam) just visible among the fine trees of its park.

New Fort
Map **14**.
Not open to the public.

Alarmed by the menace of the Turkish fleet in the year before Lepanto the Republic decided to strengthen Corfu against any further expedition and the New Fort was built on the town's landward side between 1576 and 1588, probably to the designs of Vitelli. The handsome *sea-gate* in George II Square with four rusticated columns, winged lion and original iron-studded doors is permanently closed. The navy still use the nineteenth-century British *barrack-block*, but the main structure of the fort is abandoned and overgrown. From the road which skirts the fortress on the west you can see the tremendous scale of its scarps and fosses. Inside, the logic of the honeycomb of slanting galleries, dark tunnels, bat-hung underground chambers and tall ventilation-shafts is obscured by rank undergrowth and crumbling masonry, and the place has the sinister inconsequence of a Piranesi prison.

The British passion for building immensely costly fortifications just before they leave their overseas possessions goes back well before the present century. The Walter Scott *baronial keep* which crowns the New Fort was put up in 1848 — sixteen years before the Ionian Islands were handed back to Greece. Its angled musket-slots and pull-up ladders between the floors seem to have been designed to deal with a popular uprising like that of 1848 in Cefalonia rather than a French or Russian attack.

CHURCHES

Church of St Spiridon
Map **13**.

The church was started in 1596 to replace an earlier church pulled down when the New Fort was built. It stands on the left of *Ayiou Spiridonas Street*, which leads into the Esplanade at the north end of the Liston (*Map* **16**). A dull building outside, its High-Renaissance interior manages to be both florid and sombre. The impressive stone screen imitates the façade of a church. The gilt-scrolled and painted ceiling is the work of Panayotis Doxaras (1699–1729), but the panels were overpainted in the mid nineteenth century.

St Spiridon, the island's patron saint, was a Cypriot bishop who took part in the First Oecumenical Council of Nicaea in 325. His remains were early on transferred to Constantinople and thence, before its fall in 1453, brought to Corfu together with the body of St Theodora by a priest called Kalokheretes. St Theodora's remains were soon bestowed on the community and now rest undisturbed in the Orthodox cathedral; but St Spiridon's, a source of considerable revenue, remained the private property of the Voulgaris family (who had acquired them from Kalokheretes's sons) until so to speak nationalized by the Republican Government in 1927. St Spiridon is believed to have saved the town of Corfu four times by his miraculous interventions, once from the Turks in 1716, once from famine and twice from the plague. On Palm Sunday, Easter Even, August 11th and the first Sunday in November these occasions are commemorated by services in the church and processions in which his mummified body is carried round the town in a glass-fronted palanquin, preceded by bands and followed by officials, dignitaries, contingents of the armed services, boy scouts, girl guides and schoolchildren in their Sunday best. Between 1815 and 1864 the Protestant British authorities very sensibly took over from the Catholic Venetians the custom of taking part in these Orthodox processions, and earned themselves the acid comment in Murray's *Handbook* of 1840 that 'the absurd affectation of compliance with the prejudices of the people, which occasions much annoyance to both officers and men, has been adopted with a view to conciliate the affections of the natives.' Before and after the processions, the palanquin containing the saint stands in front of the church screen, so that (as Wheeler put it in 1823) 'Greeks in their pious zeals struggling and swearing with each other to get up to the saint first' can approach and kiss his embroidered slippers. The saint's body rests normally in a silver coffer in a chapel to the right of the screen, hung with a profusion of lamps and silver votive offerings among which the models of early steamers are charming. The number of Corfiots named Spiro after the saint can lead to confusion. If one were to call 'Spiro!' loudly in any restaurant, the owner, two of the waiters, five people at near-by tables, the itinerant seller of lottery tickets and the dozing cab-driver outside would probably all look round.

Pandokrator Church
Kambielo Quarter; Map **6**.

Badly damaged by bombs during the last war, this plain seventeenth-century building has recently been restored and may eventually house the collection of icons at present shown in the palace and kept in the archbishopric. The carved *stone screen* with gilded cherubim dates from about 1720, and the mannerist *wall-paintings* in the niches on either side of the apse from about 1658. The delicately carved *stone angel* on the pediment of the church is by Giuseppe Torretti (1694–1774).

Church of the Panayia Kremasti
Kambielo Quarter; Map **5**.

This war-damaged church contains one of the town's most richly carved stone *altar-screens*, dating from about 1650. Its name comes from an icon of the Virgin which used to 'hang' outside the south door where there is now an iron bracket and a faded wall-painting. The attractive well-head in the square was donated in 1699 by Antonio Kokkini.

Orthodox Cathedral
Map **10**.

At the head of a flight of steps, the cathedral contains several fine icons and a late-nineteenth-century chased-silver coffer holding the remains of St Theodora (p. 135).

Catholic Church of St Francis
N. Theotoki Street; Map **12**.

Although the church was founded in 1387, like all Corfu's medieval churches it was rebuilt in later years. Mass is celebrated every day.

Platitera Convent
West of Theotoki Square along road marked Exits A and B.

Founded in 1716 on the outskirts of the town, the Platitera Convent has one of the prettiest late-eighteenth- and early-nineteenth-century church interiors in the Ionian Islands, and, since the destruction of the Church of the Faneromeni in Zakinthos (p. 268) presents the most complete example of a decorative scheme by artists of the Ionian school (see p. 93). The upper tiers and the right-hand icon of the bottom tier of the white and gold screen are by Koutouzis, whose Twelve Apostles are particularly full of life and character. Most of the painted panels in the blue and gold ceiling are by Vendouras, and the two large paintings over the north and south doors are by Kandounis. The gilt frame set with amethysts on the little icon of the Virgin and Child to the right of the screen was acquired in Russia by Kapodistrias when serving as foreign minister to the Tsar. His tomb is in a sort of ambulatory which lies through the south door of the church.

SQUARES

Theotoki Square

No more than 'a little village where one went to collect milk' at the end of the eighteenth century (Grasset), and once the site of a small fort and chapel dedicated to St Rock, Theotoki Square (still commonly called Sarokko) is the pivot of the island roads, a scene of bustling traffic. The bus stops for villages in the south and centre are along its northern side, and the station for the Athens bus on the southern. In, or just off, the square, are useful petrol and service stations, agencies hiring cars and scooters, old-fashioned shops selling odds and ends, and two modest new hotels. Three streets to the north, in the fosse of the New Fort, is the fruit and vegetable market.

George II Square

The flagstones and Judas trees of George II Square provide a pleasant piazza, most of it reclaimed from the sea. Here lay the *old port*, with sea-entrances to the walled town through the Spilia Gate and to the New Fort (see p. 134). The port is now used only by the Igoumenitsa ferries and the Paxos caiques; but most of the shipping, ferry and travel agencies have offices here. Lined with cafés and hotels, many modest and old-fashioned, the square is an agreeable place to sit looking across the bay to the island of Vidos and Mt Pandokrator, especially at Easter when the Judas trees are in flower. In the quarter just behind the square several modest restaurants serve typical Greek food on tables set out in the narrow side-streets, a cool and lively place to eat.

At the south-east corner of the square a street leads past the harbour-master's office to the *Orthodox Cathedral* (p. 137). If you turn left as you reach the top of the steps and walk a few metres along St Theodora's Street, you will see an ogival *Gothic mullion* set into the wall on your right. This fragment of medieval architecture, the only one which survives in Corfu, is unfortunately useless for dating this part of the town since it has been re-used in a later building.

Off the south-west corner of George II Square stands *New Fort Square*, the bus terminus for all villages north of the town. Beyond this lay the ghetto, three streets whose gates were locked every evening in Venetian times. A *synagogue* still serves the needs of the 150 or so Jews who live in the island (see p. 74).

OTHER SIGHTS

Town Hall
Map 21.

Built in 1663 as a loggia for merchants and turned into a theatre in 1720, this once elegant building has been robbed of grace and proportion by the addition of a top storey in 1903 when it was adapted to its present use. On its east wall is a mutilated *monument* to Francesco Morosini, who, setting out from Corfu in 1684 on his re-conquest of the Peloponnese, blew up the Parthenon during the siege of Athens and was made Doge for his services. Some of the carved keystones over the windows look more like portraits than grotesques.

British Cemetery

200 metres along the road which leads from Theotoki Square to Lefkimmi (Exit C on the Corfu Town map) a rough road, Koloko-troni Street, forks left. 50 metres up this road on the left is the entrance to the British Cemetery, on the site of the demolished *Fort San Salvator*. Though the monuments do not go back as far as those on Zakinthos (see p. 271), the nineteenth-century inscriptions are full of charm and interest, and the garden setting, kept up by the War Graves Commission, is enchanting. The cemetery contains the graves of British soldiers and civilians who served in the Ionian Islands during the British Protectorate, as well as those of British soldiers and sailors killed in the two World Wars. Further information from the custodian (tel. 21–411), or the British Vice-Consulate (see p. 128)

Tomb of Menekrates
Map **39**.

The experts say that this circular stone construction is not only important but beautiful. Since it sits in a sunken pit its beauty is hard to judge; a lot of people find it extremely dull. Its importance lies in the antiquity of the inscription which runs round under the eaves of the flattened conical roof and records in the Corcyraean version of the early Greek alphabet that Menekrates, consul of Oeanthe in Locris (opposite Euboea), was drowned at sea. Its date (disputed) is either sixth- or seventh-century B.C. The tomb is in the grounds of a school.

Excursion from Corfu Town

PALEOPOLIS PENINSULA

The 5-kilometre drive to Kanoni (p. 144), at the far tip of the Paleopolis peninsula, takes you through the site of ancient Kerkira (see below), skirts the luxuriant park of Mon Repos (the former royal villa, not open to the public), and passes two early churches — Paleopolis and SS Jason and Sosipater (p. 141). Kanoni itself commands the best known of all Corfu's romantic views — that looking down over the Vlakherena Convent and Pondikonisi (p. 144) and across the Khalikiopoulos Lagoon to the wooded slopes of Perama. But the peninsula has been much developed in the last ten years and large apartment blocks, five-storey hotels and the roar of jet airliners are now the accompaniments of romance.

The looping lanes which lead to Kanoni are difficult to describe clearly; for this reason the route instructions below take you only into the area of the large-scale map on p. 143. The various sights are marked on this map and described separately.

Route Leave the Esplanade by Town Route 5. Past the obelisk to Sir Howard Douglas, King Constantine Boulevard becomes a dual carriage-way (Exit D). Take the landward of the two carriage-ways and, 200 metres past the sign to the airport, fork right. (The seaside carriage-way sweeps past the suburb of Anemomilos to the Mon Repos bathing lido round the point of Garitsa Bay.)

Bus In summer buses leave for Kanoni every half-hour from the north side of the road which runs through the middle of the Esplanade towards the Citadel (V. Dousmani Street).

Accommodation and restaurants. Four hotels at Kanoni (L, A and C class) and one at Anemomilos (B class), all with restaurants.

Ancient Kerkira

Though ancient Kerkira flourished for at least 1,300 years — from its foundation as a Corinthian colony in 734 B.C. until it was sacked by the Ostrogoths in the sixth century A.D. — almost nothing survives of its buildings. This is because from the early Middle Ages until the beginning of the eighteenth century the old city was used as a building quarry for the new, and even the foundation trenches of its temples were denuded of their stones. When Wheler visited Paleopolis in 1675 there were still 'abundance of Ruins and Foundations' to be seen in the 'old City; which is now covered all over with Olive trees, and here and there an old Church standing among them'; but he also noted that 'abundance of Foundations of Temples, Arches, Pillars, and Marble Inscriptions, have been dug up here, and employed to build the new Fortifications'.

The rough topography of the town in the sixth and fifth centuries B.C. can nevertheless be deduced from a few remains and the incidental description which Thucydides gives in his account of the Peloponnesian War (Book 3). Its *acropolis* stood near the present village of Analipsis and the higher part of the town lay on the slope now largely occupied by the park of Mon Repos (*Map* 7). At the foot of the slope was the *town square*, near the eastward-facing of two harbours. Part of the *sea-wall* of this harbour was excavated in 1965 near the ruined Church of Ayos Athanasios (*Map* 2), so the town square probably lay to the west of the road which you take when you first fork off King Constantine Boulevard. The other port — known as the *Hyllaic harbour* — gave into the Khaliki-opoulos Lagoon, though exactly how far it lay along the west side of the peninsula is not known. In the fifth century B.C. the town was defended by a *wall* which ran across the neck of the peninsula. A fragment of its western end survives with an interesting built-in shrine (*Map* 8), but its precise line has not yet been discovered. The *cemetery* lay outside the town in the area of the Tomb of Mene-krates (p. 139), now occupied by the suburb of Garitsa. Potsherds of the eighth century B.C. discovered near Paleopolis Church (*Map* 6) tally well with the traditional date given by Strabo for the foundation of the colony; but no evidence has been found of any earlier occupation. The Paleopolis peninsula is not therefore a good candidate for the Phaeacian capital described in the *Odyssey* (Book 6).

The massive 'altar' of the *Temple of Artemis* (sixth century B.C.) is still in place and can be seen from the footpath which leads from the Convent of Ayi Theodori (*Map* 10) to the patch of city wall; other bits and pieces of ancient Kerkira are built into the Churches of Paleopolis and SS Jason and Sosipater (*Map* 6 and 3); but to get any idea at all of the splendid architectural embellishment of the town in the sixth century B.C. one must visit the Archaeological Museum (p. 130).

Church of SS Jason and Sosipater
Map 3.

The two inscriptions on the entrance-front record that this very pretty Byzantine church was rebuilt in the twelfth century. Its cream-coloured limestone blocks are set off by courses of tile, and between the dentilations of the cornices which decorate its three apses (two semicircular and one half-hexagonal) are tile 'inscriptions' in mock Cufic script. Inside, two of the re-used ancient columns of mottled grey marble are particularly lustrous, and the screen is made up of a hotchpotch of old marble fragments set in painted plaster. The *tombs* visible through the guichet windows at the foot of the screen are optimistically labelled with the names of the two saints; in fact they belong to the Byzantine historian George Sphrantzes, who spent his last years in the monastery attached to the church and died in about 1478, and to Catarina Paleologus, who stayed behind to die in the island shortly after 1463 while her husband — the last fleeing despot of the Morea — went on to Rome to swop St Andrew's head for a papal pension. (The Vatican returned the holy relic to Patras in 1965.) Jason and Sosipater are military saints who are reputed to have brought Christianity to Corfu. They are portrayed in two *icons* by Michael Damaskinos (*fl.* 1570–90) which hang in the *narthex*, where there is also a framed fragment of twelfth-century wall-painting depicting St Arsenius, the tenth-century bishop of the island.

Except at siesta time a caretaker is always around to open the church.

Paleopolis Church
Map **6**.

Recent excavations have shown that Paleopolis Church (known also as Ayia Kerkira) stands on a site successively occupied by a *Doric temple* of the sixth century B.C., a *public building* of the first or second century A.D. and a five-naved *basilica* of the sixth century A.D. The present ruined church is the third to have been built on the site since this basilica was destroyed by the Ostrogoths in the sixth century and occupies only the surviving central nave. It was bombed during the last war and is now roofless. The frieze of the impressive colonnaded west front carries an inscription recording that the basilica was built by Jovian, bishop of Corfu. The whole of this front comes from some other building of the second century A.D. for its two *Corinthian columns* are fluted and rounded only on their outer sides and must therefore have been attached columns in their original home. Inside the nave, the rows of *lion's-head rainwater spouts* halfway up the walls on both sides are superb works of

Corfu: Paleopolis Peninsula and Ancient Kerkira

1	Airport Terminal	8	Fragment of Ancient Town Wall
2	Church of Ayos Athanasios	9	Temple of Artemis
3	Church of SS Jason and Sosipater	10	Convent of Ayi Theodori
4	Mon Repos Bathing Lido	11	Kardaki Temple
5	Orthodox Cemetery	12	Kardaki Fountain
6	Paleopolis Church	13	Vlakherena Convent
7	Mon Repos		

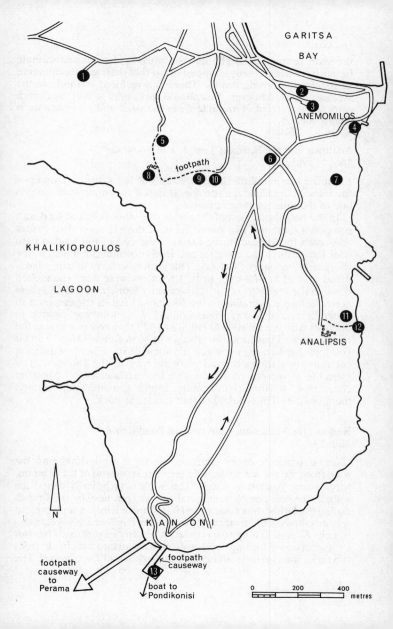

the sixth century B.C. The marble muzzles of these unfortunate beasts have been cruelly chopped off so that their gullets can serve as sockets for ceiling beams. There is a restored example in the Archaeological Museum. You should apply here to visit the church since its west front is invisible from the road and its enclosure is always locked.

Analipsis and the Kardaki Temple and Fountain
Map 11 and 12.

From the seaside bluff 100 metres east of the village of Analipsis the view of the Citadel in profile against a mountain back-drop is one of the most striking in Corfu.

In the neighbourhood of Analipsis (the site of ancient Kerkira's acropolis) there are two minor relics of the old town. Just before you reach the kerbed traffic-island at the end of the road, a path goes left through the cottages and leads down in 5 minutes to the shore-side *fountain of Kardaki.* This is more ancient than its dilapidated *lion of St Mark* suggests. Its waters were once channelled through the precincts of the sixth-century Doric *temple of Kardaki* above before descending to the fountain. English frigates used to water here, and it was while Colonel Whitmore was digging to discover why the spring had failed in 1822 that he came across the temple ruins. They lie in the grounds of Mon Repos (*Map* 7) and if you look hard enough you can see some of its rather insignificant columns over the park wall on your way to the fountain. The exquisite terracotta roof-fittings in the Archaeological Museum come from another sixth-century *temple* (possibly the Heraion mentioned by Thucydides) farther inside the park.

Kanoni, the Vlakerena Convent and Ponḍikonisi
Map 13.

'The beau-monde every afternoon perform a pilgrimage on the road from the parade to the little convent at the end of the promontory,' wrote Ansted in 1863. 'This walk is technically called the walk to the one-gun.' The original gun was put here by the French during the British blockade of 1810–15, and a Russian replacement was installed on the terrace of the *Tourist Pavilion* a few years ago to help *Kanoni* live up to its name. A century of postcards has not yet succeeded in turning the view from Kanoni into a cliché. In front of you lie the two little islands of *Vlakherena* and *Ponḍikonisi.* The first is no more than a stone raft just wide enough to carry one cypress tree, a whitewashed church and a long slope of weathered tiles. The second — 'Mouse Island' — rides out to sea like a perfectly proportioned Japanese *bonsai* of dwarf trees, rocks and ivory pagoda arranged on a celadon tray. You can reach the late-seventeenth-century *Vlakherena Convent* by a causeway below the Kanoni turning-place, and a motor-boat will take you on from the convent to Mouse Island and back for Drs 25. But their magic dissolves once you set foot on their shores: the Vlakherena church turns out to be crowded with bad icons and cheap lamps, and the nineteenth-century chapel on Pondikonisi can boast of nothing but a series of marble plaques recording royal visits. Much better then to keep to the spellbinding distance of Kanoni and watch the shadows of Perama lengthen on the water as you sip your evening drink.

ROUTES ON CORFU

For general information on island routes and roads see p. 103. Corfu has many more tarred roads than the other Ionian Islands and this means that you can explore it very thoroughly in what, for Greece, must be reckoned considerable comfort. The map on pp. 148–9 shows how the five routes radiate north, west and south from the capital to cover the main part of the island. In several cases two of these routes can be combined to form a round trip: Routes 1 and 2 and Routes 3 and 4 are linked at their far ends and Routes 5a, 5b and 5c all meet within a few hundred metres of each other.

Route 1: Corfu to Kassiopi

Several stretches of the drive up the east coast to the Angevin Fortress of Kassiopi (37 km.) are as beautiful as any in the Ionian Islands. The first 16 km. are crowded and built up; but once past the bays of Gouvia, Dassia and Ipsos the road winds round the steep olive-wooded spurs of Mount Pandokrator high above a magical succession of caves and beaches.

An expedition to the summit of Mt Pandokrator (35 km.) is worth making for the wild flowers and the view, but involves a rough ride.

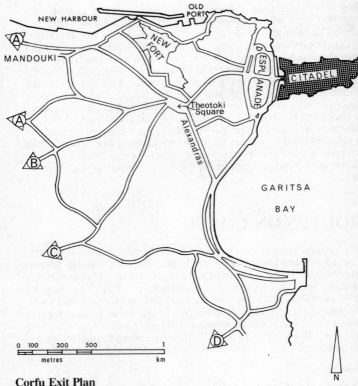

Corfu Exit Plan

A route to:
Kassiopi
Sidari
Roda
Dassia
Ipsos
Paleokastritsa

B route to:
Glifada
Ermones
Pelekas
Mirtiotissa

C route to:
The Akhillion
Ayos Matheos
Ayos Gordis
Ayi Deka
Gardiki
Perama
Benitses
Moraitika
Kavos

D route to:
Kanoni

Route Leave Corfu by Exit A on the town exit plan. Turn right at Tzavros (9·5 km.) and fork right at the second hairpin bend after Piryi (16 km.).

From Kassiopi you can follow the coast road for a further 16 km. to Roda and from there return to Corfu by Route 2 or, 5 km. before reaching Roda, take the hidden left turn at Akharavi and follow the mountain road through Episkepsis back to join Route 1 at Piryi.

Bus 4 day-return services to Kassiopi and 6 as far as Piryi.

Accommodation and Restaurants Hotels at Alikes (A and C class), Kondokali (A class), Gouvia (A and C class), Kommeno (L class), Dafnila (A class), Dassia (L, A and C class), Ipsos (B, C and D class), Piryi (C and D class), Nisaki (A class), and Ayos Stefanos (C class); rooms and restaurants all along the route but particularly frequent before Piryi, and at Kassiopi itself.

Caique For details of the daily caique see p. 108.

Holiday Camps At Dassia and Nisaki (see pp. 150–51).

Youth hostel At Kondokali.

Camping Sites At Kondokali, Kommeno, Dassia, Ipsos, and Piryi (see p. 116).

Once clear of the town and suburbs, the road skirts the coast for the first few kilometres, past the mud flats and shallows at the mouth of the River Potami. Across the bay, beyond the islet of Lazaretto (formerly the quarantine station), looms the bulk of *Mt Pandokrator*.

[6·5 km.] The main road turns inland, and what used to be the old road forks off to the right to run along the coast through Kondokali and rejoin the main road 2·5 km. farther on just past Gouvia. Kondokali is an old village with an attractive main street on the Bay of Gouvia, a lagoon sheltered from the open sea by a neck of land planted with pines. Its pleasant holiday life will be enlivened when a huge new fenced-off marina in the bay is finished. The entrance to this is at the far end of the first curve of the lagoon; and here, appropriately, a lane to the right leads in 100 metres to the three roofless naves of a *Venetian arsenal* where, in the eighteenth century, shipwrights repaired the galleys of the Levant squadron. Grasset says that it was linked to the town by a 'chemin roulant'. From here you can look across to the floating *chapel of Ipapandi*.

[9·5 km.] The main road reaches **Tzavros**, where you turn right. (The way to Paleokastritsa (Route 3) and Sidari (Route 2) is straight on.) For the next 6·5 km. the road is nearly as noisy and touristic as at Perama; but the hinterland of rolling hills and dense olive groves behind Dassia provides an easy escape from the brashness of the coast.

[10 km.] A road to the right runs round the north side of Gouvia Bay and out to the villas and hotels on Cape Kommeno.

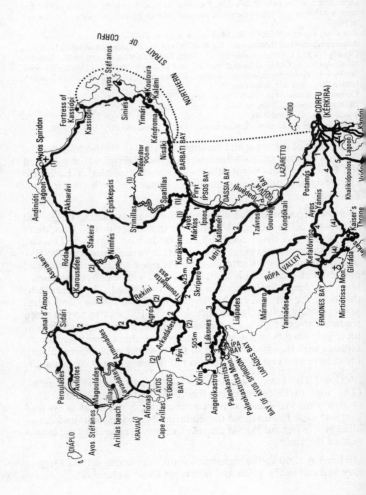

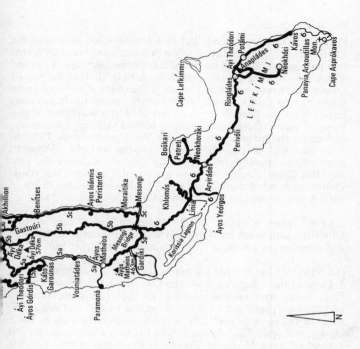

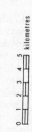

[13 km.] A cross-road leads left in a few hundred metres to the *Castello Hotel*, a successful imitation of a fourteenth-century Venetian palace built in 1880 by the Italian Count Mimbelli. The road which goes right at the cross-roads leads in 0·5 km. to the *bay of Dassia* where restaurants and hotels in the shade of an olive grove line a narrow shingle beach. At the north end of the beach flags flutter from the flagpole of the *Club Méditerranée*, bronzed and bikinied water-skiers twist and turn behind skidding speedboats, and under the luxuriant trees of the club's private cape Tahitian straw huts look thoroughly at home. On the far right a Venetian manor-house stands by the water's edge; and ahead, across the wide bay, lies Corfu Town — as good a view of it as any. The sea is shallow and, a few metres out, sandy-bottomed; but the beach, a narrow one, is popular and crowded throughout the summer.

[15 km.] **Ipsos**, a village at the south end of a very narrow kilometre-long beach lined with hotels, lodging houses, restaurants and camping sites as far as Piryi, the hamlet at the far end.

[16·5 km.] At the first hairpin bend after Piryi a road leads left for 1·2 km. to the village of **Ayos Markos**, where the *Church of the Paṇḍokrator* contains wall-paintings of 1576 (the most complete and the best preserved of this date on the island) and some fine icons of the same period. The Church is normally locked, but a villager will open the door for you. In the valley below, the locked *Chapel of Ayos Merkourios* contains fragments of wall-painting dated 1075. (You must arrange a visit to the latter beforehand at the Archaeological Museum in the town.) The road continues for 3 km. to Korakiana (and shortly afterwards joins Route 2), a particularly attractive walk or drive under the steep southern slope of the mountain.

[17 km.] Back on the main route, at the second hairpin bend after Piryi a road strikes off up the coast to the right; this is the way to Kassiopi. The left fork (marked to Spatillas) leads in 18 km. to the summit of *Mt Paṇḍokrator*. From this bend you should allow 2 hours for the return trip to the top of Corfu's highest mountain (906 metres). Only the first 8 km. are tarred, and the last few hundred metres are so steep and rocky that you will need a car with a good clearance and have to use first or second gear. 1·5 km. beyond the superbly sited hill-village of **Spatillas** (6·5 km.) and over the saddle of the mountain, a rough road forks right and

leads in 5 km. up to the village of **Strinillas**. 0·8 km. beyond this
village a rough road strikes off right. Fork right again after another
0·8 km. and in a further 2·5 km. you will reach the summit.

The view from up here is extraordinary: the north-west corner of
Corfu, the Othonian Islands, Albania with the lake of Butrinto, the
centre of the island and the town, the hills of the Lefkimmi peninsula, and, on an exceptionally clear day, Paxos, Lefkas and even the
toe of Italy can all be seen. Alpine swifts zip past with a sound of
rending gauze, and yellow asphodels and orchids are still flowering
in early June; only a little earlier in the year *Fritillaria ionica*, and
many other uncommon plants are still in flower. Below you bare
hill-farms with a bloom of green on them as evanescent as a shadow
are belted with solitary walls.

Of the remains of the Angevin monastery on the summit nothing
obviously of the thirteenth century survives, though the plain
barrel-vault of the church (which has two layers of obscure and
damp-damaged wall-paintings) may be original. The façade, and
the podium of the monastery, are late-nineteenth-century. Pilgrims
camp in the row of dilapidated cells during the week preceding the
Feast of the Transfiguration (August 6th).

[19·5 km.] Back on the Kassiopi road, a lane runs down through
tourist villas built among the olive trees to the long and beautiful
pebble beach of *Barbati*. Beyond this bay the bulwarks of Pandokrator begin to push out towards the sea; but olives grow even on
the steeper slopes, potted out in neat crescent-shaped terraces.

[22·5 km.] Just before **Nisaki**, a lane on the right slants down the hill
to three restaurants on a rock separating twin coves. You can swim
in one of the coves, or walk under the olives to more secluded bays
farther up the coast. The caiques from Corfu and Kassiopi call here
every day. There are rooms to rent both here and up in Nisaki itself,
which is dominated by the huge Ilios hotel belonging to the Club
Méditerranée.

[24·5 km.] The drive down to the very large but better designed
Nisaki Beach hotel is on the right.

Between Nisaki and Kouloura lies the prettiest stretch of the
drive, especially in the afternoon when the sun strikes obliquely
through the dark, hanging olive woods, and the ochre, white, and
mulberry-washed houses with biscuit-coloured tiles are dappled in
shade.

[27 km.] **Kenḏroma.** From this village, in spring, you can see the snow-felted ridges of Albania.

[30 km.] From **Kouloura** you look down on the most thoroughly romantic of all the little coves along this coast, where pale-green sprays of eucalyptus and dark jets of cypress surround still water and a pebble beach, and a horseshoe jetty shelters red and blue fishing-boats. All this stretch of road is high above the sea; but at Kouloura there is a tarred lane down to the port, with its fortified *Venetian manor-house* and taverna, and the next-door *bay of Kalami.* Here and at Nisaki you can often find a fisherman to take you up or down a stretch of coast made famous by Lawrence Durrell in *Prospero's Cell.* The caiques from Corfu and Kassiopi call at Kouloura every day.

After Kouloura the hills become barer and in early summer copses of golden broom load the air with their scent of honey.

[32 km.] At **Sinies** the road cuts inland, and winds down a long valley to Kassiopi.

[37 km.] **Kassiopi.** After the luxuriance of Kenḏroma and Kouloura, Kassiopi, round the corner on its own, looking north to the bleak coast of Albania and the Forty Saints, seems bare and Cycladic. Thistles and sea-squills grow on its brown headlands where the olive trees stand askew from the wind. But the water-front houses are tucked under the lee of the fortress hill, and here in the heat of the day you can sit in the shade of a huge elm and a plane tree.

Of the Kassiopi where Nero sang in front of the altar of Jupiter Cassius nothing remains but the name. But the vestiges of the thirteenth-century *Angevin fortress* on the promonotory north of the village are impressive, and one can still count eighteen semi-circular, square or rectangular towers on its circuit. A path leads from opposite the church to the main eastern entrance; here, be-tween flanking towers, an outer portcullis defended the massive inner gateway. Scops and Little owls nest in the walls, and summer nights in Kassiopi are measured by their regular and melancholy cries.

The *church* is a strange sawn-off sort of place with a priest's room in an unusual gabled tower over it. Traditionally built on the site of the temple of Jupiter, it was sacked by the Turks in 1537 and 1571 and rebuilt in 1590, as a Latin tablet records. In the Middle Ages

Our Lady of 'Cassopo' was the most famous shrine in the island and homeward-bound ships, once they had 'toed out of the Straight' like John Locke's in 1553, used to salute it with a cannon shot. 'This little church,' wrote George Wheler in 1675, 'is famous for a Picture of Our Lady to which they attribute Miracles, and whereof I had a mind to try the skill. The way is thus: Strangers, that have a mind to know whether their Friends are alive or dead, go to the Picture, and clap a piece of money upon it, thinking of some friend. If the person they think of be alive, the piece will stick fast, but if dead, it will drop down into a Sack placed underneath; so that, dead or alive, the Priest is sure of the money.' Wheler's icon may be the fine late-sixteenth-century one set in a marble frame on the wall to the right of the screen; but it is now largely concealed by a silver casing. Opposite, there is another icon Wheler must have seen: painted by Theodore Poulakis in 1670, it records the miraculous healing of a blind villager. Unfortunately the church has been garishly restored.

Kassiopi is an object lesson. Twenty years ago, two eating places and a handful of cottage rooms offered about a dozen people a holiday of great charm and simplicity two hours' bumpy drive from the city. So that more people could share Kassiopi's seclusion a wide, tarred road was built to it, part of the harbour was filled in so that cars and coaches could turn round, and discos, bars, cafés, boutiques and crazy paving were developed to entertain these numerous visitors.

The pleasantest bathing is from rock shelves north of the port and from shingle beaches round behind the fortress promontory. The water is far brisker and cleaner than anywhere inside the Corfu strait.

Route 2: Corfu to Sidari

Though the north-west of the island is quite well served by tarred roads and is becoming more popular, it is less developed than the centre. In some ways it is the most beautiful corner of Corfu, with a richer and more Italianate landscape than the centre, and, open to the sea breeze, a fresher climate. Its marly soil retains more moisture than the red earth of the limestone areas, and until well into summer the tall unfettered olive trees cast an indescribably Virgilian shade over grassy slopes and deep combes of bracken. The jumble of wooded hills are free of scrub and here and there are capped by flat mesas of sandy rock. The easy earth of the valley bottoms and plains is arranged in neat agricultural quarterings of maize and barley, hay and yellow marrow-flowers, melons and tomatoes. There are many eighteenth- and nineteenth-century houses in the well-built villages, handsome churches and a few old Venetian manors announced by self-important gateways or high garden-walls. There are excursions to the bays of Ayos Yeorgos, Ayos Stefanos and Arillas on the west coast and to Astrakeri, Roda and the Andinioti Lagoon on the north. Except at Ayos Yeorgos, the sea is shallow and the beaches are of soft brown alluvial sand.

Route Leave Corfu by Exit A on the town exit plan; go straight on at Tzavros [9·5 km.] (see Route 1); turn right over the bridge at Iatri [13·5 km.]; at the fork [22·5 km.] on the far side of Troumbetta Pass go left for Ayos Yeorgos [32 km.], Arillas [39 km.], Ayos Stefanos [40·5 km.] and Sidari [35·5 km.]; right for Astrakeri [35·5 km.], Roda [37 km.] and the Andinioti Lagoon [45 km.]. In 1980 the last few kilometres to Ayos Yeorgos, Arillas and Ayos Stefanos were untarred. From Roda it is 17 km. on to Kassiopi (see Route 1).
Bus 4 day-return services to Sidari and Avliotes but only one Sunday day-return to Roda.
Accommodation and Restaurants Hotels with restaurants at Sidari (2 C and 2 D class), Roda (1 B, 2 C and 1 E class), Arillas (2 C class), Ayos Stefanos (1 C class) and Akharavi (1 C class without restaurant); rooms at all the above and at Peroulades, Avliotes and Astrakeri.

The road west from **Tzavros** runs across the park-like waist of the island, golden with buttercups and corn-marigolds in early May, or purple with vetch and marsh-orchids, and later scented with hay and roses.

[13·5 km.] Turn right over a bridge at a place called *Iatri* ('doctors') after two Italian brothers who killed each other in the nineteenth century. The way to Paleokastritsa (Route 3) is straight on.

[16 km.] A road on the right leads in 1 km. to **Korakiana**, a well-built village in a pretty site.

[18·5 km.] **Skripero**, a village with one or two attractive arcaded houses under the lee of the mountain, the only place on Corfu where the villagers eat frogs. From here the road zigzags up to cross the mountain range.

[21 km.] It is worth stopping just before the windy pass called *Troumbetta* ('Trumpet') to look back over the middle of the island, spiked with Lear's black exclamatory cypresses. Over the pass the view opens to the Othonian Islands and Albania.

[22·5 km.] Turn right for Karousades, Astrakeri and Roda. 4 km. down this road to Karousades, across a bridge over a stream in Rekini, a road branches off to the right and runs through endless olives for 9·5 km. to a left turn just beyond the village of **Sfakera**. From here it is 1 km. to **Roda**, once a hamlet on a plain by the sea, with a waterfront giving on to a long sand beach, now rapidly building up into a resort village, though still bare and unplanted. The large *Roda Beach* hotel is out of sight 1·5 km. away.

From the turn beyond Sfakera it is 16 km. by a fast new road to Kassiopi, past the yellow flags and feathered reeds of the *Anḍinioti Lagoon* (where you may see a Great White heron or a Black-winged stilt), and then along steep rocky shores to the Angevin fortress. At **Akharavi** (an uncompleted 'new town' for holiday-makers 3 km. along this road) a concealed right turn signed to Ayos Panḍeleimon leads by a very attractive mountain route of 19·5 km. back to Piryi on the east coast. In 1980 the new coast road also ran west from Roda for 4 km. to Karousades (see below) and will eventually continue to Sidari.

Keeping straight on at the Rekini fork, it is a 9 km. up and down drive to the substantial village of **Karousades**, and a further 1·5 km. down a decayed tarred lane to the beach at **Astrakeri**, a remote and pretty corner, where there are a few rooms and you can get something to eat.

For Sidari keep left at the fork below Troumbetta Pass.

[24 km.] Continuing along the main road, you come to **Arkadades**. If you turn left at the T-junction in this village a tarred lane will take you in 4 km. to **Payi**, a delightful drive under the north slopes of the mountain. Just beyond Payi a cascade (the last of three) spouts down — in the late spring at any rate — from pinnacles and buttresses of rock, one pierced with an arch. This 'eighteenth-century Gothick' arrangement is set off by the sombre olive trees of the area, whose trunks and leaves are sadly but picturesquely blackened by disease. Beyond Payi a rough lane descends in just under 4 km. to the *beach of Ayos Yeorgos*, one of the finest on the island but with no facilities other than a summer-hut which provides simple refreshments. At the far end of the bay, **Afionas** — the site of a Bronze Age settlement — sits high on a promontory joined to Cape Arillas by a narrow corridor of land.

Turning right at the T-junction in Arkadades you wind down along the foothill spurs to **Agros**.

[26·5 km.] A hidden left turn at the beginning of this long village leads to Afionas in 12 km., Arillas in 13 km. and Ayos Stefanos in 14·5 km. After Dafni and Armenades this side-road comes to a T-crossing on the far side of a valley, signed left to Kavvadades. A few metres up the turn to the left another left turn is signed to Afionas, 4·5 km. away. **Afionas** is a village in an impressively steep and narrow site at the end of the promontory, with fine views south to Cape Arillas and south-west over St George's Bay. 2·5 km. before reaching Afionas an earth lane to the left goes snaking down to the sands of this bay; there are summer eating places and rooms to rent. Just before this left turn there is a right turn which leads down in 3 km. to the pebble beach and hotels left **Arillas**; and from Arillas a road (untarred in 1980) goes on to **Ayos Stefanos**, 1·5 km. away, with another hotel, a fine sand beach, and heather growing above its clay cliffs. From Ayos Stefanos one can reach Sidari in about 9·5 km. either via Avliotes or via Magoulades. In both cases the first three kilometres or so were untarred in 1980.

Back on the main route, the road winds down from Agros to the river bottom and runs level for the last 5 km. to Sidari.

[35·5 km.] **Sidari**. Sidari is a collection of houses, restaurants and small hotels grouped on a flat jut of sand with a breakwater, a jetty and a few poplars. It has become one of the most popular tourist spots on the island. Some of the restaurants have pleasant pergolas where coach-loads of tourists eat looking out across the sandy bay. For the best bathing turn right a few hundred metres along the road beyond the village (the turning is signposted to the Canal D'Amour Kendro), and then cross the river by a bridge; on the coast beyond, the sea has eroded the pancake strata of clay and marl into deeply indented coves and worn a tunnel through a promontory — the *Canal d'Amour*. In the summer the *kéndro* by the bridge provides drinks and simple food. The swimming here is in brisk, shelving waters, whereas the rest of the bay is uniformly shallow.

Beyond Sidari the road continues to Peroulades, where there are some handsome but dilapidated village houses, and — by a fork to the left — to Avliotes. Both villages offer rooms to rent, but the sea is difficult to get to.

Route 3: Corfu to Paleokastritsa

Since 1829, when Sir Frederick Adam built the road to it, Paleokastritsa (25 km.) on the west coast of the island has been Corfu's most visited beauty spot.

Route Leave Corfu by Exit A on the town exit plan and go straight on at Tzavros [9·5 km.] (see Route 1) and Iatri [13·5 km.] (see Route 2). The road is well-made and wide. You can return to Corfu either by the new fast road via Liapades and the Ropa Valley to Kefalovrisso, and thence by Route 4, or by a road to Marmaro and Ermones in the Ropa valley and thence by Route 4.

Bus Three day-return buses to Paleokastritsa and Lakones leave from New Fort Square.

Accommodation and restaurants Seven hotels (A, B, C and D class) and numerous rooms at Paleokastritsa; most of the hotels have restaurants. One C class hotel with restaurant at Liapades.

Camping site At Paleokastritsa (see p. 116).

[19·5 km.] A road forks left, signposted to Liapades. Continuing straight on you will see ahead of you the rusty red and grey cliffs which tower over the valley leading down to Paleokastritsa.

[21·5 km.] The left turn leads to Paleokastritsa. A tarred lane on the right snakes up in 3 km. to **Lakones**. To get a bird's-eye view of Paleokastritsa you should drive through this village and on a further 1 km. to a café called *Bella Vista*, built like an opera box over the bitten-out bays below with their pale-green shallows and dark-blue depths. Surprisingly you can see the Citadel of Corfu, which perhaps explains the site of *Angelokastro* on its 300-metre sugar-loaf peak to the west; for from here signals could be sent of approaching enemies. Probably built between 1236 and 1259 by the despot of Epiros, Michael Angelos II, the castle is architecturally disappointing and hardly worth the 2·5 km. drive on through **Krini** and a 20-minute climb; for what appear from a distance to be substantial walls turn out to be the steep natural rock-faces of the hilltop and little masonry survives.

If you keep left at the turn to Lakones, the road dives seaward into a valley dark with cypresses and many-eyed olive trees and then winds along the *bay of Liapades*.

[25 km.] **Paleokastritsa**. Though the clover-leaf *bay of Alipa* has been spoilt by huge hotels, souvenir stands and villas (each enclosed in its private zoo of wire) and the final *cove of Ayos Spiridon* is no longer 'a quiet bay, where the carriage waits, and luncheon may be eaten on the sands' (Murray, 1900), Paleokastritsa remains beautiful — if one can ignore one's fellow-visitors and the trippery atmosphere. Edward Lear couldn't: he wrote in 1862 (*The Letters*),

> At this beautiful place there is just now perfect quiet excepting only a dim hum of myriad ripples 500 feet below me, all round the giant rocks which rise perpendicularly from the sea: — which sea, perfectly calm and blue stretches right out westward unbrokenly to the sky, cloudless that, save a streak of lilac cloud on the horizon. On my left is the convent of Palaiokastrizza, and happily, as the monkery has functions at 2 a.m. they are all fast asleep now and to my left is one of the many peacock-tail-hued bays here, reflecting the vast red cliffs and their crowning roofs of Lentisk Prinari, myrtle and sage — far above them — higher and higher, the immense rock of St Angelo rising into the air, on whose summit the old castle still is seen a ruin, just 1,400 feet above the water. It half seems to me that such life as this must be wholly another from the drum-beating bothery frivolity of the town of Corfu, and I seem to grow a year younger every hour. Not that it will last. Accursed picnic parties with miserable scores of asses male and female are coming tomorrow, and peace flies — as I shall too.

In the summer months 'scores of asses' still arrive every day in buses to crowd the beach and fill the many restaurants with their orders for lobster, the delicious but expensive local speciality which is kept alive in sunken fish-safes until needed. The bathing in the bay of Ayos Spiridon is as good as any on Corfu. Dinghies and motor-boats will take you farther afield or to various caves in the near-by cliffs.

The *Monastery of Paleokastritsa* on the right-hand promontory is said to have been founded in 1228. A pleasant eighteenth- and nineteenth-century building, it is well worth visiting for its spectacular bosky setting on the clifftop, the sparkling white-washed pinnacles and arcades of its courtyard garden, and the exquisite carved gilt rococo frames of many of the icons in the church, which is hung with silver chandeliers and has a painted ceiling. The reputedly fiteenth-century icon is eighteenth century or later, but there are one or two interesting seventeenth-century icons in a room which has been turned into a small museum. The monastery's chief feast-day — one of the island's most popular *panayíria* — falls on the Friday following Orthodox Easter.

Victor Bérard, the French Homeric scholar, has suggested that Paleokastritsa is the site of the Phaeacian capital described in Book 6 of the *Odyssey*. He places Alkinous' palace on the monastery promontory, the town on the other, and the two ports Homer mentions in the bays of Ayos Spiridon and Alipa. It is a pleasant idea which no single archaeological find has yet substantiated (see pp. 48 and 83).

Route 4: Corfu to Ermones

There is a string of splendid sandy beaches on the west coast of Corfu. Three of these (in descending order of merit) — Glifada (14·5 km), Mirtiotissa (15 km.) and Ermones (15·5 km.) — are neighbours and can be compared during one exploratory afternoon. Above the hill-village of Pelekas — along the side-road to Glifada — there is a superb viewpoint; and at Mirtiotissa an enchantingly sited monastery.

Route Leave Corfu by Exit B on the town exit plan. For Pelekas and Glifada turn left 6·5 km. from Corfu. For Ermones go straight on at this turn; keep left in Kefalovriso, and ignore all left turns until you have crossed the bridge over the drainage canal in the Ropa valley [14·5 km.]. Mirtiotissa lies halfway between Glifada and Ermones and can be reached from either (see below).
Bus For Ermones: 4 day-return services to Vatos; the turn-off to this village is 2·5 km. short of the beach.
    To Pelekas: 5 day-return services.
    To Ayos Yannis: 11 day-return services.
Accommodation and restaurants 2 hotels at Glifada (A and B class), and 1 at Ermones (A class); beach restaurants at both places; rooms and restaurants at Pelekas; eating place above Mirtiotissa.
Youth hostel At Ayos Yannis.
Camping site At Ermones.

The first five kilometres of this route are dull; but then there is a pretty stretch where a winding steam, a copse of trees by a broad meadow, a range of stone barns and two or three neglected manor-houses suggest the eighteenth century.

[6·5 km.] Fork left for Pelekas and Glifada. This road takes you up in 5·5 km. to the attractive hill-village of **Pelekas**. With many rooms to let and several eating places, it is a popular place to stay for those who cannot afford Glifada itself. 50 metres after a hairpin bend to the left by the church which faces you as you arrive, the road forks to either side of a second church. If you go right you can drive by a tarred road to a *belle vue* 1 km. above the village, a favourite spot of the German Emperor (see p. 164) and now known as the *Kaiser's Throne*. In the early evening the spread of the sea westwards is silvered to a mirror by the setting sun, and you can look east across the island to the *Citadel* and the *Epirot mountains*. Forking left at the second church, it is 5 km. down to the middle of the long gold beach of *Glifada*, backed by an olive grove. For sea, sand, solitude and a simple life, there used to be no better place on Corfu. A huge A class hotel has now imposed its life-style at the south end of the beach; but the north end, with its small new B class hotel and beach restaurants, is still attractive.

Halfway up to Pelekas as you return from the beach a lane signposted Ermones, strikes off north — a short cut of 2·5 km. to rejoin the main route to Ermones and one way to Mirtiotissa (see below).

[6·5 km.] Continuing straight on at the fork to Pelekas the road winds through particularly rich and gentle countryside.

[8 km.] You come to **Ayos Yannis**, a hamlet where a rough road on the right leads in 0·5 km. to a rather grand country-house of the 1820s now used as a *youth hostel*. The very handsome architecture, the wild and scented garden, the informal family atmosphere and the excellent bus service to 'Ay. Yanni' more than compensate for this hostel's isolated position.

[11 km.] You reach **Kefalovriso**, a hamlet on the edge of the flat *Ropa valley* which was a malarial swamp until finally drained in the 1920s and converted into fertile pasture. Here the fast road to the right runs up the east side of the Ropa valley to join the Paleokas-tritsa road 11 km. away.

[12·5 km.] A road to the left is signed to Pelekas.

[14·5 km.] Another road to the left is signed to Pelekas and Glifada; this is the way to Mirtiotissa. 1·5 km. along this road (as it swings left up a hill after passing two cottages), an earth lane leads off right through the olive trees and after 1 km. begins to descend towards the sea. In 1980 it was too steep and rough for cars from this point; but it is only 5 or 10 minutes' walk down to the beach.

The water is even shallower than at Glifada but the sands are enlivened by a scatter of smooth grey boulders, and you can wash off the salt of your bathe where fresh water drips from cliffs sprouting with pines and tussocky rock-plants. A 10-minute walk up the path which starts at the northern end of the bay will bring you to the whitewashed *Monastery of Our Lady of the Myrtles*, traditionally founded in the fourteenth century by the captured son of a Turkish bey who became a Christian. The church, rebuilt after a rock-fall, is modern; but the site, looking down over olive, orange and even banana trees to the blue water, is a peaceful and lovely one.

[15 km.] Back on the main road you reach the bridge over the drainage canal. Here the road to the right leads in a few hundred metres to the clubhouse of the Corfu Golf and Country Club whose attractively landscaped 18-hole course is famous for its billiard-table greens, grassed with Penncross Bent. The road to the left runs 1 km. to the edge of the plain where a gate cut in the rock allows the water to escape and cascade down from pool to pool to the sandy beach of *Ermones*. A rough track winds down to the sea; but the beach restaurant (some way away on the other side of the stream) is reached by a different rough track which strikes off the main road *before* the bridge over the drainage canal. The bathing is not as good as at Glifada and Mirtiotissa, and the background of bare cliffs is rather forbidding. And in spite of some good planting, the bungalows of the huge Ermones Beach hotel on the hill to the north and its funicular lift to the sands, do not improve the landscape. Victor Bérard maintains that it was here that Odysseus swam ashore and that to these pools Nausicaa drove across the Ropa valley from Paleokastritsa with her laundry-laden wagon (see pp. 82 and 159).

Route 5a: Corfu to the Mesongi Bridge via Ayos Matheos

This is the most westerly of the three routes between Corfu and the Mesongi Bridge. Its chief interest is the fine west coast beach of Ayos Gordis (18 or 19·5 km.) reached by alternative steep but well-made side roads. The Byzantine fortress of Gardiki is described at the end of this route, but can just as easily be reached by way of Route 5b or 5c (see pp. 163 and 165) and all three routes can be used as ways to the far south (see Route 6).

Route Leave Corfu by Exit C on the town exit plan; keep straight on at Vrioni [5 km.] where Route 5c forks left to Benitses and the easterly route to the Mesongi Bridge; keep straight on at the next tarred left fork [7 km.] to Gastouri and the Akhillion (described in Route 5b); and straight on where Route 5b forks left [8 km.] to Ayi Deka and the central route to the Mesongi Bridge. The quicker of the two routes to Ayos Gordis is via Sinarades.

Bus 4 day-return services to Ayos Gordis.

Accommodation and Restaurants 3 hotels (A, C and D class), many rooms, and 8 beach restaurants at Ayos Gordis; D class hotel, eating place and a few rooms at Paramona.

[8 km.] Past the left turn to Ayi Deka the road continues along a particularly luxuriant valley where wild clematis and dog-roses scramble up the cypresses.

[10 km.] A road on the right leads up in about 3 km. to Sinarades, on the outskirts of which a road (signposted) leads a further 4 km. down again to **Ayos Gordis**, a beach which has been developed only in the last ten years: the lodging houses and hotels are particularly garish and un-Corfiot. At the south end of the beach, just beyond the huge hotel, the background of rocks, cliffs and trees is attractive and dramatic. The beach itself is sand but a broad underwater belt of stones stretches along most of it.

[12·5 km.] Back on the main route you reach **Ayi Theodori**, a village on a col looking back to the city and west to the bay of Ayos Gordis.

[15 km.] For **Ayos Gordis**, take the right fork down a good tarred road signposted to **Kato Garounas**; from this village the road takes you 3 km. down to the middle of the beach.

At the Ayos Gordis fork the road on the left runs down the west side of a long inland valley. In 1980 the first 6·5 km. of this road, the stretch to Ayos Matheos, were unsurfaced.

[17·5 km.] **Vouniatades**.

[21·5 km.] **Ayos Matheos**, a very large village on the slopes of one of the island's main peaks (554 metres). At the beginning of the village a rough road to the right leads, in 3 km., to the sandy beaches of Paramona where there are a few rooms, an eating place and a small hotel.

[24 km.] A metalled road leads right in about 0·5 km. to the Byzantine *fortress of Gardiki* on a hummock among the olives just after the track forks left. It consists of an octagonal circuit-wall strengthened by eight square towers. The southernmost tower on the wall which faces you as you arrive, and the tower beyond, have decorative courses of tile, and quoins and bonding-courses of fine-worked stones. These probably come from some ancient building. This may have been a spring-house sited by the perennial pool of sweet water which explains the castle's unusual low-lying site. Stylistically the castle seems to date from the early thirteenth century and this tallies with an island tradition that it was built by the despots of Epirus.

The rough roads which fork to either side of the castle rejoin to form a 4-km. loop serving the rich farming land which stretches right up to the sandy beaches north of the Korissia Lagoon.

[26 km.] You rejoin the main road to the south just beyond the Mesongi Bridge. From here you can return to the town by Route 5b or 5c or continue to Kavos (see p. 167).

Route 5b: Corfu to the Mesongi Bridge via Ayi Deka

This central route of the three to the Mesongi Bridge (23 km.) is the hilliest and provides several attractive views. Its highlight is the detour to the Akhillion (9 km.), which in 1900 Murray could describe without surprise as 'a country seat erected for the Empress of Austria, containing a few modern works of art, but chiefly remarkable for the beauty of its gardens'. The Akhillion now contains a museum, a restaurant and a casino.

Route Leave Corfu by Route C on the town exit plan: keep straight on at Vrioni [5 km.] where Route 5C – the coastal road to Benitses and the Mesongi Bridge – forks left; for the Akhillion, turn left at the next fork [7 km.]: for Ayi Deka fork left at the next fork after this [8 km.]. From here the road is narrow and pot-holed as far as the Mesongi Bridge. From the Akhillion a road winds down for 1·5 km. to join the coast road 0·8 km. north of Benitses (see Route 5C).
Bus There are day-return buses to the Akhillion, but none to Ayi Deka.
Accommodation and Restaurants Hotel (C class), rooms and restaurants in Gastouri.

[7 km.] From the left turn 2·5 km. beyond Vrioni it is a winding climb of about 1·5 km. up lovely wooded slopes to the attractive village of **Gastouri**, at the far end of which *the Akhillion* stands on a knoll surveying the sea, the town, and the gentle valleys of the interior.

The Akhillion

Open Museum and gardens: all the year 08.00–19.00. Entrance free.
   Restaurant: March 15th–October 31st 20.00–04.00.
   Casino: March 15th–October 31st 19.00–0400.

Kirkwall records that in 1861 Elizabeth of Austria 'stayed several months in the country-house of the Lord High Commissioner'. It was her second escape from the nightmare punctilio of the Habsburg court, the infidelity of her husband Franz Joseph and the spiteful persecution of her mother-in-law. Twenty-five years after that first taste of Corfu she commissioned a house of her own which would embody her romantic conception of Achilles and his sea-mother Thetis. But between 1892 when the building was completed and her assassination in 1898 Elizabeth in fact spent little time in Corfu. In 1907 Kaiser Wilhelm II of Germany bought the empty house, left its style unchanged and until 1914 came to it regularly for his summer holidays. At the end of the First World War the property passed to the Greek state and in recent years has been leased, restored and turned to its present use.

One is expected by Corfiots to find the Akhillion either horrifying or side-splittingly amusing. But it is not really quite extravagant enough of its kind to be either. Europe has more outspoken testimonies to the architectural taste and social attitudes of the period, and the charm of the Akhillion lies in its incongruity with its surroundings, whether this appears in daytime in the Lake Como marble balustrades and statuary or at night in dance music, bright lights, whisky and roulette. Both are exhilaratingly absurd in the heart of rustic Corfu.

Downstairs the neo-Pompeian rooms hold a few evocative souvenirs of the Empress — china, silver, photographs and a charming portrait — and of the Kaiser — one of his writing-saddles, water-colours of ironclads lying off Corfu and so on. The ornate façade of the house is undistinguished even for its period, but the architects showed ingenuity in burying the building in the side of the hill so that the various floors give on to different levels of the lovely terraced gardens. The lawns of the top terrace run like the decks of a ship along the ridge. At the south end, against the house, a peri-style shelters nine entertaining marble Muses and an earnest row of ancient writers and sages. From here one can look into the rooms of the upper floor (closed in day-time) and see the toffee-tin fresco of the 'Triumph of Achilles'. At the north end of the terrace the Kaiser's idea of Achilles — a vast mechanistic bronze (Berlin

1909) — forms a striking contrast to Elizabeth's melancholy *fin-de-siècle* conception of the dying hero nearer the house in marble.

The *Casino* provides roulette, baccarat, chemin de fer and, in a sort of servants' hall of gambling downstairs, fruit-machines. Passports or identity cards and coats and ties are necessary. The Casino has its own free bus service which runs from the Ionion Hotel every hour from 19.00 until midnight, stopping at the Old Port, Esplanade, Corfu Palace Hotel and Theotoki Square.

[8 km.] Keeping straight on at the Gastouri turn you fork left at the next turn and climb tortuously for 3 km.

[11 km.] **Ayi Deka**, a pretty hill-village on the slopes of the mountain of the same name, Corfu's second highest peak (576 metres), and one of the best viewpoints on the island, for the Khalikiopoulos Lagoon and the town are laid out below you and Mt Pandokrator and the Albanian mountains stand beyond. From a little farther along there is another attractive view down over the fishing village of Benitses and across the sea to the mountains of Epiros; but after that the road is dull: a long descent down the eastern side of a broad inland valley shut off from the sea on the west by the hills around Ayos Matheos.

[23 km.] You join the coastal road — Route 5c — just before the Mesongi Bridge. From here you can return to Corfu by Route 5a — visiting Gardiki en route (see p. 162) — or 5c or continue to Kavos (see p. 167).

Route 5c: Corfu to the Mesongi Bridge via Benitses

Between Perama (6·5 km.) and Moraitika (19·5 km.) a corniche road, backed by the hills of the Ayi Deka range, dips up and down along Corfu's Costa Brava, past an almost unbroken succession of hotels, restaurants, villas, rooms, bric-à-brac shops, bars, discos and scooter-hire stands. At Perama and Benitses (10 km.) the coast is irretrievably spoilt by the jazzy vulgarity of mass tourism; elsewhere you can still catch a glimpse of cottages, gardens and olive groves and there are even one or two small and not yet wired off shingly coves from which to bathe.

Route Leave Corfu by Exit C on the town exit plan and turn left at Vrioni [5 km.].
Bus A dozen day-return services to Benitses, but only one a day as far as Mesongi.
Accommodation and Restaurants Hotels at Perama (1 A class, 2 B class, 4 C class), at or
near Benitses (2 A class, 2 B class, 1 C class, 3 D class, 2 E class), at Moraitika (1 L class,
1 A class, 1 B class, 1 C class) and at Mesongi (3 C class); rooms and restaurants all
along the route. Holiday camp hotels at Ayos Ioannis Peristeron.

[5 km.] Turning left at Vrioni you cross the *Cressida stream* —
where Corfu's wild strawberries (*fráoules*) are grown — and soon
complete the circuit of the Khalikiopoulos Lagoon. In former times
an aqueduct took the water of the Cressida spring all the way round
the head of the lagoon to Ancient Kerkira.

[6·5 km.] From **Perama**, on the corner, there are good views of
Pondikonisi and the Vlakherena Convent (see p. 144). From here
you can walk to Kanoni by the causeway.

[8·5 km.] You pass the water-gate of the Akhillion and the destroyed bridge which led to it. Dolphins sport in a choppy white
marble sea on the piers of a jetty and to the right a stepped alley of
cypresses looks up over tiers of pavilions to the demure statue of
Elizabeth of Austria.

[9·5 km.] A tarred road on the right comes down (one way only)
from the Akhillion itself (see p. 163).

[10·5 km.] **Benitses**. This is the only real fishing-village on the
island. In the late afternoon a panting caique tows out the scarlet
fishing-boats in schools of six with acetylene lamps perched on their
poops. Behind the main street are the remains of a Roman villa,
probably of the early third century A.D. The apsed *caldarium* has a
damaged geometric mosaic floor and the vault of the deep bath-
house next door is still intact. If you ask to see the *mosaiká*, you will
be shown where the owner lives. He will expect a tip for the trouble
of showing you over. The charm of Benitses lay in the proportions
of its gentle curve of houses separated from the sea by a village
street shaded with elms, mulberries and silver poplars; and in spite
of the widened road, the cemented waterfront, the concrete jetty,
the cramped hotels, the advertisements and the tourist parapher-
nalia some of this visual charm still survives.

[14·5 km.] By the hamlet of Ayos Ioannis Peristeron a tunnel goes
under a headland occupied by the Yaltour hotel (belonging to the

Club Méditerranée), possibly the ugliest bit of large-scale building on the island.

[17·5 km.] You pass the *Miramare Beach Hotel* in a narrow grove of olives between the road and the sea, its beautifully mown lawns, paved paths and sun-bathing occupants laid out to the passer-by like a brochure come to life.

[18·5 km.] On the outskirts of the picturesque village of **Moraitika**, by the right of the road, you can see more *Roman remains* of about the same date as those in Benitses. This unexcavated building shows traces of brick squinches suggesting that it once had a dome. The remains here, at Benitses and at Petreti (see p. 168) seem to show that the east coast of Corfu was as popular a stretch for villas in Roman times as it is today.

[19·5 km.] At the end of Moraitika a road runs left for under 1 km. to the Mesongi Beach Hotel and other small hotels and restaurants on a rather bare alluvial plain to the north of the mouth of the River Mesongi. Beyond Moraitika, where the road turns sharply inland along this river, at the height of summer pent-up water and a dinghy or two, nose into the reeds, present an unexpected sight.

[20 km.] A road on the left crosses the river and runs for 1·5 km. through fine olive groves to **Mesongi**, a shady village on the sea with hotels and restaurants.

[21 km.] You reach a T-junction just before the main Mesongi Bridge. From here you can continue to the south (see below), or return to the town by Route 5a or 5b. Gardiki at the end of Route 5a (p. 162) is only 4 km. away.

Route 6: The Mesongi Bridge to Kavos

Apart from the ruined Arkoudillas Monastery, the far south of the island has little to tempt the explorer. But in the last ten years Kavos itself has become an attractive resort; and between the Mesongi Bridge and Aryirades there are one or two worthwhile excursions to beaches on the east and west. (The distances below are from the Bridge, not from Corfu Town.)

Route Of the three roads to the Mesongi Bridge, Route 5c is the shortest [21 km.] and in best repair, but is much busier than 5a [26·5 km.] or 5b [23 km.].
Bus 2 day-return services to Kavos and 5 to Lefkimmi (see p. 169).
Accommodation and Restaurants C class hotel and restaurants at Boukari; rooms and restaurants all along the route, and at Kavos, Petreti and Ayos Yeorgos beach.

[0·5 km.] A few hundred metres beyond the Mesongi Bridge a tarred road branches right for Ayos Matheos (see Route 5a). 2 km. along this side-road a metalled road on the left leads in less than 1 km. to the Byzantine fortress of Gardiki (see p. 162). Continuing southwards along the main road, you climb a little and look out over the west coast and the Korissia Lagoon (see below).

[6·5 km.] In the hamlet of **Linia**, opposite a left turn signed to Khlomos, an untarred lane leads right for 1·5 km. through fine olives and then across a plain planted with maize and wheat to sand-dunes which block you from the sea. If you walk 200 metres north from the end of this lane you will get a close look at the Korissia Lagoon, which is fed by the sea through a narrow canal. This is palisaded to trap the grey mullet from whose roe the Corfiot variety of Greek caviar, or *avgotárakho*, is made. Corfu, at first sight a unanimity of olives, abounds in corners which give the impression of different countries. This littoral plain, with sedges and streams, munching cows, and the sound of the wind in the reeds and the rusty sawing of warblers, is one of them: a good place for picnics, and — over the dunes — for uncrowded bathing. But not for long, to judge from the rate of development at Ayos Yeorgos.

[7 km.] Another road to the right leads in 2·5 km. to the long sand beaches of *Ayos Yeorgos*. Rough roads run for 1 km. north and south along the coast; this, like the plain behind it, is disfigured by haphazard building, mostly rooms for rent and restaurants. There is little shade but good underwater fishing among the shoals out to sea.

[9·5 km.] **Aryirades**, a long village with a bright blue and crimson campanile. Halfway through the village, a road to the left takes you in 5 km. to the fishing-hamlets of **Petreti** and **Boukari** on the east coast. 1·5 km. from Aryirades you go through the village of **Neokhoraki**, then descend to a little plain and drive on to a T-junction at the far side of it, ignoring a right turn signed to Ayos Nikolaos. For Boukari go left at this T-junction and, after climbing through two villages, wind down through splendid olive groves to the sea. Apart from the modern hotel and its beach taverna, there is another restaurant in a handsome old house with a walled orange orchard, standing in the shade of eucalyptus trees by a wooden jetty. It is a deliciously peaceful site with views north along the wooded slopes to Mesongi. For Petreti go right at the T-junction and 1 km. later, fork left. The village itself has mushroomed from nothing in the last ten years and is unattractive. As you come in you will see the remains of a round *Roman brick piscina* on your right, probably part of a villa of about A.D. 200. At the end of the village a seventeenth-century manor house offers very simple accommodation to young people, and beyond it fine olive groves line a deeply curving bay of shallow water. There are many rooms to rent in the newer part of the village and fish tavernas on the sands.

[14·5 km.] Back on the main road, you come to **Perivoli**, where the grazing ponies seem glossier than elsewhere. After this village you swing east again past pale grey hummocks like old china-clay workings through **Ringlades, Anaplades, Ayi Theodori** and **Potami** — an unattractive but important agglomeration of villages known jointly as **Lefkimmi** or, more colloquially, *Ta Léfki*.

[19·5 km.] As you cross the river at **Potami** you may see caiques unloading corn on to the river quays, a strange Dutch sight for the Ionian Islands. From here the road is level to Kavos.

[26 km.] **Kavos**. Standing among a real Old Guard of olive trees with tremendous trunks and shakos of silver-grey foliage, even two storey houses in Kavos allow the trees the ascendancy the eye delights in and the mind desires. No hard roofline sticks up above them and hardly a single one has been cut to fit in the houses, bars and restaurants. There are rooms to rent and in 1980 a B class hotel was being built which will be only slightly out of scale.

Beyond Kavos there is a delightful walk or drive along a lane which runs first through a magnificent park of olives and bracken, then out on to the scrub-covered cliffs, then in again over the lip of a hidden valley full of luxuriant ilexes, laurels, junipers and cypresses. The lane ends about 4·5 km. from Kavos; but from here you should walk 100 metres along a shade-packed path to a Baroque *stone gate* with a rusticated arch, a keystone carved with a mask, a bunch of grapes and the date 170(?) — the last figure has vanished. Above it rises a belfry whose swirling curves end in neat coils of stone like draughtsmen — the earliest example of a type common all over the island (see p. 90). The gate leads to the small fortified *Monastery of the Panayia Arkoudillas*, of which little remains but a crumbling range or two. But it is a remarkable site: from among the old mulberries and unpruned almond trees you look down into a sunlit valley, quite unaware that 6 metres behind your back the white eroded cliffs from which the Lefkimmi peninsula takes its name plunge 90 metres into the sea. Somewhere near here the Corcyraeans may have put up the trophy which marked their victory over the Corinthians in the sea battle which opened the Peloponnesian War (Thucydides, Book 1).

PAXOS (PAXI)

Paxos (*i Paxi* in Greek — a masculine plural name) is the smallest of
the Ionian Islands, with an area of 31 square kilometres including
Antipaxos. It lies about 16 kilometres south of Corfu and is
administered as a subdistrict (eparchy) of that island. In 1980 it had
a population of 2,253 and Gaio, its capital (officially known as
Paxos), contained 450 inhabitants.

INFORMATION FOR VISITORS

Information
Kinotikó grafío (see p. 30) (tel. Gaio 7), a three-storey building back from the water-
front about seventy-five metres north of the main square. The office staff speak Greek
only but are used to inquiries about rooms (*domátia*).
Post Office and Cable Office (O.T.E)
In one building on the water-front about a hundred metres south of the main square.
Clinic
At Bogdanatika 2·5 km. along the Lakka road. Ask for the *iatrío*.
Feast-day
August 15th (Assumption of the Virgin). Service in the morning on Panayia Island
(with a traditional distribution of beef broth) and dancing and feasting in the main
square of Gaio in the evening.

GETTING TO PAXOS

Sea

Car Ferries
From Brindisi via Corfu: The *Ionis* leaves at 23.00 every other day
between June and September. Journey time: 10 hours.
From Corfu (Old Port): the small *Kamalia* leaves every day except
Sundays and sometimes Thursdays; the larger *Paxi* leaves three
times a week; both go to Lakka only.
From Ithaca: the *Ionis* leaves at 01.45 every other day between
June and September. Journey time: 3¾ hours.

Caique
From the Old Port of Corfu (see Corfu Town map on pp. 122–3) to
Lakka, Longos and sometimes Gaio. Every day except Sunday at
about 14.00 (Mondays 17.00). Journey time about 4 hours to Gaio.
Coffee and soft drinks are available on board but no food. Between
Kavos and Lakka there is often a heavy swell.

From Parga on the mainland (June to September): On most days of the week at about 17.00.

Day Trip
The *Paxi* (see *Car Ferries*) leaves Corfu Old Port at 09.00 for Lakka and returns at 16.15. This allows time to bathe at Lakka and also to take a bus to Gaio and back.

TRANSPORT ON THE ISLAND

Buses

For rates see p. 22. There are four or five day-return services from Gaio to Lakka, calling at Longos on the way there and back. The journey takes about 20 minutes.

Excursion

On most days of the week from June to September it is possible to cross over to the mainland opposite and spend a day in Parga, a charming little town with a Venetian castle and a lovely beach. The journey by caique takes about two hours.

Taxis

There are five taxis on the island. For rates see p. 23.

Scooter and bicycle hire

Scooters and mopeds are available in the three main villages at prices comparable to those in Corfu. Bicycles from D. Vlakh-opoulos, at the back of Gaio.

ACCOMMODATION AND RESTAURANTS

Town hotels

E class   *San Giorgio*. 15 beds in two-floor building overlooking the sea on the north edge of Gaio. No restaurant.

Country hotels

B class   *Paxos Beach*. Open April 1st to October 31st. 54 beds in bungalows in seaside olive grove 1 km. south of Gaio. Own beach, water ski-ing, launch excursions. Restaurant.

Villas

The Greek Islands Club (see p. 115) have about 70 houses, villas and apartments in all parts of the island, mostly near the sea.

Rooms in private houses

In 1980 there were about 20 rooms in Lakka and Gaio.

Restaurants

There are four or five tavernas in each of the three main villages of Gaio, Lakka and Longos, and a summer eating place on Mongonisi island.

Specialities

Lobster and vin rosé (see pp. 100–1).

SPORT

Bathing

Rock shelves at a place called *Ioannás* about 0·5 km. south of the town; pebbles in many coves along the east coast, some accessible on foot (Longos; *Paxos Beach Hotel*), most only by boat; pebble and sand at Lakka (p. 177), on Mongonisi island (p. 178) and in Antipaxos (p. 179).

A small boat goes to an Antipaxos beach every day from Gaio.

Water sports

Yachts, Wayfarers, Toppers and Windsurfers can be hired from the Greek Islands Club Sailing Centre at Lakka. Water ski-ing is available there and at the *Paxos Beach Hotel*. Good underwater fishing off Antipaxos.

INTRODUCTION TO PAXOS

Nine and a half kilometres long by three kilometres wide, Paxos floats on the blue depths of the Ionian Sea like a fragment of some prelapsarian garden — an enchanting working-model of an island across which, like Gulliver, you can step in a stride or two. Until a few years ago it was untouched by tourism and the twentieth century. Now it is a popular port of call for yachts; buses and cars hired in Corfu move up and down newly tarred roads; an attractive beach-hotel has been built out of sight of, but close to, Gaio, the capital; and in 1968 water was piped to the town from a new bore. Until then the islanders had to rely on rainwater, for there are no springs on Paxos; Davy says that in the last century they used to wash their clothes in the sea, using a special type of marl as soap. There are no monuments of any note, and Paxos' tourist features are its Lilliputian capital, its well-tended olive groves, its crystalline waters, its succulent lobsters and its blue sea-caves.

GAIO

The charm of Gaio lies in a series of contrasts: though officially a town, this doll's-house capital has a population of less than 500. But though no larger than a village, it has houses three or four storeys high, with oeil-de-boeuf windows to ventilate their attics and tiled string-courses which give their upper storeys a mansardish and towny look. But again, in this village that pretends to be a town there is little traffic (except at the height of the tourist season), and you can stroll uncaring in bare feet along smooth-paved alleys. It is this last contrast that is the most captivating, for in Gaio, alone of Ionian towns, you feel as though you have walked back into the unmotorized age of Lear and Cartwright. The Gothic-Revival window-paning of the church in the middle of the stone-flagged *platía* and the former British Residency add to this nineteenth-century air.

There is another contrast: though Gaio is on the sea it appears to be on a river, for you arrive at the town as it were up a narrow carriage-drive of water which sweeps up to the forecourt of the town. But though Gaio seems to be on a river, no other town in the Seven Islands depends so much on the sea. Boxes of twitching lobsters are sent off every day to Corfu, and in the early mornings the fishermen spill out their catch of dogfish and spider-crabs, cuttlefish and mullet, rock-fish and conger-eels on to two slab-tables off one corner of the square.

PRINCIPAL SIGHTS

Former British Residency

The finest building in Gaio is the former British Residency, which stands on the water-front a little to the north of the square. It is a delightful product of the Mediterranean Regency — a five-bay house three storeys high with attic pavilions linked by an arcade, pale-green shutters and trellised ironwork to its balconies. It is now used by the harbour police.

Castle on Ayos Nikolaos Island

Hire or borrow a dinghy and you can row from the former Residency to a dilapidated stone quay on St Nicholas's Island in two or three strokes of your oars. The island is private property and you should first ask for permission to visit it at the *kinotiko grafio* (see p. 171). From a little way up the cobbled path you will get the best view of the town; almost nothing has changed since Lear sketched it from here in the 1860s. Farther up the path and through the pine trees on the left are the remains of the castle built by the Sant' Ippolito family in 1423 and restored by the French in 1810 after a British frigate had threateningly bombarded the town. If you make your way through the choke of brambles to the ramparts, you will get the view to the mainland and the sea breeze of which the town is deprived.

EXCURSIONS FROM GAIO

There are few more idyllic ways of spending an afternoon in the Ionian Islands than to walk among the olive groves south of Gaio. The tarred lanes and nineteenth-century gravel drives meander from one handful of cottages to another, each with a village church and a tongue-twisting Paxiot name: Makratika, Veliandatika, Fanariotatika. There is no map of Paxos large enough to show quite how these lanes behave (but see under Routes on Paxos below), and having started up the tarred road to Lakka and branched off left along one of them you must follow your nose. All sense of direction is lost in an underworld of shade without land- or sky- or sea-mark. Occasionally the sun strikes through the roof of leaves on to the orange-and-white stucco of a cottage, a lemon tree by a cistern, or a great ribbed water-jar like an ancient pithos; and sometimes, through a gap, you catch a glimpse of a grey campanile or a cypress spire sunning itself above the treetops on the other side of a valley. The olive groves are as ordered and well-kept as an Italian garden, the red earth raked clean of stones to provide an easy landing-ground for the tiny black Paxiot olives.

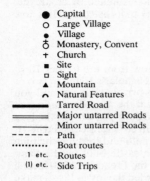

Route Map of
Paxos (Paxi)

- ● Capital
- ○ Large Village
- ● Village
- ⚵ Monastery, Convent
- ✝ Church
- ■ Site
- □ Sight
- ▲ Mountain
- ∩ Natural Features
- ▬▬▬ Tarred Road
- ▬▬▬ Major untarred Roads
- ───── Minor untarred Roads
- ----- Path
- ·········· Boat routes
- 1 etc. Routes
- (1) etc. Side Trips

All the plain whitewashed churches you pass have the same idiosyncratic moulding round their doors — consisting of deeply cut lozenges, almost always painted ochre. How their plain nineteenth-century interiors would delight Sir John Betjeman: touchingly bad icons, polished brass candelabra stuck with bees-wax candles, spotless tiled floors, and carved deal stalls. Another nineteenth-century feature is the village cistern built, dated and inscribed during the British Protectorate. Fresh water was once so scarce that a town crier (the *ḍelális*) would announce the brief hour during which a particular cistern could be drawn from.

Up on the wind-scrubbed cliffs which look over the mazarine sea to the west, the limestone slabs (which split naturally into courses as regular as any mason's) are built up into six-foot walls along both sides of paths paved with the natural bedrock, so that you walk blindly along stone corridors over the tops of which lurch sprays of wild white dog-roses.

ROUTES ON PAXOS

Three routes are described: the first, from Gaio to Lakka by the morning caique to Corfu; the second, back from Lakka to Gaio by the island's spine-road; and the third, round the island by hired motor-boat (see map opposite). Routes 1 and 2 can be combined in either order to make a pleasant day's outing, using caique or bus in either direction or walking one way. Route 3 depends on the weather: the sea must not only be calm but swell-less.

Paxos walking and wild flowers by Martin Sands contains some detailed itineraries and an excellent map.

Route 1: Gaio to Lakka by caique

Caique Leaves Gaio daily at about 11.00 (see also p. 171). The journey takes about 35 minutes.

As you leave the narrows you pass the island of **Panayia** where a lighthouse, a chapel, and — in summer — a copse of blazing yellow broom are belted by a white wall. **Longos**, 15 minutes up the coast, is a pretty little port at the end of a horseshoe bay. Its white cottages have dark green shutters, and until 1967 Victorian oil-lanterns used to hang from brackets on the quayside buildings.

After loading and unloading, the caique sets off up the east coast again, skirting the shore only 40 metres out. Every 200 metres or so, between headlands where shelves of rock are coiled like Chelsea buns, a miniature valley full of olives runs down to a white pebble beach. The hills are covered with scrub, olives and stands of wild cypress.

Lakka, the northernmost of Paxos' three ports, is another 10 minutes away. Whether you arrive from Gaio or Corfu, its oval lagoon is invisible until just before you pass through its narrow neck. You can bathe from an olive-shaded strip of pebble beach and either picnic or eat in one of the village's tavernas.

Route 2: Lakka to Gaio

Route The two roads which leave Lakka for Gaio (8 km.) join after 1·2 km.

Behind Lakka there is, for Paxos, a wide valley, where the olive trees are extraordinary. Their long snaking branches trail upwards to the air like water-weeds, and in their subaqueous shade you feel as though you were walking at the bottom of the sea. A steepish climb brings you to the pretty little *Church of Ayos Konstandinos* in **Mastoratika**, dated 1720 and washed white with navy-blue architraves. Just before this hamlet, where the two roads from Lakka join, a road to the left takes you down in 1·5 km. to Longos (see Route 1). After Mastoratika, another less tiring gradient brings you to **Magazia**, a long hamlet with three churches. Just before Magazia, a lane on the right takes you to **Manessatika** and thence by a stepped path down to *Ipapandi*, the site of the only old well on the island and of the *Metropolitan Church*, a Byzantine building with two domes but so restored and disguised with enthusiastic paint as to be hardly worth visiting, except, perhaps, for a case containing a bishop's robes, mitre and staff of 1849. There is a typical Corfiot-style *campanile* next door, with pillared belfry and elongated crimson dome, from the top of which you can look down the valley to the Lakka lagoon.

After Magazia a final climb brings you out below the crest of the island (230 metres) and in sight of the sea to the west. For a kilometre or so the road runs in the sun, and the hot air is full of the aromatic scent of cypress resin. From the ridge you go slowly down through several more hamlets, two with tall campaniles, past a clearing where prospectors tried for oil some years ago and left a cemetery of olive trunks, and down a last steep slope into the valley behind Gaio.

Route 3: Round Paxos by boat

Boat Journey It takes under 2½ hours to circumnavigate Paxos in a motor-boat without stopping, but the pleasantest way of making the trip is to hire a local fishing-boat; visit Antipaxos (*Andípaxi*) first for a bathe and picnic in a cove as you go round the main island. The Greek Islands Club run excursions of this sort.

The sheer western cliffs of Paxos are full of spectacular sea-caves, some so huge that a motor-boat can move about inside them when the sea is calm, others smaller but deeper where the water is dark electric-blue and glitters with phosphorescence.

Starting south from Gaio, in less than 10 minutes you pass the Paxos Beach Hotel in a secluded valley, and in another 10 reach **Mongonisi Island**, separated from Paxos at its southern end by a channel you can step across. On the coast a little way north of the harbour made by this island you can bathe in a stinking but therapeutic rock-cut bath coated with yellow sulphur-flowers. The channel between Mongonisi and the next islet, **Kaltsonisi**, is wide enough for the boat to glide through over glassy water and a white-sand bottom. Gazing at the still beauty of these narrows is a hermit's whitewashed chapel backed by the dark glazed green of myrtles and holm-oaks. From here it is no more than 15 minutes to the northern tip of **Antipaxos**, and 5 minutes down its east coast to the fine white sand and pale blue water of *Voutoumi Bay*, the most Caribbean of all Ionian beaches.

Of the twenty-five or thirty caves or curiously shaped rocks up the west coast of Paxos five or six stand out. For colour the blue ribbon goes to a small cave on Mongonisi Island, only about 200 metres west of the Kaltsonisi channel. Here the water — 'full fathom five' at least — glows unnaturally in the slanting sunlight like illuminated copper-sulphate crystals. 15 minutes farther along is the great *arch of Tripito* under a flying buttress to the cliff. Another 10 minutes away, the beach at *Galazio* is the best place to land for a picnic, though the water is slightly sulphuretted. 20 minutes beyond, the *Ortholithos* — a magnificent obelisk of rock 30 metres high — rises abruptly from the sea; it is best seen from inside and framed by the mouth of the *cave of Petriti*. The *Stakhai caves*, 5 minutes farther along, form a triple cavern, one with a hole in the roof; here, and round the next point at *Erimitis*, the highest cliff, are coves to which the villagers descend by interminable steps to bathe. Davy records a curious nineteenth-century custom, now happily no longer found: 'And, should the season of the year be spring, the traveller may have an opportunity of witnessing a singular species of angling, in which I was informed, the natives indulge from the lofty cliffs, not in the sea beneath for fish, but in the air for birds — swallows — which then crowd about the cliffs, and which they catch with a fly, attached to a fine hook and line, thrown and managed very much in the same manner as in common fly-fishing.' In *Ipapanḍi cave*, 10 minutes from Erimitis one can often see seals resting; opposite, a rock like a submarine lies awash in the sea.

From Ipapanḍi, it takes 15 minutes more to reach Lakka (see Routes 1 and 2).

LEFKAS

With an area of 293 square kilometres and a 1971 population of 24,581 (excluding the dependent island of Meganisi), Lefkas is the fourth largest of the central Ionian Islands. Its capital — also called Lefkas — contains 6,818 inhabitants. The island's Greek name of *i Lefkás* becomes *tin Lefkáda* in the accusative and *tis Lefkádos* in the genitive.

INFORMATION FOR VISITORS

Information
Lefkas Travel, Dörpfeld Street (*Map* 1) (tel. 22430).
Post Office
Map 15.
Cable Office
Map 7.
Hospital
Map 13. (tel. 336).
Bus station
Map 18.
Feast Day
Feast of the Holy Ghost on the seventh Monday after Orthodox Easter. Service at Faneromeni Monastery in the morning, dancing and feasting in the town in the evening. Two-day festival at Karia, starting on August 11th, in honour of St Spiridon.
Festivals
International Music and Folk-Dancing Festival in August. Teams from foreign countries and several parts of Greece, as well as Lefkas' own orchestra and dance group, take part in this event which is, however, less high-powered than its name suggests.

GETTING TO LEFKAS

You reach Lefkas by driving to its capital from the mainland, crossing by a chain-ferry, or by air from Athens to Aktion, and thence by road to Lefkas.

Air

From Athens there are three flights a week to Aktion on the mainland, 16 km. by road from Lefkas. Frequent buses connect Aktion to Lefkas.

Road

From Athens: via Corinth, Rion-Antirion car ferry (every half-hour during daylight, less frequently at night, paying, crossing time 20 minutes), Mesolongi, Agrinion and Amfilokhia (total 362 km.). The chain-ferry at Lefkas is constant during daylight, free, crossing time 3 minutes, and operates as the need arises during the night. From Corfu via Igoumenitsa: via Margariti, Morfi, Kanaliki and Preveza (total 122 km.). This involves taking the Preveza-Aktion ferry (continuous, crossing time ten minutes).

Bus

From Athens (see p. 20): Two morning buses and one evening bus a day along the route above. Journey takes about 9 hours.
Athens Office of the Lefkas K.T.E.L.: 100 Kifissou Street (tel. 5133583).
From Igoumenitsa: There are several buses as far as Preveza but only one sure connection with the service from Aktion to Lefkas.

TRANSPORT ON THE ISLAND

Buses

The bus station (K.T.E.L.) is off Ayos Minas Square (*Map* **18**), tel. 22364. Apart from the usual village services there are clockwise and anti-clockwise buses every morning along the ring road to Vasiliki, where they stop for 3 or 4 hours. This means that you can spend most of the afternoon in either Nidri or Vasiliki.

Caiques

Caiques run daily between the capital (*Map* **5**) and Nidri (see p. 192), and also down the canal to the beach at the north end of the Yiro.

Taxis

There are about 40 taxis in the island, most of them based on the capital. For rates see p. 23. The three ranks are in Ayos Minas Square (tel. c/o 22353) on the quayside at the north end of the main street (tel. c/o 22629), and in King George II Square (tel. 22215).

Car, scooter and bicycle hire

Cars from Lefkas Travel, Dörpfeld Street (*Map* **1**) (tel. 22430), E. Grapsa, Ayos Minas Square (tel. 22883), and Lefkas Tours, 9 Bei

Street (opposite the K.T.E.L. — *Map* **18**) (tel. 22817); scooters at *Map* **4**; bicycles at *Map* **17**.

ACCOMMODATION AND RESTAURANTS

Town hotels

B class   *Lefkas*. Medium-sized waterfront hotel. Restaurant.
            Nirikos. Small waterfront hotel. Snack-bar.

C class   *Santa Maura*, 2 Spirou Vlanti Street. Small central hotel in typical Lefkas style. Hot and cold water in all rooms. No lift. Cake shop and wine garden. Outdoor summer restaurant.

D class   *Byzantion*, Dörpfeld Street. Central two-floor building in typical Lefkas style. Some views of sea and castle. Central heating.

E class   *Averoff*, Dörpfeld Street. Top two floors of central late-nineteenth-century three-floor building in typical Lefkas style.
            Patras, King George II Square. Second and third floors of typical Lefkas building in central square.

Country hotels

C class   *Nidri Beach*, Nidri. Small village hotel behind beach.

Rooms in private houses

The number of rooms available in 1980 was approximately as follows: 100 in Lefkas town, 70 at Liya, 120 at Nikiana, 250 at Nidri, 30 at Sivota, 120 at Vasiliki and 40 at Ayos Nikita.

Camping sites

There is an attractive camping site at Desimo Bay (p. 197) and a less comfortable one at Poros Beach (p. 198).

Restaurants

In Lefkas Town there are two or three restaurants in or near George II Square and a number of grilled-meat places along the main street. For restaurants in the country see the Route Instructions.
Specialities: *savóro* in spring and autumn (see p. 100), salami (ask

for *nopó* salami which is made from unfrozen meat), small soles (*glósses*) and pale yellow lentils from Englouvi.

Breakfast: a common Lefkadian breakfast is hot milk with thick Melba toast (*friganiés*); cold rice-pudding (*rizógala*) is also a favourite.

SPORT

Bathing

Sand or sandy shingle between Liya and Nidri (p. 195), at Desimo Bay (p. 197), on the Yiro (p. 189), at Ayos Ioannis (p. 206), at Vasiliki (p. 199) and at Ayos Nikitas (p. 206); pebbles at Rouda Bay (p. 198).

INTRODUCTION TO LEFKAS

Lefkas is neither quite naturally an island nor quite naturally a peninsula. Though the long sand-spit of the Yiro nearly links it to the Akarnanian shore, you drive to it along a man-made causeway; and though it is surrounded by water, only a canal dredged through the shallows of the Sea Lake makes it circumnavigable. Linked by the umbilical cord of its sand-spit to the primeval womb of the mainland mountains, Lefkas seems however to contain more of the earthy mystery of the ancient world than its sea-weaned neighbours do, and in variety of natural beauty even Corfu seldom surpasses it.

Ruled sometimes from the sea as an island and sometimes from the mainland as a peninsula, Lefkas is as a result half Ionian and half Western Greek. It is Ionian in its greenness, its olive forests, its eighteenth-century Venetian costumes, the façades of its churches, its castle, its brass band and its British Residency; but it is Western Greek in the fish palisades and canoes of its muddy lagoon, its two hundred years of Turkish rule (with their legacy of dark looks and scimitar noses), its Epirot music, its timber-framed houses and its ramshackle capital.

If Lefkas has gained a little of both worlds by its geographical ambiguity, it has lost a lot from its inaccessibility. Though its land is fertile and its peasants renowned for their skill and industry, it is a poor island. For lack of a proper port its Venetian and British rulers could not easily fit it into their maritime scheme of things; and since 1864 successive Greek Governments have found it equally difficult to develop its remote economy. In the last ten years good roads to Amfilokhia and Igoumenitsa, air services to Aktion, electric light in the hill-villages, and an international folk-dance festival have all done something to bring the modern world to Lefkas; but with only three modern hotels and a few hundred rooms to rent it remains the least sophisticated of the Ionian Islands proper — and also the least spoilt.

LEFKAS TOWN

Lefkas started in the early sixteenth century as a collection of warehouses at the landward end of the aqueduct then built by the Turks across the lagoon to their capital in the castle. In 1704 an earthquake shattered the water conduit and the capital moved to its present site, then (and until this century) known as Amaxikhi, perhaps from the carts (*amáxia*) which gathered there to load and unload their produce.

No early traveller had a good word to say of Amaxikhi. Sibthorp remarked on the 'little attention paid by the police to cleanliness' in 1795; in 1814 Kendrick thought the streets 'narrow and ill-built'; in the 1860s Lear (*Views*) found little to praise 'either as to situation, architecture, or cleanliness'; and as late as 1872 Murray commented on its 'wretched appearance'. Today, when asphalt and reinforced concrete have imposed their eye-bruising monotony on nearly every mainland town, Lefkas' watery site and gimcrack architecture strike one as strange and captivating. A floating town it seems at first, where caiques ride high above the quayside on the waveless lagoon and the gutters of the narrow streets run with water like the scuppers of a laden ship. The houses increase one's mystification; it looks as if they had all been temporarily patched up after the great earthquake of 1948, for their upper works consist of sheets of zinc, hardboard or corrugated iron, resting on a first floor of masonry. But it turns out that such seemingly provisional materials have always been chosen for the upper storeys in Lefkas because they place a lighter burden on foundations constantly shaken by earthquakes; and corrugated iron is only the practical modern equivalent of the plaster-daubed calamus-reed screens used in the early nineteenth century. It is extraordinary what an air of Regency elegance this traditional shanty-town material acquires when it is painted in pleasing shades of pale apricot, lime-green or sky-blue and white, especially when the houses are decorated with fluted wooden pilasters or elegant wrought-iron balconies. As curious as the upper works are the bottom storeys; these are lined, even in the case of churches, with timber posts and beams standing inside the masonry like the framework of a ship inside its planking. This resilient inner structure not only carries the top of the house safely through all but the worst of earth tremors, but prevents the masonry from falling inward on the inhabitants. Though hundreds of houses were damaged in the 1948 earthquake only two people were killed.

Apart from a main street and a waterside road the town contains nothing but narrow sanded alleys, few of which have names or are wide enough for cars. At its seaward or causeway end the main street starts obscurely as a lane too narrow for double traffic before debouching into the town's main square. This has the Prefecture on one side and the Church of Ayos Spiridon (1685) on another. From here the street broadens and runs like an Oriental bazaar for almost half a kilometre to a fork at the far end of the town. There is no street in the Ionian Islands so bursting with food and drink and wares of every kind: pots and pans, mirrors, plastic bowls, buckets, rope, sacks of beans and rice and chick-peas, bales of cloth and suits and dresses, bottles, barrels, bunches of local salami, books, tins, piles of bread behind dusty guichet windows and racks of fruit and vegetables. There are few modern shop-fronts and the low houses on either side hang out over wooden arcades. Under these arcades you peer through doors and windows into downstair rooms where butchers flense the lard off huge pigs hanging from the ceiling joists, or at window-sills where cauldrons of tripe and offal simmer on a stove, while behind, at dark café tables, workmen make late breakfasts off noisy and nourishing soup. The Lefkadians are great pork-eaters and as one walks up the street in the evening one is enfiladed by the rich aromas of pigs spitted over charcoal grills. 'Wretched' this street may be in the sense that few of its wooden houses have been replaced by rectangular cement façades and that little traffic disturbs the village women striding unselfconsciously about their business in their best coming-to-town Venetian costumes of dark blue, bottle-green or mocha satin. But interest, colour and character it does not lack, especially in the evening when the townspeople take it over for their volta (p. 78). And there are one or two very attractive buidlings. The pink and white façade of the *Church of the Isodia tis Theotokou* (Presentation of the Virgin) (*Map* **14**) halfway up on the left, is one of the most original and satisfying neo-classical exercises which have survived in Greece, and it is perfectly set off by two tall pine trees. A little before this, the ornate façade of the *Church of the Pandocrator* (*Map* **10**) represents the seventeenth-century style. Country cousins of their sophisticated Zantiot relations, even when first built in the late seventeenth and early eighteenth centuries, the town's churches have been re-erected many times after earthquakes and their provincial features have been further coarsened by nineteenth-century restorations. But they survive; and their carved altar-screens (often economically over-painted white rather than regilded), panelled walls and painted ceilings provide numerous and pleasant, if uninspired, examples of the 'Ionian Baroque' type (see p. 90).

Up at the south end of the street on the right stood the grandest, until gutted by fire, *Ayos Minas*. Its iron belfry, like a miniature Eiffel Tower, was put up after the 1948 earthquake; several churches have similar structures. The road to the right beyond this church is the main traffic route round the town; it runs down to the cathedral square, past the former British Residency and Courthouse — twin buildings of 1825 in a pleasant Anglicized Lefkadian style — and then along the side of the lagoon to the castle causeway.

PRINCIPAL SIGHTS

Museum and Public Library
Map **6**.

Open Weekdays *Summer* 08.00–13.30
               Winter 09.00–14.00
          Monday, Wednesday and Friday 17.00–1930
          Closed on Sundays.
Entrance: Free.

The museum is housed on the ground floor of a substantial nineteenth-century house and to visit it you must apply to the librarian of the public library on the floor above. But in 1980 it was closed completely for major repairs to the structure. It contains a large and interesting collection of icons by such eighteenth- and nineteenth-century Lefkadian artists as Roussos, Dze and Vendouras. The two finest paintings are an anonymous fourteenth-century 'Entry into Jerusalem' and a 'St Dimitrios' by P. Doxaras (see p. 92). A gold-embroidered stole reputedly presented to an archbishop of Lefkas by Catherine the Great and some Russian icons from Pontus are also worth looking at.

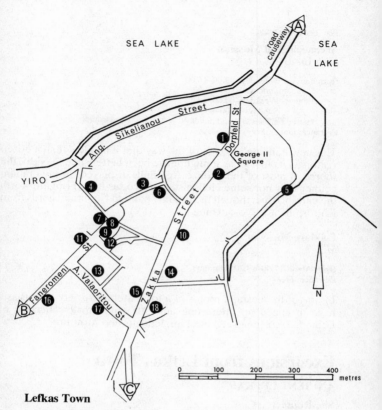

Lefkas Town

1 Tourist Information Office
2 Prefecture
3 Folklore Museum
4 Scooter hire
5 Nidri and Yiro Caique Berths
6 Museum and Public Library
7 Cable Office (O.T.E.)
8 Court House
9 Former British Residency
10 Church of the Pandokrator
11 Town Hall
12 Cathedral
13 Hospital
14 Church of Isodia tis Theotokou
15 Post Office

16 Archaeological Museum
17 Bicycle hire
18 K.T.E.L.

A route to
    Castle of Ayia Mavra
    Yiro Beach
B route to
    Ayos Ioannis
C route to
    Vasiliki
    Ancient Lefkas
    Nidri
    Karia
    Sappho's Leap

Archaeological Museum
Map **16**.

Open *Summer* Weekdays 09.00–15.00
　　　　　　Sundays 10.00–16.00
　　　　Winter　Weekdays 09.00–15.30
　　　　　　Sundays 10.00–16.30
　　　Closed on Tuesdays and holidays.
Entrance: Drs 25. Free on Sundays.

This new building is so out of the way that it had less than a dozen
visitors in its first year; it might have been better sited in Nidri, the
source of most of the Bronze Age finds displayed. In my opinion
neither they nor some Hellenistic terracottas from Frini are worth
the entrance fee, though the brightly painted Neolithic sherds from
Khirospilia are eye-catching (see p. 199).

Folklore Museum
Map **3**.

Open About 17.00–19.30 most days.
Entrance: Free.

In one of the upstairs rooms of a local literary society enthusiasts
have arranged an interesting and attractive small collection of
Lefkadian costumes, textiles, implements and furniture.

Excursions from Lefkas Town

ANCIENT LEFKAS

See Route 1.

CHAPEL OF THE PANAYIA ODIYITRIA

See Route 2.

AYOS IOANNIS

See Route 4.

CASTLE OF AYIA MAVRA AND THE YIRO BEACH

For Major Church (later General Sir Richard), who stormed the
castle in 1811 after a gallant defence by French and Italian troops,

Ayia Mavra was 'that diabolical castle seated like a magician's fortress in the middle of the sea' (Lane-Poole). To see it with his eyes one must imagine the lagoon without the road causeways which now run past the castle from the island to the mainland shore. A visit can be combined with a bathe from the splendid Yiro beach just opposite.

Route Leave Lefkas by Exit A on the town plan and drive to the chain-ferry at the end of the causeway (1·5 km.).
Key The key to the castle can be obtained from the café next to the chain ferry.

As you drive out along the causeway across the Sea Lake you can see the submerged piers of the *Turkish aqueduct* on your left, picked out in calm weather by perching sea-gulls. This aqueduct ran out on 260 arches and served as a dangerous causeway until 1825. In the seventeenth century Wheler said that it 'would make the stoutest man tremble in passing it', and Leake who walked along it in 1806 says that it was 'so narrow, that when the wind is very strong it sometimes happens that careless or drunken men fall, or are blown over into the water and smothered in the mud'. Apart from the *deep-water canal* to the right of the causeway (first dredged by the British in the nineteenth century), the water of the Sea Lake is seldom more than a metre deep and can be navigated only by flat-bottomed pirogues with projecting riggers. Though these are still called '*monóxila*', they are no longer dug-out canoes, as the name implies they were in earlier days.

Behind the unsightly wine factory at the mouth of the canal, a modern tourist *periptero* provides changing-rooms, food and refreshments for bathers using the beaches which run all along the outer edge of the Yiro, as this long sand-spit is called. A road runs all round it and back to town (5 km.). When the north-west winds relent, the water here is deliciously brisk and clean.

The entrance to the *castle* (free) is across the chain-ferry. The entrance gate is to the right of the great polygonal tower which faces you as you disembark from the chain ferry. When Wheler visited Santa Maura in 1675, the castle was 'separated by a ditch of thirty, or forty foot wide from two little Islands, which are as the suburbs to the Fortress, and are inhabited by Turks or Greeks'. At that time there were 'Five or six thousand Inhabitants in the Cittadel and Suburbs'. The eastern ditch survives, but the western — once cross-ed by a wooden foot-bridge — has been swallowed up by the new canal; every vestige of the populous suburbs has disappeared.

The stages by which the castle developed to its present size are obscure. A plan published by Coronelli in 1687 shows a citadel with square towers and surrounded by an inner moat in the north-east corner of the present circuit. This citadel was probably the full extent of the original fortress which, on July 10th, 1300, Charles II of Naples gave John Orsini permission to build on Letorna (as the Yiro was known in Italian). Walter de Brienne — who took the castle in 1331 (and as Constable of France was later killed by the English at Poitiers) — had no reason to enlarge this now-vanished early building during the brief Angevin tenancy; and it was almost certainly the Tocco family who extended the circuit to its present size after they had ousted the Angevins in 1362.

Between 1479 when the last Tocco fled in front of the advancing Turks, and 1684 when Morosini took the place for Venice, there must have been many repairs to walls and towers damaged by earthquake and bombardment, and perhaps some major building. The Venetians certainly patched it up during the year they held it between 1501 and 1502, and the Turks, who owned it for over two hundred years, must have kept it in repair even if they did not enlarge it. It is difficult to say on stylistic grounds whether the great *polygonal tower* by the western entrance is early Turkish or late Tocco handiwork; and there is the same uncertainty about the inner part of the eastern entrance which has a distinctly Oriental look. But the *tower* under the modern lighthouse — which has a fine stone vaulted chamber inside it — is certainly Frankish work of the fourteenth or fifteenth century. On top of the remaining base of this tower is the tomb of Major-General Davis, Adjutant-General of the British Forces in Sicily, who died here on his way home in 1813. The eastern side of the castle, with its two rectangular bastions, was rebuilt by the Venetians in the early years of the eighteenth century, when they added the echeloned outerworks beyond the moat. The eighteenth-century *chapel* in the south-eastern rectangular bastion is of no architectural interest; but it stands on the site — outside the

Route Map of Lefkas

●	Capital	⌒	Natural Features
○	Large Village	━━━	Tarred Road
●	Village	═══	Major untarred Roads
ŏ	Monastery, Convent	────	Minor untarred Roads
†	Church	- - - -	Path
■	Site	··········	Boat routes
□	Sight	1 etc.	Routes
▲	Mountain	(1) etc.	Side Trips

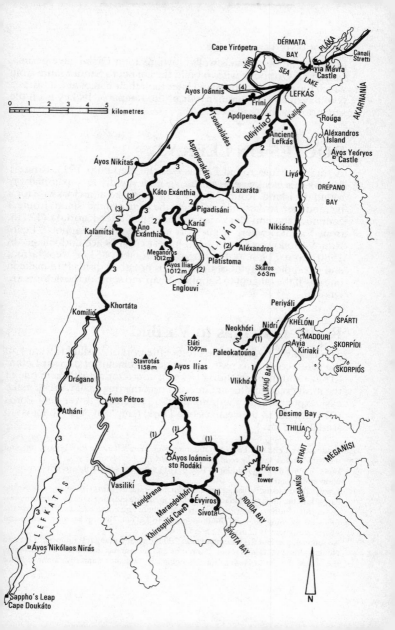

original Catholic castle's walls — where John Orsini gave permission to his Orthodox wife to build the chapel to Santa Maura from which the castle and the island later took their name; and it offers a cool haven after a summer tour of the ramparts. Its key is on the same ring as the castle key.

ROUTES ON LEFKAS

A ring road runs round Lefkas (see the map on p. 191). Route 1 follows this clockwise as far as Vasiliki, slightly less than halfway round the island. Route 2 follows the ring road anti-clockwise for a bit, and then strikes off to Karia in the centre of the island. Route 3 continues the anti-clockwise run until just after Khortata (17 km. from Vasiliki) where it goes off at a tangent to Sappho's Leap. Route 4 follows a new road to a west coast beach and village. In 1980 about 71 km. of the ring road's total of 85 km. were tarred; and a complete circuit of the island is not at all difficult to make in one day if the tangent to Sappho's Leap and some of the detours are ignored.

Route 1: Lefkas to Vasiliki

This clockwise route to the pretty little port of Vasiliki (39 km.) on the south coast runs past the intriguing remains of ancient Lefkas (3 km.) and through Nidri (18 km.), now a tourist village in one of the most graceful sites in Greece. From the ring road you can make easy expeditions to the remains of a Hellenistic tower near Poros (27 km.) and to the vestiges of a Doric temple at Ayos Ioannis sto Rodaki (35 km.).

Route Leave Lefkas by Exit C on the town plan, keep left at the fork 1·5 km. out, and thereafter follow the ring road to Vasiliki [39·5 km.].

Bus Counting the ring road buses (see p. 181) there are several day-return services to Nidri and Vasiliki.

Caique There is a useful caique service from the capital to Nidri. Three caiques leave the east side of the town (see Lefkas Town map) in the late morning or early afternoon; two go on from Nidri to Meganisi, stop the night there and come back to Nidri early the following morning, when all the three return to Lefkas. The trip between Lefkas and Nidri takes about 1½ hours.

Accommodation and Restaurants About 200 rooms and many restaurants at Liya and Nikiana; hotel (C class), about 250 rooms and several restaurants at Nidri; camping site and restaurant at Desimo Bay; camping site, bungalows and restaurant at Poros beach; about 30 rooms and two restaurants at Sivota; and about 120 rooms and four restaurants at Vasiliki.

[2·5 km.] *Megali Vrisi* — the 'great spring'. A small *church* under the hill on your right and ancient niches carved in the rock-face mark the importance of this source of water. The Turks piped it to Amaxikhi and thence carried it out to the castle by their aqueduct. It still provides the modern capital with all its needs. A few hundred metres beyond the spring the road turns sharply to the right round a spur called *Kaligoni* ('good corner'). Up this spur runs the northern wall of the ancient Corinthian town of Lefkas.

Ancient Lefkas

The town of Lefkas or Nerikos was founded by Corinth in the second half of the seventh century B.C., probably to take the place of Korkyra as a staging-post on the route up the Adriatic once that colony had revolted in 664 B.C. Strabo says, 'The Corinthians dug a canal through the isthmus of the peninsula and made Leucas an island; and they transferred Nericus to the place which, though once an isthmus, is now a strait spanned by a bridge, and they changed its name to Leucas.' Though the existence of this Corinthian *canal* (or 'Dioryctus') is vouched for by many ancient authors, its site remains a vexed and rather fascinating question. For the traveller arriving on Lefkas by road today it is natural to assume that 'the isthmus of the Peninsula' is that formed by the sand-spit of the Yiro, and that the Corinthians made their cut through this, somewhere near the castle of Ayia Mavra and the present deep-water canal. But many of the ancient accounts do not tally with such an interpretation. Recounting the Roman siege of 197 B.C., Livy says,

> Leucas is now an island, cut off from Akarnania by a shallow channel dug by hand; then it was a peninsula, joined to Akarnania by a narrow neck of land on its western side; this neck of land was about five hundred paces long and not more than one hundred and twenty paces wide. In this constricted place lay Leucas, clinging to a hill facing the east and Akarnania; the lower parts of the town were flat, lying along the sea which separates Leucadia from Akarnania. On that side it is vulnerable by land and sea, for the shallows are more like a pool than the sea and the whole country is flat and favourable for siege works.

Since Livy accurately describes the site of the ancient city, and since the distance between this and the mainland is here very little more than 'five hundred paces' (while the Yiro is more than five kilometres long), it is reasonable to suppose that the *isthmus* too was here, that it has subsided and that if the Yiro also existed as a barrier two thousand years ago the natural gap between its tip and Akarnania was then navigable. In Livy's time Strabo's *bridge* (probably a work of Augustus) had not yet been built, but its line — exactly opposite the city — is well known, and parts of the causeway leading to the piers which must have supported arches spanning the canal still lie a few feet under the Sea Lake. Goodisson inspected this 'very ancient and interesting ruin' before 1822 and recorded that 'At about the middle of the narrow road leading to the bridge is a little islet, upon which are the foundations of several small square buildings of cut stone, and probably belonging to some little temple, or perhaps it was a sort of toll-house.' This little islet (which was blown up in about 1900 when the canal was deepened) further clinches the position of the canal and therefore the isthmus, at any rate in Roman times. For Dionysius of Halicarnassus, writing in the first century B.C., says that Aeneas and the Trojans landing in Lefkas 'built a temple to Aphrodite, which stands today on the little island between Dioryctus and the city'.

The remains of the perimeter walls of the town lie on the olive-shaded terraces of a gentle hill and not among disheartening scrub and rocks as on Ithaca, Kithira and Cefalonia. So to trace their line — while boats with lateen sails or stout donkey-engines pass up and down beyond the flat meadows below you — is a pleasure and not a sight-seeing duty.

If you walk back a few metres from the Kaligoni corner and take a zigzag path which starts up the hill opposite a track which joins the road from the other side, you will see a fine stretch of wall, built from polygonal blocks, only a little way up, by two small cottages. You can follow this wall up to the top of the hill without any great difficulty, and thence along a ridge for about 0·5 km. until, on a further rise, you reach the base of a tower where Hellenistic and Byzantine stones overlie the early masonry. More Byzantine walls on the east of this rise suggest that it must have been the strongpoint of the Byzantine capital before the Orsinis built Ayia Mavra castle. Though less easy to follow beyond this point, the wall continues along the ridge until after another 0·5 km. you swing left up to a small peak crowned by the bottom courses of a round classical *tower*. From this south-west corner and high point of the ancient city the wall runs down to the road at Spazmeni Vrisi (see below) and out across the flat coastal strip to the sea. Just below the tower is a stretch of wall which Dörpfeld (see p. 196) qualified as the most ancient on the site. It consists of roughly rectangular, almost unworked blocks piled rather than fitted on top of each other.

[3 km.] Back on the road at *Kaligoni*, you can see how a wall also ran out to the sea at the north end of the town; its line is now followed by a water conduit leading to a mill close to the shore. As you continue along the ring road through what is in fact the middle of the town, you will see many shaped blocks of stone in the fields on either side.

[4 km.] *Spazmeni Vrisi* — the 'broken fountain'. The southern limit of the ancient town is marked by a bank which runs down to the sea beside a lane on the left.

[5 km.] A track goes left to the salt-pans of *Alikes*, worth a visit in September to watch the peasant women raking up the salt, or later to see it stored under long tiled roofs, as though of houses which have settled down to their eaves in quicksands. These pans have been producing salt of excellent quality since the Middle Ages. On **Alexandros Island** beyond, formed when the modern canal was dredged through the sand-spit, stands a little *fort* built by the Russians in the early 1800s to counter the threat of Aly Pasha's grandiose construction on the hill across the channel. Named after Tsar Alexander, it is a rare relic of the Russian presence in the Ionian Islands.

The stretch of road between Alikes and Nidri is dotted with new houses advertising rooms to let, often over restaurants. Though in 1980 their number was not oppressive, the speed with which they have gone up in the last few years is an ominous sign for the future of this coast.

[6·5 km.] **Liya**, a fishing hamlet by a jetty on the beach. Hereafter the road runs for 6·5 km. through gentle olive-wooded countryside reminiscent of the east coast of Corfu, with the more open waters of the *bay of Drepano* sparkling on a series of small shingly beaches.

[11 km.] **Nikiana**, a seaside hamlet with a small beach in a pretty olive-wooded site. A kilometre or so after, the road climbs a little to squeeze past the bare toes of *Mt Skaros* and you see the island of Sparti (see below).

[16 km.] **Periyali**, an attractive hamlet from which you can look down on the tiny wooded islet of **Kheloni** — 'turtle'.

[17·5 km.] **Nidri**.

Backed by *Mt Elati* (1,100 metres) to the west and the high hill of *Skaros* (580 metres) to the north, Nidri stands at the outer end of a long fiord — *Vlikho Bay* — protected from the sea by a promontory whose splendid skyline dips hesitantly to a final knoll a few hundred metres across the water from the village. The Ionian Islands possess three surprising inlets — the bays of Vathi, Argostoli and Vlikho — but none is so serene and gentle as the last, its slopes waving with the silver and grey of olives and studded with dark cypress trees, its shallow, pale blue waters ruffled by no rude wind. To the left of the knoll of *Ayia Kiriaki* is the islet of **Madouri** where, like a Palladian temple on an island in an eighteenth-century lake, the house built by the poet Aristotelis Valaoritis (1824–79) presents its elegant pedimented façade embowered in trees. (Valaoritis' works celebrated the Greek struggle against the Turk and the Ionian struggle for independence from Britain). Beyond, are the larger islands of **Sparti** and **Skorpios** (once owned by Aristotle Onassis, who is buried there).

Nidri was for many years the home of the German archaeologist Wilhelm Dörpfeld (1853–1940), who was persuaded that Lefkas was the Homeric Ithaca (see p. 81). He lived in a prefabricated house sent out to him by the Kaiser in 1907 and is buried under a simple stone on the promontory of Ayia Kiriaki. The finds of his many season's digs on the island are now in the archaeological musuem in town. They come chiefly from two grave-plots in the plain, one circular and surrounded by a wall, the other rectangular. Dörpfeld interpreted and dated the finds to agree with his conviction that Nidri was the site of Odysseus' capital, but modern archaeologists put them many hundred years before the traditional date of the siege of Troy.

Nidri's main street is the most cosmopolitan in the island: discos, boutiques, car-hire offices, travel agencies and restaurants all give it the unmistakable stamp of the miniature package tour resort which it has become in the last few years.

Excursions from Nidri

From Nidri you can catch a daily caique to near-by Meganisi, a wonderfully unspoilt island with untouched coves and beaches but virtually no facilities for visitors.

At the southern end of Nidri a road on the right will take you in 2·5 km. to **Paleokatouna** in the foothills behind the plain, and then by steep, rough zigzags a further 2·5 km. up to **Neokhori** for a magnificent view over the plain, the village, the north end of Vlikho Bay, the Nidri islands and across the sea to the distant mainland scarp with its runnels of white scree.

Beyond Nidri the road continues across the plain past orange groves and vines, and then through a splendid forest of olives.

[21 km.] **Vlikho** is a boat-building village at the foot of sloping rockstrata which reminded Goodisson of 'a half-fallen pack of cards'. Small cargo steamers tie up in the deep water which comes up to the long quayside road.

[22·5 km.] A rough road on the left forks left after 1 km. to run round Vlikho Bay to Dörpfeld's grave at Ayia Kiriaki, and right to Desimo Bay where there is a camping site with all the usual facilities, including a restaurant, behind a splendid beach. After this turn the main road begins to climb, and there are lovely views back over the apparently landlocked fiord where white egrets stalk the shallows.

[26 km.] At the saddle a road forks left to **Poros** 2·5 km. away; it runs round the top of a valley which looks south to Rouda Bay, and frames Arkoudi (Dörpfeld's Asteris), Ithaca and Cefalonia in its arms. If you climb for 10 minutes up the steep cemented paths from the middle of Poros towards the *church* which stands by an outcrop of rock on the spur due south of you, pass to the left of it and walk for another 10 minutes round the corner of the hill, you will come to the remains of a *tower* of the fourth century B.C., one corner of which still stands some 4·5 metres high. Beyond it, among the olives, the cypresses and the ploughed terraces, are the bottom courses of substantial buildings, ancient millstones and cisterns, which suggest a Hellenistic olive-press. 500 metres back along the road from Poros to the saddle you can take a snaking earth road which runs down for 1·5 km. through a delightful jumble of grey rocks and thickets of cypresses to the long pebble and shingle beach of Rouda Bay (also known as Poros beach) where there is a camping site, bungalows and a restaurant.

[28 km.] Continuing along the ring road from the saddle, you come to a right fork, signposted to Sivros, which leads in just over 6·5 km. to the *Monastery of Ayos Ioannis sto Rodaki*, built on the foundations of a Doric temple. (Having turned off, go left at the next fork.) The road traverses the maquis-covered skirt of Mt Elati for a while, then swings round a spur guarded by a little chapel into the Sivros valley. 4 km. from the ring road a rather hidden track leads off left (less alarming than it looks) and brings you in under 3 km. to a knoll where the monastery stands among two or three fine ilexes looking over the Vasiliki plain to Ayos Petros. The monastery buildings (eighteenth century and ruined by earthquakes) are of no interest, but in the courtyard are numbers of fine blocks of ancient stone, and the north wall of the chapel itself, built on the site of the *cella* or inner temple, contains two or three courses of the original wall. Let into the outer wall of the apse are fragments of Doric and Ionic or Corinthian column, while inside in the sanctuary are two Doric column drums, and a Doric capital forms the top of the altar. The wall-paintings in the apse are early-seventeenth century, the others eighteenth. Dörpfeld, who partly excavated the site in the 1900s, says that the temple was bigger than the Theseion in Athens or the Temple of Poseidon at Sounion. Its dedication is unknown but is ascribed to Demeter since in the nineteenth century farmers still used to bring their ploughshares to be blessed in the monastery church.

From where the track turns down to Ayos Ioannis the road continues to the hill-village of **Sivros** just over 1·5 km. away. Here the women collect water from the fountain in round-bottomed copper basins called *pinyátes* which they balance gracefully on their heads. From Sivros you can climb 5·5 km. by a metalled road to the mountain village of **Ayos Ilias**, an attractive drive with magnificent views, though the village itself is uninteresting; or follow the tarred road down to a bridge over a rushing stream and then skirt the plain by a rough route which rejoins the ring road just outside the Vasiliki (see below).

[31 km.] Continuing along the ring road you come to a road on the left which leads down in 2 km. to **Sivota**, a fishing hamlet with an eating place but with nothing else to recommend it except its astonishing landlocked bay — a wonderful haven for yachtsmen.

Dörpfeld believed this was the Bay of Phorcys where Odysseus was put ashore by the Phaeacians (*Odyssey*, Book 13).

[32 km.] Another lane— slanting left up the hill— will bring you through the top of **Marandokhori** (a split-level village) and, in just over 1·5 km., to the small village of **Evyiros**. It hangs above a large fertile 'sump' over whose seaward edge you can see Cefalonia and Ithaca. From here— with a villager to show the way— it is 5 minutes' walk down to the *cave of Khirospilia*, where Dörpfeld found Late Neolithic tools and pottery from habitation levels dating to the third and second millennia; the finds are in the archaeological museum in town. Apart from its archaeological significance the cave is dull.

Back on the ring road, you drive through the bottom of Marandokhori and the village of **Kondarena**, with a plane-shaded fountain.

[38·5 km.] Having climbed a ridge you pass a right fork to Sivros. The first 4 km. of this rough side road make an attractive wooded drive or walk past two strange hummocks like huge tumuli on one of which Goodisson found the remains of a portico and 'many square blocks of stone'. These and the 'fragments of cyclopean walls' he saw nearer the sea are no longer visible and are not mentioned by Dörpfeld. But they lend credence to Leake's suggestion that the plain of Vasiliki may be the site of the city of Pherae, described by Scylax (fifth century B.C.?) as being opposite Ithaca.

[39·5 km.] **Vasiliki**.
With its saffron- and cyclamen-coloured fishing-nets hung out to dry along a stone quay shaded by plane and eucalyptus trees, and some very prettily coloured half-timbered houses, the village of Vasiliki is the most attractive in the island. There are about 120 rooms and, in summer, four restaurants. Beyond the harbour a sea-walk leads to a rebuilt church in a grove of plane trees, and here and farther back water gushes from perennial springs. Good bathing is to be had from pebble coves 10 minutes' walk beyond the church (where a new B class hotel was being built in 1980) and from the huge sand and shingle beach which runs across the bottom of the plain. This plain is the largest and richest in the island. Planted with maize, clover, vines, vegetables, corn, olives and fruit trees, it is watered in winter by two torrents, and in summer by artesian wells. To the north the slopes of *Mt Stavrotas* rise in one long

upward sweep to its summit at 1,145 metres; this unbroken wall of mountain with the unexpected size of the plain gives the valley a continental scale and grandeur which you meet elsewhere in the Ionian Islands only on Cefalonia. To the south the arms of the bay frame Ithaca and the Fiskardo peninsula of Cefalonia — huge blue-grey backs emerging from the sea.

From Vasiliki it is just over 7 km. along the ring road to the large village of Ayos Petros, halfway up the ridge on the far side of the plain, and another 7 km. to the left turn to Komilio and Sappho's Leap (see Route 3).

Route 2: Lefkas to Karia

Karia (15 km.) is a hill-village on the edge of a tremendous hollow in the middle of the island. Behind it you can take your car up a further 300 metres or so into the mountains for a series of spectacular views. The late Byzantine Chapel of the Odiyitria is worth stopping for at the beginning of the route if arrangements to visit it can be made with the caretaker of the Archaeological Museum.

Route Leave Lefkas by Exit C on the town plan and take the right fork 1·5 km. out. This is the beginning of the westward-running ring road. Fork right at Lazarata [10·5 km.] and left at Asproyerakata [12 km.].
Bus There is a day-return service to Karia.
Accommodation and Restaurants The inn at Karia is a *pandokhíon* and should be used only in emergencies; but there are two eating-places in the main square.

[3 km.] From the third hairpin bend after the end of the flat olive forest, you will see on your right the deserted and half-ruined *Monastery of the Panayia Odiyitria*, founded in 1450 by Heleni Palaeologina, the mother-in-law of Leonardo Tocco III. Built of cream-coloured stone set off by courses of tile, the small damaged *chapel* is the only surviving Byzantine building on the island. It is architecturally interesting because, though constructed in these traditional Byzantine materials, its basilica plan is, at this late date, purely Western. The fine contemporary *wall-paintings* in the apse have recently been restored and, like the building itself, are in a style halfway between Italian and Greek.

From the convent you wind up for 8 km. by spurs and valleys covered with cypresses and olives to the group of villages known as Sfakhiotes, traditionally settled by Cretans after Morosini's recapture of the island in 1684. It is worth stopping more than once on the way up to look back at varying angles and from different heights to the Sea Lake, with the great elbow of the Yiro running out to the castle and enclosing the western lagoon, the causeway arrowing across the shallow-coloured water, the dikes protecting the deep-water canal from the silt of the eastern lagoon, and — beyond the castle — Aly Pasha's little fortress and the Akarnanian hills. Immediately below you lies a land-lagoon of olives, its unruffled surface broken only by the cypresses of the cemetery.

[10·5 km.] At **Lazarata**, the first of the Sfakhiot villages, you fork right and drive along a narrow cultivated plain. Vineyards run right up to the brows of the hills on either side, and in the middle of October you will see big baskets of osier and split calamus-reed full of grapes by the sides of the roads. These are collected by lorries and taken first to a weighing station, so that each individual peasant's contribution can be recorded, and then to a co-operative wine-press. The houses in the string of villages which flank the road are generally of roughly quarried stone with dressed-stone arches over the wide doorways of the stable undercrofts.

[12 km.] At the end of the valley, past three or four fine old plane trees round the well of **Asproyerakata**, you should fork left. (The right-hand fork leads to the west coast and Sappho's Leap — see Route 3.) Keeping to the right at the next fork you drive through the attractive terraced village of **Pigadisani** on the edge of the most spectacular of the Ionian 'sumps' — the huge sunken *valley of Livadi* — whose flat-bottom lands are broken by hillocks crowned with abandoned windmills and become a shallow lake in winter. There is something very strange about the way in which one's eye has to switchback down into this great sink, up over its eastern rim, down to the sea beyond, and up again to the distant barrier of the Akarnanian hills.

[15 km.] A road leads off to the right by which you can climb for 7 km. to a fork where signs mark the limit of a forbidden telecommunications station. Annoying though it is not to be able to explore the prohibited peaks, before the huge communicative dishes were installed near the summits of *Mt Meganoros* (1,010 metres) and *Mt Ayos Ilias* one had to climb for hours on foot for the extraordinary views to the north and east which one can now enjoy in minutes. In 1872 Murray described the view from the hill of Skaros — much lower down to the east on the other side of the Livadi — as 'one of the finest prospects of Greece'; and though reason cries out that this is pitching praise too high it is impossible to be dully reasonable when confronted with the hills and inlets, mountains and lagoons which stretch away to Preveza and the Gulf of Arta in an enchanted mystery of water, land and sky.

Beyond the fork to the summit the tarred road continues for 0·8 km. to a military camp. From here a very rough and narrow track crosses the hummocky and eroded plateau and winds 4 km. steeply down to the cottages and orchards of Englouvi (see below), a welcome contrast to the Dr Strangelove installations above.

[15·5 km.] **Karia**.
This is the largest village on the island. But once you have refreshed yourself in the cool air of its *platía*, deliciously shaded by plane trees and surrounded by cafés, you will have exhausted all its possibilities unless you happen to arrive there on 11th or 12th August, when a festival in honour of St Spiridon is held.

Excursions from Karia

Beyond Karia the road is negotiable for a further 7 km. to **Englouvi**, a village tucked into a niche of the mountains behind Nidri and under the cone of Mt Ayos Ilias. The 11-km. circuit of the Livadi sump — down from the Englouvi road to Platistoma and then through Alexandros and back to Lazarata — is confusing and in parts very rough.

Route 3: Lefkas to Sappho's Leap

According to Menander (342–291 B.C.), 'Sappho is said to have been the first to fling herself with a leap from the far-seen rock' (Strabo, Book 10) at the south-west tip of Lefkas. It is fifty-five kilometres away and not an easy place to get to, but once there your reward will be solitude, white cliffs, indigo sea, the scent of junipers, and — if you let your imagination loose — a cry of despair, a flutter of wings, a splash and the echo of panicking oars.

Route Leave Lefkas by Exit C on the town plan. Follow Route 2 as far as Asproyerakata and there fork right. 3 km. beyond Khortata [28·5 km.] fork right on to a rough road which runs through Komilio [32 km.] and Dragano [36 km.]. If you have a small car and can negotiate the narrow, steep and rough passage between the houses here you can drive on for 16 km. by a rough track to the lighthouse at the end of the peninsula and the

Leap itself. It is not an expedition to undertake as an afterthought on your way round the island. Between the turn-off to Komilio and Vasiliki the ring road is being remade, and only one short stretch of the 14·5 km. is tarred.

[12 km.] **Asproyerakata**. Forking right, you climb up the south side of a deep cleft — the first of three which cut into the island's long western massif — and look down the V-sight of the valley to the distant sea. A little later, rounding the shoulder of the range towards the south, you will suddenly glimpse — a surprising distance below you — a valley full of olives folded from the sea by a low coastal ridge, a few rooftops, and a glitter of white sand: Ayos Nikitas. Tricked by the flat interval of the Sfakhiotes plain, one does not realize how high one has climbed: here and as far as Khortata the road runs at between 460 and 600 metres.

[18·5 km.] A road forks right into the village of **Kato Exanthia** (or **Drimonas**) built round an amphitheatrical valley hidden by the hillside ahead of you. From here a very steep and stony road goes down to Ayos Nikitas, 8 km. below you on the coast (see Route 4).

[20 km.] A second road leads down to Kato Exanthia, now visible from above. The limestone pebbles of the steep hillside vineyards here are as white as chalk.

[22·5 km.] **Ano Exanthia**, the next village, is tucked into the armpit of *Mt Meganoros* (1,010 metres), whose steep grey screes rise straight up from the road on your left. Like the other hamlets along this route it is scruffy but picturesque, with cottages clinging to the hillside among quince and almond and cherry trees.

[25 km.] 0·8 km. beyond a second deep eroded valley you pass a right fork to **Kalamitsi**, whose sheets of almond blossom are worth driving 3 km. or so to look down on in February. 1·5 km. farther on you round a corner to find a third and last great valley ahead; this turns out to run both west to the sea and east to the plain of Vasiliki and thus divides the long Lefkatas peninsula from *Mt Stavrotas* (1,145 metres), the culmination of the massif along which you have been driving and the highest mountain on the island.

[28 km.] **Khortata** is the last of these west-coast villages perched high on the afternoon-baked mountainside with nothing to break the huge dazzle of sea but the blue shapes of Paxos and Antipaxos.

[31 km.] Across the narrow saddle which spans the valley below Khortata you reach a right turn to Komilio. This is the route to Sappho's Leap. If you follow the ring road straight on, it is 7 km. down to Ayos Petros and another 7 km. to Vasiliki — see Route 1 — a long, rough but beautiful descent above 'a landscape which for richness and beauty of scenery is hardly to be exceeded in any country' (Goodisson).

[32 km.] **Komilio**. From the plain of Vasiliki the *Lefkatas peninsula* looks like a bare and uninviting ridge; but as you drive south from Komilio it turns out to be scooped and runnelled by a narrow and well-planted valley.

[36 km.] **Dragano**. Below this village the olive groves have collected in dark and silent pools which are prevented from spilling out over the cliffs by a dam of rising ground.

[38·5 km.] **Athani**, whose wine is one of the best on the island and whose cliffside-tethered sheep are as famous for their flavour in Lefkas as Brittany's *prés-salés* in France.

[50 km.] *Ayos Nikolaos Niras*, a chapel off the road to the left. From here the track winds up and down over the knobs in the undulating tail of the island to the final hump of the promontory, at first through thickets of lentisc and arbutus and then through dense and fragrant junipers. From the top of the slope to your right the white cliffs from which Lefkas (like Albion) takes its name plunge vertiginously down into blue-black water.

[55 km.] *Sappho's Leap*
At the end of the peninsula, according to Strabo, stood 'the temple of Apollo Leucatas, and also the "Leap".'
   It is impossible to say with certainty whether this Leap took place from the cliff-top where the lighthouse now stands or from the higher hump to the north of it. From the vestigial remains which he found on both sites Dörpfeld deduced that the remains of the temple must lie almost exactly under the lighthouse. (One or two of its foundation stones lie on the slope to the south, rolled out of the way of the new building.) If so, it seems possible that the few stones on the higher hump are part of a ritual launching-pad. For the Leap was an annual spectacle. Strabo says,

It was an ancestral custom among the Leucadians, every year at the sacrifice performed in honour of Apollo, for some criminal to be flung from this rocky look-out for the sake of averting evil, wings and birds of all kinds being fastened to him, since by their fluttering they could lighten the leap, and also for a number of men, stationed all round below the rock in small fishing-boats, to take the victim in, and when he had been taken on board, to do all in their power to get him safely outside their borders.

The crowds who must have come to witness this scapegoat cere-mony would have seen the full drama only if they were looking back at the higher cliff from the temple platform.

The remoteness of this place is such that Ithaca and Cefalonia across the water to the south seem nearer than the north of Lefkas, and a tourist ship frothing past at least three thousand years away.

Route 4: Lefkas to Ayos Nikitas

Ayos Nikitas (12 km.) is a fishing hamlet at the end of a long curve of sand, the first of a string of magnificent but otherwise inaccessible beaches which stretch almost unbroken under the western cliffs of Lefkas as far south as Athani. The seaside hamlet of Ayos Ioannis (3 km.), off the road to Ayos Nikitas, boasts an Angevin chapel.

Route Leave Lefkas by Exit B on the town plan.
Accommodation and Restaurants About 40 rooms and two eating places at Ayos Nikitas.

As you leave the town, you pass through the suburb of *Neapolis*. Here, after the 1948 earthquake, new houses were fitted into the existing grid-plan of old olive trees, and the householders sitting out in this forest garden used to look as though they were taking part in a never-ending *fête champêtre*. Now most of the trees have been cut down for yet more houses and the suburb is as characterless as any other.

[1·5 km.] At a white roadside chapel an untarred road leads in 1·5 km. to a turning-place about 100 metres from the village of Ayos Ioannis. As you walk into it from the turning-place, the *Chapel of Ayos Ioannis Andzousis* is on your left. Its name is probably a corruption of the 'Angevins' who built it in the first quarter of the fourteenth century. Its barrel-vaulted nave is shaped under a solid rock roof, and there is a tradition that the first Christian church in the island was earlier built in the same cave. The only thing of note now is the highly formalized *double-headed eagles* carved on a tombstone in front of the screen. From Ayos Ioannis you can climb down to the beginning of the long beach which sweeps all the way up the Yiro. In summer the owners of the nail-and-driftwood huts along the beach move out with a mattress, a plastic water-bottle and some food and sit in their pyjama trousers enjoying the breeze.

Beyond the turn to Ayos Ioannis the road climbs up past Frini to a scarp where the uninteresting post-earthquake church of the island's most notable monastery, Faneromeni, has a fine view back over the Sea Lake.

[5·6 km.] **Tsoukalades**, once a 'potter's' village, hidden in the rich olive groves of the plateau. From here the road winds down by a route sliced through steep pine-forested slopes to the beginning of the long beach which ends at Ayos Nikitas.

[12 km.] **Ayos Nikitas**. Until 1980, when the new coast road was finished, it was 26·5 km. to Ayos Nikitas, eight of them down a very stony track from the mountains: and the crumbling, untidy and neglected hamlet has not yet had time to transform itself into the tourist resort which its position seems to dictate. How long will it be before the still dazed and not very friendly villagers are tempted to sell to developers parcels of the very attractive olive grove which runs back in a fold of ground sheltered from the sea? A rough road runs up this little valley, and where it turns left to climb to Kato Exanthia and Kalamitsi (p. 203), a bulldozed track goes right over the low coastal ridge and down to other splendid and deserted beaches.

ITHACA (ITHAKI)

Ithaca (*i Itháki*) lies parallel to and only three or four kilometres away from the long northern promontory of Cefalonia. With an area of 90 square kilometres (not counting the scattered Ekhinades Islands), it is the sixth largest of the Ionian Islands and in 1971 had a population of 6,318. It is 27 km. long, and nowhere more than 6·5 km. from east to west. Its capital is also officially called *Ithaki* but is commonly known as *Vathi*; in 1971 it had 2,257 inhabitants.

INFORMATION FOR VISITORS

Information
The Town Hall (*Map* 4) (tel. 32795) do what they can to help, but mostly in Greek.
Post Office
Map 9.
Cable Office
Map 8.
Clinic
Map 11.
An unsigned wooden bungalow with a red corrugated-iron roof about 300 metres up on the left of the road to Arethusa's Fountain.
Feast-Day
August 15th (Assumption of the Virgin). Morning Service in the Kathara Convent, evening feasting and dancing in Vathi.
Festival
Modern Theatrical Festival every other year in August.

GETTING TO ITHACA

Sea

Car Ferries
From Patras via Sami on Cefalonia: Every day the *Kefallinia*, starting at Patras at 13.30 goes on to Ithaca from Sami at about 17.30 and stops the night at Vathi. Journey time: From Sami to Vathi, about 1 hour; from Patras to Vathi about 6 hours.

Every other day between June and September the *Ionis*, starting at 21.00, goes on to Ithaca from Sami at 00.30 on its way to Brindisi. Journey time: 4½ hours.
From Brindisi via Corfu and Paxos: Every other day between June and September the *Ionis*, leaving at 23.00, goes on to Ithaca from Corfu at 07.30 and from Paxos at 09.15. Journey time: 13½ hours.

Road

From Athens via Corinth to Patras: total distance 222 km.

Bus

From Athens: The K.T.E.L. buses for Ithaca are the same as those for Cefalonia (see p. 225). Since these buses drive straight on to Argostoli from Sami you should take your luggage off them when you embark at Patras and keep it by you on the ferry.

Train

From Athens: Seven trains (S.E.K.) a day to Patras. Journey time 4 to 5 hours. (The Cefalonia/Ithaca car ferry berth in Patras is about 0·5 km. from the railway station.)

TRANSPORT ON THE ISLAND

Buses

For general information about island buses see p. 22. There is one useful day-return service as far as Kioni, and two to Perakhori.

Caique

A caique comes in every day from Kioni to meet the ferry.

Taxis

There are about 16 hire-cars on the island, half based on the main square of Vathi, the remainder on Perakhori and villages in North Ithaca.

Scooter and bicycle hire

Scooters from D. Kanellos (tel. 32035) behind the main water-front square; bicycles from S. Refalas close to the Town Hall.

ACCOMMODATION AND RESTAURANTS

Vathi

B Class   *Mentor*. Open all year. 36 rooms in three-floor water-front block. Breakfast obligatory. Central heating. Sea visible from all balconies. A class restaurant.

Odysseus. Open all year. 10 rooms in two-floor water-
front block, most facing the sea. A class restaurant.

Villas

The Greek Islands Club (see p. 115) have a few villas at Kioni.

Rooms in private houses

The number of rooms available in 1980 was approximately as
follows: 250 in Vathi, 60 in Kioni, 50 in Perakhori, 12 in Stavros
and 12 in Frikes.

Restaurants

There are three restaurants and a grilled-chicken place in the centre
of Vathi, and summer eating places by the town bathing beaches, at
Perakhori and at Dexia (Excursions). For restaurants in the country
see the Route Instructions.

SPORT

Bathing

Vathi: There are two or three small beaches near the outlet of Vathi
Bay. Though the shingle is sticky with oil and the water far from
clear, any bathing is better than none on a hot day. In summer,
motor-boats ply to these beaches from the quayside near the main
square, or you can reach them by the water-side road along the east
side of the bay. Loutsa, the farthest, is 2·5 km.

Elsewhere: Sand and shingle at Sarakiniko (see p. 213) shingle at
Ayos Ioannis (see p. 219), pebbles at Piso Aetos (p. 218), Polis Bay
(p. 221) and between Frikes and Kioni (p. 223) and deep water at
Frikes (p. 223) and Polis Bay.

INTRODUCTION TO ITHACA

There are two versions of Ithaca, one poetry, one prose. The prose
version makes poor reading, for Ithaca is an island in decline. Since
1900 emigration and seafaring have drained it of youth and energy
and its present small population is largely middle-aged. Some are
remittance-men back from the States who can at last afford to rule
the coffee-house roost and put up their wickerwork shoes. Others,
after a lifetime at sea, have at last returned like Du Bellay's hero

'vivre entre ses parents le reste de son âge'. A few still struggle to carry on the old back-breaking ritual of olive, corn and vine; but with no young hands to help it is a losing battle, and many a once grape-laden terrace is now overgrown with scrub. Ithaca has none of the assets which can turn an agriculturally intractable island into an idle pleasure-ground for tourists; its bathing is indifferent, its roads steep or rough, its terrain austere (apart from three valleys), and its accommodation modest and old-fashioned. Its archeological remains are insignificant and its Homeric topography is disputed by scholars and archaeologists alike.

The poetic version of the island is as rich as the imagination of each traveller. For the name of Ithaca — a knapped flint of a name — has become a talisman and is now so old and rubbed by credulous hands that in its glassy core you can see ancient peoples moving, sun glinting on bronze, water and oars. Reason is powerless against the magic of this name, and as you climb the long hill-walks by steep goat-tracks the arguments of scholars are drowned by the sound of goat-bells and the scent of thyme. This high and narrow land, dreaming beside a sunlit street of water, may — like Odysseus himself in Plato's Myth of Er — have renounced ambition and become the home of ordinary men, but around its empty bays its former master's words still echo: 'My home is under the clear skies of Ithaca. Our landmark is the wooded peak of wind-swept Neriton. For neighbours we have many-peopled isles with no great space between them, Dulichium and Same and wooded Zacynthus.' (*Odyssey*, Book 9.)

VATHI (ITHAKI)

Nothing so becomes Vathi as one's first mysterious landfall. By the time you have left Sami in the late afternoon and are thrumming up the wild and uninhabited east coast of Ithaca the sun will have dropped far enough to drag all the hot-blooded colours of the day over to the other side of the island, and though a sudden burst of sun-fire may still dazzle you out to sea, inland the summer shooting-war is over. The hazy pennants of light which stream over the saddle of Aetos and the higher Cefalonian ridge of Erissos behind are those of a departing multitude, and when you turn in to the huge fiord of the Gulf of Molos it will be as desolate as a recently-filled arena, with empty tiers of mountainside presiding over dark and silent water. There is no sign of a port, and not a

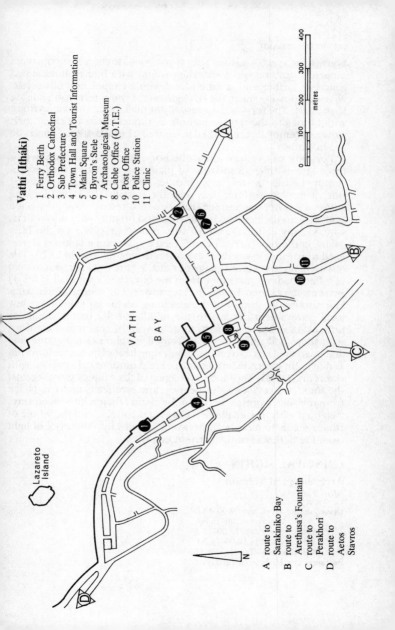

Vathí (Itháki)

1 Ferry Berth
2 Orthodox Cathedral
3 Sub Prefecture
4 Town Hall and Tourist Information
5 Main Square
6 Byron's Stele
7 Archaeological Museum
8 Cable Office (O.T.E.)
9 Post Office
10 Police Station
11 Clinic

VATHI

BAY

Lazareto
Island

N

A route to
   Sarakiniko Bay
B route to
   Arethusa's Fountain
C route to
   Perakhori
D route to
   Aetos
   Stavros

metres

0   100   200   300   400

house to be seen. And then your ferry swings to the left and through a narrow gut you see a sparkling sound with houses horseshoed round its farther end, a little island with a chapel, and olive trees alive and glowing still in the last light on the warm terracotta hillside to the east. The ferry ties up casually at the kerb of the water-front, with houses to the right — its bulk as thoughtlessly blocking their view as a removals van parked in front of a bijou cottage — and you are in Vathi.

For most of the way round the horseshoe Vathi is only two or three streets thick, a mixture of plain and attractive nineteenth-century houses and less happy post-earthquake buildings. The east side of the bay suffered less than the west in 1953, and looking across the water one can see from two or three pale colour-washed houses, with their curved biscuit-tiles and brigh'ly painted shutters, why Murray called the town 'very pretty' in 1900. To the little island in the bay (first a prison, then a quarantine station) Byron used to row out every day for a swim during his visit in 1823. The town's main street is the quayside road. Where this kinks out to take in a flat quadrant reclaimed from the bay, the Town Hall (*Map* 4) presents its odd neo-Bavarian clock-tower. The central *platia* (*Map* 5) lies round the corner of the quadrant, on the far side of the new local government offices. In the middle of the day it would be difficult to imagine a square more devoid of charm and comfort, with shops and cafés like glass-fronted warehouses along one side and not a single tree to relieve the sizzling heat of its concrete apron. But at night it is transformed into a great outdoor café decked with chairs and tables. The laddered rigging of the caiques sways against the stars; waiters like water-beetles skim erratically up to and back from invisible frontiers between the chairs, their white-metal trays freighted with frosted glasses, cakes and coffees; and the whole of Ithaca seems to have been drawn like moths into this pool of light from the darkness of the surrounding island.

PRINCIPAL SIGHTS

Archaeological Museum
Map 7.

Open *Summer* Weekdays 09.00–15.00
                 Sundays 10.00–16.00
      Winter Weekdays 10.00–15.30
                 Sundays 10.00–16.30
    N.B. Closed on Tuesdays and holidays.
Entrance: Drs 25. Free on Sundays.

This new building houses finds made in South Ithaca, chiefly at Aetos in the 'thirties. The collection of proto-Corinthian pottery (eighth to sixth centuries B.C.) is one of the largest and most varied anywhere and thus of particular interest to archaeologists and scholars. But you do not have to be a scholar to admire the grace of some of these pots and the extraordinary fertility of their designs. There are also objects in bone and ivory, coins, and a large number of small bronzes, particularly of horses.

A few metres east of the museum a stele in the town's war-memorial courtyard commemorates Byron's visit in August 1823. It carries an emotional but nevertheless typically lordly quotation: 'If this island belonged to me I would bury all my books here and never go away.'

Excursions from Vathi

CAVE OF THE NYMPHS, MT AETOS AND PISO AETOS

See Route 1 (4 km., 5 km. and 6·5 km.).

SARAKINIKO

On the east coast of the promontory which encloses Vathi Bay are numbers of attractive bathing coves. Most of them can be reached only by boat, but to the most sheltered of them, Sarakiniko, there is a road.

Route Leave Vathi by Exit A on the town plan. Fork left a few hundred metres out and follow the concrete road up to the ridge (1·5 km.) and the rough road down to the second cove (1·5 km.).

Two coves of white pebbles, sand a little way out to sea, brilliant blue water and shady olive trees used to make Sarakiniko a delight-ful place for a bathing picnic. But a community of about 100 young Germans, who have bought the land at the second cove and hope to live off it, have rather changed the scene with their beds of lettuces, tents, laundry and parked minibuses. The name Sarakiniko (or variations of it) is common in the Ionian Islands and records either the raids of North African Saracens in the eighteenth century, when Venice's naval power was in decline, or earlier Arab piracy. During late Byzantine and medieval times Ithaca was often virtually taken over by pirates of one nationality or another.

ARETHUSA'S FOUNTAIN

Since Gell (p. 81) first 'identified' it in 1806, a spring at a place called Perapigadi has come to be associated with Arethusa's Fountain (5 km. and 20 minutes on foot), where Eumaeus watered his pigs (*Odyssey*, Book 13).

Route Leave Vathi by Exit B on the town plan, signposted to Arethusa's Fountain. 5 km. out, park your car on the ridge from which you can first see the sea to the south-east. Take the path which strikes left down the hillside 50 metres beyond the bend on the ridge, and traverse the slope in a south-easterly direction, rounding two spurs. The untarred road is one of the worst in the island and the path no more than a foot-trace.

The valley behind Vathi is the largest reasonably flat space in the island and is well planted with vines and olives; but cultivation stops abruptly as you reach the ridge, a sharp maquis-covered shoulder-blade which slants down eastward to a coast as indented as a piece of jigsaw puzzle.

As the footpath from the ridge rounds the second spur you will come to a narrow gorge overhung with wild olive, myrtle and kermes oak and echoing with the cries and wing-beats of birds. On your right the gorge narrows to a cleft, and enough water drips into a ledge formed by the rather remarkable strata of shaly rock for hornets, bees and wasps to drink at. High above is a line of creamy-white cliff stained with red — the Homeric Korax or 'Ravens' Crag'. The spring or 'fountain' itself emerges from a small hole in a slope of scree a few metres to the right of the cleft. It could be cleared. When Gell was here he saw 'a cavity penetrating about ten feet into the mountain, probably made by art at some distant period, and containing a reservoir of excellent water, collected in drops from the roof and sides of the grotto'. What water there is today would hardly quench the thirst of one young pig; but those who believe that the *Odyssey* is a factual record of events can comfort themselves with the thought that in the Late Bronze Age oak forests must have retained the winter's rains and increased the spring's flow. Though the remains of the two stone dams which are now covered by fallen rocks below the cleft both seem quite modern, they suggest how 'deep pools' could have been filled by winter torrents and kept topped up by the fountain in summer. As to the difficulty of watering some 360 boars and 600 sows in litter, all folded several hundred steep feet above on the plateau of Marathia, Bronze Age pigs were small and agile and quite unlike the ponderous and specially bred animals of today. Travellers without any strong interest in Homeric topography may find the place rather disappointing. Though there is a certain grandeur about the cliffs above the spring and the gorge below, not every present-day visitor will agree with Byron's verdict (recorded in 1823) that the site would 'alone be worth the voyage' from Cefalonia to Ithaca.

From the bend where you left your car the road continues for 1·2 km. to the red-soiled plateau of *Marathia*, inhabited by one solitary goatherd. If you arrive very early in the morning you can watch this contemporary Eumaeus milk his stone-corralled herds, their coats clipped *en pelisse*, their necks encircled by collars of bent and whittled holm-oak. When you have watched goats pent up like this together and listened to their groans of lust and squeals of jealous rage you will quickly see why the satyr was given his goat-like form.

PERAKHORI

Perakhori (4 km.) is near Palaiokhora, the former capital of the island and one of three hamlets which sprang up after the resettlement of 1503.

Route Leave Vathi by Exit C on the town plan. The untarred right fork a few hundred metres outside the town is a steep short cut if you are walking.
Accommodation and Restaurants About 50 rooms and 2 summer *kendros*.

Though there is nothing much to see in Perakhori, it is about 300 metres above the summer heat of Vathi and a pleasant place to walk to late in the afternoon. At the top of the village you can sit in the shade of *Mt Merovigli* (690 metres) and look down on the valley and a corner of the town. The masts of the caiques will still be in sunlight, and over the top of the promontory which shuts Vathi off from the open sea the Ekhinades Islands and the mainland lie in an apricot-coloured evening haze. Cocks crow; donkeys bray; the waspish buzz of a motor-scooter comes up from the town below; and you will not have to sit here long before you hear a woman's strident voice calling 'Tilemakhos!' or 'Pinelopi!'

Beyond the village a rough road continues for 2·5 km. to the uninteresting *Taxiarkhis Monastery* on the plateau, an attractive walk. On the way down from Perakhori, if you fork left at the first hairpin below the *kendros* and then fork right off this concrete road behind a church, a signed path will lead you in ten minutes to the ruined village of Palaiokhora, the original capital, on a site commanding the bay.

ROUTES ON ITHACA

Ithaca's very simple road-system is covered in one route between South and North Ithaca (see the map on p. 217). Places of interest in the north are described in a series of excursions from Stavros.

Route 1: Vathi to Stavros

North Ithaca is in many ways more sympathetic than the south, with several small villages scattered around a fertile valley, bays facing east and west and north, and a more Homeric feel. The route to Stavros (17 km.), its capital, makes a spectacular drive, and there are detours to the 'Cave of the Nymphs', to an ancient town on Mt Aetos, and to beaches below the village of Ayos Ioannis.

Route Leave Vathi by Exit D on the town plan.
Bus See p. 208.
Caique See p. 208.
Accommodation and Restaurants Rooms in Stavros (20), Frikes (20) and Kioni (60), where there are also villas; restaurants in all three villages; and a beach taverna on the Bay of Dexia.

[1·5 km.] A metalled road on the left leads in 2·5 km. to the *'Cave of the Nymphs'*. A signed path which starts on the left of the turning-place (as you face the hill) will take you to its narrow doorway in two minutes. A small antechamber leads by iron steps to the main chamber, dimly lit by a cleft in the roof. You will need a powerful torch to get down safely and to make out the one fine columnar stalagmite. Though it corresponds well enough to the description in the *Odyssey* (Book 13) — as do a great many caves in Greece — this 'Cave of the Nymphs' is much farther from the sea than Homer suggests, and one does not envy Odysseus the task of lugging his bronze tripod-cauldrons and other presents up to it. It is a fairly recent addition to Ithaca's topographical folklore, and nothing about it is as suggestive as Gell's brief account of the vanished cave of Dexia (see below) or the archaeological finds in the cave of Polis (see p. 221).

[2·5 km.] The horseshoe-shaped *bay of Dexia* on the right is now sign-posted Bay of Phorkys; Gell was the first to identify it with the harbour where Odysseus was beached by the Phaeacians (*Odyssey*, Book 13). In 1806 there were the remains of a cave at sea-level

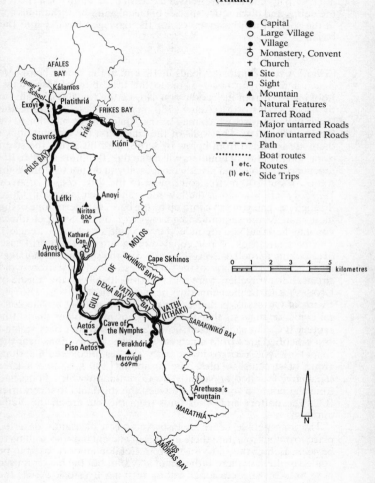

Route Map of Ithaca
(Itháki)

- ● Capital
- ○ Large Village
- ● Village
- ☉ Monastery, Convent
- † Church
- ■ Site
- □ Sight
- ▲ Mountain
- ⌒ Natural Features
- ▬▬ Tarred Road
- ═══ Major untarred Roads
- ≡≡≡ Minor untarred Roads
- - - - Path
- ·········· Boat routes
- 1 etc. Routes
- (1) etc. Side Trips

AFÁLES BAY

Homer's School

Kálamos

Exoyí

Platithriá

FRÍKES BAY

Stavrós

Fríkes

Kióni

PÓLIS BAY

1

Léfki

Anoyí

Níritos
806 m

Kathará Con.

MÓLOS

Áyos
Ioánnis

1

SKHÍNOS BAY

Cape Skhínos

GULF OF

DEXIÁ BAY

VATHÍ BAY

VATHÍ
(ITHÁKI)

SARAKINIKÓ BAY

Aetós

Cave of
the Nymphs

Píso Aetós

1

Perakhóri

Merovígli
669m

Arethusa's
Fountain

MARATHIÁ

ÁYOS
ANDREAS BAY

0 1 2 3 4 5 kilometres

N

whose roof had recently fallen and which was being used as a quarry. In his 'anxiety to discover a cavern near Vathi' Gell cleared the debris and disclosed 'a species of basin' and 'small channels cut in the rock, which have served for the passage of water into the basins'.

[3 km.] A road on the left leads in 1·5 km. to the saddle below *Mt Aetos*, and in a further 1·5 km. to the little port of **Piso Aetos**. Looking west from the saddle you can see the remains of walls on the steep slopes of Mt Aetos (380 metres). These belong to the lower half of a town which may be the Alalcomenae mentioned by Strabo (Book 10). The walls of the citadel on the summit above them are screened from below by scrub; and this scrub, the steep slope and the litter of boulders will make the 20-minute climb to the top a very arduous and prickly business if you do not take the right route. About 100 metres south-west of the little *chapel of Ayos Yeorgos* there is a gap in the low rock-cliff which faces you. Once through this gap you can climb up by the barer southern slope of the mountain. At the summit and gazing down on the Strait of Ithaca you may feel that you are indeed in an eagle's nest (*aetós*, 'eagle'). The best stretches of polygonal walling are on the north-east, overlooking a wood of evergreen oaks and the saddle. Earthquakes have dislodged the whole of the south-west side of the narrow ovoid circuit. Early travellers were told that this citadel was the 'Castle of Ulysses', and Schliemann dug here enthusiastically in 1867 in search of Odysseus' bedpost (see p. 81). But present archaeological evidence suggests that the town is not much older than fifth-century B.C. The saddle itself, however, seems to have been treated as a sanctified area from much earlier times. Excavations near the chapel of Ayos Yeorgos in the early 'thirties uncovered a curious group of structures which date to about 1200 B.C., and a later sanctuary, founded apparently by Corinthians, which flourished from the ninth to some time between the third and first centuries B.C. The pottery and other finds from the site are in the Vathi museum.

The long pebble beach at Piso Aetos is a pleasantly deserted place to bathe from, and there are bits of ancient harbour walling to be seen. Before the war visitors from Cefalonian ports used to be landed at the jetty here rather than at Vathi; but the haven is used now only by an occasional caique ferrying livestock across the channel.

[3 km.] Back on the main road you skirt the *Gulf of Molos* at the water's edge and then climb to the top of the narrow isthmus which joins the two halves of the island. There is a strange moment when the road runs along the very roof-ridge of the isthmus and you can look down the slopes of its steep gable to the sea on either side.

[8 km.] A rough road on the left leads down in 1·5 km. to a T-junction in the hamlet of **Ayos Ioannis**. From here the overgrown road to the left runs down in 0·8 km. to a dead-end only 100 metres above a string of small coves whose clean shingle and brisk sea provide some of the best bathing on Ithaca. The overgrown road to the right climbs for about 3 km. to rejoin Route 1 outside Lefki. A few hundred metres along this road you will see a ruined mill below you on the left; here a path leads in about 200 metres to other good shingle beaches.

[8·5 km.] A metalled road to the right takes you in 4·5 km. to the nineteenth-century *Monastery of Kathara*, the shrine of the island's patron saint, the Virgin Kathariotissa, whose feast day is September 8th. Though of no architectural interest, the monastery was pleasantly rebuilt on a smaller scale after the 1953 earthquake, and its courtyard is green with pines and bright with pots of geraniums and fuchsias. The official guest room has two bedrooms opening off it, which you may be invited to stay in or use for a siesta. And the view is splendid. To the south-east you look up through the neck of bottle-shaped Vathi Bay to see Vathi at the bottom; to the south Aetos stands silhouetted against the mountains of Cefalonia and the Gulf of Sami; and to the west lies the Fiskardo peninsula with the sea-bleached hem of its ruffled coastline showing.

[13 km.] The rough road up from Ayos Ioannis joins you on the left.

[13·5 km.] **Lefki**, the only hamlet you pass through on this high traverse of North Ithaca's west flank. Its corrugated asbestos roofs are a reminder that Ithaca too suffered in the 1953 earthquake. From here you can see the islet of **Daskalio** over against the coast of Cefalonia. It is an unconvincing candidate for the island of Asteris where the suitors lay in wait for Telemachus (*Odyssey*, Books 4 and 16), but the only one there is.

[17 km.] You reach Stavros.

STAVROS

On a ridge 120 metres above sea-level, Stavros is a cooler summer place to stay in than Vathi. The café with rooms over it was built as a hotel by a former steward on the Archduke Salvator's yacht (see p. 71). With the exception of one Venetian house with a flared skirt to its walls, no building in Stavros is much older than late-nineteenth-century. But the village stands on a site which may be that of the town which lay below Odysseus' palace. Excavations in the 'thirties established that a settlement flourished on *Pelikata hill* — the highest point of the Stavros ridge — from about 2200 to 1200 B.C., and indirect evidence suggests that this high point was once occupied by a substantial Mycenaean building of worked masonry. This archaeological confirmation that Stavros was a better candidate for Odysseus' capital than Aetos gave North Ithaca a lead in its prestige battle with the south, and a rather impressive modern bust of Odysseus was soon put up in the small public garden by the café to mark the victory.

The finds from the Pelikata ridge, and from a cave in the near-by bay of Polis (see below), are housed in a little *museum* 0·8 km. from the village on the road to **Exoyi** and close to the site of the settlement. Its key is normally kept in the school halfway down the main street on the right, and the schoolmaster can make arrangements for you to be taken to it at most times of the day. Apart from Early Middle and Late Bronze Age sherds, the most suggestive exhibits come from the Polis cave and consist of a fragment of a terracotta mask of the first or second century B.C., scratchily inscribed 'Votive offering to Odysseus . . . dedicated it', and many large bits of beautifully decorated solid bronze legs belonging to tripod-cauldrons. None of these is earlier than about 1000 B.C. and most of them are eighth-century. Curiously, there are pieces of twelve tripods, and a thirteenth is said to have been found at the site some years before the excavation. What were these thirteen tripod-cauldrons doing in a small cave-shrine in Ithaca? Herodotus tells us that 'It used to be customary at the Games of the Triopian Apollo to give bronze tripods as prizes, and the winners were not allowed to take them away, but were required to dedicate them on the spot to the god' (Book 1). It is possible that a similar custom prevailed in Ithaca. We know from an inscription that games were being held in the island at the end of the third century B.C., when they were called — significantly — the Odysseia. And there is no reason why such games should not have been held much earlier. Traditionally, the Olympian Games were not founded but *re*-founded in 776 B.C. With these considerations in mind, and assuming that the *Odyssey* was composed in the seventh century B.C., the archaeologist who discovered the tripods, Miss Benton, concludes in her report (*Annual of the British School at Athens*, Vol. 35) that 'Their existence would have been enough to account for Homer's story that Odysseus brought thirteen tripods with him from Phaeacia, and hid them in a cave near his landing-place on Ithaca. The fact that one of the tripods was on wheels provides a further link with Homer.' (*Iliad*, Book 18.)

The site of the Pelikata settlement is about 250 metres due north of the museum. Round the hilltop ran an imposing wall of cyclopean masonry, some of whose colossal blocks can still be seen in the terrace-walls.

EXCURSIONS FROM STAVROS

Bay of Polis

Route Between the café and the public garden a road leads down in 1·2 km. to the bay of Polis.

This is the closest bathing-place to Stavros. The pebbles of the main beach are treacled over with oil, but to the south of the jetty the shore is cleaner. 100 metres or so to the west of the north end of the beach you may be able to make out the outline of a large seaside cave. Its roof fell in some time after the end of the first century A.D. and it is not worth visiting. It was used as a shrine from the Early Bronze Age until Hellenistic times and a third-century B.C. potsherd in the Stavros museum shows that it was dedicated to the 'nymphs'. *Pólis* ('town') is a very rare place-name in Greece and its survival here suggests that a town of great fame must once have stood in the vicinity, i.e., Odysseus' capital on the ridge.

At Polis you can sometimes find a fishing-boat to take you to Fiskardo on Cefalonia.

'Homer's School'

Route Fork left at the north end of the main street in Stavros and 1·2 km. farther along fork left again up the rough road to Exoyi. A few hundred metres up, fork right on to an earth lane which brings you in 10 minutes to a new chapel. Pass it on the downhill side and join a cobbled path which bends left and climbs in a minute or two to the tumble of ruins.

'Homer's School' is the nickname given to the only ancient building on Ithaca (apart from Aetos) whose remains are still visible above ground. Two or three courses of some of its walls, of polygonal masonry, form the foundation of the nineteenth-century *Chapel of Ayos Athanasios* which was destroyed by the 1953 earthquake. It stands on a great boulder which juts out over the valley like a miniature acropolis, and in a cleft in the middle of the boulder a rock-cut stair descends to end in mid air. In the neighbourhood are further walls and rock-cut tombs, and a vaulted spring-chamber in which one or two late-Mycenaean sherds were found during excavations in the 'thirties. Whatever the purpose of the building and its age, it is an intriguing site, looking out over the bay of Afales as though from the bridge of a ship.

Spring of Kalamos

Route Fork left at the end of the main street in Stavros and, 1·2 km. farther on, right to Platithria. This brings you in 0·8 km. to a place called Yefira, where a bridge spans a gully and the road divides into three. Take the rough road left, go left at the next fork and right at the fork after that.

The road ends 2·8 km. from Stavros by a house which, before the 1953 earthquake, was a small hotel. In front of it three spouts of the most delicious water gush into a trough under a modern portico and spill away to irrigate oranges and tangerines, melon patches, loquats and knee-high grass in a valley whose luxuriance reminds one of Corfu. This spring of Kalamos is North Ithaca's contender for 'Arethusa's Fountain'; above it a line of low cliffs has been known as *Koraka* (Raven's Crag) at least since Leake was here in 1806 and completes the canonical picture. A footpath continues beyond the spring, a shady walk with Sappho's Leap across the water to the north and slanting tables of smooth rock to the west on the other side of the dark blue bay of Afales. On your way back to Yefira you can see an attractive bit of Grandma Moses architecture on your left — an obelisk of twenty-five old millstones put up as a 'monument in memory of the past generation who cultivede the soil of Ithaca to remain here to the end of time'. That the present generation cultivate other soils is shown by the names of their retiring villas — 'South Africa', 'The White House', 'North Queensland Bungalow' — and the abandoned and overgrown terraces on the hill of Exoyi to your right.

Anoyi

Route Leave Stavros by the road which runs east opposite the café. In 1980 the new road being bulldozed to Anoyi (6·5 km.) was almost unusable. Beyond Anoyi a very rough road continues past the Monastery of Kathara to rejoin Route 1 just before the isthmus (14·5 km.)

Once you have climbed out of the fertile Stavros valley and rounded the shoulder of Mt Niritos, you will find yourself on a very curious upland plateau, so covered with huge boulders and immense puddles of stone that corn and vines can grow only in the small pockets and long crannies between them. Anoyi is a mountain hamlet which has lost ground steadily to Kioni, down below it on the coast. Already in 1806 Gell noted that more and more families were being 'tempted by the convenience of the port to forsake the security which the mountain offered'. The crumbling ribs of an earlier village, Anoyi's sixteenth-century ancestor, lie a little way up the mountainside. A few minutes' walk below the café stands the rain-runnelled *'Boulder of Hercules'* like a fluted Norse helmet. It looks so artificial that only a close inspection will persuade you that it is not the solitary survivor of a vanished stonehenge. Down here the plateau is so level that you cannot see by what steep slope, if any, you are anchored in the world, and you seem to hang suspended 450 metres above the distant Ekhinades Islands and the gleaming sea. At the far end of the village a restored church on the right is full of sombre wall-paintings dating from 1670.

Beyond Anoyi the comforting buttress of the plateau shrinks to nothing and the road clings to a slope which plunges straight down to the waters of the Gulf of Molos.

Frikes and Kioni

Route Fork right at the north end of the main street in Stavros and, in Frikes [2·5 km.], right again along the water-front to Kioni [7 km.].

[2·5 km.] In **Frikes** there are a couple of café's, a place to eat and good deep-water bathing from the end of the mole. Beyond it a corniche road runs past several white-pebble bathing-coves to Kioni.

[7 km.] Built on the irregular slopes of an olive-clad valley which surrounds a wide indented bay, **Kioni** is the most attractively sited of all Ithaca's villages. From a ridge where the oldest houses and two dilapidated mills stand in the wind, you wind down to the sheltered port by a cemented road. Behind the trees along the quayside are summer eating places where there is always plenty of fish. With its rooms and villas, and its bus and caique services to Vathi, Kioni is a good place for a simple seaside holiday.

CEFALONIA (KEFALLINIA)

Cefalonia (*i Kefallinía* in Greek) lies opposite the mouth of the Gulf of Corinth and is the largest of the Ionian Islands (689 square kilometres). Though farthest out to sea it is the central island of the group. In 1980 it had a population of 31,790. Argostoli, the capital (7,060 inhabitants in 1971), is 24 kilometres from the main port of Sami, on the far side of a range of mountains.

INFORMATION FOR VISITORS

Information
National Tourist Organization office (*Map* **6**).
Post Office
Map **11**.
Cable Office (O.T.E.)
Map **8**.
Hospital
Map **14** (tels 252 and 515).
Feast-Days
First Sunday after Easter, August 16th and October 20th: processions in honour of St Yerasimos in the Omala (see p. 246).

GETTING TO CEFALONIA

Air

Daily flights from Athens to Argostoli.

Sea

Car ferries to Sami
From Patras: The *Kefallinia* leaves at 13.30 every day. Journey time: 4 hours.
   Every other day between June and September the *Ionis* leaves at 21.00 en route to Brindisi.
From Ithaca: The *Kefallinia* leaves at 07.00 every day. Journey time: about 1 hour.
From Brindisi (via Corfu, Paxos and Ithaca): The *Ionis* (see above) leaves at 23.00. Journey time: 14¾ hours.

Car ferries to Poros
A new daily service from Killini (see pp. 259 and 260) was due to start in late summer 1980.

Road

From Athens via Corinth to Patras: Total mileage, 222 km.

Bus

From Athens (see p. 20). Two or three morning buses a day along the above route. The journey to Argostoli (including the ferry crossing) takes about 9 hours.
Athens Office of the Cefalonia K.T.E.L.: 100 Kifissou Street (tel. 5129498).

Train

From Athens: Seven trains (S.E.K.) a day to Patras. Journey time: 4 to 5 hours. (The Cefalonia/Ithaca car ferry berth in Patras is about 0·4 km. from the railway station.)

TRANSPORT ON THE ISLAND

Buses

For general information about island bus services see p. 22. For such a large island Cefalonia is not too badly served. For details of the services see the individual routes. The K.T.E.L. office and main bus station are in I. Metaxa Street (*Map* 13).

Car ferries

The frequent small car ferries between Argostoli and Lixouri save a long drive round the head of the Gulf of Lixouri (for details see Route 6).

Taxis

There are about 200 taxis and hire-cars on the island, 70 of them based on Argostoli. For rates see p. 23. The main town ranks are in Valianos Square (tels 28110 and 28505) and near the bus station (*Map* 13) (tel. 22700).

Car and bicycle hire

Cars from A. Pefanis, 4 P. Valianou Street (tel. 22338) and Budget Rent-a-Car, 3 and 5 R. Vergoti Street (tel. 23125).
  Bicycles from Garbi Bros, 130 I. Metaxa Street.

ACCOMMODATION AND RESTAURANTS

Town hotels

B Class   *Xenia.* Small hotel on north-west outskirts. Large garden. All rooms face sea. Two minutes from town bathing-lido. L class restaurant.

C Class   *Ainos*, Valianos Square. Open all year. Medium-sized hotel on main square. No restaurant.

Armonia, 1 M. Yerulanou Street. Small hotel between the main square and the water-front. No restaurant.

Ayos Yerasimos, 6 Ayou Yerasimou Street. Small side-street hotel back from the water-front. No restaurant.

Castello, Valianos Square. Small hotel on main square. No restaurant.

Cephalonia Star, 50 I. Metaxa Street. Medium-sized water-front hotel. Snack-bar.

Phocas, 3 M. Yerulanou Street. Small hotel behind the water-front. No restaurant.

Tourist, 94 I. Metaxa Street. Small water-front block. No restaurant.

D Class   *Aigli*, 3 March 21st Street. Small hotel between main square and water-front. No restaurant.

Allegro, 2 A. Khoida Street. Open all year. Small hotel. No restaurant.

Dido, 3 D. Lavranga Street. Small hotel on corner of main square. Snack-bar.

Emborikon, 2 L. Mitaki Street. Small side-street hotel. No restaurant.

Khara, 87 Vergoti Avenue. Small hotel on outskirts. Vine arbour. No restaurant.

Paralia, 144 I. Metaxa Street. Small water-front hotel above restaurant (B class).

Parthenon, 4 Zakinthou Street. Small side-street hotel. No restaurant.

Country hotels

A Class   *Méditerranée*, Lassi. (*Excursions from Argostoli*) Open April–October. Very large beach-side hotel, own beach, night-club, restaurant, swimming pool, water ski-ing and tennis.

White Rocks, Platis Yalos. (*Excursions from Argostoli*) Large air-conditioned hotel and bungalows. Open May–October. Own beach, restaurant, night club, water ski-ing, tennis.

B Class   *Iraklis*, Poros. *Route* 2. Open April–September. Small cliff-top hotel; no restaurant, water ski-ing.

Irinna, Ayia Pelayia. *Route* 1. Open April–September. Large seaside hotel. Own beach, restaurant, terrace, swimming pool.

C Class   *Ionian*, Sami. *Route 3*. Small hotel two hundred metres from sea. No restaurant.

Pylaros, Ayia Effimia. *Link route B*. Small water-front hotel. Restaurant.

E Class   *Ionios Avra*, Lixouri. *Route* 6. Small hotel on main square. No restaurant.

Khoropoula, Lixouri. *Route* 6. Small hotel above restaurant in main square.

Krinos, Sami. *Route* 3. Bungalow hotel fifty metres from sea. No restaurant.

Sami, Sami. *Route* 3. Water-front hotel over café. No hot water. No restaurant.

Rooms in private houses

For general information see p. 27. In 1980 the number of rooms to rent was approximately as follows: 70 in and around Argostoli, 10 in Katelios, 30 in Skala, 200 in Poros, 40 in Sami, 10 in Ayia Effimia, 20 in Assos and 60 in Fiskardo. Less than a third of these are A class rooms.

Villas and flats

There are one or two flats above Makris Yalos and a large number of villas (mostly small prefabricated bungalows) at Poros (Poros Village Villas, tel. 52351).

Restaurants

In Argostoli most of the best restaurants are in or near Valianos Square, with cheaper places on the water-front. For country restaurants see the Route Instructions.

Specialities: Red and white *robóla* (p. 101), *Kefalonitikípitta*

(p. 100), *bacaliaropitta* (salt-cod fish pies), *mándoles* and *ortzáta* (p. 101), Krani melons and currant grapes.

SPORT

Bathing

Town bathing is from the quayside opposite the *Xenia Hotel* (café, snack-bar and changing cabins).

Sand beaches at Platis Yalos and Makris Yalos (p. 236), Lourdata (p. 242), Ayos Thomas (p. 242), Mirtos (p. 252), Katelios (p. 243) and near Assos (p. 252).

Shingle beaches at Nea Skala (p. 243) and Assos (p. 252).

Pebble beaches at Poros (p. 245), Sami (p. 248), Karavomilo (p. 257) and near Fiskardo (p. 254).

Rock bathing at Fiskardo.

INTRODUCTION TO CEFALONIA

Cefalonia is an island for explorers. It is the largest and least densely populated of the Ionian Islands. Apart from half a dozen fertile valleys, some flat meadow-land near Argostoli, some pockets of currant vine round Lixouri and a few small littoral plains, the whole island is solid mountain — a huge Empty Quarter with the dark pine forest of Mt Enos for an oasis at its heart and peak. In 1953 the villages which had over the centuries found toe-holds in the crannies of this mountain were uprooted by earthquake, and the sites of their old stone growths are now littered with unlovely prefabricated seedlings. But here and there a village, port or castle has survived and blossoms still like an uncollected plant — Assos, Fiskardo and the castle of St George.

Cefalonia has a name like a flag snapping at a mast-head; but you would not guess that it was a nautical island. Its sailors journey between other ports (as they have since the time of Odysseus) and those of them who come back to settle turn their hands from hawsers and paint-chipping to donkey-loads of vine-prunings and the plough. Some stay away to get on in the world with a quarrelsomeness and push for which Cefalonians are proverbial, driven to assert themselves so restlessly elsewhere by the sheer impossibility of taming their own mountain. For on this enormous rock-garden of an island there is not much room for a man to achieve what a Cefalonian — with his belief in Science, Learning and the Modern

World — regards as his rightful stature. No island in Greece boasts a list of past and present university professors as long as Cefalonia's.

Because of its size and its mountains Cefalonia is a difficult island to develop as a tourist centre and its three large seaside hotels are all close to Argostoli. But if there is little luxury and less lotus-eating elsewhere in Cefalonia, there *is* accommodation of a sort in nearly every worthwhile corner, and the reward of the traveller who journeys round this small continent is a succession of unexpected and hospitable settlements, a few ancient sites of unrivalled beauty and innumerable sea and mountain vistas of astonishing splendour.

ARGOSTOLI

Argostoli became the capital of Cefalonia in 1765 when an earthquake forced the Venetian garrison and *provveditore* to abandon the town of St George. Though Grasset thought it a miserable little village at the end of the eighteenth century, by all accounts it was a pleasant enough place before the 1953 earthquake; photographs in the Koryalenios Museum show handsome and substantial houses, a theatre, and an imposing neo-classical courthouse; and in 1834 the Rev. Richard Burgess described the town as 'a little Naples'. Now, apart from some graceful palm trees, the new town has little of note about it except its site — a strange one for the capital of an island famed for ship-owners and merchant-sailors. For Argostoli turns its back firmly on the high seas and gazes inland across a neck of water towards pine trees and mountains. A long stone bridge spans the middle of this inlet in a picturesque but most un-seamanlike way; and the absence of any shipping larger than rowing-boats and yachts adds to the illusion that the town lies on a lake.

In the late afternoon of a calm day the harbour has an almost Alpine air. Napier (*The Colonies*) says,

> The sounds of music, and of oars, with the songs of boat-men, float along its smooth surface in the softness of a summer's evening with the most pleasing effect. The bright colours in which most southern nations love to dress, increase the liveliness of the scene; and added to the wildness of the overhanging mountains, with their changing evening tints, create a picture in which masses of rocks, water and people, are so grouped as to produce a beauty of scenery that this harbour has no claims to at any other period of the day.

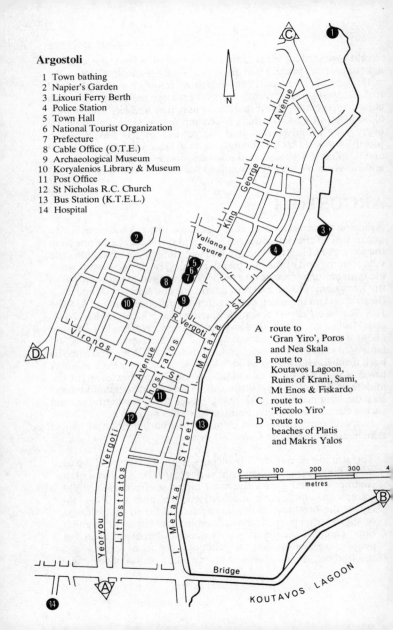

Argostoli

1 Town bathing
2 Napier's Garden
3 Lixouri Ferry Berth
4 Police Station
5 Town Hall
6 National Tourist Organization
7 Prefecture
8 Cable Office (O.T.E.)
9 Archaeological Museum
10 Koryalenios Library & Museum
11 Post Office
12 St Nicholas R.C. Church
13 Bus Station (K.T.E.L.)
14 Hospital

Valianos Square

King George Avenue

St

Metaxa

R. Vergoti

Vironos

Lithostratos St

Avenue

Vergoti

I. Metaxa Street

Yeoryou

Lithostratos

A route to
   'Gran Yiro', Poros
   and Nea Skala
B route to
   Koutavos Lagoon,
   Ruins of Krani, Sami,
   Mt Enos & Fiskardo
C route to
   'Piccolo Yiro'
D route to
   beaches of Platis
   and Makris Yalos

0   100   200   300   4
         metres

Bridge

KOUTAVOS LAGOON

From the north end of Argostoli, King George II Avenue leads the prevailing breeze straight into the heart of the town — the paved and tree-planted Valianos Square, surrounded by cafés and restaurants. West of the square, on the hillside, an attractive public garden commemorates General Sir Charles Napier (1782–1853), who, as a young colonel, was Resident from 1822 to 1830. It is sad that no stone, plaque or obelisk now records the name of this warm-hearted and impulsive soldier, the ablest and the most human of all the administrators during the British Protectorate. Devoted to Cefalonia he confided to his diary in 1825 'that every hour not employed to do her good appears wasted' (*The Life*). His statue was defaced during the Italian occupation and has not yet been replaced.

The street that runs south from the middle of the square passes four modern buildings — the Town Hall, the Prefecture, the Museum and the Law Courts — before giving up its pretensions to be a boulevard and continuing as a narrow shopping thoroughfare through the remaining length of the town. This was the main street of the Venetian capital and is still popularly known as the *Lithóstrotos* ('stone paved') because, until 1953, it was paved with Roman blocks brought by sea from Sami. Not far along on its left is the Post Office, and farther down on the right the Catholic church of St Nicholas. The old masonry of Argostoli's Orthodox churches has not been re-used as in Zakinthos but many of the new concrete shells contain the original eighteenth-century screens, unfortunately often regilded. On Cefalonia church screens often display five or six rather than four principal icons (see p. 92). Many of the paintings are seventeenth-century. The Cable Office is at the beginning of the main traffic route through the town — Yeorgou Vergoti Avenue — which runs parallel to and inland of this shopping street. Most of Argostoli's hotels lie between Valianos Square and the water-front, or on the water-front road itself. This runs past the main market and the bus station (K.T.E.L.) to the bridge over the Koutavos Lagoon.

PRINCIPAL SIGHTS

Koryalenios Historical and Cultural Museum and Public Library
Map **10**.

Museum open: 10.00–12.00 and 16.00–20.00
                          Closed on Sundays
Entrance: Free

Library open: 08.00–12.00 and 16.00–20.00
                  Closed on Sundays.

Library

Marinos Koryalenios was a cultured and wealthy Cefalonian merchant who died in London in 1910 leaving numerous philanthropic bequests, among them one for this public library, whose collection of French, German, Italian and English works should keep rainbound tourists happy. It also contains an interesting collection of Napier's papers.

In a separate room (which will be unlocked on application) hangs a collection of icons bequeathed by another Cefalonian, Spyridon Kharakopou. Though there are some interesting works among them, particularly those by minor or unknown hands, in my opinion the uniform way in which their late owner had them cleaned, framed and varnished stifles much of their vitality. There are also a few attractive pieces of Ionian Island furniture.

Museum

The museum that opened in 1968 as an afterthought in the library basement must now be one of the most attractive of its kind in Europe. In twelve years its director, Mrs Eleni Kosmetatou, has steadily increased its contents and improved its displays until it now reminds one of some permanent and particularly successful exhibition at the Victoria and Albert. One does not know which to admire the most: the flair with which the exhibits are presented or the meticulous historical documentation which accompanies them. Everything that can be found to illustrate life in Cefalonia, chiefly during the nineteenth century, is here arranged, lit and labelled in Greek and English in the most captivating way: table silver, china, glass, furniture, kitchen utensils, musical instruments, models, photographs, and pictures. The collection of nineteenth- and early twentieth-century costume, and of needlework, crochet and lace is especially large, and among the many good icons the four large gold-ground works by Stephen Tzangarola from the church at Sision (p. 242) are noteworthy.

On the left of the bottom floor a unique collection of archives covering practically the whole period of Venetian rule (1500–1797) can be inspected on application. The documents are still being sorted and catalogued.

Archaeological Museum
Map **9**.

Open *Summer* Weekdays 08.00–13.00 and 15.00–18.00
              Sundays 09.00–13.30 and 16.00–18.00
        Winter 10.00–16.30
        N.B. Closed on Tuesdays.
Entrance: Drs 25.

The main feature of the museum is a room full of late-Mycenaean pots (see p. 47) from tombs excavated in various parts of the island: Kokolata, above Assos; Prokopata, in the foothills across the water from Argostoli; Mavrata and Katelios, in the south-east corner of the island; and Lakithra, Metaxata and Mazarakata, in the area south of St George's Castle. Scores of provincial Late-Mycenaean pots make a dreary display, and they are very badly labelled. No effort has been made to explain the Mycenaeans' presence in the island, their funerary customs or their pottery styles. There are also cases showing Mycenaean gold jewellery, seals, beads and bronze swords again without any useful comment. In another room are cases of Byzantine and Classical coins, including coins from the four ancient towns of Cefalonia, and Hellenistic and Roman finds from Sami, among them a fine life-size bronze portrait head of the first half of the third century A.D.

Excursions from Argostoli
TOUR OF THE KOUTAVOS LAGOON AND THE RUINS OF KRANI

'The walls of the Cranii are among the best extant specimens of the military architecture of the Greeks, and a curious example of their attention to strength of position in preference to other conveniences, for nothing can be more rugged and forbidding than the greater part of the site' (Leake). Most visitors will wish to take his word for the 'greater part of the site' and satisfy themselves with a stretch or two of the walls at their most accessible point halfway round the Koutavos Lagoon and 2.5 km. from the town.

Route Leave Argostoli by Exit B on the town plan, fork right on to the Sami road once over the bridge, and right again 100 metres or so farther on.

The *bridge* which divides Argostoli harbour from the shallows of the Koutavos Lagoon was built in 1813 'in the Greek mode of construction, without cement' by Lt.-Col. de Bosset, a Swiss-born officer in the British Army who was military commander of the island from 1810 to 1814. The four sides of the *obelisk* in the middle originally carried a vaunting inscription in Greek, Latin and English: 'To the glory of the British Nation. The inhabitants of Cephalonia 1813.' On the outskirts of a fine eucalyptus grove, halfway round the lagoon, you pass a little spring-house on your left just before a rough road forks left. Leave your car here if you want to climb for 5 minutes to see the walls.

Krani

We know from Thucydides that in 431 B.C. Krani, Pali, Sami and Proni formed a tetrapolis. Despite Leake's strictures, the site is the best one in the area — beside a sheltered harbour and with access to a spring copious enough to provide the needs of the whole of modern Argostoli. This spring must always have been the focal point of any settlement; and recent excavations have shown that the town goes back at any rate to the sixth century B.C. To reach the nearest stretch of walls you should take the faint zigzag path which starts up the hill a few metres south of the spring-house. This is the ancient ascent, as its retaining walls show. Following it up and *away* from the pine trees, past four hairpin bends, you will arrive at the north end of a ridge from which a much-tumbled spur-wall of large irregular stones runs down westward to the lagoon. From this corner you can walk southwards along a sort of ramp which is faced with masonry on both sides until you reach a gap in a medieval wall which joins you at right angles from the left. Through the gap you will find yourself on a terrace; and if you climb down off this to the right you will see the best section of *retaining wall* in this area, a twenty-metre stretch which has been cleared of prickly evergreen oak to reveal neatly fitting irregular polygonal masonry. If you walk farther along the terrace and round the corner to the left, you will see another, probably later, *spur-wall* running south-eastward down the hill to the meadows below. In Grasset's day the Krani meadows and the eucalyptus grove were an unhealthy swamp, and it was only in the 1830s that the area was drained and reclaimed; so it may be that this spur-wall defended a port where there are now fields. The knoll on which you are standing was a secondary strong-point; the *main acropolis* stood on the scrub-covered hill 0·8 km. to the east. A 5-kilometre circuit of walls enclosed the whole of the upland hollow to the north-east as well as linking the two strong-points. A long stretch of the *north-east wall* still stands and can be visited more easily from a side-road off Route 3 (see p. 246).

From the spring-house the road continues round the lagoon, passes the municipal sports ground, and re-enters Argostoli at the south end of the bridge.

THE 'PICCOLO YIRO'

In the age of carriage promenades the 8-kilometre drive round the tip of the Lassi peninsula was known as the *Piccolo* or *Mikro Yiro* — the Short Circuit. The road passes the famous Sea Mill (2·5 km.) and the neo-classical lighthouse of Ayi Theodori (3 km.).

Route Leave Argostoli by Exit C on the town plan and follow the coast road between pine woods and the sea.

[2·5 km.] The *Sea Mill* stands beside a modern *kéndro* on the point of the peninsula opposite Lixouri. In 1835 an English resident, Mr Stevens, was walking by the sea when he heard a noise of running water under his feet. He had the site excavated and discovered a stream of sea water flowing inland at such a rate that he decided to build a corn-mill on it. A second mill was put up in 1859, and in 1926 a survivor of one of these two mills had been adapted to provide Argostoli with its supply of ice. Throughout the nineteenth century persistent attempts were made to find out where the water reappeared; but it was not until a team from the University of Graz had experimented for several months in the early 1960s with large quantities of yellow dye that the mystery of these *katavóthres* was finally solved. Astonishingly, the water comes up sixteen kilometres away on the other side of the island at Melissani (see p. 257), having plunged beneath the main range of mountains. One of the old mill-wheels has been repaired and the site has been turned into a sort of rockery with paved paths and bridges. Unfortunately the 1953 earthquake greatly reduced the flow of water and the leisurely revolutions of the iron wheel would not now ice a single lemonade. There is a small bathing beach near this mill.

[3 km.] You pass the pretty little *lighthouse of St Theodore*, designed as a Doric rotunda by Captain Kennedy, R.E., in the 1820s. Rebuilt after 1953, it is now the sole survivor of several fine neo-classical buildings with which Napier and this gifted Sapper embellished Lixouri and Argostoli.

From the lighthouse it is 3 km. through olive groves and a pine avenue to the junction with the road between Argostoli and Platis

Yalos, and a further 1·5 km. back to the town's main square (see below).

THE BEACHES OF PLATIS AND MAKRIS YALOS

Argostoli is lucky to have two of the loveliest beaches in Cefalonia — or, indeed, the Seven Islands — only 3 km. away.

Route Leave Argostoli by Exit D on the town plan.
Bus In summer, buses run between town and beach about every hour until 15.00. You can catch them in Valianos Square.
Accommodation and Restaurants A class hotels at Lassi and Platis Yalos, restaurants there and in between, and a few rooms and villas in the area.

[0·8 km.] At the top of the ridge behind the town a road forks left to Lakithra (see Route 1).

[1·5 km.] A road forks right to circle the Lassi peninsula (see the 'Piccolo Yiro' above).

[2·5 km.] A road forks left to the cave which St Yerasimos found too social for a hermitage in the sixteenth century (see p. 246).

[2·8 km.] The drive to the *Méditerranée* hotel is on the right.

[3 km.] *Platis* and *Makris Yalos*. The farther and smaller of the two beaches — the 'Broad Sands' — has been appropriated by the *White Rocks* hotel.

To the nearer and more beautiful beach — the 'Long Sands' — you must descend by steps at the end of a signposted lane which you pass a few hundred metres before reaching Platis Yalos. At both, the fine sand shelves under the sparkling water neither too suddenly for children nor too slowly for proper swimming. In front of you lie the plate-like island of Vardiani and the flat jut of the Paliki.

From these two beaches it is 8 km. on to Metaxata (see Route 1).

ROUTES ON CEFALONIA

For general information on island routes and roads see p. 103. Cefalonia's size and mountains make it a tiring island to explore in a series of day expeditions from any one place. Three of the six routes which the map on p. 238 shows radiating from Argostoli are therefore linked by subsidiary routes to Sami, which can be used as an alternative base.

Route 1: The 'Gran Yiro'

In the nineteenth century the *Gran Yiro* was the name of an excursion which took the rider east from Argostoli to the Castle of Ayos Yeorgos (9 km.), then south to the village of Metaxata (10·5 km.) and back to the capital by either a ridge road or a coastal road. It is still an excellent route to follow.

Route Leave Argostoli by Exit A on the town map and drive out across the Krania meadows to Travliata.
Bus Day-return services to Travliata and Metaxata.
Accommodation and Restaurants Hotel at Ayia Pelayia (B class) and Platis Yalos (A class), restaurants at Lakithra and between Platis Yalos and Argostoli, and an eating place at Metaxata.

[7 km.] As you approach the castle hill, a road signed to Troiannata forks left. If you fork right off this in 0·8 km. a rough road will take you up in 0·8 km. to the main gate. This northern approach runs up through the ruins of the old capital — broken churches with their frescoes showing and cottages on olive-shaded slopes — and is more picturesque than the signed road up from Travliata.

[8 km.] **Travliata**. At the cross-roads on the outskirts of the village take the road to the left which zigzags for 0·8 km. up to the main street of the old capital — a ridgeway running from a church to the great east bastion of the *Castle of Ayos Yeorgos*.

The Castle of Ayos Yeorgos

Open *Summer* 08.30–12.30
               16.00–18.00
               Sundays and holidays 09.00–15.00
               Winter 09.00–13.30
               14.00–16.00
Sundays and holidays 10.00–16.30
Closed on Tuesdays.
Entrance: Free.

The caretaker (who lives in the last cottage on the left) should appear to unlock the door in the restored portcullis-gateway as you

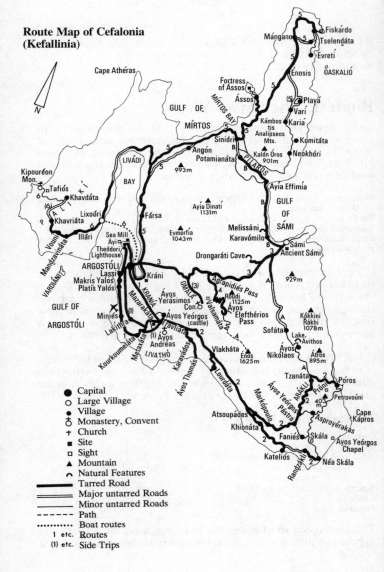

Route Map of Cefalonia (Kefallinia)

Cape Athéras

GULF OF MÍRTOS

MÍRTOS BAY

Fortress of Assos

Ássos

Mángano

Fiskárdo

Tselendáta

Evretí

Énosis

OÁSKALIÓ

Playá

Vari

Kámbos tis Analípseos Mts.

Kariá

Kalón Óros 901m

Komitáta

Neokhóri

PILAROS

Sinióri

Angón Potamianáta

993m

Ayia Effimía

GULF OF SÁMI

LIVÁDI BAY

Fársa

Ayia Dinati 1131m

Evmorfía 1043m

Melissáni

Karavómilo

Sámi

Ancient Sámi

Drongaráti Cave

929m

Kipouréon Mon.

Tafiós

Khavdáta

Lixoúri

Illári

Khavriáta

Vouni

Mandravúnda

VARDÁNI

Sea Mill

Ayii Theódori Lighthouse

ARGOSTÓLI

Lassí

Makrís Yalós

Platís Yalós

Kráni

KRANIA

Mazarakáta

Ávyos Yerásimos

Con.

Ávyos Yeórgos (castle)

Vlakháta

Agrapidiés Pass

Roúdi 1125m

Ávyos Elefthérios Pass

Sofáta

Kókkini Rákhi 1078m

Lake Avithos

Ávyos Nikólaos

Átros 895m

Miniés

Lakíthra

Metaxáta

OMALA

Ávyos Andréas

LIVATHÓ

Lavriáta

Karavádos

Kourkoumeláta

Vlakháta

Énos 1625m

Ávyos Thomás

Lourdáta

Markópoulo

Tzanáta

Póros

Petrovoúni

Cape Kápros

Ávyos Yeórgos Pastra

ARAKLI

Próni

40?

Asproyérakas

Atsoupádes

Khionáta

Faniés

Skála

Ávyos Yeórgos Chapel

Katéliós

Néa Skála

Randzáki

● Capital
○ Large Village
• Village
⌂ Monastery, Convent
+ Church
■ Site
□ Sight
▲ Mountain
⌒ Natural Features
━━ Tarred Road
═══ Major untarred Roads
⎓ Minor untarred Roads
----- Path
········· Boat routes
1 etc. Routes
(1) etc. Side Trips

0 2 4 6 8 10 kilometres

arrive, and if he shows you round will expect a tip of about twenty drachmas.

When seen from Argostoli in the afternoon light, St George's Castle on its dunce's cap of a hill, a dark topknot of pine trees standing above its circlet of grey walls, looks like an illustration to a Provençal Romance. It is the best-preserved and most attractive castle in the Ionian Islands.

In Byzantine times the site seems to have been known only by the name of the island, and the first mention of a castle 'of St George' comes in a document of 1264 in the time of Richard Orsini. Under the Orsini and their richer and more powerful successors as Palatine Counts, the Tocci, the castle vied in feudal splendour with the Frankish strongholds of the Morea; but island life must have been lonely and provincial, for Froissart records how exceeding glad the Tocci ladies were when, in the first years of the fifteenth century, the Comte de Nevers stayed on his way home to France and they had a sophisticated royal guest to talk to.

Though the castle one now sees is entirely Venetian, rebuilt immediately after the island had been taken from the Turks in 1500, the hilltop site (322 metres) is quite untypical of the Republic's seaside fortifications and the whole feeling of the place is medieval. The circuit is in almost perfect condition, its smooth stones weathered red-gold and mottled with saffron-coloured lichen, the scutcheons of the *provveditori* still legible to anyone prepared to scramble round outside.

Inside, little that is recognizable survives: the shell of the *Latin Cathedral of St Nicholas* at the end of the pine avenue as you enter; a well-head dated 1572; and a few vaulted rooms and magazines. The finest bit of architecture is the round tower to the west with wavily indented corbels; it contains a spring-chamber to which you can descend by a flight of worn steps. In the great flaring bastion which guards the main entrance to the east are dungeons which you can also visit if you have a good torch. The view from the walls is superb: north-west to Argostoli and the Gulf; east to Mt Enos; and south-east to Zakinthos. At the foot of the hill to the north is a field so beautifully cleaned and levelled that it is tempting to think that it must once have served as a jousting-yard.

At the bottom end of the ridgeway which runs down from the castle gate, an ornate stone *belfry gate* stands like a triumphal arch in front of the *Church of Evangelistria* (Our Lady of the Annunciation), whose golden stone and oeil-de-boeuf windows recall the church architecture of Zante. The signifcance of the three little stone men who hold their hands on their heads above the belfry arch is unknown. These two late-sixteenth-century survivors of the 1953 earthquake are almost unique on the island.

[8 km.] Back on the main road in Travliata two roads go south: one opposite the southern ascent to the castle, the other a few metres farther on. You should take the second.

[8·5 km.] A rough road crosses the route. 0·5 km. along the road to the right, on the far side of a low scrub-covered ridge of rock on the right, are the late-Mycenaean rock-cut *tombs of Mazarakata.* (The place is easily recognizable from the ineffective wire fence.) The sixteen chamber-tombs, of various sizes, are each approached by a dromos and contain rows of rock-cut graves. The pottery found in them when they were excavated in 1909 is late- or sub-Mycenaean ware of the twelfth century B.C.

[9·5 km.] You reach a T-junction. Turning right you come almost immediately to a cross-roads. The road ahead leads in 2·5 km. to **Lakithra**, just beyond which a restaurant in a grove of pines on the ridge to your right, surveys Mt Enos, Zakinthos and the flat coastal strip of land below you to the south. Inconclusive excavations carried out early in this century suggest that Lakithra may have been the acropolis and centre of the considerable late-Mycenaean settlement to which the tombs at Mazarakata, Metaxata and other near-by places all bear witness. By the ridge-road which continues beyond the restaurant it is 5 km. to the road which links Argostoli to Platis Yalos, and another 0·8 km. down into the town (see Excursions from Argostoli). From this ridge-road there are attractive views north to the Krania meadow-lands and the Koutavos Lagoon.

[10·5 km.] Turning left at the cross-roads, you reach a T-junction in **Metaxata**, a village looking down over the rich land of the Livatho. Here several rich ship-owners and sea-captains have built themselves country villas. Byron, who stayed at Metaxata from August to December 1823 waiting for letters from the Committee in England and advice from the Peloponnese before sailing for Mesolongi, describes the night-time view: 'Standing at the window of my apartment in this beautiful village, the calm though cool serenity of a beautiful and transparent moonlight, showing the Islands, the Mountains, the Sea, with a distant outline of the Morea traced between the double Azure of the waves and skies, has quieted me enough to be able to write . . .'

Byron's stay is commemorated by a small marble slab set in a garden wall and inscribed 'Lord Byron's ivy'. The ivy still flourishes, but the house he lived in has vanished.

If you fork right at the T-junction in Metaxata a tarred road will take you down in 0·8 km. to **Kourkoumelata**, a model post-earthquake village with an Olympic-sized sports stadium, vast school and clinic, and rows of tidy little Californian houses surrounded by green lawns, all financed by one wealthy Cefalonian.

[11 km.] The left fork at the bottom of Kourkoumelata will take you into the adjoining village of **Kaligata** where the south façade and screen of the church (1804) are good examples of Cefalonia's late and florid baroque.

[12 km.] A road forks left to the *Irinna* hotel, 1·5 km. away on the coast at a place called Ayia Pelayia.

[14·5 km.] A road on the left beyond Minies leads in 0·8 km. to the airport, and just after this point the luxuriant countryside of the Livatho gives way to the bare seaward-facing hillside of the ridge behind Argostoli.

[18·5 km.] **Platis Yalos**. For this beach and the road back to Argostoli see p. 236.

Route 2: Argostoli to Poros and Nea Skala

At Nea Skala (40 km.) there are interesting Roman mosaics and a fine sand-and-shingle beach and at Poros (43·5 km.) — Cefalonia's nearest approach to a bathing resort — a pebble beach. But what makes the drive worth while is not so much what you will find in these two east-coast villages as the scenery en route. Between the sea and the high-running road which skirts the uninhabited grey screes of Mt Enos, thatched with a dark and jagged forest of primeval firs, a narrow coastal plateau is laid out for your inspection, whose cornfields, cypresses and olive groves, ploughed land and meadow reveal a gentler and more luxuriant landscape than one would have thought could exist in an island so uncompromisingly mountainous and stony. Across the open sea to the south-east lies Zakinthos, its high western cliffs picked out by the afternoon sun.

Route Leave Argostoli by Exit A on the town plan and follow Route 1 as far as Travliata [8 km.] where you go straight on. For Nea Skala, fork right 24 km. out from Argostoli. For Poros keep left at this fork and continue straight on through several villages to Tzanata [40 km.]. Just past Tzanata the road forks. Go right here for Poros; the left fork will take you along Link Route A to Sami. In 1980 a 5 km. stretch of the road to Nea Skala was being widened in readiness for tarring.
Bus Day return services to both Nea Skala and Poros.
Accommodation and Restaurants Summer eating places at Ayos Thomas and Lourdata; rooms (10) and restaurants at Katelios; rooms (30), restaurants and a small hotel at Nea Skala; hotels (B and C class), rooms (200) villas and restaurants at Poros.

[8·5 km.] In **Peratata**, the village immediately following Tavliata, a lane on the right leads in a few hundred metres to the *Convent of Ayos Andreas*, where the older of the two churches houses a series of twelfth-century wall-paintings (recovered from a third church and transferred to canvas) as well as its own superimposed sixteenth-, seventeenth- and eighteenth-century frescoes. The new church also houses what is claimed to be the saint's velvet-shod left foot and some fine icons.

[9·5 km.] Beyond Peratata a signed road leads right in 1·2 km. to **Karavados** and forking left in this village continues for another 1·5 km. to the coast at a place called Ayos Thomas. It is a pretty spot with a summer eating place, a trickle of water, a small beach of particularly fine sand, and flat ledges of sedimentary rock from which you can dive into deep water. These ledges seem to have been pushed up by some comparatively recent spasm and contain shells which have only just had time to fossilize.

[16 km.] **Vlakhata**. A road on the right leads down through **Lourdata** to a very beautiful sandy beach 2·5 km. away. With a narrow strip of irrigated vegetable-gardens, orange, lemon and olive trees behind it, a stream of water and a summer eating place, this is a perfect spot for a bathe. The development of Poros as a seaside resort instead of Lourdata is one of the 'mysteries of Cefalonia'.

[21 km.] A rough road on the right is signed to the ancient *Monastery of Sision*, whose name recalls its Frankish dedication to St Francis of Assisi. Completely destroyed in the 1953 earthquake, it is no longer worth visiting.

[24 km.] Take the right fork for the main route to Nea Skala 16 km. away. This leads you down in 3 km. to the rich coastal plateau around **Khionata**, where there are magnificent olive trees. The road then drops steeply down again to the plain of Katelios and brings you in another 4 km. to the fishing-hamlet of **Katelios**, a 0·5 km. detour to the right, where the combination of red and blue boats, eucalyptus trees, a stream, mountain and meadow-land is inexplicably attractive. There are rooms to stay in, miles of surfy golden beach, and a fine seventeenth-century screen in the church of Ayos Andreas. Across the river-bed with its thirsty plane trees, you climb up again for 4 km. to **Randzakli** and thence dip in and out of several moist ravines choked with olive trees. The soil on this last 5-kilometre stretch is a sandy clay; *Serapia lingua* litters the roadside ditches and *Cistus salviaefolius* covers the banks with its white-starred clumps in May and June.

Nea Skala

In the last ten years luxuriant gardens and rustling windbreaks of scented pines have softened the hard edges of this post-earthquake village, and it has now become an attractive and sleepy place for a seaside holiday, with endless miles of sandy beach as its chief draw. But it also has a Roman villa set in a dip to the south. Ask at the new hotel for the key to the shelter which covers its mosaics.

The mosaic in the main hall of the *villa* shows a young man being torn to pieces by a lion, a tiger, a puma and a leopard; and the long inscription below, signed by the artist Krateros, suggests that this scene was an allegorical warning to guests not to allow themselves to be devoured by envy of their host's prosperous villa. Another mosaic, in rather worse condition, depicts the same triple sacrifice of ram, bull and boar which Odysseus was told by Teiresias to make to Poseidon (*Odyssey*, Book 11). The mosaics date from the second half of the second century A.D.

From new Skala you can drive up in 4 km. by a very rough and steep road to old Skala, a ghost-village of earthquake-riven houses in a very beautiful olive-shaded site looking out to Zakinthos. A vast oak tree and an undamaged sixteenth-century Venetian *belfry-gate* stand on the left as you leave the village. From here, keeping left at the next fork, you can rejoin the Argostoli-Poros road at Pastra, 4 easier kilometres away. This rough short cut saves the long return to the original fork off to Nea Skala.

[26 km.] Shortly after this first Nea Skala fork off the main Poros road you pass through the shaded village of **Atsoupades**.

[29 km.] **Markopoulo**, a village on the corner of Mt Enos, is said to be the original home of Marco Polo's ancestors. It is also renowned for a phenomenon which no ophiologist has yet explained. Every year, during the week preceding the feast of the Assumption of the Virgin (i.e., August 8th–15th), snakes with black crosses on their heads and with skins like silk are caught near and in the village church. Seen at no other time or place, the snakes are not only harmless but are credited with thaumaturgic powers and the villagers drape them round their necks.

At Markopoulo you turn in along the splendid valley of Katelios, whose water mills once ground most of the island's corn.

[32 km.] **Pastra**. Fork right here for a rough 8 km. route through old Scala to new Scala (see above).

[33·5 km.] **Ayos Yeorgos**. From this village you wind down by hairpin bends to the great *vale of Arakli*, surrounded on all sides by mountains and particularly beautiful when, in spring, the terraced hillsides descend in narrow treads of bright green corn. The fertile and now well-settled valley was inaccessible and unexploited until Napier built his network of roads and brought skilled Maltese farmers in to grow fruit and vegetables. 'Heracles here is finer than any part of Zante,' he wrote in 1823 (*The Life*), 'But nothing save goats can get there.'

[40 km.] **Tzanata**. Just past a grove of plane trees in this well-watered village, a rough road forks left for Sami, 22·5 km. away by Link Route A. The last 0·8 km. of the road on to Poros is spectacular, for the valley's outlet to the sea between Mt Atros (796 metres) to the north and Mt Petrovouni to the south is through a short but dramatic gorge, and the road squeezes through beside a torrent-bed which, in spring, is a race of limpid waters.

[43·5 km.] **Poros**. Outside the gorge on a narrow strip of land by the sea, Poros has snowballed in the last ten years from a post-earthquake core of prefabs into a little seaside resort. In July and August the place fills up with holiday families and there is a companionable air. But for most of the year the hotels are shut and the village deserted; then the close steep background of mountainside, though always green, seems lonely and forbidding. The best bathing is from the long beach north of the village centre, reached by a bridge across the river-bed. Though the large pebbles are hard on the feet the water is clear and invigorating.

Under Cape Sarakinato, two hundred metres to the south of the modern village, is an older fishing hamlet on a sheltered, sandy bay. Here, in 1980, a jetty was being built for a new ferry service to Killini on the mainland.

On a knoll known as *Pakhni*, a little below the summit of Mt Petrovouni, stood the classical *city of Proni*, one eye on the sea, the other on its hidden valley. Its coins bore the impression of the club with which its citizens liked to think that Heracles had struck open the gorge when he accompanied Amphitryon on his expedition against the ox-stealing Teleboans. To climb to the not very interesting remains of its walls from the centre of the village you will need a guide and a good 50 minutes.

In summer, boat-trips from Poros to Nea Skala are sometimes arranged. The return trip, with time long enough to see the mosaics, takes something under 3 hours. Halfway there you pass *Cape Kapros* where, at the end of the eighteenth century, the naturalist Sibthorp noted that the local fishermen were still making an incantatory libation mentioned by Pliny. '"Health, Cape Capro, to your wife" (making the first libation). "To your children" (making a second). "You fish, Melanouros, eat the cake" (making a third).' Sibthorp records them chanting in demotic Greek (Walpole, *Memoirs*). The place was certainly a holy one in ancient times, for a little farther along the coast, by the solitary *Chapel of Ayos Yeorgos*, the remains of a Doric temple of the sixth century B.C. have been discovered.

Route 3: Argostoli to Sami

The road between the capital and the ferry-port of Sami (24 km.) is a national rather than an island responsibility and is kept in good repair. Even so, the climb over the island's steep spine in the middle of a summer day can easily bring a car to the boil. There are excursions to the north-east wall of Krani (5 km. and 20 minutes on foot), the Convent of Ayos Yerasimos (12 km.) in the Omala, the summit of Mt Enos (23 km. plus 1 hour on foot: described separately in Route 4), and a cave full of stalactites at Drongarati (21·5 km.).

Route Leave Argostoli by Exit B on the town plan and turn right a few metres north of the Koutavos bridge.
Bus 4 day-return services to Sami which call at the Omala en route.
Accommodation and Restaurants 1 C and 2 E class hotels in Sami where there are 40 rooms and four restaurants.

[1·2 km.] A road forks right to encircle the Koutavos Lagoon (see Excursions from Argostoli).

[4 km.] A rough road on the right is signposted to the cyclopean walls of **Krani** — a misleading sign since the track ends 0·8 km. away by the *Chapel of Ayos Ilias* and no further sign shows you what to do then. You should walk approximately south by a path which soon peters out, aiming at a point where the left-hand slope of the steep hill on the right and ahead of you begins to flatten out. After 20 minutes you will cross the line of a wall which runs south-east from the hill for about 1 km. Seldom more than a course or two high, it is often obscured by scrub. Its frequent towers and varying styles of masonry suggest a hurried and unfinished work of about 300 B.C. — an extension made probably to protect herds driven in during times of siege. (For other parts of Krani see Excursions.)

[8 km.] As you reach the pass over the first range of hills, a road forks right into the broad *valley of the Omala* — the largest of all the many upland 'sumps' in the Ionian Islands — and after a level run along a fine avenue 'nearly a mile long and sixty feet wide' which Napier recalls (*The Life*) laying out for the Abbot in the early 1820s ends at the *Convent of Ayos Yerasimos*, 4 km. from the main road. St Yerasimos Notaras, the island's patron saint, was born in Trikala in the Peloponnese in 1509 of an old and wealthy family. He took his vows as a monk on Mt Athos in his early twenties and thereafter spent many years travelling from one monastery to another all over the Levant. In Jerusalem he was ordained deacon and priest by the Greek Patriarch, but after twelve years at the Church of the Holy Sepulchre left in search of a more ascetic life which he found first at Mar Sabbas above the Dead Sea, then on Crete, then on Zakinthos (where he spent five years as a hermit) and finally on Cefalonia. Here he set up in a cave between Platis Yalos and Argostoli, but disturbed by constant visitors moved up to the Omala, where he rebuilt a ruined church and was persuaded by the villagers to establish a nunnery for their unmarried daughters. As well as being a healer especially gifted in casting out devils, and a saintly man,

St Yerasimos seems to have had green fingers and to have been a water-diviner, and the legend that the water in the well under the plane tree which he planted at the centre of the avenue rises when his remains are carried there on the first Sunday after Easter may be based on the memory of a successful well sunk at his direction. His death on August 16th, 1579, and beatification two years later on October 20th, are also commemorated with services and processions. As on Corfu and Zante, the saint's mummified remains have two homes, a permanent silver coffer and a glass-fronted processional palanquin.

Neither the new and richly-furnished church nor the modern hostels are at all attractive, and it is the broad sweep of the valley, the fine avenue, and the towering slopes of Mt Roudi and Mt Enos to the north and east which, for the un-Orthodox, make the place worth visiting.

[8 km.] Back on the main road to Sami you cross the Omala valley and climb the mountain range.

[13 km.] *The pass of Agrapidies.* A road on the right leads to Mt Enos (see Route 4). From the pass you can free-wheel 8 kilometres down to the Sami valley, looking out to Ithaca and Lefkas and the island-circled sea.

[21 km.] In the valley bottom a road joins you from the left and leads in about 0·5 km. to the *cave of Drongarati* (open 07.00–19.30 April to September; entrance: Drs 20). A guide will lead you by easy cement steps and paths past stalactites which hang from the roof like folds of tripe from a buther's hook or bunches of candles from a chandler's ceiling. The floor of the huge lower cavern has been levelled with the idea of holding subterranean concerts.

[22·5 km.] A road forks right to Poros (see Link Route A).

[23·5 km.] A road forks left to Karavomilo, Ayia Effimia and Siniori (see Link Route B).

[24 km.] You reach Sami.

SAMI

Rebuilt with British help after 1953, Sami's main street and water-front houses are all on the same pattern with double decks of square arcades. The impression this uniformity gives of a planned and prosperous port is not entirely a façade. Its small C class hotel is often taken over entirely by successive groups in summer, and the car ferries which call at least once a day and go on to Corfu and Ithaca make it a busy place. Sami falls nevertheless between two stools. Too much of a port to be a peaceful seaside resort, it lacks the life and bustle of a town. The pebble beach which runs round the Gulf of Sami is too vast, impersonal and exposed for bathing at its best, and the *kéndro* at Karavomilo (see Link Route B) — a pleasant place to dine on a summer night — is 2·8 km. away. But though Sami is not so good a base as Argostoli, it is a handy and pleasant place for an overnight stay before setting off for Poros, Assos or Fiskardo, or in which to wait for the ferry to Ithaca.

At the back of the town are the remains of a *Roman bath* of the early third century A.D., with a dull mosaic floor just visible from outside the wire enclosure. The fine bronze head in the Argostoli museum was found here. In the neighbourhood you can visit the cave at Drongarati (see above), the pot-hole of Melissani (see Link Route B) and the remains of the ancient city of Sami.

ENVIRONS OF SAMI

Ancient Sami

In the fifth century B.C. Sami formed part of the four-towned Cefalonian confederation mentioned by Thucydides; its earlier history is unknown. In 188 B.C. it refused to surrender to the Romans and was stormed and sacked after a four-month siege. Thereafter it seems to have been abandoned for a century or so, since Strabo says that it no longer existed in his time; but it was resettled and flourished during the first three centuries A.D. The town lay in the valley between the two foothills which stand directly behind the present village. As you arrive by ferry you can see a line of wall running down from the summit of the northern hill towards the valley. This linked strong-points on the summits of each hill.

The remains of a tower and a large stretch of wall on the southern summit (known as Ayia Fanendes from the name of a now ruined monastery on the site) are 50 minutes' steep climb from the town.

Route About 100 metres south along the water-front from the jetty you come to a traffic square. Take the road that runs in from this towards the hill and turn left up the last lane which crosses it. About 50 metres up this lane take a narrow path which strikes off on the right by an old olive tree. Fork left after 2 minutes and right after another 15 minutes. Shortly after passing through a grove of pines you will see the tumble of the monastery above you on the left.

The path leads directly to an impressive stretch of wall behind the monastery. Its great blocks of bossed masonry are Hellenistic, probably of the third century B.C. To the north of the church, and set into the wall, are the bottom five or six courses of a handsome tower which looks a century older. Nineteenth-century travellers described and illustrated a curious tunnel which ran through the tower, but this is now hidden under the debris of a fallen campanile. The wall runs to the north edge of the summit and starts down into the valley, where it must have joined its opposite number from the other hill. Further disconnected stretches of the town wall, mostly of polygonal masonry, can be seen below and to the left of the path as you leave the monastery on the way down.

Route 4: Argostoli to Mt Enos

Cefalonia is the only island in the whole of Greece to retain a dense and sizeable chunk of its original forest, and it is an exhilarating experience to drive into the heart of it (23 km.) and then climb to the summit of Mt Enos through its ancient trees (1 hour each way).

Route Leave Argostoli by Exit B on the town plan and follow Route 3 to the pass of Agrapidies [13 km.]. Here turn right. 19 of the 23 km. are tarred.

[13 km.] The road which forks right at the pass of Agrapidies runs high up along the bare southern side of *Mt Roudi* (1,125 metres). Down below you in the Omala, the deserted site of old Valsamata looks like a bomb-obliterated wartime target; in the stony *terra rossa* of the vineyards high on the other side of the valley grow the grapes from which the best *robóla* is trodden out in autumn; and over the rim of the valley to the south-east lies Zakinthos, baring its western cliffs with a ferocity which no visitor to that gentle island would suspect it of possessing.

[17·2 km.] The *pass of Ayos Eleftherios*. Various signboards on the right proclaiming 'No entry', 'No photography', etc. in increasingly dramatic terms, do *not* mean that you must turn back.

[13 km.] You reach a notice forbidding you to follow the tarred road farther round and up to a telecommunications installation; here you must fork left on to a dirt-track which climbs over stony slopes bare even in spring of all vegetation but yellow umbels of spurge and thick scatters of *Orchis provincialis* and *quadripunctata*. Ravens in numbers perch on boulders or croak and soar and tumble in the wind which cuts across the ridge.

[20·6 km.] As you reach the edge of the forest the ecology of the mountain changes with a suddenness which is almost incredible. In the space of a few metres the harsh scree of stones is embedded in mossy lawns and, in spring, drifts of pale blue *Anemone blanda* lie like sky-reflecting pools under the silver firs. These magnificent cedar-like trees, hung with Spanish moss and a home for jays, take their botanical name of *Abies cefalonica* from this particular forest, which must once have covered the whole mountain-range. Confined now to 202 hectares on the summit of Roudi and 890 hectares along the ridge of Enos, the forest was six times as large in 1500, when the tempo of tree-felling quickened suddenly to keep pace with the production-line of galleys turned out by the Arsenal in Venice. But even the Venetians' depredations did nothing like the damage caused by two fires kindled by disgruntled peasants at the end of the sixteenth and eighteenth centuries. The second, in 1797, lasted two weeks and lit the night-time streets of Argostoli. The wind is said to have carried the burned embers as far as Zakinthos, and the peasants harvested sixty-fold yields of corn from the rich humus of the charred slopes. By a curious legacy of British rule the forest now belongs to a Cefalonian philanthropic society and for lack of proper attention shrinks imperceptibly every year.

[21·5 km.] A pink-washed forestry station is a good place for a picnic.

[23 km.] The road ends at an earthquake-shattered hotel. The way to the summit is by a path which forks off right along the ridge just before you reach this building. It is an up-and-down walk rather than a climb and can easily be done in 1 hour each way. In early spring, the loveliest time, the glades on the northern slopes are full of hard-packed snow. Until the great fire of 1797 this used to lie as late as August, and even in Napier's time it was packed in caves till May and then brought down to Argostoli in the summer months or sent across to Zante to cool the negus and the punch at the Resident's evening parties. The summit (1,555 metres) is marked by a little *block-house*, and from here the views are quite spectacular: north-east past Ithaca and Lefkas to the snow-capped peaks of the Pindus range; east to the mountains on either side of the Gulf of Corinth; and south, 1,500 metres straight down the steep pitch of the mountainside to Lourdata (p. 242).

Route 5: Argostoli to Fiskardo

The extraordinary fortified peninsula of Assos (38·5 km.) on the wild west coast and the pretty little port of Fiskardo (53 km.) at the northern tip of the island can be visited in one day. But it is not only more restful but far more rewarding to find a room in one or the other and spend a night or two away.

Route Leave Argostoli by Exit B on the town plan and once across the bridge over the Koutavos Lagoon keep straight ahead. There is nothing of note to stop for on the road which runs for 13 km. up the east side of the bay of Livadi; but look back as you pass through Farsa [17 km.] at the sunlight streaming through the eye-sockets of the ruined houses, and across the bay at the clustered hill-villages of the Paliki. In 16 km. you pass the left fork to Lixouri, better reached from Argostoli by the ferry (see Route 6). Turn left at Siniori [29 km.] and, for Assos, fork left 6·5 km. beyond this village.
Bus A day-return service to Fiskardo and a one-way bus to Assos; but in summer there are coach tours to Assos as well.
Accommodation and Restaurants In Fiskardo: a very small B class hotel, 60 rooms, and 5 restaurants. In Assos: 30 rooms and 2 restaurants.

[1·2 km.] Shortly after the bridge you pass the *British cemetery* on the right. (It is the first of three cemeteries in a row and the key is kept in the cottage next to it.) Not as evocative as the Corfu cemetery or as romantic as the one on Zakinthos, many of its stones mention death by 'fever'. It was on Cefalonia that Private Wheeler recorded that 'The cause of not firing over the grave of a soldier in this country is that when the sickly season sets in the number of deaths are generally very great and that so much firing would dispirit the men.'

[19·5 km.] As you cross the neck of the Paliki peninsula a splendid view stretches in front of you up the west coast of the Fiskardo peninsula to the distant bulk of Lefkas; and from here you drive for 8 km. along a bare and precipitous mountainside with the ecstatic blues of the *Gulf of Mirtos* nearly 335 metres beneath you — kingfisher, peacock and butterfly, edged with slivers of white beach. The Assos peninsula grows more and more distinct, until you can make out the brown stone walls running along its crest.

[29 km.] At **Siniori** you fork left across the col which bridges the deep and richly planted *valley of Pilaros*. 100 metres or so after this turn a rough road on the left takes you down in 4 km. to *Mirtos beach*, a huge and dazzling stretch of white sand. There is neither café nor shade and the best time to bathe there is in the morning before the summer sun has got you squarely in its sights.

[35·5 km.] Fork left for Assos, 3 km. down a snaking road.

Assos

Strabo writes of Cefalonia that 'where the island is narrowest it forms an isthmus, so low-lying that it is often submerged from sea to sea', a description which can apply only to the spit of land which joins the rocky lump of Assos to the rest of the island. On the sheltered cove formed by this spit and the peninsula is the picturesque little village of Assos, its white and colour-washed houses running a little way up either side of a fertile valley which flattens out by a shingle beach into a village square of beaten earth, shaded by fine planes and silver poplars. The skeletons of one or two handsome nineteenth-century houses are the only reminder of the 1953 earthquake. After the long hot traverse of the mountainside, the simplicity and freshness of Assos is delicious, and if you stay you will feel much more of a guest than a client as your landlady shows you to her scrupulously clean spare room, brings you water in a pitcher and sets your table with wine from her own vineyard, country bread and, perhaps, a mackerel cooked with garlic and rosemary.

From the village it is almost 2·5 km. by a narrow, twisting lane up to the gate of the *fortress*, built between 1593 and 1595 as a refuge for the population of the area. Leake mentions 'a piece of Hellenic wall in the modern castle', but no later visitor has been able to find this or other evidence of early occupation. The only bit of architectural sophistication about the rough quarry-faced revetments which protect the vulnerable landward side of the fortress is the elbowed *entrance-corridor*, a typical example of Venetian panache. Elsewhere the fortress relies on the sheer cliffs and steep slopes of the peninsula and the circuit-wall is nowhere very impressive. But one should certainly make the climb up to the castle. From the top there is an enchanting view down to the cove, the village and the beaches north of it; and the line of tremendous white cliffs stretching round the dark blue waters of the Gulf of Mirtos to the west and south provides 'one of the sublimest scenes in the Seven Islands' (Lear, *Views*). And this is not all. The barren outer slopes of the peninsula hide a deep bowl of fertile land (tended by the inmates of an agricultural prison until 1953, but since largely neglected) and the terraces of olives and of vines, the waist-deep grasses, the wild flowers and the birds make one feel that one has here strayed into a sort of Ionian Xanadu. The pleasure-dome of the Venetian bailey has crumbled; the twice five miles of walls are here no more than three; and huge cisterns do duty for the sacred river; but the contained poetry of the place is similar.

[35·5 km.] Continuing north along the main road from the fork down to Assos, you clear the last spurs of a mountain 900 metres high, with the lovely name of *Kámbos tis Analípseos* (Field of the Ascension), and, moving over to the other side of the ridge, see the stern coastline of Ithaca across the strait to the east.

[42·5 km.] At **Enosis** an untarred right turn leads in 3 km. to **Playa** (go right or left at the fork before this village; the roads re-join) and in another 3 km. to **Vari**, where the tiny *Chapel of the Panayia Kouyanna* — the only surviving Byzantine building on the island — contains the remains of remarkable late-fifteenth-century wall-paintings. (Stop by the large church on the right at the end of the village and ask for the caretaker and the chapel key at the café opposite. The chapel is 5 minutes' walk away.) On the north wall of the transept three magnificent life-size hierarchs confront you eye to eye. The colour has gone from all but their gold haloes, but the *sanguine* outlines of the figures are swift and self-assured. The screen is the east wall of the transept itself, pierced by one small door and divided into painted arches. Here a little more colour survives — rose, pale blue and yellow — and the faces of the Twelve Apostles are drawn with exceptional liveliness. The fading of the correct iconographical colour-scheme has had the freakish effect of enhancing the strangeness and appeal of these paintings, whose tones must once have been more like the glowing clarets, dark greens and blues of the Last Judgment on the north wall of the nave. Underneath this an engaging cartoon-strip of unsophisticated doodles in dark brown on white (seventeenth-century?) depicts the torments of the damned.

Beyond Enosis on the main road the stony upland country, terraced for corn and vines, grows greener with thickets of kermes oak, tree heath and arbutus.

[48 km.] **Mangano**, a large village with shops and cafés at the head of a cleft-like valley. The supermarket here caters for the visiting yachtsmen of Fiskardo and is better stocked than any in Argostoli. At Mangano the road makes a loop round the northern tip of the island through increasingly thick stands of cypress, with views north to Sappho's Leap on Lefkas (see p. 204).

[53 km.] **Fiskardo**

Fiskardo is named after Robert Guiscard — the Weasel — whose death here of the plague in 1085 put paid for fifty years to the Sicilian Normans' expeditions against Byzantium. There is a story that his men began to build a church worthy for him to lie in but left it unfinished when they later decided to sail back to Italy with his body. Perhaps this bit of folklore was inspired by the remains of a *sixth-century basilica* on the point across the harbour above the pretty round *Venetian beacon-tower*. For its two towers flank the west front in a typically Norman way.

Fiskardo is the only village on the island which survived the 1953 earthquake almost untouched, and the weathered tiles and nicely worked lintels, sills and quoins of its eighteenth- and nineteenth-century houses are immensely restful after the prefabricated huts and new cement of the other villages. (The one or two damaged houses are the result of a wartime British raid on Italian shipping in the harbour.) Less than a hundred people live here, and in winter the stone quay is deserted and the houses, belonging mostly to seafaring people, are firmly shuttered. But from spring to autumn the harbour is often full of yachts, and in summer the awning-shaded water-front restaurant is packed with holiday-makers. As in the whole district of Erissos, fresh water is in short supply. For a bathe you can walk north or south to secluded coves where the cypresses march down to flat shelves of rock which serve as sun-bathing tables.

Route 6: Argostoli to the Kipoureon Monastery

The roads in the Paliki — as the southern bulge of the Lixouri peninsula is called, after the ancient town of Pali — are in worse condition than those in the rest of the island, and the only place there worth the discomfort of the drive is the Kipoureon Monastery (17 km.), magnificently sited on the cliffs of the west coast.

Route The car ferries which cross Livadi Bay in half an hour seven or eight times a day in each direction make it an easy matter to reach Lixouri from Argostoli. The ferry terminal is to the north of the customs and port officials' enclosure (*Town Map* **3**).

Leave Lixouri by the road which runs south from the south-west corner of the main square. The rather roundabout route goes through or past the villages of Illari, Mandzavinata, Vouni and Khavriata. 2·5 km. past Khavriata (where the tar ends), and just before a sign announcing Khavdata, take the even rougher road which forks left up into the bare range of hills.

Accommodation and Restaurants D and E class hotels in Lixouri and two restaurants. Guest-rooms at Kipoureon Monastery (take your own food).

The hot little town of **Lixouri** will tempt few visitors to stay. In the central square the sunlight on white paving, whitewashed walls and kerbs to the pavements, and whitewashed tree-tunks is almost blinding. The *ruins of Pali* (1·5 km. north of the town between the coast road and the sea) are too vestigial to repay a visit.

Between Lixouri and Khavriata the landscape presents 'one of the most curious and extraordinary scenes imaginable' (Davy), cut and eroded into spikes, tables and ridges of naked white marl over which the road climbs as long-windedly as an ant over chalky ploughland. In the hot craters and gullies the currant vine and the olive flourish. Distance softens the lunar landscape you have traversed into a gentle green and white plain and from the top of the range of hills the view back over the bay to the rest of Cefalonia is splendid. Over the brow of the last hill you will see the trees and ruined walls of the deserted *Tafios Monastery* at the head of a terraced valley on the right; and as you wind down you will glimpse below you, on a shelf of land 100 metres above the sea, the tiled roofs of the quadrangle of Kipoureon, a palm tree by its belfry entrance.

Monastery of Kipoureon

Founded in 1744 as an offshoot of the much older foundation up the valley, Kipoureon was hardly touched by the 1953 earthquake, and its galleried courtyard used to be charming and picturesque, though of no great architectural distinction. But during the last ten years the monastery has been misguidedly restored by its hard-working resident monks. The floor-tiles — lilac edged with dark blue and typical of Cefalonian churches — have been replaced by concrete. However, other treasures have survived. On the walls next to the screen there are two fine icons from Tafios, of Christ as High Priest and of the Virgin and Child, both possibly of the sixteenth century; and in the monastery's museum are the remains of a fine seventeenth-century altar-screen, one or two interesting icons, a few manuscript gospels, and a lot of nineteenth-century Russian church plate and embroidery. There is a row of guest-rooms, and if you decide to stay the night you should take a few provisions, and, of course, slip a more generous offering into the church collection-box. From the belvedere on the cliff-tops you can watch the sun settle into the empty sea, and next morning climb down to the cove to bathe.

Link Route A: Sami to Tzanata

This is a link route for those who want to visit Poros while based on Sami. Only about 6·5 of the 22·5 km. to Tzanata are tarred but the road to Sofata is being remade; after Sofata it is narrow, rough and steep.

Route Leave Sami by the main Argostoli road and fork left after 1·5 km. at the signpost for Poros.

[11 km.] After an easy sweeping climb you reach the head of the valley at a fork in the road outside **Sofata**. Behind the small building on the right as you enter are the remains of retaining walls of polygonal masonry supporting a flattened area which commands the valley. A semicircle of dressed stones standing on this platform suggests the podium of a Hellenistic tower or temple. Sofata is on the watershed between the Poros and Sami valleys, and this point may have marked the frontier between the towns of Proni and Sami in antiquity. There is a good view of the thick forest on the moist northern slopes of Mt Enos.

[16 km.] On the outskirts of the large village of **Ayos Nikolaos** a track on the left is signposted to *Lake Avithos*. If you walk down it for about 50 metres and then strike left through the olives for the same distance, you will come out above the reed-fringed pool whose dark blue waters, continually renewed, irrigate the whole valley.

   Back on the road, fork right a few metres farther on to avoid the village. From here it is 6·5 km. down to the *vale of Arakli* beside stream-beds increasingly choked with plane and cherry trees.

[22·5 km.] You reach a T-junction in **Tzanata**. From this point it is 3 km. left to Poros, and 40 km. right to Argostoli (see Route 2).

Link Route B: Sami to Siniori

This is a link route for those who want to visit Assos and Fiskardo from Sami. Apart from the strange and beautiful pot-hole of Melissani and the seaside pool of Karavomilo there is nothing to stop for.

Route Leave Sami by the main Argostoli road and turn right in 0·8 km. at the sign for Ayia Effimia and Assos. In Ayia Effimia [9·5 km.] there is a road going left as you enter the village, but the way up to Siniori is along the road which forks left by the petrol pump at the far left-hand end of the open water-front. This starts off on the north side of the valley, then swings across to the south.
Accommodation and Restaurants C class hotel, a few rooms and a restaurant at Ayia Effimia and a restaurant at Karavomilo.

[2·7 km.] Towards the end of the village of **Karavomilo** a signposted lane on the right takes you down in 50 metres to the reed-fringed seaside pool at Karavomilo fed from Melissani (see below). There is a pleasant modern *kéndro* on a eucalyptus-shaded terrace by the beach where people from Sami come to dine and dance on summer evenings. On the left, ten metres out to sea, a froth of foam marks the upsurge of an underwater spring, one of the many which make the bathing here icy and invigorating, though the stones are hard on one's feet and when the prevailing *máestros* churns up the bottom the water is far from clear.

[3 km.] A concrete lane on the left takes you in 200 metres to the water-filled *pot-hole of Melissani* (open April to September 07.00–19.00; entrance: Drs 20. Café). A modern rock-cut tunnel, like the approach to a Pharaonic tomb, slants down to the water-level; and here you take a rowing-boat across the sunlit and intensely blue water into a dark cave as large again as the open crater, where mossy stalactites writhe from the roof like roots, this way and that, all out of true, as though blown awry by a Stygian wind. In this pot-hole, rim-hung with olive trees and skimmed by swallows, the sea-water which plunged underground at the Sea Mill near Argostoli (see p. 235) comes up for air, now fresher than before though still too salt to drink, and then runs underground again to the pool at Karavomilo.

[9·5 km.] **Ayia Effimia**, a little port serving the rich valley of Pilaros, flourishing in the nineteenth century but now eclipsed by Sami. Its honey (*méli*) is famous, but is sold in bulk so take your own container.

[17 km.] **Siniori**. Towards the end of the village there is a signposted fork right for Assos and Fiskardo, 9·5 km. and 24 km. away respectively. If you go straight on it is 29 km. back to Argostoli (see Route 5).

ZAKINTHOS (ZANTE)

Zakinthos (*i Zákinthos* in Greek) is the most southerly of the Ionian Islands proper and the third largest, with an area of 435 square kilometres. It lies a few kilometres off the west coast of the Peloponnese and is reached by air from Athens or car ferry from Killini. In 1971 the island had a population of 30,187 and the capital (also called Zakinthos) contained 9,339 inhabitants. The Venetians (and their British successors) called both town and island Zante, and though this name is now seldom used in everyday conversation it is kept alive in the jingle 'Zante, fior di Levante'.

INFORMATION FOR VISITORS

Information
Tourist Police, Solomos Square (*Map 15*) (tel. 22550). An exceptionally hard-working, helpful office, though without any English speaker.
Post Office
Map 15.
Cable Office (O.T.E.)
Map 8.
Hospital
At Perivola, behind the town (tel. 515).
Feast-Days
Easter (see p. 77); August 24th and December 17th, processions in honour of St Dionisios (see p. 268).

GETTING TO ZAKINTHOS

Air

In winter there are three, in summer five flights weekly in each direction between Athens and Zakinthos. The Olympic Airlines office is in King George II Square (tel. 28611).

Sea

Car ferries
From Killini (71 km. south of Patras): At 13.00 and 17.30 in winter, at 10.00, 14.00 and 18.00 in spring, and every two hours between 08.00 and 20.00 in summer. Crossing time about 1½ hours.

Road

From Athens: Via Corinth and Patras to Killini. Total 293 km.

Bus

From Athens: See p. 20.
Two morning buses along the route above (they can be boarded at Patras). Journey time 7½ hours.
Athens Officeof the Zakinthos K.T.E.L.: 100 Kifissou Street (tel. 5129432).
Patras Office: Opposite the railway station (tel. 277556).
Zante Office: *Map* 17 (tels. 22656 and 23776).

Train

From Athens: S.E.K. — One morning train to Killini via Patras (where it can be boarded). Journey time about 8½ hours.

TRANSPORT ON THE ISLAND

Buses

For general information about island buses see p. 22. In summer there are useful return services to all the main beaches; for details see the individual routes. The K.T.E.L. bus station (both for the island and for Athens) is at 42 Filita Street (*Map* 17).

Taxis

There are about 60 taxis on the island, almost all of them based on the capital. For rates see p. 23. The two main ranks are opposite the Cable Office (*Map* 8) in All Saints' Square and at the east end of the Platia Rouga.

Car, scooter and bicycle hire

Cars: From D. Plessa Bros., 1 Vasilis Konstandinou Street (tel 28258).
Scooters: From D. Kardianos, 'O Faros', Platia Inglesi (tel. 22309).
Bicycles: From V. Vosos, 1 Filita Street.

ACCOMMODATION AND RESTAURANTS

Town hotels

B Class   *Strada Marina*, 14 Lomvardou Street. Medium-sized water-front hotel opposite ferry berth. Rather noisy site. Roof garden. Most rooms have a sea view, al canned music. No restaurant.

Xenia, 66 D. Roma Boulevard. Medium-sized sea-front hotel. All rooms have sea view. L class restaurant.

C Class   *Adriana*, 6 N. Kolyva Street. Small water-front hotel. No restaurant.

Aigli, K. Lomvardou Street. Small water-front hotel. No restaurant.

Angelica, Kryoneriou. Small water-front hotel opposite bathing lido. No restaurant.

Astoria, 1 Rizospoton. Annexe of Phoenix. No restaurant.

Diana, 11 Capodistriou Street. Central, medium-sized hotel. No restaurant.

Phoenix, Solomos Square. Medium-sized hotel in main square. Some rooms with sea view, eight double suites. Café and cake shop. No restaurant.

Zenith, 44 Tertseti Street. Small back-street hotel. No restaurant.

D Class   *Alfa*, 1 Tertseti Street. Small back-of-town hotel. No restaurant.

Diethnes, 102 Ay. Lazarou Street. Small outskirts house. No restaurant.

Ionian, 18 A. Roma Street. Small hotel on main street. Top-floor rooms have sea views. No restaurant.

Kendrikon, 25 L. Zoi Street. Central side-street hotel. No restaurant.

Kharavgi, 3 Xanthopoulou Street. Small side-street hotel. No restaurant.

Ouranion, 7 Ay. Eleftherion. Open June to September. No restaurant.

Rezenda, 36 A. Roma Street. Small main street hotel. No restaurant.

Country hotels

B Class   *Galaxias*, Laganas. *Route* 2. Open April 1st to October 31st. Large beach-side hotel. L class restaurant.

Khrisi Akti, Argasi. *Route* 1. Medium-sized seaside hotel. Beach. A class restaurant. Tennis.

Mimosa Beach, Argasi. *Route* 1. Open April to October. One-, two- or (in the case of single) four-room seaside bungalows with central public rooms. Beach and water ski-ing. No restaurant.

Zante Beach, Laganas. *Route* **2**. Open April to October. Very large hotel on grassed and planted beach-side site. Restaurant, discotheque, swimming pool, water ski-ing, mini-golf, tennis.

C Class *Anetis*, Planos. *Excursions*. Small beach-side hotel. Restaurant.

Argasi Beach, Argasi. *Route* **1**. Small beach-side hotel.

Asteria, Alikes. *Route* **5**. Open Easter until end September. Small beach-side hotel. Restaurant.

Asteria, Laganas. *Route* **2**. Small beach-side hotel. Restaurant.

Ionis, Alikes. *Route* **5**. Small beach-side hotel. Restaurant.

Ionis, Laganas. *Route* **2**. Medium-sized, back from beach. No restaurant.

Montreal, Alikes. *Route* **5**. Medium-sized beach-side hotel. Restaurant.

Oraia Eleni, Planos. *Excursions*. Small hotel set back from beach.

Tsilivi, Tsilivi. *Excursions*. Medium-sized, back from the beach. Restaurant.

D Class *Alikes*, Alikes. *Route* **5**. Small beach-side hotel. Restaurant.

Hermes, Laganas. *Route* **2**. Small beach-side hotel. Restaurant.

Thalassia Avra, Laganas. *Route* **2**. Small beach-side hotel. Restaurant.

Porto Roma, Vasiliko. *Route* **1**. Small bungalow hotel above the beach. Restaurant.

Flats

The *Castello Marino* at Argasi has 20 double or triple bed flats in a beach-side site, and there are several blocks of flats at Laganas.

Rooms in private houses

The number of rooms available in 1980 was approximately as follows: 230 in Zakinthos town, 30 at Bokhali, 80 at Planos and Tsilivi, 100 at Argasi, 40 at Vasiliko, 230 at Laganas, 70 at Mouzaki and 100 at Alikes.

Holiday camp

The *Club Méditerranée* (see p. 28) have a site on the Vasiliko peninsula but in 1980 had not yet done anything with it.

Restaurants

The best restaurants in town are in or near St Mark's Square (*Map* 7); but there are simple grill-rooms in other parts where you can get draught *verdéa* with excellent grilled chicken and a salad. On the way up the Castle hill and at Bokhali are *kéndros* where you can hear *kantádes*.

For country restaurants see the Route Instructions.

Specialities: *Sáltsa* (see p. 100), *mandoláto* (see p. 101), *verdéa* (see p. 101), currant grapes and wild strawberries (*fraoules*).

SPORT

Bathing

Soft sand beaches, particularly suitable for children, at Tsilivi and Planos (p. 273), Porto Roma and Yerakas (p. 277), Alikes (p. 286) and Laganas (p. 277).

INTRODUCTION TO ZAKINTHOS

'Zant is but a little Island; But to make amends, is one of the most fruitful and pleasant places I ever saw.' So judged Wheler in 1675 and his verdict is still true. It is an island conveniently divided into two: a distant half, discreetly hidden, whose wild hills can either be explored or ignored; and, near at hand, a great fertile plain ringed round with foothills and margined at each end with sandy beaches. 'The old nursery rhyme:

> "If all the world were apple-pie
> "And all the trees were bread and cheese"

supposes a sort of Food-landscape hardly more remarkable than that presented by this vast green plain, which may be, in truth, called one unbroken continuance of future currant dumplings and plum puddings,' wrote Lear in 1863 (*Views*). In spring the plain is

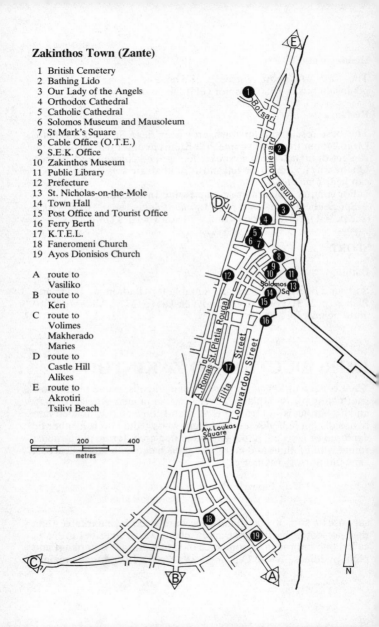

Zakinthos Town (Zante)

1 British Cemetery
2 Bathing Lido
3 Our Lady of the Angels
4 Orthodox Cathedral
5 Catholic Cathedral
6 Solomos Museum and Mausoleum
7 St Mark's Square
8 Cable Office (O.T.E.)
9 S.E.K. Office
10 Zakinthos Museum
11 Public Library
12 Prefecture
13 St. Nicholas-on-the-Mole
14 Town Hall
15 Post Office and Tourist Office
16 Ferry Berth
17 K.T.E.L.
18 Faneromeni Church
19 Ayos Dionisios Church

A route to
   Vasiliko
B route to
   Keri
C route to
   Volimes
   Makherado
   Maries
D route to
   Castle Hill
   Alikes
E route to
   Akrotiri
   Tsilivi Beach

0   200   400
metres

Botsari

Roma Boulevard

A. Romas St. (Platia Rouga)

Filita Street

Lomvardou Street

Solomos Sq.

Ay. Loukas Square

N

like a garden with its flowers and blossom, and by the tarred and level roads which lead across it from the capital you can visit much of the island in an afternoon.

Over the capital itself the melancholy of past beauty and lost grandeur hang in the air. Until its destruction in 1953 Zante was Venice's chief monument in Greece, surpassed only by Dubrovnik in its wealth of architecture. Poetry, painting and music flourished on the island as they did nowhere else in the Ionian Sea and though the old town is irrevocably gone you are reminded of its sophistication at every turn. In the museum and behind the baroque façades of rebuilt churches are dozens of icons and carved altar-screens, and statues of poets gaze at you from each square, a famous line or two inscribed on the pedestals below. On balmy evenings on the Castle Hill, or in the summer at the end of the harbour mole, passionate *bel canto* voices will serenade you with local *kantádes* to an accompaniment of guitars and mandolins. These local folk-songs are sometimes satirical, sometimes sentimental, sometimes as jangly as a Neapolitan barrel-organ.

ZAKINTHOS TOWN (ZANTE)

At about midday on August 12th, 1953, a stupendous earth-tremor levelled the churches, palaces and colonnades which had earned for the town of Zante the title of 'Venice of the Ionian Sea'. Almost immediately, a fire, catching in the wind from the spilt embers of a *tavérna* grill, ran blazing through the debris of a large part of the town, devouring the icons, gilded altar-screens, fine furniture and painted ceilings on which the Zantiots had spent their huge revenues from the currant trade in the seventeenth and eighteenth centuries. Only three present buildings survived the earthquake — the Church of the island's patron, St Dionisios (*Map 19*), a bank and a school — and apart from them and a few restored churches the town one now sees is entirely new. New in construction if not in plan: for the scheme to build a bold new Mediterranean city properly divided into residential, working and shopping zones, foundered on the resistance of private-property owners; and the town preserves the street plan which evolved at the end of the sixteenth century. The Venetian governor complained then in his increasingly deserted castle that 'all the well-off citizens (and those who live with them) are setting up on the shore, where they have built a remarkable new town and grow rich on commerce by the sea.' It is a long thin town stretching for more than three kilometres along the narrow edge of the bay beneath the Castle Hill with room for only one row of houses at its northern end between Cape Krioneri and the sea. Where the road doubles the National Tourist Organization have built an attractive bathing lido backed by lawns and flowers. The first part is free; the second, where there are changing cabins, tennis courts and a snack-bar charges a small entrance fee. Here, up wind and up current of the town, both sea and air are admirably clean.

From the straight inner road you can turn right by the large whitewashed Church of Ayia Triada to the old *British Cemetery* (*Map* 1). One hundred and fifty metres or so farther in towards the centre of the town, between the two roads, stands the very pretty little *Church of Our Lady of the Angels* (*Map* 3). The curved seaside road marks the original margin of the sea, now pushed back by rubble from the devastated town. Following this road you reach a paved garden where a marble bust commemorates Andreas Vesalius, the father of modern anatomy, who died in Zakinthos in 1564 after being shipwrecked in Keri Bay on his way back to Brussels from Jerusalem.

The north side of Solomos Square beyond is filled by the *Public Library* (*Map* 11) (which houses a collection of photographs of Zante before and after the earthquake) and the *Church of St Nicholas-on-the-Mole* (*Map* 13); the *Zakinthos Museum* (*Map* 10) fills the west side, and the *Town Hall* (*Map* 14) stands on the south. Upstairs on its landing is a bronze relief of 'Minerva embracing Truth and banishing Falsehood' by the Danish sculptor Thorwaldsen, which once decorated a statue of Sir Thomas Maitland.

Off the north-west corner of Solomos Square, through All Saint's Square (Cable Office; *Map* 8), are the paved *piazza of St Mark*, the site of the *Catholic Cathedral* (*Map* 5) and the *Solomos Museum* (*Map* 6). There are very few Catholic families in Zakinthos now, and the church is open only during the occasional visits of a priest from Corfu. Art historians who can get hold of the key will be able to test their expertise on the alleged Titian over the altar.

St Mark's Square is the terminus of Zante's main street, the *Platia Rouga* ('Broad Street'), once lined with seventeenth- and eighteenth-century *palazzi* and, until 1953, unique in Greece. If its present stiff cement arches inevitably fail to recapture the charm of the old stone colonnades, at least they provide welcome shade, the balconies overflow with scents of jasmine, carnation, gardenia and geranium, and many of the houses have an attractive square green ceiling of vines suspended above them on a frame of wire and calamus-reeds.

The campaniles of the *Churches of Ayos Dionisios* (*Map* **19**) and *of the Faneromeni* (*Map* **18**) mark their positions at the south end of the town, the first topped by a pyramid of red tiles, the second by a sandstone-coloured pepper-pot dome. They are most easily reached by the quayside road.

CHURCHES

Church of the Kiria ton Angelon (Our Lady of the Angels)
Map **3**.

This enchanting little church was built in 1687 by the hairdressers' guild and well restored after 1953. Its stone façade is richly carved with almost plateresque ornament, and over the door are cryptic symbols of the sun, moon and stars. Inside, the two angels (*c.* 1600) on the side-doors of the seventeenth-century altar-screen are particularly fine. (Key with the priest of St Nicholas-on-the-Mole.)

Church of Ayos Nikolaos sto Molo (St Nicholas-on-the-Mole)
Map **13**.

In 1483 this was a chapel on an island; in 1560, when the fisher-men's guild asked permission to rebuild it as their church and meeting-place, it stood on the mole; and for many years after the area of the present square was reclaimed from the sea, a lamp hanging on its vanished campanile guided the fishing-boats back to the harbour. Particularly well rebuilt after 1953, it is the oldest church now standing in the town and for centuries has been the starting-point for Zante's solemn and splendid Easter processions (see p. 77).

It is a plain but handsome building of golden blocks and pale curved tiles. The stones of the north wall — set in courses of tile — are a faithful reconstruction; they suggest that the sixteenth-century builders copied this Byzantine feature from the original chapel. Constant earthquakes have made 'anastylosis' second nature to the Zantiot masons.

Church of Ayos Dionisios (St Dionisius)
Map **19**.

The neo-Byzantine exterior of the huge building has little to recommend it; but there is a convincing touch of Venice about its tall white campanile when seen across the calm water of the harbour.

The inside is spacious and impressive. The silver casing (1820) of the left-hand icon on the altar-screen, depicting scenes from the saint's life, is by Baffas (see p. 94), as is the splendid rococo coffer in which the saint lies in the newly gilded chapel on the right. On August 24th and December 17th his remains are transferred to an eighteenth-century glass-and-silver sedan-chair and carried round the town in solemn procession.

St Dionisios Sigouros, born in Zante in 1547, came of a noble Zantiot family which survived in the island until quite recently. Archbishop of Aegina and then of the united province of Cefalonia and Zakinthos, he spent his last years as abbot of Anafonitria Monastery (see p. 284) where he added to his reputation for sanctity by sheltering his brother's assassin. He died in 1622 and was beatified in 1703. In 1717 the monastery in the Strofades Islands, where he was buried, was sacked by an Ottoman fleet; but two monks of the Order of St Basil escaped with his remains to Zakinthos, where the present church, finished not long before the 1953 earthquake, is the third built to house them.

Church of the Faneromeni
Map **18**.

Until it fell in 1953 and lost a remarkable screen, a unique painted ceiling and many important icons in the fire that followed, the Church of the Faneromeni was Zante's richest and most splendid building. It was completed in 1659, at the apogee of the island's prosperity. The name 'Faneromeni' comes from a 'manifestation' of the Virgin in the form of a small icon found hanging in the seaside rushes in the thirteenth or fourteenth century. The church has been rebuilt with many of its original stones, and one can admire the sophistication of its main north façade which is divided into three tiers: the first of blind arcading; the second of alternate blind and open windows; and the third of twelve blank oeils-de-boeuf in scrolled frames under a dentilated cornice.

MUSEUMS

Zakinthos Museum
Map **10**.

Open *Summer*   08.00–13.00 and 16.00–19.00
　　　　Sundays   10.00–13.00 and 16.00–19.00
　　　　Winter   09.00–13.00 and 14.30–17.00
　　　　Sundays   10.00–13.00 and 15.00–18.00
　　　　N.B. Closed on Tuesdays.
Entrance: Drs 25.

The museum contains many fine and interesting icons and serves as
an excellent introduction to the church art of Zante between the
twelfth and nineteenth centuries (see p. 91). In the central and
left-hand ground-floor rooms the clear colour and swift stylized
drawing of the 'Prophets' which N. Doxaras painted in 1757 for the
Church of the Faneromeni are as refreshing as poster art beside the
academic Italianate works of N. Kandounis, though the latter's
damaged 'Descent from the Cross' shows how capable if derivative
he was. In the central hall the long painting by J. Korai (1756)
started a fashion on the island for such panoramic pictures. It
depicts the procession of the relics of St Kharalambos and was
painted for the church dedicated to that saint (see p. 274). Despite
its solemn subject, the painting is full of life and gaiety and presents
a lively view of the social hierarchies of the period. In the right-hand
room there are two of the seventeenth-century carved gilt altar-
screens for which Zante is famous; one is from the Church of
Pantocrator and dated 1681, the other from the church of St James
of Kollas and dated 1690. One should look closely at the lively little
figures which clamber among the gilded scrolls as well as stand back
to admire the effect of the whole screen as a glowing frame for the
icons it displays. Upstairs, the sombre blues and reds of the fragmentary twelfth-century wall-painting from the former *Catholic
Cathedral of the Redeemer* in the Castle are much more satisfying
than the hot chrome, puce and green of a whole churchful of
seventeenth-century wall-paintings from the Church of St Andrew
in Volimes, the only frescoes of this period remaining on the island.
The heart of the museum is an upstairs room full of mostly
anonymous but splendid sixteenth-and seventeenth-century icons,
beside which their eighteenth-century successors next door appear
flaccid and uninspired, though an 'Ecce Home' by N. Kalleryis is
effective in a sentimental way.

Solomos Museum and Mausoleum
Map **6**.

Open Daily throughout the year 09.00–12.00 and 17.00–19.00
　　　Closed on Wednesdays.
Entrance: Free.

In the mausoleum downstairs stand the gold-inscribed marble tombs of two of Zante's three great poets — Dionisios Solomos (1798–1857) and Andreas Kalvos (1792–1869). With the publication in 1822 of his second poem in Greek — the 'Hymn to Liberty' — Solomos was immediately acclaimed as a national poet far beyond the shores of Zante. 'The second edition of the Hymn was printed in Paris in 1824 . . . Hugo, Lamartine and Chateaubriand hailed it with delight. Manzoni applauded and spread the fame of his pupil in Italy. Goethe christened the poet the "Byron of the East" ' (Jenkins). In 1863 the first two stanzas of the hymn were adopted as the national anthem of Greece. Kalvos's work is little known outside Greece. He married an Englishwoman and died in London; their remains were brought back to Zakinthos in 1960.

Zante's third great poet, Ugo Foskolo (1778–1827), wrote in Italian and was well known in Europe. In *Our Village* Miss Mitford calls him 'that prince of amateurs'.

The museum upstairs contains manuscripts, portraits and mementoes of the three poets and other Zantiot notabilities, the arms of forty-two Zantiot families inscribed in the Libro d'Oro, and one or two pieces of local furniture. In the eighteenth and nineteenth centuries cabinet-makers in both Zakinthos and Corfu produced some very attractive furniture in the Italian, French and English taste, but fine examples are rarely seen outside private houses.

OTHER SIGHTS

Platia Solomou (Solomos Square)

Solomos Square is the town's main square, rebuilt in its previous grandiose way, so that except at Easter, when magnificent crowd-scenes are achieved by the thousands of extras who arrive from Athens, it too often resembles an empty stage. A few cheerful cafés under the Library arcades and a *períptero* or two would humanize the place and satisfy the town's need for a social focus. At present there is none; and this lack — in a Greek town of all places — makes for a depressing evening. Poor Zakinthos! Tall pine trees and graceful palms, and the stone, stucco and terracotta of Ziller's magnificent neo-classical theatre, once gave colour and movement to this scene.

A model and a charming water-colour of the theatre stand in the entrance hall of the Zakinthos Museum (p. 268).

The British Cemetery
Map 1.

In a rare burst of enthusiasm, Grasset wrote that there was 'nothing more picturesque than this resting-place for the dead'. It lies just beyond the head-high ruins of the *Church of Ayos Ioannis*, and a householder near by will unlock the padlocked churchyard and take you through. Here, under urns and canopies, carved tombstones and simple slabs, lie consuls and honest merchants of the Levant Company, wives and children of officers of the nineteenth-century garrison, Wesleyan missionaries and soldiers of the 36th Foot. The earliest monument is the Inigo-Jones-ish grotto of Clement Harby — 'Consul Anglicanus in Peloponenso et Insula Zacynthi' — where worn tritonesses are now clothed in ivy and earthquakes have dislodged the royal arms of Charles II; the latest is the modest slab of '2nd Class Instr. of Musketry William Brown' who died in the year Britain gave back Zakinthos to Greece.

Excursions from Zakinthos Town

CASTLE HILL

Immediately behind the town rise the eroded white spurs and runnels of the Castle Hill, 'so high and ragged, that it will tyre any man or ever he be halfe way up' (Locke). Half of it is said to have sheered off and subsided in a great earthquake of 1514, burying the remains of a classical city beneath the fallen acropolis of Psophis and leaving the present harsh white scarp to the south and west. According to Pausanias (Book 8), 'The acropolis of Zacynthus is also called Psophis because a man of Psophis [in Arcadia], Zacynthus, son of Dardanus, was the first who sailed across to the island and colonized it.'

Two views of the town in the Museum, painted in the early years of the British Protectorate, show the fortress hill bare of trees. In places it still presents rather a desolate and forbidding sight from the town and plain; but nothing could be gentler and more refreshing than the olive groves and orchards of Bokhali on its shoulder, or the pine wood on its eastern slopes and inside the castle walls; and the bird's-eye views of the town and plain from the summit are among the chief delights of Zante.

Route Leave the town by Exit D on the town map and take the left turn at the cross-roads on the brow of the hill 1·5 km. out.

Accommodation and Restaurants A large new hotel was being built on the hillltop in 1980; rooms and *kéndros* at Bokhali and on the way up. In one or two of these restaurants you can listen to *kantádes* while you eat.

Halfway up the hill by the road which climbs from behind St Mark's Square, a lane joins you from the left by which you can reach the *Jewish cemetery* (interesting medieval tombstones), and the little *Chapel of Ayos Yeorgos tou Latinou*. Here in 1819 and 1821 the local patriots of the Friendly Society swore secretly to fight for union with Greece. The left-hand turn on the brow of the hill takes you up 0·8 km. to the hamlet of **Bokhali** where, from the parapet by the campanile of the *Church of Khrisopiyi*, you can survey the minute activities of the town below you. Across the harbour bay, the crumpled and intriguing slopes of *Mt Skopos* (485 metres) are topped by the 'sentinel' rock from which it takes its name and the white dome of a monastery church. Away to the right, across the dusty cornfields of the southern plain, the hump of Marathonisi Island breaks the low line of Keri Bay; and to the north the Frankish castle of *Khlemoutsi* or *Glarentsa* stands out clearly above the not too distant coast of the Morea. In the church is an icon brought long ago from Crete and reputed to have been painted in 848 by the Byzantine artist Panisalkos. Most of it is now covered by a jewel-encrusted silver-gilt casing hung with a grateful line of gold rings and wrist-watches, and the only visible parts of the icon — the faces of the Virgin and Child — look as though they had been restored when Kandounis (see p. 93) painted the scene on the reverse of the icon in 1815.

The Castle

From Bokhali it is 5 minutes' walk up to the Castle. Frequent earthquakes have destroyed all obvious evidence of the Byzantine, medieval and early Venetian fortifications which must have stood here at one time, and the steep and impressive grey limestone revetments which face you on arrival, covered with gold lichen and artemisium, date from a major rebuilding of 1646. But the round *bastion* at the north-east angle, which you pass on the left on your way up to the gate and which you see from the town, and a stretch or two of wall on the west are probably sixteenth century or older. Inside the castle, a massive *powder-magazine* up towards the precipitous southern end and the crumbling apse of the *medieval cathedral* are the only recognizable remains apart from the often dangerously unprotected *well-heads* of numerous cisterns and a few nineteenth-century British buildings. The seventeenth-century *main gate* three-quarters of the way along the east wall is now blocked up and invisible from inside, but its *triple entrance*, with blazons, inscriptions and rusticated arches, still makes a crumbling architectural display when seen from the outside. To reach it, fork left before the first bastion on your way up from Khrisopiyi to the present entrance and follow a narrow path between the pine trees on the hillside and the foot of the east wall. Apart from the ruined splendour of this gate and the massive terrepleined ramparts on the north, the chief pleasure of the castle now lies in its shady pine wood full of *Ophrys lutea* and *sphegodes* in the spring, and the views west and south from its battlements over the plain, 'divided into Vineyards, mixed with olive, Cypress trees, and Summer-houses of Pleasure' (Wheler).

AKROTIRI

Akrotiri, the olive-wooded headland to the north of the Castle Hill, is a delicious place for an afternoon stroll, full of birds and peaceful rustic activity even though next door to the town. In the 1820s Sir Frederick Adam built himself a *summer villa* here, much to the indignation of Charles Napier, then Resident in Cefalonia, who, trying to run his island on a shoestring budget, thought a *third* palace for the Corfu-based Lord High Commissioner a shameful extravagance. The villa (partly destroyed in 1953 and rebuilt as a private house) later became the home of the island's famous poet, Solomos.

Route Leave the town by Exit D and take the right turn at the brow of the hill 1·5 km. out. By the road to the left at the T-junction 0·4 km. on you can reach Tsilivi or return to Krioneri (see below).

TSILIVI

When the prevailing northerly wind is not blowing too fiercely, the closest good bathing outside the town is at the long sand beach of Tsilivi (5·5 km.).

Route Either follow the coast road beyond Cape Krioneri to the north of the town (Exit E on the town map) and drive through the pretty olive groves of Akrotiri, or take the winding road to the right halfway down the far side of the Castle Hill (see Route 4) and immediately fork right.
Accommodation and Restaurants Hotels (3 C class) and rooms (about 70) at Planos (the name of the village at the north end of the beach); restaurants there and at the south end; rooms along the coast road of Akrotiri.

ROUTES ON ZAKINTHOS

The five routes described fan out from the central hub of the capital (see the route map on p. 275).

Route 1: Zakinthos to Vasiliko

The drive along the south-eastern promontory to Vasiliko (15 km.) makes a pleasant excursion. A touristic garden suburb of new hotels reaches as far as Argasi (4·5 km.), but after that the stretch which winds over the shoulders of Mt Skopos is one of the prettiest on the island, with kermes oaks, cypresses and luxuriant myrtles growing in the ravines and glens. At the tip of the promontory there is excellent bathing.

Route Leave the town by Exit A on the town plan and ignore all forks to the right.
Bus In summer, frequent day-return services to Argasi (leaving from the large kiosk at the Solomos Square end of Lomvardou Street) and one day-return to Vasiliko (leaving from Ay. Loukas Square).
Accommodation and Restaurants Hotels (2 B and 1 C class), flats, rooms (about 100) and restaurants at Argasi (with several new hotels being built in 1980); a D class hotel, rooms (about 40) and restaurants at Vasiliko; rooms along the route.

A few metres after crossing the bridge beyond the Church of Ayos Dionisios you will come, on your left, to the *Church of Ayos Kharalambis*, whose baroque stone mouldings and architraves (of 1728) have been fitted into a new concrete shell. A few hundred metres farther on, after a sharp bend to the left, you pass the little *Church of Ayia Ekaterini* on the right. A dependency of the Monastery of St Katherine in Sinai, it was built in 1664. There are several works by Michael Damaskinos on the elaborate altar-screen of 1665: the top half and the lower two panels of the central door are certainly, and the 'Three Hierarchs' on the far left, probably by him. Most of the icons have recently been restored and make a very rich display. Outside there is a memorial tablet to Damian Zagorisky, the Russian vice-consul in 1803 when Zante's currant trade justified the presence of consuls from Austria, England, France, Holland, Naples and Ragusa as well.

[2 km.] A road on the right leads in 4·5 km. to **Kalamaki**, a scattered group of cottages at the still unfrequented north end of Laganas beach. (But in 1980 a large new beach hotel was being built there.)

Route Map of Zákinthos (Zante)

Korithion

Skinaria

ALIKÉS
BAY

Káto Volimes
Méso
Volimes   Ano Volimes
Áyos   4   Orthoniés
Yeórgos Mon.
Anafonitria Mon.   4   Alikés
                                                                              5
                         3   Áy. Ioánnis   Ánd Yeráki   Planos
                                         Mon.   Tsiliví Beach
                    Mariés   Katastári   Káto Yerák   AKR
                                                              5   Cape Krionéri
                Exokhóra   Girion   Kalipádo   Bókhali
                              3   Áyos Dimítrios   Vanáto   5
        Kampi   Áyos León   ZÁKINTHOS (ZANTE)
                          IRAKHIONAS MTS.   Mt. Sinai   Gatáni
                                         Mon.   Melinádo   Argási
                                     3   (3)   Xirokástello
                                      Makherádo   Skopós   Pórto
                                              3   492m   Vasiliko   Róma
                                   Áyos Nikólaos   Mouzáki   (2)
                                                                                       PELOÚZO
                              2   Sarakína   Laganá   Kalamáki
                         Agalás   ÁYOS SÓSTIS
                                              2   Lithakia   Cape
                                         Pitch   MARATHONÍSI   Yérakas
                                         Spring
                                    2   KERÍ BAY
                              Kerí

0   2   4   6   8   10
kilometres

N

●	Capital
○	Large Village
●	Village
⛪	Monastery, Convent
†	Church
■	Site
□	Sight
▲	Mountain
⌐	Natural Features
————	Tarred Road
═══	Major untarred Roads
≡≡≡	Minor untarred Roads
- - - -	Path
••••••	Boat routes
1 etc.	Routes
(1) etc.	Side Trips

It is a pretty drive, past one or two hillocks standing up among the olive trees as abruptly as in a Chinese painting.

Round the cape beyond this turn to Kalamaki the sea has mysteriously encroached on the shore, eating away half a church and leaving a three-arched *Venetian bridge* standing absurdly in the shallows on its own.

[4·5 km.] **Argasi**, a favoured site because of an abundant spring on Mt Skopos. This once watered only the terraces which provide the town with the succulent vegetables and wild strawberries which are such a delicacy between Easter and the end of June. Now it irrigates a crop of new hotels. But for a year or two, until the place becomes as built up and noisy as Perama in Corfu, Argasi will remain a pleasant place to stay, the only one with views back to the capital, the Castle Hill and Cefalonia in the background. Beyond it the road climbs up and down for 3 km. over the spurs and ravines of *Mt Skopos.*

[8 km.] **Xirokastello**. Here the road leaves Mt Skopos behind and winds slowly down into a more open countryside of olives, orchards and cornfields backed by a long ridge, in places richly wooded with stone pines. In the summer flocks of turkeys sprint after grass-hoppers in the stubble, sheep lie in the shade and donkeys gaze dreamily out to sea. At the end of the eighteenth century Sibthorp remarked that 'the Turkies, running in the olive-grounds, become exceedingly fat, and acquire an excellent flavour from the fruit which they pick up' (Walpole, *Travels*).

[13 km.] You drive through a pine wood by the sea, bought by the *Club Méditerranée* as a site for a holiday camp.

[15 km.] **Vasiliko**. The road comes to a triple junction in Vasiliko, a scattered hamlet shaded by poplars, eucalyptus and stone-pines. This is a good place to stay for those who want a simple swimming-holiday. To the right a negotiable lane goes on for 0·8 km. through a grove of cypresses and olives, and out to a gorse-covered bluff. Walk forward 50 metres and you are on the cropped turf of a cliff-top looking over the open sea to the south and, to the left, down to a surfy golden beach backed by the curious red and white cliffs of Cape Yerakas; to the right the islets of Pelouzo and Marathonisi break the expanse of Keri Bay. The central lane leads down in 0·4 km. to the bluff above the middle of Yerakas Bay, where there is a summer eating place. And the left-hand road at the triple junction will take you an easy 0·8 km. down to a very simple hotel above a beautiful sandy beach at *Porto Roma*, the affectionate nickname of a cove where Alexandros Romas, the Zantiot politician and soldier, liked to fish, swim and moor his yacht at the turn of the last century. Both here and at the magnificent but shadeless beach at Yerakas, turtles used to swim warily in to lay their eggs on summer afternoons; their tank-like tracks are a give-away to the whereabouts of the pits they scoop out deeply and then cover with a low mound of sand.

Route 2: Zakinthos to Keri

The drive to Keri (20·5 km.) takes you across the currant chess-board of the plain of Zante and up into the southern tip of the island's western range of hills. There are excursions to the beach at Laganas (9·5 km.) and to the pitch springs which were described by Herodotus (17 km.).

Route Leave the town by Exit B on the town plan.
Bus Hourly day-return services to Laganas in summer, and one day-return service to Keri.
Accommodation and Restaurants Hotels (2 B, 14 C and 5 D class – not all listed in this book), rooms (about 200), flats, and many beach restaurants at Laganas; rooms and restaurants at Lithakia, Mouzaki and Keri, and along the route.

[5 km.] A road on the left leads in 0·8 km. to the airport.

[6·8 km.] A road forks left to Laganas, but that described below is quicker and straighter.

[8 km.] A second road on the left leads in just over 1·5 km. to **Laganas**, the island's chief bathing-resort. Along both roads to Laganas (and in other parts of Zakinthos) you will see many curious little thatched huts on stilts in which the peasants sleep in the heat of summer. In earlier and more suspicious centuries these *kalíves* were built as watch-towers over the currant vines and melon patches. Ten years ago these were the only buildings on the plain. Now it is dotted all over with little houses to raise summer catch-crops of tourists in. At Laganas itself the fine brown alluvial sand packs down hard enough to turn the eight-kilometre beach into a road which used to be used by farmers in their wooden carts as well as by cars. But a fast new road now runs behind it all the way to Kalamaki (p. 274) at its northern end; and the wired off plots between it and the sea suggest that it will not be long before hotels stretch from one end to the other. Of the twenty or so already built only the *Zante Beach* has any style. The water is clean but very shallow; and at the Laganas end the creamy rocks of Ayos Sostis and the island of Marathonisi relieve the monotony of the bare sweep of sand.

[8 km.] Back on the main road a road on the right, signposted to Mouzaki, leads in 4·8 km. to Makherado (see Route 3). From various points along the next 3 km. of road beyond this turn you can see across the fields, to the left, on a ridge, the pink-washed façade of *Sarakina*, the Lunzi family's eighteenth-century country house, before 1953 the stateliest home on the island, now shattered and unsafe but still impressive from a distance. If you take the drive to it from the main road, you will discover a colony of peacocks, now the villa's only inhabitants, a sculpture gallery of ancient heroes under the staircase, the shattered remains of wine and olive presses in the west wing and an intact chapel containing the tombs of the Lunzi family. Then the road begins to skirt the hills and as you climb there are pretty views down over hillocks planted with clumps of pine, eucalyptus and cypress trees and across the bay to Mt Skopos.

[15 km.] **Lithakia**, a village with several restaurants and rooms to rent. Roads lead down in 3 km. to the beach, and up in 8 km. to the hill village of Agalas (see p. 43), where two or three handsome pre-earthquake village houses are still standing.

[16 km.] Having cut inland, you come out above a deep enclosed valley at the bottom of which a road to the left is signposted to Keri Lake, the way to the *pitch springs*, still used by local fishermen to caulk their boats. The chief spring is hard to find, and it is best to drive first to the sea 0·8 km. away at the end of the lane. Here by a mole on the right are two pitch-scummed wells dug by exploration companies between the wars. But these are hardly inspiring; and turning back along the lane you should stop at the first little stone building on your right, go down to the end of the olive grove, and walk for about 40 metres towards the sea along the edge of the swamp which fills the valley. Here, at the head of a stream, you will come across a shallow pool no bigger than a tea-table and edged with stones. Its insignificance is at first rather disconcerting; but though the scale is small the phenomenon is absorbing. At the bottom of a foot of crystal water black tentacles of pitch writhe in the current in a most sinister and living way, occasionally budding off like polyps into glistening bubbles and globs which float off among the virulent green felts of weed. The swamp has silted up since Herodotus' time when there were a number of ponds, the largest measuring 23 metres each way and 4 metres deep. He describes the collection of the pitch as follows (Book 4),

> The process is to tie a branch of myrtle on to the end of a pole, which is then thrust down to the bottom of this pond; the pitch sticks to the myrtle, and is thus brought to the surface. It smells like bitumen, but in all other respects it is better than the pitch of Pieria. It is then poured into a trench near the pond, and when a good quantity has been collected, it is removed from the trench and transferred to jars.

The swamp is a good place for birds: Red-rumped swallows and Sand martins swoop over the reeds and redstarts and whitethroats are two a penny.

[16 km.] From the turn down to the pitch springs the road winds up a rocky ravine and past a fertile upland valley.

[20·7 km.] **Keri**. There are a few rooms to rent and a couple of restaurants in this village, but the pleasantest place to stay and eat at is probably the *Apelati*, an inn 1·5 km. before Keri.

The seventeenth-century *church*, 5 minutes' walk down in the valley to the right, has one of the handsomest façades on the island, consisting of six windows and a door all framed by Corinthian half-columns and topped by broken semicircular pediments. The baroque black and gold screen is particularly fine, with the icon of Our Lady of Keri richly framed, supported and canopied up against it. There is a typical Zantiot processional painting under the women's gallery, and two or three attractively urbane early-nineteenth-century religious pictures on the walls.

Route 3: Zakinthos to Anafonitria Monastery

From the Castle Hill it looks as though the runnelled range of hills beyond the plain forms a narrow coastal cordillera to the west, and that the whole of the island is thus within easy scope. In fact an extensive upland lies beyond these summits; this is the 'wooded Zakynthos' of the Odyssey, entirely different in feeling and appearance to the rest of the island. Though most of the many cottages and churches which survived the earthquake here are unsafe and are gradually being replaced, enough still stand to give an idea of the traditional architecture of the hill villages. This route crosses the plain to Makherado (11 km.), where the church has the most elaborately decorated interior on the island, and then strikes up into the hills and runs over a rolling plateau out of sight of the sea to the medieval monastery of Anafonitria (38·5 km.). Apart from the monastery and a particularly fine church-screen in Exokhora (30·5 km.) there is nothing to stop for after Makherado, but the countryside is wild and unspoilt and in places very attractive.

Route Leave the town by Exit C on the town plan and in 5 km. take the second turn to the left, signposted to Makherado. In Makherado turn left immediately before the church and, after a couple of hundred metres, right to Lagopodon.
Bus Several day-return services to Makherado and at least one to Maries; but carless visitors to Anafonitria would do better to use the frequent services to Volimes along Route 4.
Accommodation and Restaurants Very few rooms along the route; kéndros at Ayos Leon and just before Anafonitria village.

[2·5 km.] A road forks left to join Route 2.

[5 km.] Fork left to Makherado.

[11 km.] **Makherado**, where the *church* beyond the cross roads as you arrive is worth a special visit. Though much restored both inside and out in the late nineteenth century, its interior is the most sumptuous on the island, with a late-eighteenth-century screen, painted walls and ceiling, delightful *bombé* lattice-work above the women's gallery, rich silver chandeliers and candelabra and an early-seventeenth-century carved gilt lectern. The bells in the towering campanile, which has an octagonal turret, have a lovely tone. The great treasure of the church is the *icon of Ayia Mavra*, an exceptionally beautiful Italianate work of the late fifteenth or early sixteenth century. Its nineteenth-century silver-gilt casing is finely done and, with garlands of gold and jewelled offerings hung in front of it, sets off the austere beauty of the exposed face; but it is a pity that it conceals so much of the painting.

Makerado has another, unrestored, seventeenth-century church well worth walking round: *Ipapandi*, only a few metres along the road to Melinado if you turn right as you arrive. Its north façade has very richly carved door and window surrounds, and the arched and rusticated belfry, of about 1700, must be the best example still standing in the island.

[11·5 km.] The recently built conventual *Church of the Panayia Eleftherotria*, just after the right turn to Lagopodon, houses an attractive early screen from a destroyed church in Katastari. From here the road winds up the hillside and there are good views back over the southern half of the plain, to the Castle Hill, Mt Skopos and Keri Bay.

[14·5 km.] The road forks, but only to offer alternative routes up a steep gradient.

[18·5 km.] **Ayos Nikolaos**, a small hill-village rather shut in on all sides by barish hills, but with one or two pre-earthquake cottages and a mass of walnut trees. The façade of the recently rebuilt nineteenth-century *church* looks more like that of a bishop's palace, and the late-nineteenth-century *campanile* has strange carved stonework in the top two of its five storeys (the upper one octagonal): caryatids flanking niches which contain carved crucifixes and *memento moris* on a giant scale. From up here a loudspeaker summons villagers to the telephone. At the village crossroads a rough road to the left leads in 8 km. to Agalas (see p. 278).

[20 km.] A little beyond Ayos Nikolaos a rough road on the right leads in 3 km. to the locked and deserted monastery of Mount Sinai in a long flat valley hidden between folds of the hills.

[24 km.] A road on the right leads up in 6·5 km. to **Loukha**, and in another 1·5 km. to **Girion**. At nearly 610 metres they are the islands two highest hill villages.

[24 km.] **Ayos Leon**, another hill-village, beyond which the undulating countryside is almost uninhabited, a few olives and stone-walled vineyards being the only signs of life among scrub, heath, cypresses and pines.

[29·5 km.] A metalled but (in 1980) untarred road leads down to rich bottom land round the village of **Kampi**. Just under a kilometre beyond the village a track ends above cliffs which plunge magnificently about 100 metres into the sea.

[30·5 km.] **Exokhora**. The *Church of Ayos Nikolaos*, on the right of the village green of Exokhora — a grassy expanse with a wide-spreading plane tree in the middle — contains a particularly fine mid-seventeenth-century screen. A row of buxom nude-breasted angels act as miniature caryatids to the second tier of icon arches, and below them is an unusual frieze of carved foliage and animals, including elephants.

[32 km.] The outskirts of **Maries**, a village in lovely park-like countryside. Beyond it the rolling hills are covered with dark and full-grown forest.

[36 km.] At a T-junction the road to the right joins the Katastari/Volimes road (Route 4) just over 1·5 km. away; that to the left leads to the village and monastery of Anafonitria. (For the monastery fork left in 0·4 km. and follow the earth road for 2·5 km.)

[38·5 km.] *Monastery of Anafonitria*
Founded by the ruling Tocco family in the early fifteenth century, the monastery was badly damaged in 1953, and all that remains of the monastic ranges is a magnificent square *medieval tower* with a skirted base, entered at first-floor level from steps inside the unlocked courtyard. Two of the sweet *tenor-bells* hanging in the belfry above were given in 1669 and 1689 by Clement Harby, the English consul (see the British cemetery). The small three-aisled *church* contains seventeenth-century wall-paintings (mostly covered by whitewash) and a miracle-working icon of the Virgin discovered not far away on the coast near the wreckage of a Constantinopolitan merchant-galley. The pigments have oxidized and blackened; but what remains visible is finely painted and the icon may be as early as the late fifteenth century. To visit the church, ask at the large and unsightly *kéndro* which has been built almost on the monastery's doorstep.

    If you turn right where the earth road forks off, you will come to a large silver poplar in the middle of the cross-roads in the village of Anafonitria. The very rough track straight ahead leads in 3 km. to the *Monastery of Ayos Yeorgos Kremna*, slightly more easily visited from Volimes (see Route 4).

Route 4: Zakinthos to Volimes

This route runs by the main tarred road up the length of the plain to Katastari (16 km.) and on to the large hill-village of Volimes (33·5 km.) in the north-west corner of the island. In the plain there is a worthwhile detour to the church at Makherado (see Route 3), and another to the beach at Alikes, which can also be reached by Route 5. In the hills there are possible expeditions to the three ancient and attractive monasteries of Ayos Ioannis (19·5 km.), Anafonitria (32 km.) and Ayos Yeorgos.

Route Leave the town by Exit C on the town plan.
Bus Frequent day-return services to Volimes.
Accommodation and Restaurants No rooms; restaurants at Katastari and near the turn-off to Anafonitria.

[2·5 km.] A road forks left to join Route 2.

[5 km.] A road forks left to Makherado (see Route 3). 50 metres farther on another road forks right through Gaitani to join Route 5.

[6 km.] Another road on the right joins Route 5 at Vanato.

[8 km.] You come to **Ayos Dimitrios**, on rising ground, where the church has a good *campanile*.

[16 km.] You reach **Katastari**, the island's third largest village, on a hillside looking down over the salt-pans of Alikes. A road on the right as you come into the village will take you down in 1·5 km. to Alikes beach (see Route 5). From Katastari the road climbs up into the hills which border the Bay of Alikes.

[19·5 km.] After rounding a sharp turn to the left, you can leave your car by the side of the road and take the track on the left which climbs in 5 minutes to the *Monastery of Ayos Ioannis o Prodromos* (St John the Baptist), founded shortly after 1452. The entrance, round behind a walled orchard, leads into a courtyard. On the right a flight of stone steps leads to a *refectory*. Beyond the steps is the *main entrance*; above its handsome rusticated portal, dated 1666 on the keystone of the arch, there is a clenched stone hand to hold a flag-staff; near by are the foundations of a sixteenth-century *round tower*. There is a very fine early-seventeenth-century carved gilt lectern inside the rather plain *church* in the courtyard; and on the left of the eighteenth-century altar-screen there is a silver casing (to an icon of the beheading of St John the Baptist) by Arvanitopoulo which is interesting because it is earlier (1800) and more classical than the rococo work of Baffas (see p. 94), and technically nearly as accomplished. The icon of St John on the wall next to it, by the Cretan, Theodore Poulakis (1622–92), is one of the most note-worthy on the island for its thoroughly Western rendering of a traditional Byzantine theme.

The monastery is poor and contains nothing else of great interest. When the last two very old monks were alive they lived in a rather touching room with a hill of round priest's loaves in one corner, a map of the Holy Land, bunches of great iron keys, a saw, a mouse-trap and a sink. Since their death it is not easy to get into the church, and you should ask in Katastari for the whereabouts of the key-holder.

Back on the main road and 1·5 km. beyond the monastery you will reach a spur from which there is a good view back over most of the south-eastern half of the island. Here you swing inland and climb up between hills bare of all but a crew-cut of maquis to a jumbled plateau where walled fields of corn, vines and pasture are interspersed with copses of stunted cypresses, and the grey stone villages merge into the hillsides.

[26·5 km.] A road on the right leads up in 0·8 km. to **Orthonies**; 2·5 km. beyond the top of the village, lost in a hidden valley over the hill, stands the half-ruined *Monastery of the Panayia Spiliotissa*. Promising from a distance, it turns out to contain nothing to make the descent to it worth while.

[27·5 km.] A fork left leads in 5·5 km. to Maries and to the *Monas-tery of Anafonitria*, just over 4·5 km. away (see Route 3). The grass-covered, rounded hilltops hereabouts are unusual enough to catch the eye. They show that throughout antiquity this part of the island was never deforested for long enough to become eroded.

[33 km.] A fork leads right in 0·8 km. to **Ano Volimes**, the 'upper' part of this triple hill-village. In **Meso** ('Middle') **Volimes** (straight on at the fork) the seventeenth-century *Church of Ayia Paraskevi*, with curly, shell-topped pediments to its windows, has a good *témplo* and lectern and attractive dull-white and wine-red painted eighteenth-century wooden panelling round its walls.

Environs of Volimes

From Meso Volimes it is a 3-km. walk to the lovely solitary site of the *Monastery of Ayos Yeorgos Kremna*. Once a villager has started you off on the right route you will not need a guide. The nearly level track leads for most of the way through attractive empty country-side, but for the last 5 minutes runs through thick pine woods which slope down to cliffs looking out over the Mediterranean. If the last resident monk is in you will find the door unlocked. Inside the courtyard there is a nicely treaded double stone *staircase*, and a mid-sixteenth-century *round tower* which still preserves part of its louvered cornice for dropping stones and boiling oil — neither, one suddenly realizes, hard to come by in the Greek countryside. The simple little church has an unexpected and enchanting eighteenth-century grisaille ceiling with a motif of swans and seahorses, and a *trompe l'oeil* coffered apse.

A track scraped through the heathery moorland leads on from the monastery to the village of Anafonitria (see Route 3). Both these ways to Ayos Yeorgos are slowly negotiable by car.

Route 5: Zakinthos to Alikes

The plain of Zakinthos is no longer quite such a flat-plum-pudding land as it appeared to Lear a hundred years ago: corn, maize and olives are now as common as currant-vines, and hummocks of noble silver poplars break its even lines. In April the young vines in their cane-palisaded yards are up to their ears in wild flowers, the green cornfields are splattered with the magenta dabs of *Gladiolis segetum*, and below the bare bodices of the mountains the flaring skirts of the foothills are embroidered all over with golden gorse. At its northern end the plain squeezes between converging hills to a narrow outlet on the sea at the beach of Alikes (17 km.) Route 4 is in fact a quicker way to this beach but Route 5 is prettier, and from it there are short expeditions to an early-nineteenth-century church at Kalipado (8 km.) and to a good viewpoint at Ano Yeraki (13 km.). From here you can also return to town by a road which runs close to the coast.

Route Leave the town by Exit D on the town plan.
Bus Frequent day-return services to Alikes.
Accommodation and Restaurants Four hotels (2 C and 1 D class) with three restaurants between them, and about 100 rooms (half of them A class) at or near Alikes.

[1·5 km.] The turns to left and right at the brow of the Castle Hill go to Bokhali and Akrotiri (see Excursions). Just beyond this cross-roads a lane on the right will take you in a couple of hundred metres to *Strani Hill*. Here a stele and a bust mark the site where in 1822 Solomos composed his 'Hymn to Liberty', later adopted as the Greek national anthem.

[2 km.] A road turns sharp right to Tsilivi (see Excursions). As you drive down the far side of the hill, look up to the left for a glimpse of the castle's north-western walls.

[3 km.] A road on the left leads through Gaitani to join Route 4.

[5·5 km.] **Vanato**, on the right. Another road on the left also joins Route 4.

[7·5 km.] **Kalipado**. Here the Vultso family *Chapel of Ayos Ioannis* has been restored and taken over by the state. Its white-painted panels and gilded scrolls provide an ornate and light-hearted frame for a whole series of damaged canvases by the painter-priest Koutouzis (1741–1813), and the general effect is of a pretty little opera-house rather than a church. To visit it apply at the museum in town.

[11 km.] **Kato Yeraki**. At the far end of this village a right fork will take you up in just over 1·5 km. to the village of **Ano Yeraki** above which the hilltop *Church of Ayos Nikolaos* provides a splendid viewpoint over the plain and across to Cefalonia. (On your way up keep left at the triple fork.) If you fork right on the way up you will reach Meso Yeraki in 1·2 km. From here you can follow a road for 8 km. through pleasant but uneventful olive groves to Planos (see Excursions). The last five kilometres run parallel to the sea, and here and there signed earth lanes lead down to beach tavernas.

Back on the main road and forking left at the end of Kato Yeraki, you wind down a very pretty valley full of olive and lemon trees and after running along a reed-fringed stretch of canal arrive in the hamlet of Alikes.

[17 km.] **Alikes**. Four hotels, several restaurants and numerous rooms by a long sand-beach make Alikes a pleasant alternative to Laganas for a holiday or a day's outing by the sea. The water is as shallow as at Laganas but you have the mountains of Cefalonia as a background to your bathe. Channels cut through the sand-dunes allow sea-water to fill the salt-pans, which cover about four hectares behind the beach. From Alikes it is 1·5 km. up to Katastari on Route 4.

KITHIRA

Kithira lies between the two southernmost prongs of the Peloponnese, where the Ionian, Aegean and Cretan Seas converge. Geographically speaking it is not really an Ionian Island at all (see p. 38), but when included ranks as the fifth largest. Not counting Antikithira, it has an area of 277 square kilometres and in 1979 had a population of 2,874. Its capital (469 inhabitants) is more often known by the popular name of Khóra than by its official name of Kithira. Kithira (*ta Kíthira* in Greek — a neuter plural name) is no longer referred to by its Venetian name of Cerigo.

INFORMATION FOR VISITORS

Information
For tourist information in general, see p. 30. In Ayia Pelayia: shop under the *Kythireia* hotel. In Khora: the Mayor's office off the main square. For rooms: the Police Station in the outer ward of the castle precinct in Khora.

Post Office
Next to the colonnaded market-building towards the bottom of the main street.

Cable Office (O.T.E.)
In the main square at the top of the main street.

Clinic
In Potamos (tel. Potamos 3).

Feast Day
August 15th (Assumption of the Virgin); service in the morning at Mirtidia Monastery and dancing in the evening at Potamos.

GETTING TO KITHIRA

Air

Olympic Airways operate one flight a day in each direction (sometimes two in summer) between Athens and Kithira, using a small light aircraft. Flight time: 1 hour. For the airport see Route 4.

Sea

From Piraeus to Ayia Pelayia via Monemvasia: Car-ferry *Ionion* on Thursdays, passenger ship *Kanaris* on Saturdays (Maleas Shipping Co., 4 Akti Tzelepi, Piraeus, tel. 4124900). Journey time: 11 hours.

Hydrofoil launches ('Flying Dolphins') leave the Zea port of Piraeus every day in summer. Journey time 5 hours.

From Neapolis to Ayia Pelayia: The *Elaphonisos* (a small landing-craft type ferry) leaves at 08.00 daily in summer, three times a week in winter. Journey time: $1\frac{1}{2}$ hours.

TRANSPORT ON THE ISLAND

Buses

For general information about island bus services see p. 22. There is no printed timetable or bus station on Kithira. Buses leave from the main square. In the summer holidays the island's four buses are used for morning excursions to beaches at Kapsali and Ayia Pelayia, calling at various villages for passengers. At other seasons school services provide the only regular connections between Khora and Potamos.

Taxis

There are about 15 hire-cars based on different villages on the island. For rates see p. 23. In Khora the rank is in the square at the top of the main street.

ACCOMMODATION AND RESTAURANTS

Country Hotels

C Class   *Kythereia*, Ayia Pelayia. 7 rooms on second floor of water-front block. No restaurant.

Country inns

E. Kominos's, Kapsali. *Excursions.* 12 A and B class rooms over water-front restaurant.
Pefkaki, Livadi. *Route* **1**. 14 A class rooms over restaurant in central inland village.

Rooms in private houses

For general information see p. 27. In addition to the inn rooms, in 1980 the number of rooms available was approximately as follows: 50 in Ayia Pelayia, 28 in Kapsali, 24 in Avlemona, 20 in Khora and 32 in various inland villages.

Villas and flats

For general information see p. 29. There are about 14 holiday houses at Kapsali (information from the Mayor's office), 14 at Livadi (information from the Pevkaki Inn), 12 at Ayia Pelayia (information from the Kythereia Hotel) and 6 at Skandia.

Restaurants

All year: In Livadi, Kapsali, Ayia Pelayia and Potamos. Summer only: In Khora (some years), Platia Ammos, Avlemona, and Tsikalaria (beyond Livadi). There are also simple eating places in Milopotamo and Diakofti.
Specialities: Garlic sausages (*loukánika*) and honey in the comb (*melópita*).

Camping sites

The National Tourist Office is preparing camping sites with all the usual facilities in a pine wood above Kapsali and on the bare litoral at Avlemona. The first was due to open in 1980, the second in 1981.

SPORT

Bathing

Soft sand beaches at Ayia Pelayia (p. 304) and Diakofti (p. 306), sand and shingle at Kapsali (p. 293), shingle at Platia Ammos (p. 304) and sand and pebbles at Kastri and Skandia (p. 308).

INTRODUCTION TO KITHIRA

Quelle est cette île triste et noire? – C'est Cythère . . .
Regardez, après tout c'est une pauvre terre.

Sent off round the world in disgrace in 1841, Baudelaire was no doubt in a glum mood when his boat called at Kithira. But he was not the first traveller to be deceived by the legendary birthplace of Aphrodite and mythical honeymoon-home of Helen of Troy. 'Were we to frame an Idea of this place from the fame of these Beauties, we might imagine it one of the most charming places of the World,' wrote Wheler in 1675; 'But on the contrary the greater part of it is a barren, rocky and mountainous Soil, ill-peopled, and can beg of no plenty.'

Kithira is still ill-peopled. Though three times as large as Ithaca it has a smaller population, and more people of Kithiran descent now live in Australia than on the island itself. But because the population is scattered among many hamlets, and these — though half-empty — stand untouched by earthquakes, parts of the central plateau seem cheerful and densely settled. On a late summer afternoon you can look across soft-earth fields hazed with the greeny yellow of wild fennel to half a dozen villages with pink roofs, stone walls and dark clumps of fig trees, while cloud shadows move slowly over the sombre moorland beyond, obliterating one by one the white smiles of the monasteries. Though you can see half of the Kithiran upland from some of these monasteries, on no Ionian Island is the sea so often out of sight. Only between Kastri and Avlemona — a bare and ancient shore of rock-cut Minoan tombs and quarries from which the stones of Aphrodite's temple were once hewn — does the road run beside the sea.

There is only one small hotel on Kithira; and in summer unless you have booked a room ahead in one of the few inns you may find nowhere to stay. The island is also difficult to explore unless you take a car or scooter with you from Piraeus or travel chiefly by taxi, for although the roads are good there are hardly any buses.

Kithira's chief features are Khora, its picturesque capital; its many fine Byzantine churches, some extremely early, others decorated with striking wall-paintings, nearly all of them distinguished by double apses (a rarity elsewhere); the bare and lovely sweep of its hillsides and its unfrequented shores; and, above all, the character of its inhabitants. They combine the politeness of the Ionian Islands, the upstanding pride of the Cretans and the warm hospitality of the Cyclades.

KHORA

Khora is more of a Cycladic than an Ionian village. High above the sea, its mostly flat-topped houses are spilt like lumps of sugar along a narrow spur which leads out to the commanding promontory of the castle hill. From one side of the spur you look down to the port of Kapsali, and from the other across a separate valley to a different stretch of hills and sea. The town's single street climbs narrowly from the gateway of the castle precinct to a little tree-planted square. At one place it is bridged by an old house and when you first arrive the scutcheoned arch is a useful reminder of the where-abouts of some otherwise indistinguishable shop or other. To the left and right, flights of steps lead up and down to sinuous alleys where some of the houses have attractive architectural features: chimney-stacks built up on jutting corbels, marble blazons and fine stone doorways. The churches are all barrel-vaulted and often have airy arcaded belfries and one or two fine icons. *Stavromenos*, the first you pass on the left as you arrive from Kapsali, is typical; its screen (eighteenth century but regilded) fills the whole curve of the vault with what looks like a genealogical tree of Bible notables, and the icon of the Virgin and Child at the west end has an exceptionally beautiful carved gilt frame. On the way up the main street you pass the *Post Office* on the left just before a little colonnaded *market-building* built by the British in 1834, and the old curiosity shop of a *museum* on the right just before the archway over the street.

Though Khora is the capital of the island it is smaller than Potamos and less cheerful than Ayia Pelayia; out of sight of the village-dotted central plateau, it has become rather a forlorn and empty place in the last few decades and its height above the sea is also frustrating in summer, unless you have your own car. But perched up in the air with its castle standing out on a great acropolis, it is the most dramatically sited of all Ionian villages.

PRINCIPAL SIGHTS

The Kastro

The entrance to the castle precinct (open day and night) is through the undercroft of a house at the bottom of the main street, and there are some interesting old houses and scutcheons in the quarter just inside the gateway.

The *castle* was rebuilt in 1503, a year after the Venetian Republic had again taken back the administration of the island from the Venier family. Its style is plain and rectangular compared with other Venetian architecture of the early sixteenth century and it is clear that on the seaward side the Venetians merely strengthened the castle which the Venieri had begun to build in 1316. But the date cut deeply into a foundation stone shows that the landward bastion was built from scratch in 1503. Apart from the impressive soar of the early walls and a vaulted Venetian entrance-corridor the fortifications have no particular distinguishing features. But the clifftop site is magnificent and from the eastern parapets there is a dizzy view down to Kapsali Bay and out over the saurian tail of the Trakhilas peninsula to the lump of Avgo Island.

Both the outer ward which formed the original fortified nucleus of the town (on the northern and eastern slopes of the castle hill), and the castle circuit itself, hold an astonishing number of ruined churches. Built in the same sophisticated style as those of Paliokhora (p. 302) and Kato Khora (p. 299), many of them contain rather dull seventeenth- and eighteenth-century wall-paintings and are locked; the curator of the museum (see below) has the keys to them. The finest is the *Church of Ayos Vasilios* with a shattered round drum, stone beading under its windows and nicely cut relieving arches.

Museum

Open Weekdays 07.30–14.00
Sundays 10.00–13.00
N.B. Closed on Mondays.
Entrance: free.

Kithira may eventually have a new museum, and when it does the sepulchral statue of a lion of the sixth century B.C. found at Paleopolis and now in the Athens National Museum should return to its island home. Meanwhile, one small room houses a pleasant confusion of coins, amphorae, flags, marble scutcheons, official seals and crates of broken pottery excavated at Kastri (p. 308). Three show-cases contain whole pots and steatite vessels; these are mostly local wares of the Middle Minoan period. But there are one or two Cretan pieces, a Late-Minoan stone lamp and a Mycenaean stirrup-jar.

EXCURSION FROM KHORA

Kapsali

Route Leave Khora by the south end of the main street.
Bus In July and August a bus takes bathers down and up again for an hour or two before lunch.
Accommodation and Restaurants Inn, villas, rooms, camping site and three restaurants.

From Khora it is 2·5 km. down by a winding road to the port of **Kapsali**. On the way to its two glittering blue bays you pass dusty aloes with their candelabra of dull yellow flowers and crickets sizzling in the trees. At midday the parabola of cliffs behind the port focuses the sun on you like a burning-glass, and unless you swim out a little way from the sand-and-shingle beach the water is not cold enough to be refreshing. A few eighteenth-century warehouses or chandler's magazines survive and the style of their interiors, with great internal arches supporting joists under an earth roof, can be seen in the *Kamares* restaurant, recently converted into the pleasantest place to eat and drink anywhere in the island. Halfway round the second bay the cells of the *lazaretto* (1817) now provide refuge only for donkeys. In the evening Kapsali becomes an enchanted place as the sky behind the Kastro turns conch-pink, Venus makes her brief curtsy to the left of Khora's jumbled skyline — here of all places in perfect rapport with the land — and the latticed belfry of *Ayia Anna* stands out black and Gothic-looking against the fading violet of the sky.

ROUTES ON KITHIRA

For general information on island routes and roads see p. 103. Kithira's routes branch left and right off a central spine-road (see the map on p. 295). Of the island's roads only the last part of Route 4, Route 5, and the whole of the link between them, are in bad condition. The best of two or three good maps (that of E. Sophios, on sale in Potamos) shows several negotiable roads not mentioned in this book. In 1980 there were petrol stations at Khora, Livadi, Konḍolianika and Potamos.

Route 1: Khora to Mirtidia Monastery

Mirtidia Monastery (13 km.) on the west coast of the island is a mid-nineteenth-century building which enshrines the island's most precious icon. The frescoed twelfth-century Church of Ayos Dimitrios in Pourko and the Convent of Ayia Elesa — a remarkable viewpoint — lie on the same side-road.

Route Drive north from Khora. Ignore the right fork at the far end of Livadi [4 km.] and keep straight on for Kalokernes [9 km.]. Here you should again ignore a right fork (by which you can join Route 2) and keep straight on.
Accommodation and Restaurants Inn with restaurant, other rooms, and villas at Livadi.

[4 km.] **Livadi**, a village named after a little upland 'plain' which used to provide most of the island's vegetables. The Pefkaki inn

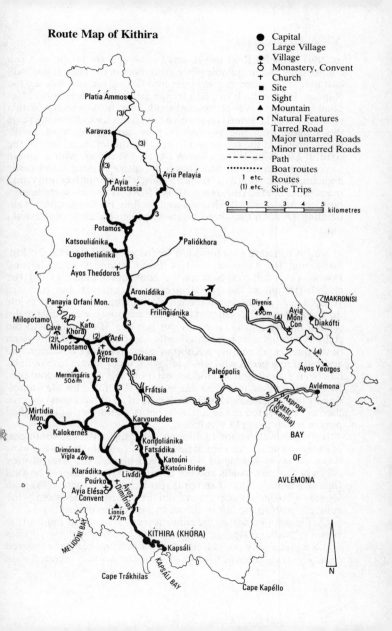

Route Map of Kithira

●	Capital
○	Large Village
•	Village
⚭	Monastery, Convent
†	Church
■	Site
□	Sight
▲	Mountain
⌒	Natural Features
	Tarred Road
	Major untarred Roads
	Minor untarred Roads
- - -	Path
· · · · ·	Boat routes
1 etc.	Routes
(1) etc.	Side Trips

0 1 2 3 4 5 kilometres

Platía Ámmos
(3)

Karavás
(3)

(3)

† Ayía Anastasía

Ayía Pelayía

3

Potamós

Katsouliánika

Logothetiánika

3

† Áyos Theódoros

■ Paliókhora

Aroniádika
4

4

Frilingiánika

Diyenís 490m
(4)

Ayía Móni Con
4

MAKRONÍSI

Diakófti

(4)

Panayía Orfaní Mon.
(2)

Milopótamo
Cave
(2)

Káto
Khóra
(2)

Aréi

Milopótamo

† Áyos Pétros

• Dókana

Paleópolis

Áyos Yeórgos

Avlémona

Mermingáris 506m

2

3

5

Frátsia

5

Ásproga
Kastrí (Skandía)

Mirtídia Mon.
1

BAY

Kalokernés

2

2

Karvounádes

OF

Drimónas Vigla 469m

1

2

Kondoliánika
Fatsádika

AVLÉMONA

Klarádika

Poúrko

Livádi

Katoúni

† Áyos Dimítrios
Katoúni Bridge

Ayía Elésa Convent

Liónis 477m

1

KÍTHIRA (KHÓRA)

Kapsáli

MELIDÓNI BAY

Cape Trákhilas

KAPSÁLI BAY

Cape Kapéllo

N

(p. 289) is useful if all the rooms by the sea are taken, and is a comfortable and hospitable place at all times of the year. If you look east across the plain as you come into the village you will see the *Katouni Bridge*, built in 1826 by the British Resident John Macphail to carry a never-completed road down to Avlemona. With a total length of 120 yards and twelve tall arches it was for many years the longest and finest — and is now surely the most pointless — bridge in the whole of Greece. On the left-hand side of the road in Livadi itself the *Church of Ayos Andreas*, with a square tower and pyramidical roof, has a deceptively modest and rustic appearance. Starting as a basilican church in the ninth century, and many times altered (most recently in 1628), it contains some important patches of newly cleaned and well-lit twelfth-century wallpainting. (Ask for the whereabouts of the key-holder at the Pevkaki inn.)

[5 km.] A concrete road forks left for the village of **Pourko**, 2·5 km. away, and the *Convent of Ayia Elesa*, visible 0·8 km. beyond Pourko on a hill-top. Neither the conventual buildings nor the church (rebuilt in the 1870s) are of any interest; but they are vertiginously perched on the edge of a cliff and there is a fine view northwards over the centre of the island and south-west down to the sea. In the latter direction you can just see *Melidoni Bay* to the right. A curious story is attached to this deep inlet. In the early years of the nineteenth century a Kithiran sailor dying in Constantinople confessed to a priest who was a fellow-islander that in his youth he had been a pirate and had hidden two pots of gold in Melidoni Bay. In 1825 the priest retrieved this booty and fulfilled his life's ambition by building a new church on the site of an old monastery above the bay. Cemented to the top of its belfry stands one of the ribbed pots in which the gold was found.

It is worth walking for 15 minutes to the top of the rise south-east of the convent, for the capital lies behind it, and the bird's-eye view down on to its jumble of whitewashed houses, the straight grey edges of the castle walls and the twin blue bays of Kapsali beyond (like two hungry bites at an apple) provides an epitome of Aegean scenery. (To find the path, start from the cistern at the bottom of the concrete path to the left of the main gate of the monastery.)

On the way down from the convent you will see in the fields to the right of Pourko a strange unformulated building with two domes and a mysteriously undulating whitewashed and cement-rendered roof. This is the ancient *Church of Ayos Dimitrios*, 5 minutes' walk from the village by a path some way after the last house on the right. It consists of four distinct but connected chapels of different dates, and its plan is made more confusing by the fact that they are not all at right angles to each other. Between them these chapels contain a remarkable collection of damaged *wall-paintings* which have recently been restored and which are of at least three different dates from the twelfth to the fouteenth centuries. The largest patches of painting are in the main barrel-vaulted chapel with twin apses. The key is kept in Pourko.

Continuing along the tarred road again, you reach the next village in 3 km.

[8·8 km.] **Kalokernes**. The tarred road which forks right at the end of this village joins Route 2 to Milopotamo in just over 1·5 km. Keeping straight ahead you wind down a very inhospitable moun- tainside (whose bleak slopes are however increasingly disguised by a pine forest planted fifteen years ago), cross a small but typical Macphail bridge of 1821, and reach a scarp from which you can look down on Mirtidia Monastery a hundred metres or so below on a flat flare of plough-land planted here and there with olive and almond trees.

[13 km.] *Mirtidia Monastery*
According to island tradition the monastery was founded when a shepherd boy found a miraculous icon on the site in the fourteenth century. In the eighteenth century the icon was taken to Khora for safe-keeping in an age of corsairs, and the present sumptuous but uninteresting church was started shortly after it had been brought back in 1841. The pigments of the icon have completely oxidized and the heads of the Virgin and Child are no more than black spaces outlined by the silver-gilt mount. Only two monks now remain to look after the church, the rows of cells and the green shade of a garden dutifully planted with myrtles. All in all, then, there is not much to see except on August 15th. Then the icon is carried in procession round the precincts of the monastery, the bishop lays aside his jewelled mitre to deliver a powerful sermon and Kithirans from every village pack into cars and on to scooters to come and celebrate 'the festival of their patron saint, Our Lady of the myrtle bough, whose image borne by the waves to the island and found in a myrtle tree represents the Christian version of Aphrodite rising from the sea' (Miller).

Route 2: Khora to Milopotamo

Milopotamo (13 km.), on the west edge of the central table-land, is visually the most attractive village on the island, a mixture of sparkling whitewash and crumbling Venetian stone. In the neighbourhood, interesting excursions can be made to the Monastery of the Panayia Orfani, the fortified village of Kato Khora, Milopotamo Cave and the Byzantine Church of Ayos Petros.

Route Drive north from Khora. Take the turn to the right at the far end of Livadi [4 km.], keep straight ahead where the spine-road to Potamos forks right after Karvounades [7 km.] and go right at the fork 1 km. farther on.

Accommodation and Restaurants Rooms and eating-place in Milopotamo.

[5 km.].**Fatsadika**. If you look back over your left shoulder as you drive through this village you will see the crenellated neo-Gothic *school* which Macphail built in the 1820s on the hillside opposite. From the brow beyond the village you can see the Peloponnese.

[5·5 km.] **Kondolianika**.

[6·8 km.] **Karvounades**.

[8·8 km.] If you go left at this second tarred fork after Karvounades you will join Route 1 in just over 1·5 km. Turning right you drive through a gentle countryside of cornfields and olives. The church you see on the skyline to the right before you come into Milopotamo is Ayos Petros (see below).

[13 km.] You reach Milopotamo.

MILOPOTAMO

Below the *platía*, shaded by three big plane trees, runs a sunken lane where a washing-trough six metres long is fed by a fountain presided over by a nineteenth-century marble lion with engaging human finger-nails and eyebrows. The small barrel-vaulted *Church of Ayos Sozon*, which forms one side of the *platía*, has well-preserved late-seventeenth-century wall-paintings arranged in long cartoon-strip frames round its walls. In the shade of the plane trees you can sit and sip a coffee or eat simple food from the café opposite, and look across to the well-kept neo-classical *Church of Ayos Kharalambis*, against whose dazzling walls bougainvillaea bursts in magenta sprays. A stroll round the village reveals one or two nice architectural features: a flight of stone steps with graceful balusters and a moulded stone handrail, and tall round or octagonal chimneys with neat stone hats.

From Milopotamo you can look across the Gulf of Lakonia to the Mani and, in spring, see the snow-covered Taigetos mountains.

EXCURSIONS FROM MILOPOTAMO

The Monastery of the Panayia Orfani

Just beyond the Church of Ayos Sozon the road forks. The right-hand fork leads in 4 km. to the *Monastery of the Panayia Orfani*. At first the untarred road runs along and above the valley, which steepens suddenly into a romantic chasm full of trees. Here until early in this century most of the island's corn was ground by twenty-four water-mills turned by the stream. A little farther on, over a ridge, you glimpse the sea and follow a very steep, rough and zigzag route down through aromatic junipers to the monastery. This is built into the cliff on the far side of a short rock gorge to which the valley narrows. The modest building was completely restored in 1964 and is now surrounded by acres of cement. There are no monks, but a caretaker will unlock the church, which is inside a cave in the wall of the gorge. Its white-plastered and icon-hung walls contrast powerfully with a chocolate-coloured ceiling of natural rock, cleft and fissured, and on a hot summer day you feel as though you have stepped into a refrigerator. Whether or not you drive all the way to the monastery, it is worth going as far as the ridge, from just before which you can get an impression of the castle in Kato Khora, across a valley to the south.

Kato Khora and Milopotamo Cave

Route To reach Kato Khora (1·2 km. from Milopotamo) and Milopotamo Cave (a 25-minute walk beyond Kato Khora) take the left fork beyond the Church of Ayos Sozon and the right fork 0·4 km. farther on.

Kato Khora is a scruffy, crumbling, picturesque hamlet full of old arches and jutting corbels. In the *platía* at the end of its narrow main street you are confronted by the unexpected façade of a Lancastrian *school* built by Macphail in 1825. With its Gothic windows and stone rib-mouldings, it is an enchanting little building. The street on the left of the school leads to the entrance of a *miniature fortress*. Its gate-way has all the standard trimmings — rustication, blazons, the lion of St Mark and the date 1566 — but on a farmyard scale. Inside, among the half-acre or so of ruined houses whose undercrofts lodge squawking hens and donkeys, is a clutch of seven small stone-tiled churches of the sixteenth and seventeenth centuries, some with very fine masonry vaults and arches, and all decorated with more or less fragmentary wall-paintings done in a popular style. These have recently been restored. (Ask the museum curator in Khora about visiting them.) A curious little island Mistra, this chapel-packed fortress must have taken the place and followed the architectural tradition of Paliokhora, abandoned thirty years before (see p. 302).

If you turn right as you come out of the castle gate, follow a bulldozed track down to the bridge over the valley bottom and up the far side for a few hundred metres, you will come to a path to the right which leads by 20 minutes' fairly steep and rough descent to the locked grille of *Milopotamo Cave*. (Ask in the Milopotamo café for the whereabouts of the guide and keyholder.) Reputedly one of the four or five finest in Greece, the cave is about 250 metres deep and contains several chambers. There is a plan of it in the café at Milopotamo. In Davy's opinion it 'possesses singular beauty, which it chiefly owes to the enormous stalactites, and stalagmites in which it abounds, formed of cream-coloured marble . . . some resembling colomns, others altars, others buildings in ruins, and many resembling animals, the mimic forms, in brief, are of all kinds, and of most fantastic shapes.' You will need more than a torch to see these properly and to make your way over the slippery floors. The outer, day-lit chamber contains some of the best-preserved twelfth-century *wall-paintings* in the Ionian Islands. The crudely drawn and brightly coloured figures are painted on a low plaster-daubed dry-stone wall which forms a screen for the cave chapel of *Ayia Sofia*.

Outside the cave you can sit and warm yourself again in the sun and listen to the invisible surge of the sea below. It is a harsh, hot, precipitous coast, softened only by occasional patches of sweet-scented juniper scrub and the company of bees.

Church of Ayos Petros

The road which runs up from the *platía* in Milopotamo past the Church of Ayos Kharalambis leads in 1·2 km. to the village of **Arei**. As you come into this village a rough track on the right will take you in about 5 minutes on foot to the twelfth- or early-thirteenth-century *Church of Ayos Petros*. Though insensitively restored with blood-red tiles and hard-cement pointing, this church is a good example of the cross-in-square plan of the period, and from the outside you can see clearly how its different roof slopes and ridges mould the symbolic spaces inside it (see p. 88). The wall-paintings of St Peter in the conch of the apse, and of Apostles' heads, are contemporary. The key is kept in Arei, from which you can drive on for 1·5 km. to join the island's spine-road and Route 3.

Route 3: Khora to Ayia Pelayia

This route — the central spine-road of the island — links the capital with Kithira's second port of Ayia Pelayia (26·5 km.) on the north-east coast — the island's beach resort — and runs past Potamos (17 km.), the island's largest village. Apart from two long excursions to Diakofti and Avlemona (Routes 4 and 5), there are possible expeditions to the Byzantine Church of Ayos Theodoros, to the medieval capital of Paliokhora, and — beyond Potamos — to the beach at Platia Ammos.

Route Drive north from Khora. Turn right at the far end of Livadi [4 km.]; fork right 0·8 km. after Karvounades [7 km.]; take the right-hand of the two roads at the bottom of the hill up to Potamos [19 km.] and fork right at the top.
Accommodation and Restaurants Rooms and restaurants at Potamos; hotel (C class), villas, rooms and restaurants at Ayia-Pelayia; summer rooms and restaurants at Platia Ammos.

[9·5 km.] A bus shelter marks the rough road on the right which leads to Fratsia and Avlemona (see Route 5). Here the road enters a wild and untenanted stretch of country, full of scrub and boulders and grim stone walls. This high moorland, desolate and intractable, and sometimes even in August shrouded in dank and swift-moving clouds, runs for nearly 8 kilometres until, surmounting a final ridge, you look down to the gentler and more cultivated landscape round Potamos. As you climb the ridge you can see Cape Tenaron and the Mani peninsula over to the left — clearest when silhouetted by the sunset — and, from the brow itself, Cape Maleas over to the right.

[11 km.] **Dokana**, with a large country-house in the Cycladic style.

[11·5 km.] A bus shelter marks the road on the left which leads in 1·5 km. to Arei (see Route 2).

[15 km.] **Aroniadika**, a substantial village which extends along the road to the right. This leads to the airport, Kastri and Diakofti (see Route 4).

[16 km.] A rough earth road, which is unmarked and easy to overlook, leads right in 4 km. to **Paliokhora**, the tragic site of the medieval capital (then known as Ayos Dimitrios). Paliokhora was founded in the last quarter of the thirteenth century by the family of Daimoyannes from Monemvasia, at that time the island's rulers. Perched on top of a promontory between two precipitous valleys which converge in an impressive gorge, and scarcely visible from the sea, it seemed a refuge secure from the ravages of corsairs. Tradition has it that the seventy-two families who lived inside its walls each owned a chapel. The remains of more than a dozen of these are still visible clinging to the steep sides of the promontory, sometimes literally on top of each other. Built in Monemvasiot style with masonry of high quality and, where they survive, roofs of stone tiles, most of these churches contain fragments of fourteenth- and fifteenth-century wall paintings; those in *Ayos Antonios* (on the right as you enter the town) are the best-preserved and, for their unusual Italianate manner, the most interesting; but even they are scarcely visible under a green coat of damp. The finest and most complete church is *Ayia Varvara*, on its own outside the walls, with an octagonal dome; but even this is used by sheep. So it is the curious history of the site rather than its architecture which now justifies a visit. In 1537 the Ottoman admiral Khair ud Din Barbarossa besieged and sacked the town, carrying off 7,000 islanders. It is Kithira's most calamitous event, still remembered in folk-song and embroidered with supernatural legend. A few sheep-bells, the melancholy cries of the blue rock-thrush and the croak of ravens echoing across the grey and russet gorge are now the only sounds of life to be heard at Paliokhora — the 'old place' — deserted since that day.

[16·5 km.] A small *chapel* marks the rough road on the left which leads in less than 1 km. to the twelfth- or thirteenth-century *Church of Ayos Theodoros*. It is well worth a visit even if the priest who lives next door is away and one cannot get in. For the whitewashed Renaissance façade with scutcheon, inscribed elegy in shaky classical Greek and cusped ogival doorway, green pine tree in the courtyard and tiled octagonal dome make up one of the most satisfying compositions on the island; and on the west side of the courtyard is the shell of a handsome baroque episcopal hall. The church is the resting-place of the skull of the saintly Theodore, who died during a visit to the island in the tenth century; it rests in a mid-nineteenth-century reliquary in the shape of an Orthodox bishop's mitre. On the north wall of the narthex (which may be all that is left of an earlier church) there are some attractive wall-paintings.

[17·7 km.] A road on the left leads in 0·8 km. to the attractive hamlet of **Logothetianika** and, beyond it, to **Katsoulianika**.

[19 km.] The road forks at the bottom of a hill on the outskirts of Potamos.

[19·5 km.] **Potamos** is the largest village on Kithira. On Sunday mornings its pine-tree-shaded *platia* is the scene of a bustling country market. Though the village has no architectural interest, it is a centre of cheerful agricultural activity, and seems more of a capital than Khora.

Environs of Potamos

From Potamos you can make an excursion of 8 km. to the luxuriant valley round Karavas, and 3 km. farther to the beach at Platia Ammos.

Route Leave Potamos by the road which runs through the platia. In 1980 only the first 2·5 km. and last 1·5 km. to Karavas were tarred. For Platia Ammos turn left at the bottom of the village of Karavas.

You reach the edge of the central plateau in 4 km. at the solitary *Church of Ayia Anastasia*. The rock and maquis of the rest of the island is replaced here by schisty soil and hummocky hills covered with heather and arbutus, and terraced for young pine trees. There are good views of the Peloponnese and Cape Maleas as you wind down from Ayia Anastasia through a valley richly planted with olive, walnut, oak and almond trees and watered by many little springs. In April the carpets of scarlet anemones are astounding. The substantial and isolated farmhouses suggest that this part of the island was replanted with Albanians after Barbarossa's raid in the sixteenth century, like several of the Cyclades. In **Karavas** there is a café from whose balcony you can look out over the valley. The population has been much reduced by emigration and many fields and terraces are untended. At the bottom of the village the rough earth road to the right will take you in 5·5 km. to **Ayia Pelayia**, dipping in and out of several narrow valleys each with a thread of green calamus-reeds along the bottom. The rough earth road to the left leads in 3 km. to **Platia Ammos**, a broad curving shingle beach backed by a dozen little bungalows. The Neapolis ferry sometimes calls here on its way to Ayia Pelayia, and the large legend 'Tourist Plaz' on the wall of one building proclaims the hope that the place will become a resort. Trees have been planted but at present it is a shadeless and uncharming site. The bathing however is some of the best on Kithira. There are two small eating-places and a handful of private rooms.

If you fork right at the bottom of the hill leading up to Potamos and right again at the top of it you will come almost immediately to the second of Macphail's great bridges, built in 1825, with stone roundels between the springs of its seven arches and a carved stone swag in the centre. From here the road traverses bare and rocky uplands for 3 km. until it reaches the edge of the plateau and winds down to Ayia Pelayia. As you leave Potamos there is a magnificent view across the waters of the Lakonic Gulf to Cape Maleas.

[24 km.] **Ayia Pelayia**. Though it lacks the visual drama and Venetian antecedents of Kapsali, this northern port is open to the north-easterly breezes and a lot cooler in summer. A mole sticks out at the junction of two long shallow bays (both with fine sand beaches), and a water-front road shaded with tamarisks runs between the northern beach and the fishing hamlet behind it. Its background is greener with olive trees than most other parts of the island and with its good bathing and copious water-supply it is probably the only place on Kithira which could in time become an 'Eldorado de tous les vieux garçons' (Baudelaire). Already it has a lively holiday air in July and August, and with the mainland lit up by the afternoon sun across the water and an unending procession of great tankers in the distance it does not seem so remote from the world as the rest of the island. Beyond the port the untarred road continues for 5·5 km. to the bottom of Karavas and thence either back to Potamos or on to Platia Ammos (see above).

Route 4: Khora to Diakofti

This route to the east coast will interest a determined explorer rather than a casual visitor. For the final bliss of a bathe from the sandy beach at Diakofti (31 km.) you must pay the penance of uncomfortable roads and lonely countryside, and the rewards offered by the two excursions are small: a fine view from the Convent of Ayia Moni and the remains of an early mosaic floor in the Chapel of Ayos Yeorgos.

Route Drive north from Khora (Route 1); turn right at the far end of Livadi [4 km.]; fork right 0·8 km. after Karvounades [14·8 km.] (Routes 2 and 3); turn right at Aroniadika [14·8 km.]. For Skandia and Avlemona fork right 0·4 km. after Friling-ianika [17 km.]. In 1980 only the first 21 km. of the route to Diakofti were tarred. A rough 4-km. link road beyond the Convent of Ayia Moni makes it possible to join the coast road between Avlemona and Skandia.
Restaurant Eating-place at Diakofti.

[16·8 km.] **Frilingianika**. The rough road which forks right 0·4 km. beyond this village joins Route 5 at Skandia on the coast 9·5 km. away. Until Route 5 is tarred this is the road to follow by those visiting the coastal sites from Ayia Pelayia.

[20 km.] A turn to the left leads in 0·4 km. to the airfield. The road, which has been running for more than 3 km. across an extra-ordinarily flat and empty plateau, now winds round the head of a valley to come out above the Bay of Avlemona.

[23 km.] A road forks left and climbs in just under 3 km. to the *Convent of Ayia Moni*, on the slopes of *Mt Diyenis* (490 metres). Like Ayia Elesa (Route 1) this is a place of pilgrimage and you will often find a family or two whose cooking and laundering add a touch of colour and a scent of garlic to the high and windy court-yard. The convent was founded in the eighteenth century and its nineteenth-century church is of no interest. But the view west over the centre of the island and south to the Bay of Avlemona is a fine one. From the ridge behind the convent you can look north to Cape Maleas or down to Diakofti, where ships lie imperturbably in the lee of Makronisi Island even when the sea beyond is whitely raging. On the shoulder of the hill to the south-west you can see the Chapel of Ayos Yeorgos (see below). Beyond the convent the road con-tinues for 2·5 km. to a telecommunications installation.

After the turn up to the convent the road deteriorates rapidly.

[27 km.] A road to the right leads down in 4 km. to join the coast road between Kastri and Avlemona and thus forms a link (though a very rough and steep one) between Routes 4 and 5.

[27 km.] 100 metres or so beyond the previous turn a track strikes off across a level plateau to the right. You can drive along it for about 1·5 km. but must walk the rest of the way (½ hour) up to the *Chapel of Ayos Yeorgos*. Outside, nothing original survives of this seventh-century building (the earliest on the island) except a fragment of marble chancel-rail which has been re-used as an architrave to a window. Inside, several patches of the contemporary *mosaic floor* are in good condition and one can make out the bottom half of a man, a mounted figure, bunches of grapes, a partridge, a leopard and a quail as well as medallions in the border. The near-by cubical building with a domical vault, known as the *Chapel of Our Lady*, may be a free-standing martyrium or baptistery belonging to the seventh-century chapel, and if so is a very rare survival of its type.

From the turn off to Ayos Yeorgos the road, now very rough and stony, zigzags down to Diakofti.

[31 km.] **Diakofti**. This little port is now seldom used except by ships putting in for shelter from north-easterly gales, some — like the half-drowned tanker — only just in time to sink. There are twenty or thirty houses, a mole and a café which sometimes has a pot of hot food simmering on the stove and saucers of local rock-salt. The shallow turquoise water of the island-sheltered shore and a stretch of whitish sand would make Diakofti an admirable site for a bathing picnic were it not for its remoteness and forbiddingly desolate background. Nicias may have landed here in 424 B.C. to climb up behind Mt Diyenis and, circling south, taken ancient Kithira by surprise.

Route 5: Khora to Avlemona

Though the table-land of Kithira is eroded by several watered gullies and more or less cultivable ravines it is breached by a really expansive valley only on the eastern shore behind the Bay of Avlemona. Until the Slavs and Arabs broke the thread of the island's history in the seventh century A.D., this valley seems to have been the chief area of settlement for nearly three millennia. In Archaic and Classical times the ancient capital, Kithira (now known as Paleopolis), overlooked the valley from a fortified summit a little way inland; and by the valley's outlet to the sea stood the port of Skandia (now also known as Kastri) on the site of a Minoan colony. Route 5 runs close to both these sites and on to the little fishing port of Avlemona. At Kastri (20·5 km.) there is excellent bathing.

Route Drive north from Khora; turn right at the far end of Livadi [4 km.]; fork right 1 km. after Karvounades [6·8 km.]; take the rough road right to Fratsia by a bus shelter [9·5 km.], and at the far end of Fratsia [11 km.] turn right on to a decayed tarred road and strike off left again before a solitary church a few metres farther on. In 1980 only the first 9 km. were tarred, but the next 8 km. had quite a comfortable surface. From Skandia a rough road runs up to join Route 4 near Frilingianika and there is another even rougher link farther on.

Accommodation and Restaurants Summer villas and restaurant at Skandia (with room for campers); rooms, camping site (due to open in 1981) and restaurant in Avlemona.

[11 km.] From the church beyond **Fratsia** the road undulates down to the east; there are glimpses of the wide Paleopolis valley and at one point — framed far away like a faded tricolor — of Avlemona, its white houses sparkling on a burned foreshore by pale blue water. After about 5 km. the road cuts right over a col into a narrow valley parallel to the main one, from which it is now screened by a substantial hill to the left. This hill is the site of *ancient Kithira*.

[16·8 km.] A sharp turn which curves to the right round the head of a subsidiary gully marks the start of an unsignposted foot-trace by which you can climb in 20 minutes to the *Chapel of Ayos Kozmas* on the ridge of the hill. From the rise a few metres to the west of the chapel you can see a well-preserved stretch of ancient walling half-way up the next summit. To judge from the style of its masonry — a cross between polygonal and cyclopean — this wall, which protected the upper town, could be as old as the sixth or seventh century B.C. On the south-west slopes of the hill lay the lower town, and somewhere on the site stood the famous *Temple of Aphrodite* which Herodotus says was founded by the Phoenicians and Pausanias claims was the most ancient of all Greek sanctuaries to that goddess. Early travellers made a point of searching for the site. Schliemann (who was here in 1888) thought that the temple must have stood on the site of Ayos Kozmas itself, for the barrel-vault of this Byzantine building (eleventh-century?) is divided in an unusual and impressive way by transverse arcades which incorporate four whole and six half-columns (all unfluted) and four beautifully cut Doric capitals, all in porous stone. But while these and other built-in fragments certainly come from a small Archaic temple, modern archaeologists are certain that this is not its original site. There are a few other remains on the hillside, but it is a rough and prickly place to explore. Wheler, who came up this way botanizing in 1675, nearly came to grief. 'I went up a little higher a simpling,' he writes, 'but discerning the rest of our Fleet under sail, and our Ship ready to put out, it not only spoiled that sport, but made me like to break my neck in hastening down.'

From the hairpin bend the road (now much rougher) runs down the narrow valley for another 3 km., swings into the broad valley again not far from the sea and crosses the stony torrent-bed of the *Paleopolis river*.

[20·5 km.] *Kastri* is the name of the low ridge beyond the river-bed. It is the site of a recently excavated Minoan settlement which flourished from about 2000 to 1450 B.C. (one of the earliest Cretan colonies yet discovered) and of *Skandia*, the island's port in classical times and later. Olives, cypresses, fruit trees and wild fennel grow on the small alluvial plain which now fills the area of the ancient harbour, and the long sand and pebble beach beyond is the most attractive place to bathe in Kithira. The ruins by the perennial pool at the mouth of the river-bed are part of a Justinian fort.

[21 km.] A rough road on the left leads up in 9·5 km. to Friling-ianika (see Route 4). In the narrow fertile valley beyond, a summer restaurant and a few holiday houses profit from another attractive beach.

[21·5 km.] *Asproga*, the next ridge after Kastri, is riddled with rock-cut tombs (dating from Minoan to Roman times) 'which one of the Island pretending to be an Antiquary, assured us were anciently the Baths of Helena' (Wheler). Beyond Asproga the road comes out to the shore and runs past ancient quarries.

[21·8 km.] A road goes left by which you can join Route 4 below Ayia Moni after a steep and stony climb of 4 km. Just under 1 km. up this road there are some much more impressive ancient quarries on the left. Stepped down like inverted ziggurats, the courtyards made by these old workings are so regular that it is hard to believe that they are not part of a sunken city.

[22·5 km.] **Avlemona**. This fishing hamlet on a bleak and treeless shore was gradually being deserted by its inhabitants. But electric-ity, water and a National Tourist Organization camping site have given it a new lease of life. Its cottages are barrel-vaulted like those of Santorini, and there is a solid old Cycladic house on the shore with a sundial painted on its front. The fishing fleet from the mainland often puts in here for shelter and painted dinghies are moored to the sides of a rock-cut creek and guarded by an octagonal *Venetian fortlet*. In the eighteenth and nineteenth centuries Avlemona was the chief western port of the island, and it was to this refuge that the yacht *Mentor*, damaged by a gale off Cape Maleas, put in and sank off shore in 1802 with many cases of Lord Elgin's marbles aboard. Sponge-divers recovered them a year or two later and at Nelson's order they were transported to England in 1805. The incident reminds one of an earlier shipload of art treasures which sank in Kithiran waters between 80 and 50 B.C. on their way to another imperial capital. The contents of this wreck were also discovered by sponge-fishers, off Antikithira in 1900, but were this time repatriated. The life-size bronze youth (Paris with an apple?) of about 340 B.C. in the Athens National Museum is the finest of them.

BIBLIOGRAPHY

SOURCES OF QUOTATIONS

Ansted, D. T., *The Ionian Islands in the year 1863* (W. H. Allen, London, 1863).

Baudelaire, Charles, *Les Fleurs du mal* (Livre de Poche Classique, Éditions Gallimard et Librairie Générale Française, Paris, 1965).

Benton, S., 'Excavations in Ithaca III', *The Annual of the British School at Athens*, vol. 35 (1938).

Byron, Lord, *The Works of Lord Byron*, Letters and Journals, vol. VI (John Murray, London, 1901).

Carlisle, Earl of, *Diary in Turkish and Greek Waters* (Longman, Brown, Green, and Longmans, London, 1854).

Chandler, R., *Travels in Greece* (Clarendon Press, Oxford, 1776).

Dallam, T., In *Early Voyages and Travels in the Levant* (Hakluyt Society, London, 1893).

Davy, J., *Notes and Observations on the Ionian Islands* (Smith, Elder and Co., London, 1842), vol. 1.

Dionysius of Halicarnassus, vol. I: 'Roman Antiquities', trans. E. Cary (Loeb Classical Library, William Heinemann, London; Harvard University Press, Cambridge, Massachusetts, 1948).

Gell, W., *The Geography and Antiquities of Ithaca* (Longman, Hurst, Rees, and Orme, London, 1807).

Goodisson, W., *The Ionian Greeks* (Thomas and George Underwood, London, 1822).

Grasset, A. Saint-Sauveur, *Voyage historique, littéraire et pittoresque dans les îles et possessions ci-devant Vénitiennes du Levant* (Tavernier, Paris, 1799–1800).

Herodotus, *The Histories*, trans. Aubrey de Selincourt (Penguin, London, 1954).

Holland, H., *Travels in the Ionian Isles, Albania, Thessaly, Macedonia, etc.* (Longman, Hurst, Rees, Orme, and Brown, London, 1815).

Homer, *Odyssey*, trans. E. V. Rieu (Penguin, London, 1946).

Jenkins, Romilly, *Dionysius Solomos* (Cambridge University Press, Cambridge, 1940).

Jervis, H. J.–W., *History of the Island of Corfu and of the Republic of the Ionian Islands* (Colburn and Co., London, 1852).

Kendrick, T. T. C., *The Ionian Islands. Manners and Customs; Sketches of Ancient History* (James Haldane, London, 1822).

Kirkwall, Viscount, *Four Years in the Ionian Islands. Their political and social condition, with a history of the British Protectorate* (Chapman and Hall, London, 1864), vol. 2.

Lane-Poole, S., *Sir Richard Church* (Longmans, Green and Co., London, 1890).

Lawrence, D. H., *Selected Essays* (Penguin, London, 1965).

Leake, W. M., *Travels in Northern Greece* (J. Rodwell, London, 1853), vol. III.

Lear, E., *Views in the Seven Ionian Islands* (Edward Lear, London, 1863).

Lear, E., *Letters of Edward Lear*, ed. Lady Strachey (T. Fisher Unwin, London, 1907).

Lithgo, W., *The Rare Adventures and Painefull Peregrinations* (James MacLehose and Sons, Glasgow, 1906).

Livy, trans. Evan T. Sage (Loeb Classical Library, William Heinemann, London; Harvard University Press, Cambridge, Massachusetts, 1961), vol. IX.

Locke, J., In *Hakluyt's Voyages* (James MacLehose and Sons, Glasgow, 1904), vol. V.

Lord, W. Frewen, *Sir T. Maitland* (T. Fisher Unwin, London, 1897).

Matton, Raymond, *Corfou* (Collection de l'Institut Français d'Athènes, Athens, 1960).

Miller, W., *The Latins in the Levant* (John Murray, London, 1908).

Murray, John, *A Handbook for Travellers in Greece* (John Murray, London, 1840).

Murray, John, *A Handbook for Travellers in Greece*, 4th ed. (John Murray, London, 1872).

Murray, John, *A Handbook for Travellers in Greece*, 7th ed. (John Murray, London, 1900).

Napier, C. J., *The Colonies: treating of their value generally — of the Ionian Islands in particular: strictures on the administration of Sir F. Adam* (Thomas and William Boone, London, 1833).

Napier, Lt.-Gen. Sir W., *The Life and Opinions of Charles James Napier* (John Murray, London, 1857) vol. 1.

Pausanias, *Description of Greece*, trans. W. H. S. Jones (Loeb Classical Library, William Heinemann, London; Harvard University Press, Cambridge, Massachusetts, 1918, 1930), vols. 1 and 2.

Plutarch, *Moralia*, vol. V: 'The Obsolescence of Oracles', trans. F. C. Babbit (Loeb Classical Library, William Heinemann, London; Harvard University Press, Cambridge, Massachusetts, 1957).

Prevelakis, E., *British Policy towards the Change of Dynasty in Greece. 1862–1863* (Privately printed, Athens, 1953).

Runciman, Steven, *Byzantine Civilization* (Edward Arnold, London, 1933).

Sandys, G., *Travels* (John Williams, Junior, London, 1673).

Schliemann, H., *Ithaque, la Peloponnèse, Troie* (C. Reinwald, Paris, 1869).

Sibthorp, John, In *Memoirs relating to European and Asiatic Turkey*, ed. Rev. R. Walpole (Longman, Hurst, Rees, Orme, and Brown, London, 1817).

Sibthorp, John, In *Travels in Various Countries of the East*, ed. Rev. R. Walpole (Longman, Hurst, Rees, Orme, and Brown, London, 1820).

Strabo, *The Geography of Strabo*, trans. H. L. Jones (Loeb Classical Library, William Heinemann, London, 1924, 1928), vols. III and V.

Thucydides, *The Peloponnesian War*, trans. Rex Warner (Penguin, London, 1964).

Turner, W., *Journal of a Tour in the Levant* (John Murray, London, 1820).

Wheeler, Private, *The Letters of Private Wheeler* (Michael Joseph, London, 1962).

Wheler, G., *A Journey into Greece* (William Cademan, Robert Kettlewell, and Awnsham Churchill, London, 1682).

Yourcenar, Marguerite, *Memoirs of Hadrian* (Secker and Warburg, London 1955; Farrar, Straus and Giroux Inc., New York).

SUGGESTED TRAVELLING LIBRARY

Durrell, Gerald, *My Family and Other Animals* (Rupert Hart-Davis, London, 1956; Penguin, London, 1957).

Durrell, Lawrence, *Prospero's Cell* (Faber, London, 1945; paperback edition, 1962).

Foss, Arthur, *The Ionian Islands* (Faber & Faber, London, 1969).

Heurtley, W. A., H. C. Darby, C. W. Crawley and C. M. Woodhouse, *A Short History of Greece* (Cambridge University Press, Cambridge, 1965; paperback edition, 1967).

Homer, *Odyssey*, trans. E. V. Rieu (Penguin, London, 1946).

Huxley, Anthony and William Taylor, *Flowers of Greece and the Aegean* (Chatto and Windus, London, 1977).

Sands, Martin J. S. *Paxos walking and wild flowers* (Villa Centre Holidays Ltd., Walton-on-Thames, 1980).

FURTHER READING

The Annual of the British School at Athens, 29 (1931), 35 (1938), 39 (1942), 40 (1943) and 44 (1949).

Bérard, Victor, *Les Navigations d'Ulysse* (Librairie Armand, Paris, 1935 and 1929), vol I (for Ithaca), vol. IV (for Corfu).

Cartwright, Joseph, *The Ionian Islands* (Publisher unknown, London, *c.* 1821).

Dörpfeld, Wilhelm, *Alt-Ithaka* (Richard Uhde, Munich, 1927), 2 vols. in German.

Konomou, Dinou, *Churches and Monasteries in Zakinthos* (Ionian and Popular Bank of Greece, Athens, 1964), in Greek.

Marinatos, S. N., *Kefallinia* (Local Tourist Committee, Cefalonia, 1962), in Greek, English and German.

Procopiou, A. G., *La Peinture réligieuse dans les îles ioniennes pendant le XVIIIe siècle* (Société Hellénique d'Éditions S.A., Athens, 1939).

Riemann, Othon, *Recherches archéologiques sur les îles ioniennes* (Bibliothèque des Écoles Françaises d'Athènes et de Rome, Paris, 1879–80), Fasc. 8, 12 and 18.

Sitwell, Sacheverell, *Great Palaces* (Spring Books, Feltham, Middlesex, 1969).

Verikiou, Spirou, *History of the 'United States' of the Ionian Islands: 1815–1864* (Privately printed, Athens, 1964), in Greek.

Wace, Alan J. B. and Frank H. Stubbings (eds.), *A Companion to Homer* (Macmillan, London, 1962), especially chapter 13 (iii) for Lefkas and Ithaca.

GLOSSARY

Words are given in the number and case in which they appear in the text.

aetós	eagle
agoraíon	hire (car)
amáxia	cars, carts
angináres	artichokes
angoúria	cucumbers
apokhoritírio	W.C.
aristoú	Irish stew
áspro	white
astakós	lobster
avgá	eggs
avgolémono	soup made with egg and lemon
avgotárakho	compressed grey mullet's roe
baklavás	flaky pastry with nuts and honey
barboúnia	red mullet
bonfilé	fillet steak
bourdétto	Corfiot fish stew
bouzoúkia	type of Greek song
brizóles	entrecôte steak
delális	Paxos town crier
domátio	room
dromolóyo	timetable, itinerary
eliés	olives
éna	one
Eptánisos	Seven Islands
estiatórion	restaurant
exokhiká	country (adj.)
fakés	lentils
fangrí	sea-bream
fasolákia	green beans
féta	sheep's or goat's milk cheese
fílakas	caretaker, watchman
foúrnos	baker's (lit. oven)
fráoules	strawberries
friganiés	thick Melba toast
galaktopolíon	diary
garídes	prawns
glikó	sweet

glóssa	sole (fish)
grafío	office
graviéra	Gruyère type of cheese
iatrío	clinic
ikonostásis	church screen (lit. icon-stand)
inopolíon	wine shop
kalamarákia	small squid
kalíves	huts
kantádes	Zantiot songs
karpoúzi	water-melon
katavóthra/es	swallow-pit
kéfalos	grey mullet
keftédes	meat-balls
kénḍro/a	country eating place
khíma	draught (of wine)
khoriátiki	country (adj.)
khorís	without
khórta	wild greens (lit. weeds)
kiló	kilo
kinotikó grafío	district council office
kokkinistó	'red-cooked', i.e. with tomato purée
kokorétsi	large grilled sausage of inwards
kolokouthákia	baby vegetable marrows
komatáki	little bit
konféto	quince cheese
korfoús	peaks
kounoupídi	cauliflower
krassí	wine
láḍi	oil
lákhano	cabbage
lithríni	sea-perch
loukánika	spicy sausages
loukoumádes	deep-fried batter fritters
máestros	Ionian northerly wind
makarónia	macaroni
manḍoláto	nougat
mánḍoles	pralines
maroúli	lettuce
mayirítsa	Easter soup
meletsánes	eggplants
méli	honey
melópita	honeycomb

meltémi	Aegean northerly wind
merída	helping (of food)
méros	W.C. (lit. place)
métrio	(here) middling sweet (of coffee)
mezés/édes	hors d'oeuvre
mikrós/é	(here) young waiter (lit. small, young)
míla	apples
misó	half
monóxila	pirogue (lit. dug-out canoe)
mousakás	minced meat and vegetable pie
nomárkhis	prefect
nopó	fresh
ókhi	no
okhiá	viper
olígo	a little
tis óras	*à la carte* (lit. of the hour)
ortzáta	almond cordial
óstria	moist southerly wind
ouzería	bar selling *ouzo*
oúzo	anise-flavoured spirit
paidákia	lamb chops
panayíri/íria	Saint's Day festival
pandokhíon	cheap inn
pandopolíon	grocer's
pastítso	minced meat and macaroni pie
pepóni	melon
períptero	newspaper kiosk, country restaurant
piáto	plate
piláfi	cooked rice
pinyátes	(copper) bowls
piperiés	pimentos
platía	town or village square
pólis	town
portokália	oranges
pouláki	little bird
próedros	president (here, of local community)
protópapas	chief priest
psári foúrno	baked fish
psomí	bread
retsína	resin-flavoured wine
revíthia	chick-peas
rizógala	cold rice pudding

robóla	type of wine from Cefalonia and Ithaca
rodákina	peaches
rosólio	sweet liqueur
saítas	type of snake
saláta	salad
sáltsa	Zantiot meat dish
saprokhiá	kind of viper
savóro	Lefkadian fish salad
sinagrída	gurnet
sirókos	hot and humid southerly wind
skáras	grilled
skéto	here, sugarless (of coffee); without oil
soffríto	Corfiot meat dish
souvlákia	beef brochettes (lit. little spits)
stafília	grapes
stifádo	Greek meat stew with onions
stilvotírio	shoe-shine parlour
stratigós	here, military governor (lit. general)
stréma/ata	area of about $\frac{1}{4}$ acre
taramosaláta	purée of cod's roe
tavérna/es	simple restaurant
témplo	church screen
thémata	Byzantine administrative districts (lit. regiments)
tiflitás	type of blind snake
tiganitó	fried
tirí	cheese
toualéta	W.C.
troumbétta	trumpet
tsíntsin bíra	ginger-beer
tsoutsoukákia	meat-balls cooked in sauce
verdéa	Zantiot white wine
vólta	the evening stroll
voútiro	butter
yaoúrti	yoghurt
yígandes	large haricot beans (lit. giants)
youvarákia	meat-balls made with rice
zakharoplastíon	cake shop, patisserie

Index